New Perspectives on Prehistoric Art

New Perspectives on Prehistoric Art

EDITED BY GÜNTER BERGHAUS

Westport, Connecticut
London

Library of Congress Cataloging-in-Publication Data

New perspectives on prehistoric art / edited by Günter Berghaus.
    p. cm.
   Includes bibliographical references and index.
   ISBN 0–275–97813–3 (alk. paper)
    1. Art, Prehistoric.   I. Berghaus, Günter, 1953–
N5310.N447   2004
709′.01—dc22   2003059645

British Library Cataloguing in Publication Data is available.

Library of Congress Catalog Card Number: 2003059645
ISBN: 0–275–97813–3

First published in 2004

Praeger Publishers, 88 Post Road West, Westport, CT 06881
An imprint of Greenwood Publishing Group, Inc.
www.praeger.com

Printed in the United States of America

The paper used in this book complies with the
Permanent Paper Standard issued by the National
Information Standards Organization (Z39.48–1984).

10 9 8 7 6 5 4 3 2 1

Every reasonable effort has been made to trace the owners of copyright materials in this
book, but in some instances this has proven impossible. The author and publisher will be
glad to receive information leading to more complete acknowledgments in subsequent
printings of the book and in the meantime extend their apologies for any omissions.

Contents

Preface

This volume has grown out of a series of lectures delivered at the University of Bristol in 2001. The annual Bristol Arts Lectures were instituted in 1911 and are directed at the general public as well as members of the university. Many of the lectures given on past occasions have been published, either individually or as a group. When in 1998 I suggested the topic of prehistoric art to the committee chairman, Michael Liversidge, he invited me to draw up a list of possible speakers. As luck would have it, more people agreed to participate than I could possibly accommodate in the program. For this reason I pursued from the very beginning the idea of a printed publication, which was kindly accepted by Elisabetta Linton, commissioning editor of Praeger, a publishing company that previously issued the posthumous edition of Hugo Obermaier's book *Art in the Ice Age* (1953) and T. G. Powell's *Prehistoric Art* (1966).

Needless to say, one volume cannot possibly attempt to cover the wide variety of approaches and methods of analysis employed in the interpretation of prehistoric art. Several academic disciplines have attempted to throw light on the early artistic expressions of humankind and have yielded, as the bibliography shows, a multitude of studies of great diversity.

The massive expansion of research into prehistoric art over the past 25 years has given rise to some useful compendia and condensed treatments of the topic in a variety of languages. However, I still have not come across a comprehensive bibliography that I could recommend to my students as an introductory guide for their independent studies. I have therefore sought to complement the chapters in this volume with a fairly wide-ranging bibliography that also covers aspects and geographical areas not specifically addressed by our contributors. The task of compiling the list was greatly aided by modern, Internet-based technologies, which allowed me to verify titles in a variety of libraries across the world. Most of the editorial and bibliographic work was completed while I was visiting professor at Brown University, and I am grateful to their library staff and Inter-Library Loan department for their kind support. Furthermore, the resources of the Tozzer Library at Harvard University were an invaluable asset when it came to preparing the manuscript for print. I am greatly indebted to their librarians for guiding me though their unrivalled collection.

The Discovery and Study of Prehistoric Art

Günter Berghaus

The study of prehistoric art as a serious academic discipline is a relatively recent phenomenon. The discovery of the Franco-Cantabrian caves in the late nineteenth and early twentieth centuries prepared the way for some preliminary, but not particularly successful, attempts to pierce the shadows of paleolithic caves. A small number of specialists such as Henri Breuil or Hugo Obermaier increased our knowledge of sites and the works decorating their walls and ceilings. However, it was only in the last decades of the twentieth century that art historians, archaeologists, anthropologists, psychologists, and scholars of other disciplines established a substantial library of serious, scientific studies on prehistoric art (see the bibliography at the end of the volume).

This combined effort of throwing light on the early manifestations of human artistic expression was severely hampered by the fact that a very substantial body of works—specifically, those executed on bark, hides, textiles, and sand—did not survive into the present age, and that the no less significant ephemeral arts of music, dance, and ritual have rarely left any material traces behind. Therefore, scholars were largely dependent on nonperishable materials for their studies and had to limit themselves, more or less, to the discovery, excavation, and preservation of rock art, that is, of works painted or engraved on rock surfaces, usually found in caves, shelters, and open-air spaces. The Centro Camuno di Studi Preistorici, directed by Emmanuel Anati, has documented some 20,000 sites with more than 35 million figures worldwide.[1] All territories inhabited by human beings provide examples, with the oldest dating back some 40,000 years, and with reliable data extant from c. 34,000 years B.P. onward.

It appears that certain ways of life, attached to certain economies, produce highly similar art, irrespective of their geographic locations and times of origin. Even nowadays, some isolated communities, which still adhere to their old ways of life, continue to create rock art and interact with existing sites in a meaningful manner as part of their ritual culture. C. G. Jung suggested that the human mind operates with archetypal images expressed in a universal language. Rock art provides evidence of many local dialects of this vernacular and gives us unique insights into the intellectual world of prehistoric hunter-gatherers, who communicated with each other over time and space in a visual rather than verbal manner. The vast number of visitors to the caves open to the public, as well as the ways in which modern artists (as well as some advertising agencies) have appropriated the imagery of the past, give me reason to think that paleolithic art still provides the modern mind—satiated with images from a media-drenched culture—with experiences that resound in the human soul like no other form of art.[2]

Apart from the creations permanently fixed to rock surfaces (which Anati estimates to make up 90 percent of surviving prehistoric works of art there also exists portable art *(art mobilier)* created as sculptures, reliefs, engravings, and markings on materials as diverse as stone, bone, wood, antlers, and ivory. Artworks of a figurative nature begin to appear in the early Upper Paleolithic and are characteristic of the period from 35,000 to 10,000 B.P.; nonrepresentational, yet probably symbolic, incisions have been dated as far back as 70,000 B.P.[3] Scholars such as Alexander Marshack see in these markings the origin of art, whereas Paul Mellars, more cautiously, advises that

none of the markings so far described from Lower and Middle Palaeolithic sites in Europe shows anything approaching the degree of clarity, regularity, organization, or obvious intentionality that one would reasonable expect from consciously symbolic or "decorative" engravings. In this respect they contrast strikingly with the majority of engravings from Upper Palaeolithic sites, where the clear patterning and intentionality of the engravings cannot be questioned.... Regardless of the significance attached to any individual object ... the sheer scarcity and isolation of these objects within the Middle Palaeolithic universe as a whole makes it difficult to see this kind of symbolic expression as a real and significant component of Neanderthal behaviour.[4]

Steven Mithen has combined his research into early symbolic behavior with an examination of the cognitive architecture of the human mind. He arrived at the conclusion that archaic humans had already developed the necessary cognitive modules for different types of symbolic communication and a highly developed technical ability to express their thoughts and feelings, but that the real breakthrough, datable in Europe to around

40,000 to 35,000 B.P., only occurred when these domain-specific modules became integrated to form what he calls "cognitive fluidity":

It was the ability to integrate these processes . . . that led to a dramatic change in the complexity of the visual symbols that could be produced. As a consequence the very first representational paintings we have, such as those in the Chauvet Cave, are as technically accomplished and expressive as any painting by human-kind—there was no gradual, cumulative evolution of the capacity for art.[5]

No doubt, the debate about early human symbolism and the emergence of artistic expression in the Middle to Upper Paleolithic Transition is far from over.[6] Looking back over the past century, we can see that some of the most fundamental questions the early pioneers asked about these works of art are still left unanswered.

THE DISCOVERY OF PREHISTORIC ART

The first excavated Ice Age objects for which descriptions were published in the nineteenth century—for example, a reindeer antler decorated with chevrons from Bize, 1827; an antler shaped to resemble a budding twig from Veyrier, 1833; and a horse head engraved on a reindeer antler from Neschers, 1840—were thought to be of Celtic origin. The first person to moot the notion of Stone Age art was Édouard Lartet, who in an article for a zoological journal established a temporal relation between an image of two deer engraved on a bone found in the cave of Chaffaud and a prehistoric bear's head he had discovered in 1860 in the cave of Massat.[7] However, his suggestion that images of such high quality may have been produced by primitive cavemen caused little more than derision, and outside the small circle of paleontologists, his views were considered downright blasphemous. As long as God-fearing Christians were still convinced that God had created Adam 6,000 years ago, only a few scientifically inclined minds were capable of relating Fuhlrott's discovery of a Neanderthal skull (1856) to Darwin's theory of evolution promoted in *The Origin of Species* (1859). Therefore, the man from the Neander Valley had to be classified as simian, as belonging to a primitive and brutal race incapable of artistic creations.

Meanwhile, the finds of engraved bones and sculpted ivory statuettes continued to multiply. A few years after Lartet's assertions, an engraved image on a mammoth tusk, found in a cave with more bones of clearly extinct animals, made other people wonder whether the populations of the Ice Age could indeed have been artists. The crucial mental leap toward the concept of prehistoric art occurred with the discovery of the painted caves of Franco-Cantabria. The term "discovery," of course, is misleading here, since many caves were known to local populations, and some had been described in travelers' reports and even had made it into the guidebooks.[8] But for a long time, the paintings' ancient date was not suspected by anybody. The crucial turning point came in 1878, when Don Marcelino Sanz de Sautuola visited the Universal Exhibition in Paris, where some early portable art was on display. Don Marcelino recognized their similarity with some of the figures which he had seen in the cave of Altamira in 1875 and he returned to the cave for more systematic examinations, accompanied by his daughter María, who alerted him to the painted "oxen" on the ceiling. As the cave had only been discovered in 1868, there was no doubt in Don Marcelino's mind that these figures were of great antiquity. He published his reflections on these so-called Ice Age paintings in a modest booklet in 1880[9] and was supported in his assumptions by the prehistorian Juan Vilanova y Piera.

Until the late nineteenth century, neither of these two men was taken seriously. But then, finally, the tide began to change. The discovery of other painted caves in the 1890s attracted the attention of the scholarly community. Émile Cartailhac, who had spoken dismissively about Sanz de Sautuola's suggestions and had refused to discuss them in his volume, *Les Ages préhistoriques de l'Espagne et du Portugal* (1886), decided to investigate several of the caves known at that point, accompanied by the young Henri Breuil. As a result of this reexamination he retracted his previous pronouncements[10] and undertook a first major publication of the Altamira paintings and engravings.[11] Hermilio Alcalde del Río, who continued the excavations at Altamira after Sanz de Sautuola's death, published his findings in the same year as Cartailhac[12] and introduced the term "Sistine Chapel of Quatenary Art." Such a comparison (taken up again later by Windels in his book on Lascaux, *"Chapelle Sixtine" de la préhistoire*, 1948) contributed to the change in public perception of prehistoric art. Popular and scholarly publications presented the works previously considered to be primitive, "antediluvian art" as masterpieces of "mankind's childhood."

Once the concept and artistic significance of prehistoric art had been established, numerous scholars began to evaluate its aesthetic characteristics and determine its possible meanings.[13] The most important person in this nascent field of inquiry was Henri Breuil, a priest by training, who accumulated unrivalled first-hand knowledge of hundreds of caves and acted as a kind of pope of prehistory until his death in 1961.[14] He viewed Paleolithic art predominantly in terms of hunting magic and believed that it developed from crude, abstract, and archaic figures to sophisticated, complex, and realistic forms. Although his highly subjective and often simplistic judgments are now discredited, he was nonetheless a man of major significance, and many of his unsurpassed tracings of cave paintings are still reproduced in modern publications. In the 1960s and 1970s he found a worthy successor in André Leroi-Gourhan, an anthropologist working in the framework of French structuralism, who directed attention to the compositional structure of the caves.

Much of the research carried out in the first three-quarters of the twentieth century was concerned with establishing chronological schemas, a typology of styles, and a framework of classification. Since then, scholars have been engaged in placing the art of prehistoric times into wider ecological and cultural contexts. Valuable insights have also been gained from technical examinations of the methods of painting and engraving. Furthermore, the early focus on the Franco-Cantabrian region has finally given way to a multitude of investigations in other parts of the world. Ethnographic studies on indigenous populations, particularly in South Africa, Australia, and North America, enabled scholars to make connections with the rock art produced on those continents and to draw some generalizing conclusions, which may also be applicable to the European record.

DETERMINING THE MEANING OF PREHISTORIC ART

Although the studies mentioned above have greatly enhanced our understanding of prehistoric art, we are still in no way near to answering the absorbing question of what motivated the artists to create these works. We do not even know whether they were meant to be art, specifically made for aesthetic appreciation rather than functional purposes. In fact, it may well be that, by classifying these works as art, we are erecting mental barriers that prevent us from arriving at an appreciation of their original function and meaning.

The aesthetic concepts developed in Europe since the Renaissance period have bestowed special status on works of art and distinguished them from objects with use value. By imposing socially determined distinctions between art and artifact, artist and craftsman, fine and applied art, certain works and creations are transposed into an autonomous sphere as if they were unaffected by everyday life. Many of the early studies on prehistoric art operated with categories of interpretation taken from post-Renaissance aesthetics, assumed to be universal and applicable to all human societies. Similarly, writers of popular treatises, editors of encyclopedias, and curators of museums displayed works from the prehistoric period in the manner of coffee table books and art exhibitions. But how can an uninitiated reader or viewer arrive at an unbiased appreciation of these works when female statuettes are referred to as "Venus figurines," when the caves of Altamira and Lascaux are called "Sistine Chapels of Prehistory," when the bisons of Tuc d'Audoubert are reproduced in perfect lighting condition without reference to their spatial surroundings and without indication of how this spot in the cave can be reached? As only few works lend themselves to such distorting presentation, we regularly find a few dozen images being reproduced over and over again while the other 35 million known figures remain practically unknown. Such selective sampling has created, over time, an extremely limited iconographic canon and fostered a highly biased view on what constitutes prehistoric art.

If in today's world we find it often impossible to draw clear distinctions between the functional and the aesthetic and have to resort to hybrid categories such as *objets d'art*, then we are facing an even more difficult task with regard to prehistoric objects and images. Although many Paleolithic works are aesthetically pleasing, we should guard ourselves from privileging these over others whose artistic aspect is less pronounced but whose functions may have been the same. A great number of studies have been dedicated to elucidating the nonfunctional features of prehistoric objects. A nascent aesthetic sense has been detected in intentionally preserved minerals, fossils, or shells, in the collecting of ocher pieces for coloring purposes, or in the expenditure of labor for no other reason but to give a hand axe a balanced and symmetric appearance. In the Middle Paleolithic, we can observe an increased use of ornaments and intentional markings on bones and stones, but the symbolic language employed in these creations is largely inaccessible to us.

It appears that in the course of human evolution, from archaic to modern *Homo sapiens*, linguistic communication came to be complemented by visual representations of ideas, concepts, and feelings. The objects that testify to such systems of symbolic communication may also have had religious or social functions. Whether they qualify as art is a matter of conjecture. Some scholars prefer to use more neutral terms, such as *symbols*, *images*, or *pictograms*. In any case, these objects appeared in cultures that predate the earliest cave paintings by tens of thousands of years.

In view of this long prehistory of prehistoric art and the mass of objects displaying an aesthetic character next to as yet undetermined practical functions, it should not astonish us that the first works corresponding to our concept of art appeared in a fully developed, complex, and sophisticated fashion some 35,000 to 25,000 years before the present. There is nothing crude or primitive about the paintings in the caves of Chauvet, Cosquer, Cougnac, or Peche Merle. So if we were to look for the childhood of art, we might find it in the Middle Paleolithic, but not in the great creations of the Franco-Cantabrian region.

Many scholars have pondered over the reasons for the "creative explosion" (as Pfeiffer described it) in the European Upper Paleolithic. Suggestions have ranged from new cosmogenic concepts to changing hunting practices and socioecological challenges. The concentration of painted caves in a small geographic region may well have to do with the shrinking habitat in the last Ice Age, as this led to a concentration of population in the climatically more temperate zones north and west of the Pyrenees. Yet it does not explain why populations in central Europe did not adapt similar decorative schemes in the plenty of caves they had at their disposal. Scholars such as Gamble, Jochim, Clark et al., and Barton et al. have suggested that Neanderthalers, who lived in socially dispersed, small bands without established networks and alliances, may have had all the skills to produce art, but no need for it. It was only with the social stress resultant from the high concentration of populations during the last Ice Age in refuge areas such as Franco-Cantabria that art attained an important function in the cultural performances of the period. The social and adaptive changes under extreme glacial conditions necessitated alliance networks, social interaction and conflict resolution, and a well-functioning information exchange. Art may have played a crucial role in these increasingly complex social networks as it facilitated intragroup cohesion, served as markers for social affiliation, and improved interaction between larger social groups. One may therefore assume that the concentration of certain types of art in certain regions and certain periods had to do with specific circumstances (ecological, economic, cultural) which artists responded to in their creations. And within one culture, different media probably had their own conceptual systems attached. Thus, for example, open-air rock art may have served as signposts related to the migration paths of animals and human beings, or as spatial markers for group territories; cave art at aggregation sites may have fulfilled ritual functions (initiation rites, vision quests, totemic ceremonies); markings on portable objects may have functioned as notation systems; beads may have been ethnic markers; anthropomorphic figurines may have had religious purposes; and so on.

In view of the wide spectrum of forms, media, and possible functions of prehistoric art, it is advisable to treat all generalizing explanations with great caution. Many unsubstantiated assertions of the past century have raised more questions than they purported to answer. If, for example, female statuettes were indeed related to fertility cults, we need to know whether men or women created and made use of them. If the cave paintings were related to hunting magic, why do they predominantly depict species that were of minor significance in the population's diet? If entoptic signs were related to shamanic practices, why do they also appear in cultures that did not practice shamanism? If early human populations were indeed distributed fairly evenly across continents, why is it that the distribution of artwork is extremely patchy across the same habitats?

With so many questions still open for debate and unlikely to be answered in the near future, it may be advisable to focus our attention on the contexts in which art appears. One of these, undoubtedly, was ritual, and ritual is performative. The tentative explications of an Ur-theatre, that is, of a primordial performance art, undertaken by Hunningher, Menagh, Kirby, and others,[15] have not been followed up in recent years. Specialists in prehistoric art coming from the disciplines of archeology and anthropology have been hampered by the underdeveloped state of ritual studies and the narrow bandwidth of theater studies. Some more fruitful interdisciplinary cooperation has recently emerged from the field of performance studies, and one may hope that dance and music scholars will, in the future, participate more actively in the debate.

Prehistoric works of art were not unchanging texts but components of cultural performances, which cannot be judged by the criteria of autonomous artwork. Objects used in the context of a ritual lose their apparent semantic fixity and attain a fluid and dynamic dimension. They only develop their unique symbolic quality when being handled, utilized, or manipulated. Therefore, unless we know more about how prehistoric populations made use of their works of art, we are unlikely to comprehend their possible meanings and functions. But in this respect, we are only at the beginning of a long journey.

Compared to the early phases in the study of prehistoric art, the number of sites with works of art found in them has multiplied a thousandfold. Many of these objects and images can now be dated. Improved excavation methods allow us to make informed judgments on the context of these finds. Evolutionary biology, paleogeography, and climatology provide us with useful information about prehistoric hunter-gatherer societies. These contextual studies further our understanding of prehistoric art as a culture-specific form of communication that reflects the norms and values of the society that once produced it. And as we are discovering more pieces of the puzzle, we are beginning to make out the broad outline of the picture.

NOTES

1. E. Anati. *World Rock Art: The Primordial Language*. Capo di Ponte: Edizioni del Centro, 1993: 11–12.

2. A phenomenon related to this which is worth mentioning in this context is the sensational success of fictional works set in prehistory. Jean Auel's Ayla novels, translated into 30 languages with an accumulated print run of 36 million [census date: April 2003], is only the tip of the iceberg. Steve Trussel's *Prehistoric Fiction Bibliography* currently runs up to 963 titles (see www.trussel.com). Here are some novels and short stories focusing on the creation of prehistoric art: Emery Barrus. *Legacy of a Hunter*. Santa Barbara, CA: Fithian Press, 1995; Norman Bate. *When Cave Men Painted*. New York: Scribner, 1963; Ann Chamberlin. *Leaving Eden*. New York: Forge, 1999; Jean-Luc Déjean. *Histoires de la préhistoire*. Paris: Hachette, 1993; Dennis B. Fradin. *Cave Painter*. Chicago: Childrens Press, 1978; Michel Peyramaure. *La Caverne magique: Le roman de Lascaux*. Paris: France Loisir, 1987; Florence Reynaud. *Le Premier Dessin du monde*. Paris: Hachette, 2000; Stefano Sibella. *Lascaux, la préhistoire merveilleuse*. Paris: Réunion des Musées Nationaux, 1999; Henry Lionel Williams. *Turi of the Magic Fingers*. New York: The Viking Press, 1939.

3. See Francesco D'Errico, Christopher Henshilwood, and Peter Nilssen. "An Engraved Bone Fragment from c. 70,000-Year-Old Middle Stone Age Levels at Blombos Cave, South Africa: Implications for the Origins of Symbolism and Language." *Antiquity* 75 (2001): 309–318, and Christopher S. Henshilwood et al. "Emergence of Modern Human Behavior: Middle Stone Age Engravings from South Africa." *Science* 295:5558 (15 February 2002): 1278–1279.

4. Paul Mellar. "Symbolism, Language and the Neanderthal Mind." In *Modelling the Early Human Mind*, ed. Paul Mellars and Kathleen Gibson. Cambridge: McDonald Institute, 1996: 15–32; quotation from pp. 21 and 23.

5. Steven Mithen. "On Early Palaeolithic 'Concept-mediated Marks,' Mental Modularity, and the Origins of Art." *Current Anthropology* 37 (1996): 666–670; quotation from p. 668. See also his full-length study on these cognitive processes, *The Prehistory of the Mind: A Search for the Origins of Art, Religion and Science*. London: Thames and Hudson, 1996.

6. For some representative studies on the subject, see the writings listed in the bibliography at the end of this volume, by C. Michael Barton et al., A. Martin Byars, Philip G. Chase and Harold L. Dibble, Andrew I. Duff et al., Chris Knight et al., J. M. Lindly and Geoffrey A. Clark, Sally McBrearty and Alison S. Brooks, Paul Mellars, Ian Watts, and Ernst E. Wreschner.

7. Édouard Lartet: "Nouvelle Recherches sur la coexistence de l'hommes et des grands mammifières fossiles." *Annales des sciences naturelle (Zoologie)*. 4th series, 15 (1861): 177–253.

8. See Paul G. Bahn. *The Cambridge Illustrated History of Prehistoric Art*. Cambridge: Cambridge University Press, 1998: 1–57.

9. Marcelino Sanz de Sautuola. *Breves appuntes sobre algunos obietos preistóricos de la Provincia de Santander*. Santander: Martínez, 1880.

10. See "Les Cavernes ornées de dessins: La Grotte d'Altamira (Espagne). Mea culpa d'un sceptique." *L'Anthropologique* 13 (1902): 348–354.

11. Émile Cartailhac and Henri Breuil. *La Caverne d'Attamira à Santillane près Santander (Espagne)*. Monaco: Imprimerie de Monaco, 1906.

12. *Las pinturas y grabados de los cavernas prehistóricas de la provincia de Santander: Altamira, Covalanas, Hornos de la Peña, Castillo*. Santander: Blanchard y Arce, 1906.

13. For the period 1900–1910, see in the bibliography the publications by Henri Breuil, Édouard Piette, Salomon Reinach, Max Verworn; for the period 1911–1920, see Clarence Bicknell, Eugen Fischer, Eduardo Hernandez-Pacheco, Moriz Hoernes, Otto Moszeik, Hugo Obermaier, Henry Fairfield Osborn, Ernest Albert Parkyn, Herbert Green Spearing, Paul Wernert; for the period 1921–1930, see Henri Bégouën, Gerard Baldwin Brown, Miles Crawford Burkitt, Louis Capitan, Leo Frobenius, Pedro Ibarra y Ruiz, Herbert Kühn, Amédée Lemozi, Georges Henri Luquet, Édouard Piette, Wilhelm Paulcke, Nicolas D. Praslov, René de Saint-Périer, Robert Rudolf Schmidt, León Strube.

14. See the biographies of Alan Houghton Brodrick. *The Abbé Breuil, Prehistorian: A Biography*. London: Hutchinson, 1963; Nicolas Skrotzky. *L'abbé Breuil*. Paris: Éditions Seghers, 1964; Eduardo Ripoll Perelló. *Vida y obra del abate Henri Breuil, padre de la prehistoria*. Barcelona: Diputación Provincial, Instituto de Prehistoria y Arqueología, 1964, and his more recent study *El abbate Henri Breuil (1877–1961)*. Ma-

drid: Universidad Nacional de Educación a Distancia, 1994. Ripoll Perelló also published a posthumous *Festschrift* for Henri Breuil in 1964/65.

15. See, for example, Benjamin Hunningher, *The Origins of Theatre*. The Hague: Nijhoff, 1955; H. B. Menagh: "The Question of Primitive Origins." *Educational Theatre Journal* 15 (1963): 236–240; E. T. Kirby: *Ur-Drama: The Origins of Theatre*. New York: New York University Press, 1975.

Consciousness, Intelligence, and Art: A View of the West European Middle to Upper Paleolithic Transition

J. David Lewis-Williams

This chapter considers the origin of two-dimensional representational imagery in, specifically, western Europe at the time of the Transition from the Middle to the Upper Paleolithic. It is argued that such imagery, the well-known cave and portable art of Franco-Cantabria, was not a consequence of an aesthetic sense or inherent impulse; on the contrary, the so-called aesthetic sense in humankind is a diversely conceived social construct that followed rather than preceded the making of the first imagery. The very concept of two-dimensional imagery was not invented by especially intelligent people; rather it is wired into the human brain and is experienced in certain states of consciousness. This kind of projected mental imagery preceded its fixing on surfaces. The need for fixed imagery was socially, not psychologically, generated.

INTRODUCTION

As it appears in most narratives, the story of human cognitive evolution follows a unifying theme: the forebears of *Homo sapiens* became more and more intelligent, more and more able to cope with environmental constraints and opportunities. Tool-making *Homo habilis* (2.0–1.6 million years ago) was brighter than the preceding so-called ape-men, the Australopithecines (3.0–2.0 million years ago); then *Homo erectus* (1.8–1.0 million years ago) was able to fashion still better tools that, as human-made extensions of the body, enabled that species to gain the upper hand over animals considerably larger than themselves. *Homo neanderthalensis* (± 100,000 years ago in the Middle East to ± 30,000 years ago in western Europe) was intellectually almost there, but the millennia of the Nean-

derthals' existence (apart from their last years when they were neighbors
to fully modern people—more of which anon) were characterized by mental inertia. Finally, the most intelligent hominid species of all emerged:
Homo sapiens populations—ourselves—were clever enough to develop
complex language and symboling systems, not merely symbolic vocali-
zations and gestures, as well as a diversity of stone, bone, and antler tools,
and far-flung exchange networks.

Every advance in this historical trajectory seems to be explained by one
thing—increasing intelligence and how it was employed to control the
environment. It was essentially this factor—intelligent adaptation—in the
equation of humanity, so the received view runs, that unleashed the spi-
raling technological and social changes to which we are not entirely content heirs. Researchers see intelligence principally as facilitating the
mastering of hostile environments; indeed, this attitude permeates our
thinking—we still speak of dams that "tame" rivers, motor races that
(destructively) "triumph" over deserts, and climbers who "conquer"
mountains.

But something is missing from this tale, something that is an inescapable
part of what it is to be human. Intelligence, undeniably important as it is, is
not a sterile electronic computer. On the contrary, it is set in a matrix of shifting, mercurial—sometimes deceiving—human consciousness.

Even when researchers do consider consciousness, they see it in terms
of intelligence:[1] for them, modern human consciousness is an alert state
that facilitates rational interaction with the environment and internalized,
mental problem solving. Significantly, they define fully modern human
consciousness, the pinnacle of human evolution, as the sort of mental state
that they themselves cultivate when they are addressing the enigmas of
science. Human consciousness has, however, an unpalatable characteristic, one that researchers into human evolution have generally ignored because it seems to be antithetical to the kind of consciousness that they
most value. Consciousness is shifting, constantly moving back and forth
along a spectrum of states that range from the highly valued alert states
to introverted daydreaming of various degrees of distancing from the immediate environment, to sleep and dreaming, to unconsciousness. Fluctuations along this spectrum are cyclic and seem to be part of the
electrochemical functioning of the human brain. Consciousness is not a
discrete, alert entity to which less alert states are unfortunately loosely
appended: on the contrary, consciousness is a much more complex suite
of intergrading conditions.

To these normal, daily fluctuations that everyone inevitably experiences
must be added induced states brought on by a wide variety of factors.
These states are more autistic than, say, daydreaming and are characterized by hallucinations in all the senses. Such mental conditions are generally known as altered states of consciousness, a term that clearly points

to the belief that "real" human consciousness comprises only the alert states at the other end of the spectrum.

Because human cognitive evolution is seen exclusively in terms of intelligence, the shifting nature of consciousness and the altered states to which that quality can lead are marginalized in accounts of human evolution. Researchers believe that these could not have played any significant role in human cognitive and social change because the associated experiences do not relate to the material world. True, some writers allow that answers to scientific problems may come in inexplicable, illogical flashes of inspiration or even in dreams, but today the sources of such insights are deemed an insufficient guarantee of their validity. Penetrating ideas have—rightly—to be put to the test, empirically or mathematically, before they can be published and accepted by others.

I certainly do not advocate mystical acquisition of knowledge or the notion that altered states of consciousness are some form of higher consciousness. That would be to embrace a Cartesian residue. Despite the apparently inexplicable nature of sudden insights, dreams, mysterious inner voices, and emotionally overpowering visions, there is nothing mystical about them: they are not vouchsafed by gods or spirits; they are caused by the electrochemical functioning of the brain. If the brain in its synapses and neural circuitry is not well-stocked with relevant data, it obviously cannot produce the necessary explanations and connections. Discovery favors the prepared mind, not the purely mystical mind.

That said, we must allow that the way in which modern, scientifically minded Westerners conceive of consciousness is not universal. In the past (as is the case in other cultures today), other conceptions of consciousness, especially of states at the autistic end of the spectrum, played a formative role in human social and cognitive evolution.

A LAUNCH PAD TO MODERNITY

These introductory remarks bring me to the geographical and historical focus of this chapter: the west European Middle to Upper Paleolithic Transition, a period that lasted (in archeological terms very briefly) from approximately 40,000 to 35,000 years ago. It has been dubbed the Human Revolution and the Creative Explosion and has been subjected to intensive study.[2] It was the time in western Europe when, comparatively suddenly, the Neanderthals faded from the scene and modern human behavior begins to show up in the archeological record: *Homo sapiens* communities began to develop (or brought with them on their migration from Africa via the Middle East)[3] complex hunting strategies that involved the prediction of migrating herds and seasonal salmon runs and the social differentiations necessary for the planning and execution of such endeavors. As new tool types appeared, artifacts also began to exhibit stylistic fea-

tures that probably signaled that they were symbolic of social communities—groups of people symbolized their ethnicity by making tools of a
particular kind. *Homo sapiens* communities also made body decorations in
the form of pendants and necklaces that suggest social distinctions. They
not only buried their dead (which the last Neanderthals may also have
occasionally done) but they did so with elaborate grave goods that were
interred with the bodies. Most strikingly of all, these anatomically modern
people began, at the beginning of the Transition, to make what we call
art—two- and three-dimensional images of animals, principally, but also
of what look like human beings, though these are probably better and less
tendentiously termed anthropomorphs. No evidence has been found to
suggest that the Neanderthals made representational images, whatever
else they had borrowed from their *Homo sapiens* neighbors.

From amongst the plethora of questions raised by all these human activities during the west European Middle to Upper Paleolithic Transition,
I tease out two for consideration in this chapter (others are discussed
elsewhere):[4]

- How did people come to realize that marks on two-dimensional surfaces
  could represent animals?
- Why did Neanderthals not learn to make images?

The two questions are related: the answer to the first points us in the
direction of an answer to the second and, indeed, to much else about the
Transition.

EXPLAINING THE ORIGIN OF TWO-DIMENSIONAL IMAGERY

For some writers, the first question does not exist. They assume that the
ability to discern and make two-dimensional images is natural to human
beings, that it is in-built. Yet anthropological evidence shows that this is
not so. For example, Anthony Forge[5] found that the New Guinea Abelam
people were not able to pick out their friends in photographs if he did not
teach them how to do so. Significantly for the argument that I develop
later, the Abelam do make what we may see as two-dimensional pictures,
but they do not believe them to *represent* anything in nature (for Westerners, a curious concept) or, for that matter, in the spirit world; rather, they
are avatars of spirits. They are not what we would see as pictures; the
Abelam do not share our Western conventions for understanding two-
dimensional representations.

If the conventions for making and recognizing two-dimensional images
are learned, how and why did they come to appear suddenly at the beginning of the Transition?

A short-cut explanation is to argue that some exceptionally intelligent individuals invented image-making. This is how the French archaeologists Brigitte and Giles Delluc sum up this position: "Around 30,000 years ago, in the Aurignacian, at the beginning of the Upper Palaeolithic, someone or some group in the Eyzies region invented drawing, the representation in two dimensions on the flat of the stone of what appeared in the environment in three dimensions."[6]

In the Dellucs' view, it was intelligence that did the trick. At once, others caught on, and soon lots of people were making and looking at pictures.

There are numerous drawbacks to this initially attractive explanation. For one, the range of animal species depicted in Upper Paleolithic art was, right from the beginning, restricted: people did not make pictures of whatever they wished. They repeatedly depicted horses, bison, aurochs, mammoths, felines, and some others, but, by and large, not trees, snakes, insects, small animals, or faces. If the vocabulary of the art was restricted in this way, it follows that it was socially established and was not the product of individual whims. Upper Paleolithic art did not begin with a wide range of subject matter, as one would expect if it were simply the invention of clever individuals.

This objection applies equally to another explanation for the origin of two-dimensional images: what we may call the "eureka!" explanation. For many years, it was believed (and indeed is still believed by some writers) that early people spotted the outlines of animals in natural markings and blotches of color on cave walls and thus realized they could make pictures even without the initial stimulus of these marks. A variant of this view is that people made random scribblings, or doodles, on cave walls and then suddenly discerned animals, or parts of animals, amongst them. If that was so, we may ask why they spotted only certain species. In other words, the vocabulary of the art was established *before* they noticed the animal forms and later made the pictures. Then, too, the Abelam objection remains: it is impossible to discern images in a tangle of lines and blotches of color *if you do not already have a notion of two-dimensional imagery.*

Even if we were to accept these unlikely explanations, we should still have to ask why, once the first images had been discerned or made, people wanted to go on making them. What *value* did images have for early Upper Paleolithic communities (not just individuals)? An easy bolt-hole explanation is to say that people have an innate drive, a psychological imperative, to make beautiful things, to decorate special things. This innatist view, attractive in its very simplicity, actually sidesteps some important issues. For instance, we must remember that there is a world of difference between, on the one hand, simply decorating things by, say, smearing them with red ocher, and, on the other, making two-dimensional images: images require comprehension of conventions that go well beyond any supposed innate aesthetic sense. So, even if we were to allow for an innate aesthetic sense, we would be left with the unanswered question: how did they invent these conventions? Further, to argue that art was triggered by an innate aesthetic drive is, in fact, circular. The argument can be broken down into the following steps. How do we know that there is such a drive? We infer its existence for the fact that people make pictures and other beautiful things. We then use that inferred urge, or aesthetic sense, to explain the very objects from which we derived it. The circularity is clear.

It is at this impasse that evolutionary notions sometimes take over. Can we discern an evolving trajectory from something other than images themselves that ended up in the making of two-dimensional pictures? The Soviet writer A. D. Stoliar developed such a scheme. First published in Russian in 1972, his publication was translated into English in the late 1970s.[7] His scheme is worth examining because some of its components still appear in textbooks. Briefly, Stoliar argued that the earliest cave paintings displayed six characteristics:

- They are of standing animals.
- They are in profile.
- They are generalized to a high degree.
- They are done with confidence; there are no corrections.
- There are no details within the outline.
- The animals have two horns, but only two legs.

These features, Stoliar believed, point to carved reliefs. But what was the relationship between paintings and reliefs? Could it have been genetic? To answer these questions, Stoliar cited the so-called bear-cult caves that, at the time when he was writing, featured prominently in accounts of the Transition and the Upper Paleolithic. It was believed that a number of cave sites contained burials of the skulls of the now-extinct cave bear and contrived arrangements of bear bones. These fearsome creatures measured up to nine feet from head to tail and hibernated in the same caves that early people occupied. Stoliar provocatively called these supposed cave bear burials and bone arrangements archaic museum exhibits and believed them to have been depictive: that is, the skulls stood for the whole animal—an early form of synecdoche. But even this simple form of depiction must have had precursors. What were they?

Stoliar proposed the following stages:

- Collective social action expelled the bears from the caves.
- The heightened emotions thus generated had to find expression in rituals: people danced around the corpse of the animal. Ritual was an emotional safety valve.

- A second ritual dramatically recounted to other people what had happened—a dramaturgical view of ritual.
- Then people recorded the themes of the rituals by exhibiting the bones.
- Then, in a transitional phase, someone handling malleable clay was struck by the similarity between the shapes that he or she was forming and the shape of an animal. Magic was thus born.
- People then made life-size clay models of bears and placed them close to the cave walls to allow space for rituals. Here Stoliar cites the Montespan clay bear that is in a lying-down, Sphinx-like posture with its forelegs stretched out in front of it.
- Later, to prevent them from collapsing, the clay models were leaned against the walls. Unlike the Montespan example, these stood on rudimentary legs.
- The next stage was a gradual flattening of the figure into high relief, then low relief.
- When such clay reliefs crumbled, they left their outlines on the walls, and the makers beheld two-dimensional images.
- From here, it was a short step to the making of two-dimensional paintings and engravings without first making clay reliefs.

Certainly, all this is ingenious. But Stoliar's sequence is open to theoretical and substantive criticisms.

From a theoretical point of view, and again very briefly, we need to query the psychological view of ritual. Whatever psychological effects bear rituals (if these did indeed exist) may have had, they were essentially *social* in character. Stoliar himself says that his explanation is a social one (he adopts a Marxist position), so this reversion to psychology is something of an aberration. It can in fact be argued that rituals engender, or perpetuate, anxiety. Christian confession, for example, keeps alive, in the long term, a sense of guilt that is the foundation of Christianity. A second theoretical objection is that Stoliar adopted a speculative "if-I-were-a-horse" form of argument. He was thinking *himself* into an Upper Paleolithic situation and saying what he believed he would do, notice, or believe under such circumstances. This is especially true at the point where he postulates the supposed clay models leading to sympathetic magic. At this point he, of course, falls foul of the Abelam objection.

Interesting though these and other theoretical criticisms are, it is today the substantive objections that are most devastating. Apart from the doubt that is now thrown on the bear-skull burials and bone configurations (the early reports are contradictory, and the excavations left much to be desired), improved dating has shown that the Montespan clay bear is comparatively late in the Upper Paleolithic period. Moreover, sophisticated two-dimensional images with internal contours and details were being made right at the beginning of the Upper Paleolithic, as in the Chauvet cave (± 33,000 B.P.). Then, too, the Vogelherd statuettes carved in mammoth ivory date to the same period. In short, there is no empirical evidence whatsoever for the sequence that Stoliar postulated. There was not a long evolutionary sequence: imagery appeared suddenly and fully-formed.

METHODOLOGY

All these arguments and counter-arguments suggest that what we are up against is not simply a poverty of data but, more seriously, a methodological dilemma. We need to ask: what sort of argument (i.e., method) will lead to a persuasive explanation of the appearance of image-making?

All too frequently, archeologists, who are sometimes unfamiliar with matters of logic and the philosophy of science, speak of proof: they say, this or that explanation cannot be proven. In fact it is a simple fundamental of science that very little, if anything, outside of mathematics can be proven. The best we can hope for is a persuasive argument, one that economically (or parsimoniously, in philosophical terminology) accounts for a set of observations. To make matters worse (that is, in some researchers' minds), those observations can never be made without reference to some hypothesis, some theory, some potential explanation. We always collect data that we consider relevant and ignore observations that we consider irrelevant. But relevant or irrelevant to what? Without some hypothesis or guiding framework, data collection is impossible. That is why so much empirical work on Upper Paleolithic art is misguided. The researchers who are undertaking it believe that they are assembling a theory-free data foundation from which they will be able to infer explanations. Philosophers of science have shown time and again that this is a vain (and illogical) hope. This is not to say that empirical work is valueless, only that it will never, of itself, produce explanations. We need to distinguish between good empirical work and the false logic of empiricism.

How, then, should we proceed? To cut a long and complex story short, I merely state that the best method available to us is to intertwine different strands of evidence to constitute a strong cable.[8] Diverse evidence can be mutually supportive and mutually constraining. A gap in one evidential strand can sometimes be compensated for by another strand (the archeological record is, after all, notoriously fragmentary), and, taken together, evidential strands can exclude bizarre explanations that do not accord with what we confidently know. I therefore try in the following paragraphs to formulate an explanation for the origin of two-dimensional imagery that intertwines (a) the evidence of the archeological record with (b) the results of neuropsychological research on how the human brain works and also with (c) the results of ethnographic research on hunter-gatherer people who make images on rocks.[9]

HUMAN CONSCIOUSNESS

As I observed at the beginning of this chapter, neuropsychological re-search has shown that intelligence is set in a matrix of shifting conscious-ness. Let us now examine what we know about the "wiring" of the human brain—the organ that, of course, generates consciousness—and see how it embodies clues to an explanation for the origin of image-making at the beginning of the west European Middle to Upper Paleolithic Transition. We need not now consider the physical structure of the brain and the details of its electrochemical functioning; those matters are adequately covered by many accessible books.[10] Here, I outline a particular type of consciousness and some of its effects. This is the autistic kind of con-sciousness that too many archeologists ignore because they consider it aberrant and not germane to the business of mastering the environment.

If we imagine normal, day-to-day modern human consciousness as a spectrum, as I have already argued we should, we can add to that spec-trum a diverging branch of what I call intensified autistic consciousness. The fluctuating, day-to-day spectrum shifts from alert states to daydream-ing, and on to dreaming in rapid eye movement (REM) sleep. In doing so, consciousness grades from alert, environment-oriented states to autis-tic (inward directed) states. The intensified autistic spectrum may be in-duced by psychotropic drugs, intense rhythmic and aural driving, sensory deprivation, hunger, pain, and certain pathological conditions, and it moves from mildly altered states to deeply affecting hallucinations in which the person experiencing them believes to be participating.

This intensified spectrum of consciousness may be divided into three stages; this is what I call the neuropsychological model.[11] In Stage 1, people see entoptic phenomena (also known as phosphenes and form constants). These are pulsing, expanding and contracting, luminous geo-metric forms. They include grids, zigzags, nested U-shapes, meandering bright lines, and clouds or chains of brilliant dots. The actual forms are wired into the brain and are therefore experienced cross-culturally: they are universal. But the ones that people value most highly and the mean-ings that they ascribe to them are culturally specific. In Stage 2, people try to make sense of what they are seeing by construing the forms as objects with emotionally charged values. A Westerner, for example, may construe a set of zigzag or undulating lines as engulfing waves, if he or she is in a fearful state, whereas a South American Tukano person may identify them as "the thought of the Sun-father."[12] In Stage 3, subjects see fully developed hallucinations of monsters, landscapes, people, and so forth with whom they interact; the geometric percepts are now peripheral. The three stages are not ineluctably sequential; sometimes people are cat-apulted directly into Stage 3.

One of the ways in which the imagery of all three stages is experienced is the key to understanding the origin of two-dimensional imagery. Sometimes subjects describe their mental imagery floating in, as it were, the middle distance and visible whether their eyes are open or closed. But images are also perceived as projected onto surfaces such as walls or ceilings. Subjects liken this experience to a slide or cinema show. At such times, they feel detached from their imagery and are able to witness the forms on the surfaces before them. A comparable experience is the perception of after images. These are experienced sometimes long after the subject has returned to alert consciousness. They may be triggered by some veridical perception or by a sudden emotion or, indeed, by no mechanism apparent to the person experiencing them. They appear to float before the subjects or to be projected onto surfaces. They may remain in vision for periods ranging from a few seconds to a number of minutes.

It is important to recall that the potential to have such experiences, together with the characteristics I have noted, is "wired" into the human nervous system. Because Upper Paleolithic *Homo sapiens* people had the same nervous system as we do, they too would have had the potential to experience the projected imagery of altered states of consciousness (which may be triggered by a great many normal, pathological, and induced conditions). That *Homo sapiens* populations of the early Upper Paleolithic possessed the full range of human consciousness is a point that is not in dispute.

Further, they would, like all people everywhere, have had to come to some commonly held understanding about the spectrum of states: they would have valued some, ignored others, and, perhaps, deplored still others. Indeed, there is no option but to divide up the spectrum of human consciousness and to evaluate the segments thus produced. Each society divides up the spectrum in its own way; what some societies call madness, others value as divine inspiration or spirit possession. Upper Paleolithic consciousness would have been neurologically generated and would have followed the same in-built spectrum, but it would have been apprehended in ways that would in all probability have differed from the modern Western ways, a point that is borne out by the beliefs of hunter-gatherer communities around the world.

That being the case, we can begin to explain the origin of image-making and the problems posed by the Upper Paleolithic evidence that I have outlined.

A ROAD TO IMAGE-MAKING

We can begin with what is for some researchers a startling statement: for at least some Upper Paleolithic people, the environment was already sometimes invested with images—that is, with mental images and projected mental images. In the nature of consciousness, it seems unlikely that *everyone* would have had such experiences, but everyone would have had some inkling of what others said about their projected mental imagery, its content, and the ways in which it changed and developed, because everyone, of necessity, dreams, and dreams have much in common with the experiences of altered states. There is therefore no need to postulate the invention of two-dimensional imagery on plane surfaces by especially intelligent people. Imagery came with the functioning of the human brain.

What was required was for social circumstances to begin to place heightened value on preexisting, commonly discussed, and prized mental imagery. Then, under such conditions, people reached out to touch what were already considered powerful things and, in doing so, fixed them on the walls of caves, thus controlling them. This fixing may have been done with a finger in soft mondmilch, with a fingernail or stone artifact on harder surfaces, or with pigment (which was already in use as body decoration and thus had value in itself). What those social circumstances might have been is a point to which I return in a moment.

If the first images came to be made in the way I suggest, a number of features of Upper Paleolithic paintings and engravings are explained. First, the way in which images seem to float on cave walls and ceilings shows them to be disengaged from any kind of natural surroundings— as indeed are projected mental images. There are no associated trees, grass, hills, and so forth: the images are things in themselves, not pictures of what people saw in the countryside. The feeling of floating that the images generate is enhanced by some of the ways in which animal hooves are frequently drawn: they hang rather than stand on an invisible land surface; other images have no hooves at all; still others are depicted as if to show the underside of horses' hooves. Another point is that, in a panel of images, the individual pictures are done without regard to relative size or position—as is the case with projected mental imagery. Finally, the images are frequently integrated with features of the surface on which they were placed: a natural bulge in the rock may supply the dorsal line of a bison, or a small projecting nodule may indicate an eye, even if this means that the animal has to be oriented in a way that does not recall the ways in which real animals would be seen outside the cave. All in all, it seems that people were not representing arbitrarily selected items in their natural environment; rather, they were fixing already valued, floating, projected mental images. The painted and engraved images were, in this sense, not pictures at all. The notion of representational art in our understanding of Upper Paleolithic imagery therefore requires reevaluation.

During the Upper Paleolithic, image-making probably followed three parallel routes. First, fixed mental imagery continued to be made throughout the period. Secondly, recollected mental imagery was sought on the surfaces onto which it had been projected; in a more alert state, the evanescent images were then reconstituted. Thirdly, there was probably a type of image-making derived from contemplation of the first two streams: people realized that they could make images without ever having themselves experienced projected mental imagery. This third sort of imagery conformed to the range of accepted and acceptable motifs. At what stage people began to regard their painted and engraved images as pictures of real animals rather than manifested, visionary spirit animals is an intriguing and debatable point.

SOCIAL CONTEXT

Let us now consider the social circumstances under which the first image-fixing could have taken place. As I have argued, the fairly narrow range of motifs depicted in the earliest art—and indeed throughout the Upper Paleolithic, though with regional and temporal numerical emphases—shows that mental imagery of certain animals was valued *before* image-fixing started. The reason for this state of affairs (value placed on mental images of certain animals) may be explained by what is now generally called shamanism (despite the Siberian origin of the word). Unfortunately "shamanism" is such a heatedly disputed term that it requires careful definition—always bearing in mind that no researcher has the authority to establish once and for all what the word means. By shamanism in hunter-gatherer contexts I mean:

- A belief and experiential system posited fundamentally on a range of institutionalized altered states of consciousness.
- A system incorporating conceptions of a tiered cosmos with spirit realms above and below the level on which people live.
- People with special powers, the shamans, cultivate the ability to access the spirit realms and to interact with their inhabitants.
- The behavior of the human nervous system in altered states often creates the illusion of dissociation from one's body (sometimes understood as spirit possession).

Shamans use dissociation and altered states in general (including dreaming) to perform tasks on behalf of their communities to:

- Contact spirits and supernatural entities.
- Heal the sick.
- Control the weather.
- Control the movements of animals.

These tasks are often, but not always, accomplished by means of

- A variously conceived supernatural power or essence.

- Contact with animal-helpers and animals believed to possess supernatural power.

This list of characteristics of hunter-gatherer shamanism excludes features that some writers consider important. For instance, I do not link shamanism to any form of mental illness. Nor do I stipulate the number of shamans that a society may have; some communities have many, others only a few, often politically powerful, shamans. Nor do I stipulate any particular method for the induction of altered states. Nor do I consider instances where shamanism flourishes alongside other religions, such as Buddhism.

Much dispute and acrimony has arisen from writers' confusion of a general definition with specific empirically established sets of behaviors and beliefs. It seems to me to be a side issue whether a given community in, say, Central America can be termed shamanistic or not, though I know others feel strongly about the matter. Unfortunately, those who deny the appropriateness of the appellation all too often simultaneously discount the observed behaviors of the community and its ritual practitioners. This is the epistemological cul-de-sac into which too narrow a definition of shamanism leads. If the term Christianity can be usefully applied to Russian Orthodox churches, the Roman Catholic Church, the Coptic Church, Lutheranism, Calvinism, Anglicanism, charismatic fundamentalism, Plymouth Brethren, the Salvation Army, and the small house churches of today, then the term shamanism, too, can be used to designate belief systems that (at least in hunter-gatherer societies, the focus of this chapter) embrace the principal points that I listed above.

I am here developing an explanation for the appearance of Upper Paleolithic imagery that postulates a belief system that, in my view, can be termed shamanistic. If critics believe that the word is inappropriate, that is not a serious matter. What matters is whether the explanation I am formulating explains the empirical evidence of the Upper Paleolithic caves, and whether it is supported by neurological research and, moreover, by comparable, but by no means identical, behaviors observable around the world.[13] It should be possible to express reservations about my use of shamanism without denying the explanatory potential of my explanation.

THE NEANDERTHALS: SOCIAL IMPLICATIONS

The picture of the early Upper Paleolithic that I have sketched—*Homo sapiens* communities in contact with Neanderthals—holds implications for an understanding of why the Neanderthals borrowed some things from the incoming *Homo sapiens* communities but did not make images. The incoming people brought with them the Aurignacian technocomplex; some Neanderthals took over parts of it to form the Châtelperronian technocomplex. The position can be summarized as follows:

What the Châtelperronian Neanderthals . . .

. . . borrowed	. . . did not borrow
stone tool techniques	advanced hunting strategies
blades	
endscrapers	
burins	
bone and antler working	
some late burials	burials *with elaborate grave goods*
personal ornaments	image-making

The distinctions are illuminating. The Neanderthals probably used the first group of things that they took over, those at the top of the borrowed column, for the same purposes as the Aurignacians did: the stone tools were used to perform the same tasks—cutting, scraping, and so forth. The second group, personal ornaments and burials, poses some different issues. If the Aurignacians used body decorations and ornaments to signal social distinctions, as is generally accepted they did, the Neanderthals could not have duplicated that symbolism because they had a simpler social structure, another point on which most researchers agree. Perhaps the Neanderthals were simply mimicking the Aurignacians without fully understanding what their ornaments meant.

Then, if we allow that some Neanderthals did bury some of their dead (a point that some researchers contest), why did they not include elaborate grave goods? Finally, the key question: why did the Neanderthals not take up image-making? Could the answers to these questions be closely related? I argue that they were and that they can be traced back to two different kinds of consciousness.

Here I turn to the work of Gerald Edelman. He distinguishes two kinds of consciousness: primary consciousness and higher-order consciousness.[14] Primary consciousness is what is possessed, to varying degrees, by certain fairly advanced, nonhuman animals; higher-order consciousness is possessed by *Homo sapiens* alone.

Animals that have primary consciousness

- Are aware of their environments.
- Have mental images, but only of a narrow slice of time—the remembered present as Edelman calls it.
- Have no sense of their own past and future.
- Have long-term learning ability, but are unable to plan an extended future based on memory.

- Have no socially constructed self.
- Have only a form of protolanguage, or no language at all.

Animals *(Homo sapiens)* that have higher-order consciousness

- Recognize their own acts and emotions.
- Have complex language (with past and future tenses).
- Entertain concepts of the past and the future that influence their model of the world.
- Have a socially constructed self.
- Have long-term mental storage of symbolic relations.

Edelman himself does not say that these two types of consciousness characterize, respectively, Neanderthals and anatomically modern people, but, if this were indeed so, it would explain a great deal about the Middle to Upper Paleolithic Transition. We can therefore speak of the distinction between primary and higher-order consciousness as a *hypothesis* and then go on to explore what data it explains and what evidential strands support it.

First, we can see that Neanderthals would, with the long-term learning ability of primary consciousness, have been able to acquire the skills necessary to make most of the artifacts that their Aurignacian neighbors were making—but that is about all. Without the ability to use complex language with past and future tenses, and the kind of memory that is closely related to, and necessary for, complex language, they would not have been able to conceive of and sustain generational societies with attributed leadership, marriage rules, and so on; they would not have had the mental ability to develop all the symbolism that is necessary to reproduce such societies through time.

Nor would they have been able to remember the projected mental imagery of altered states and to reconstitute it on the rock walls of caves. Like dogs (and other animals), they would have dreamed (it is part of a necessary protein-manufacturing process of the brain) but, still like dogs, they would not have had the ability to remember their dreams and to share them socially. They would not have been able to remember a set of symbolic animals, which the evidence of Upper Paleolithic art suggests was already in place at the beginning of the period. Importantly, their society would have provided no reason or use for a symbolic bestiary. Ultimately, they would not have been able to conceive of a future, after-death spiritual state, and spirit beings inhabiting that state. For them, burial may have been a practical issue that they could imitate, but the Aurignacians' reasons for putting valuable items in graves would have been beyond their ken. In short, the Neanderthals would have been congenital atheists.

From the point of view of *Homo sapiens* communities, the Neanderthals had control of the land and knew how to survive in periods of harsh climate. At first, the two groups may have exploited different environmental niches; later they probably began to compete for resources. Under such circumstances, the differences between the two groups would have assumed increasing importance to them. The Neanderthals saw the *Homo sapiens* communities engaging in symbolic activities that they could not fully comprehend. The *Homo sapiens* people realized that their symbolic activities, those that depended on higher-order consciousness, were what gave them the edge over the Neanderthals. Under such circumstances, there was, I suggest, a tendency for the *Homo sapiens* communities to emphasize and develop the differences between themselves and the Neanderthals—what is today called a process of othering.

Homo sapiens people already had a system of belief and religious experience complete with a bestiary of powerful spirit animals. They then began to manifest that system by nailing down their mental imagery for all to see, or at any rate for those who had access to the caves and open-air locations of image-making. In doing so, they inevitably emphasized social discriminations within their own communities: between the seers of visions (and possibly amongst them the manifesters of visions) and those who experienced only dreams that, imperfectly, seemed to confirm the existence of the seers' spirit world, and then between those who were permitted (or required) to enter the deep caves and those who were excluded from what became a subterranean spirit world.[15]

In summary, the distinctions between the west European Neanderthal archeological record and that of *Homo sapiens* are explained by the hypothesis that differences in consciousness, not intelligence alone, distinguished the two species.

THE ORIGINS OF ART RECONSIDERED

It is often noted that asking the right questions is the first—and essential—step in getting to appropriate answers. If the question is badly or vaguely phrased, the answer to a problem will not be found. An implication running through the preceding argument is that the question "What was the origin of art?" is profoundly misleading.

I suggest that the concept "art," so difficult to define, did not in any way lead to image-making. On the contrary, art is a culturally situated social construct that came *after* the making of the first images. Art is a formulation of values, beliefs, and conventions that people in particular social conditions create to deal with image-making and, of course, with other comparable activities; that is why the word is impossible to define satisfactorily. In short, art is not a human universal.

This may seem an unnecessarily iconoclastic gauntlet. So let us turn to Ernst Gombrich's enormously popular *The Story of Art*. He begins by writing: "There is really no such thing as art. There are only artists."[16] Here he rightly shifts the ground of debate from philosophy and abstract concepts to more practical questions, questions about people and what they do in their particular societies. I argue that, if we follow Gombrich's lead, and ask "What was (were) the origin(s) of *image-makers*?" we shall have a better chance of finding a convincing answer.

We are thus talking about real people doing things that were socially important, not about the origin of abstract, hard-to-define concepts. That is what I have tried to achieve in this chapter: I ask about the origin of *image-makers*, not art.

Although the manifestation of mental imagery set *Homo sapiens* communities apart from Neanderthals, the activity also had internal social consequences for *Homo sapiens* societies that spiraled in ever-widening arcs through the Upper Paleolithic. The practice provided real, visual distancing between those who had the ability to enter and control altered states of consciousness and those who did not. This distinction probably started before people began to make images. From early on, probably in Africa, the spectrum of consciousness was divided up and contested; it thus became an instrument of social discrimination within *Homo sapiens* communities. Image-making and its social consequences occurred later and were substantial material stimuli for many of the changes that archeologists detect in the Upper Paleolithic.

Here was the foundation for a society that was not built exclusively on age, gender, and physical strength, a society with cross-cutting discriminations that people could manipulate in complex ways. In this way, religion, social discrimination and domination, and image-making were set on an interacting trajectory that led, eventually, to the history of humankind and to that amorphous, hard-to-define, changing concept that we, in our particular place on that trajectory, call art.

ACKNOWLEDGMENTS

I thank Günter Berghaus for inviting me to lecture at the University of Bristol and Larry and Mary Barham for being such welcoming hosts in Dr. Berghaus's absence. I am grateful to colleagues who usefully commented on drafts of this chapter: David Hammond-Tooke, Jeremy Hollmann, and Ben Smith. The Rock Art Research Institute is funded by the University of the Witwatersrand, the National Research Foundation (grant no. 2053693), the Anglo-American Chairman's Fund, De Beers Fund Educational Trust, and Anglo-Gold. Opinions expressed in this chapter and conclusions arrived at are the author's and are not necessarily to be attributed to the funders.

NOTES

1. For example, Steven Mithen. *The Prehistory of the Mind: A Search for the Origins of Art, Religion and Science.* London: Thames and Hudson, 1996.

2. See Paul Mellars, ed. *The Emergence of Modern Humans: An Archaeological Perspective.* Edinburgh: Edinburgh University Press, 1990; Paul Mellars. "The Archaeological Records of the Neanderthal—Modern Human Transition in France." In *The Geography of Neanderthals and Modern Humans in Europe and the Greater Mediterranean,* ed. Ofer Bar-Yosef and David R. Pilbeam. Cambridge, Mass.: Peabody Museum of Archaeology and Ethnology, 2000: 35–47; Paul Mellars and Christopher Stringer, eds. *The Human Revolution: Behavioural and Biological Perspectives on the Origin of Modern Humans.* Edinburgh: Edinburgh University Press, 1989; Christopher Stringer and Clive Gamble. *In Search of the Neanderthals.* London: Thames and Hudson, 1993.

3. See Sally McBrearty and Alison S. Brooks. "The Revolution that Wasn't: A New Interpretation of the Origin of Modern Human Behaviour." *Journal of Human Evolution* 39 (2000): 453–463; Christopher S. Henshilwood, Francesco d'Errico, C. W. Marean, R. G. Milo, and Royden Yates. "An Early Bone Industry from the Middle Stone Age at Blombos Cave, South Africa: Implications for the Origins of Modern Human Behaviour, Symbolism and Language." *Journal of Human Evolution* 41 (2001): 631–678; Christopher S. Henshilwood, Francesco d'Errico, Royden Yates, Zenobia Jacobs, Chantal Tribolo, Geoff A. T. Duller, Norbert Mercier, Judith C. Sealy, Helene Valladas, Ian Watts and Ann G. Wintle. "Emergence of Modern Human Behaviour: Middle Stone Age Engravings from South Africa." *Science* 295:5558 (15 February 2002): 1278–1280.

4. J. David Lewis-Williams. "Harnessing the Brain: Vision and Shamanism in Upper Palaeolithic Western Europe." In *Beyond Art: Pleistocene Image and Symbol,* ed. Margaret Conkey, Olga Soffer, Deborah Stratmann, and Nina G. Jablonski. San Francisco: Memoirs of the California Academy of Sciences, No. 23, 1997: 321–342; J. David Lewis-Williams. *The Mind in the Cave.* London: Thames and Hudson, 2002; Jean Clottes and J. David Lewis-Williams. *The Shamans of Prehistory: Trance and Magic in the Painted Caves.* New York: Abrams, 1998.

5. Anthony Forge. "Learning to See in New Guinea." In *Socialization: The Approach from Social Anthropology,* ed. P. Mayer. London: Tavistock, 1970: 269–290.

6. Brigitte Delluc and Giles Delluc. "On the Origins of Image Making." *Current Anthropology* 27 (1986): 371.

7. Abram D. Stoliar. "On the Genesis of Depictive Activity and its Role in the Formation of Consciousness." *Soviet Anthropology and Anthropology* 16 (1977/1978): 3–42.

8. Alison Wylie. "Archaeological Cables and Tacking: The Implications of Practice for Bernstein's 'Options Beyond Objectivism and Relativism.' " *Philosophy of Science* 19 (1989): 1–18.

9. Lewis-Williams. *The Mind in the Cave* and Clottes and David Lewis-Williams: *The Shamans of Prehistory.*

10. For example, William H. Calvin. *How Brains Think: Evolving Intelligence, Then and Now.* London: Weidenfeld and Nicolson, 1997; Susan Greenfield. *The Human Brain: A Guided Tour.* London: Weidenfeld and Nicolson, 1997; Susan Greenfield. *The Private Life of the Brain.* London: Penguin, 2000; Richard L. Gregory, ed. *The Oxford Companion to the Mind.* Oxford: Oxford University Press, 1987.

11. J. David Lewis-Williams and Thomas A. Dowson. "Signs of All Times: Entoptic Phenomena in Upper Palaeolithic Art." *Current Anthropology* 29 (1988):
201–245; J. David Lewis-Williams and Thomas A. Dowson. "On Vision and Power
in the Neolithic: Evidence from the Decorated Monuments." *Current Anthropology*
34 (1993): 55–65; J. David Lewis-Williams. "Wrestling with Analogy: A Problem
in Upper Palaeolithic Art Research." *Proceedings of the Prehistoric Society* 57 (1991):
149–162.

12. Geraldo Reichel-Dolmatoff: *Beyond the Milky Way: Hallucinatory Imagery of
the Tukano Indians.* Los Angeles: UCLA Latin America Center, 1978: 34.

13. For the full argument, see Lewis-Williams. *The Mind in the Cave.*

14. Gerald. M. Edelman. *Bright Air, Brilliant Fire: On the Matter of the Mind.*
Harmondsworth: Penguin, 1994; Gerald. M. Edelman and Giulio Tononi. *Consciousness: How Matter Becomes Imagination.* Harmondsworth: Penguin, 2000.

15. Lewis-Williams. *The Mind in the Cave.*

16. Ernst Gombrich. *The Story of Art.* London: Phaidon, 1950: 5.

Hunter-Gatherer Imagery in Aboriginal Australia: Interpreting Rock Art by Informed and Formal Methods

Christopher Chippindale

Australia is a continent rich in rock art painted, engraved, and made in other media such as sand and beeswax. For some regions we have a good chronology; in some regions, knowledge of rock art and even the making of rock art continues into the very present. So we have special opportunities there to see rock art in its social context, and to build with it what one can call an Archeology of the Dreamtime. Beginning with a brief survey of the range of Australian rock art, I will concentrate on a key region, the northern Top End of the Northern Territory, where the combination of chronological information with remarkable knowledge of rock art in recent times makes possible the telling of a rock-art story richer than most.

INTRODUCTION

This chapter reports and surveys features of Australian rock art and how it is studied. I have chosen aspects in which the Australian experience is unusual, or in which I believe it may be of special relevance to rock art in other parts of the world, or—preferably—both. I have emphasized work from the region of Australia I know best, the Top End, or northern part of the Northern Territory. If in my specific examples I draw on my own work, this is not done in a spirit of self-promotion, but simply because that is what I know best and can best report. In a book of words rather than pictures, I have not attempted the impossible task of offering a broad survey. Therefore, this chapter is less an account of Australian rock art than a (partial) discussion of some of the methods with which Australian rock art can be approached and the kind of knowledge which results.

AUSTRALIA, ITS PEOPLE AND THEIR ARCHEOLOGY

Australia is a singular place, the largest inhabited island or smallest continent on earth and rather removed from the rest of the world. Its geology contains great areas of archaic Precambrian rocks; its climate is characterized by a general aridity tempered by great variability. When I went for the first time to the supposedly hot and dry center, it was cold, wet, and green with lush and fresh vegetation. Together, geology and climate make for singular land forms. Australian vegetation is unique, with eucalyptus the dominant kind of tree and many endemics, including archaic types such as cycads, which are rare or extinct in other continents. Australian animals, cut off from the rest of the world by the Wallace Line running through the Indonesian archipelago, are singular; most of the mammal species are marsupials, and the reptiles are unusual and numerous.

Human beings, according to the balance of current knowledge, came to Australia when a population of *Homo sapiens sapiens* expanded from an African region of origin perhaps around 50,000 to 60,000 years ago, perhaps later. This founding population, it seems, was one of modern humans. They used ocher minerals, which may mean that they made art there from the very beginning. Australian Aboriginals, with their own knowledge of their own history, today say they have always been there. These people, like other humans of the later glacial period, subsisted by gathering and hunting. Over the last 10,000 years, people in nearly all the world have converted from that subsistence base to one of farming domestic plants and animals. Although in intermittent contact with farming peoples immediately to the north, Aboriginal Australians did not convert to this economy. Accordingly, the anthropology and archeology of indigenous Australians is, unusually, a hunter-gatherer story into modern times.

When a First Fleet of British convicts and their guards arrived in 1788 and set up a permanent colony at what is now the city of Sydney, Aboriginal Australians, after many centuries of living rather isolated from other humans, were abruptly swallowed up by the expanding European world. They were dispossessed, and today make up only a small percentage of the nineteen million Australians, who are, for the most part, descendants of European immigrants. Strikingly, the modern population of Australians is concentrated in a small number of great cities, every one on the coast, and most on the southern edge of the continent. Much of the land mass is lightly populated, and European ways of farming are not attempted across most of the country and struggle where they are implemented. This is outback Australia; one notices it is "out" and "back," rather than "in" and "central," only if one sits on the coast and looks away from Australia, say to a British former homeland, as the focus of things. Much of outback Australia is Crown Land owned by the state; some of it is being returned to its Aboriginal traditional owners in recognition of their land rights.

The materials of Australian archeology match these events. Hunter-gatherer peoples in general, and indigenous Australians perhaps more so, tend to make their social investment in complex knowledge systems rather than material objects. Great mobility means objects must be carried, whilst stationary farming populations can invest in a mass of material objects that are less often or never moved. In Australia, therefore, not much informative material finds its way into the ground. Acid and sandy soils, alternately dry and soaked, are destructive of, often, all materials other than stone. Accordingly, the Australian archeological record is dominated by its lithic remains, and those stone tools seem even less informative about human behavior and complex knowledge than are those of other regions of the world. Rock art, accordingly, has a special place in Australian archeology: there is a great deal of it, and it promises to be more forthcoming as a source of information than do the reticent lithics. There are special opportunities in ethnography and in chronology, to which I shall return below.

AUSTRALIAN ROCK ART

To create rock art one needs, first of all, rocks. A country like the Netherlands, which has very little rock, has no rock art. Australia, on the other hand, has much exposed rock, even though its mountain ranges are not very high. Importantly, much of the geology of Australia is unusually old, and many of its exposed rock surfaces are ancient deposits. One reason they have survived so long is that they are tough and erode very slowly, so they often provide fairly stable surfaces. Rock art researchers familiar with other regions, where rock is younger and less resistant, know to expect prehistoric rock art only in very protected places and favored spots; in Australia, on the other hand, old rock art seems to survive even on surfaces which are sheltered only by modest overhangs. Otherwise, the materials and techniques of Australian rock art are, for the most part, much like those found across the world.

Paintings generally use the natural mineral pigments, especially the white clays, the yellow ochers that derive from the iron mineral called limonite, and the red ochers that derive from hematite. The characteristic suite of colors is white, yellow, and red, used singly or in combination, plus some others whose use is less common or characteristic of a particular region. A mulberry hue, in the pink–purple–blue end of the red range, is common amongst the older paintings of north and north-west Australia, and is now identified as deriving from jarosite, another and rarer mineral than hematite. Researchers believe these pigments must have been combined with organic binders, or otherwise they would not have secured themselves to the rock walls and survived. Paintings are sometimes done with the fingers in a broad-line technique, sometimes in fine-line detail by narrow hair-brushes. Apart from paintings one can find *prints,* made by human hands or objects covered in pigment and pressed or thrown against the surface, and *stencils,* made by blowing pigment around a hand, a foot, or an object to make an outline image of it. *Engravings* are cut into rock surfaces, commonly where the surfaces are smooth. Although usually called engraving, the technique has little in common with the engraving with metal tools to which the word originally applied in European art. Rather, the surface is pecked, pounded, or worn away with a stone tool to make a figure of distinct areas or lines. When fresh, the engraving stands out by the contrast in color between the patinated rock surface and the freshly bruised and exposed area of engraving. When reweathered to a uniform patina, the engravings remain visible by their relief below the unmarked surface and by a difference in texture; sometimes they are clear, sometimes hard to see in ordinary light. Other kinds of rock art include figures made of *beeswax,* molded and pressed on to rock surfaces. Although regionally localized, and nowhere frequent, these beeswax figures now have importance as the only kind of Australian rock art for which the standard scientific technique of carbon dating can routinely determine precise dates. There are also regional traditions of *ground art* made in sand (which does not endure), and of *stone arrangements,* where boulders are set in lines and other more complex shapes.

Before exploring some themes in the archeology and anthropology of Australian rock art, something more pressing must be stated. Australian Aboriginal art is aesthetically rich, full of wonderfully observed images of animals and telling conventions. Hence, it is no coincidence that Aboriginal art is one of the glories of the country, and one in which all Australians take pride. It is also one of the few areas of Australian culture, alongside sports, in which Aboriginal people lead.

AUSTRALIAN ROCK ART: WHY IS THERE SO MUCH OF IT?

Australia is rich in rock art (Figure 1), especially when one realizes how small the Aboriginal population was in relation to the size of the continent. The first and most obvious reason for this, noted above, is the country's geology, which offers many rock art surfaces comparatively resistant to erosion and hence likely to endure. A second reason is that rock art continued to be made in large quantities and in many regions of Australia until recently, and sometimes is still created today. This is a decided contrast with, for example, Europe, where rock art largely ceased to be made

Figure 1
Thirty major rock art regions of Australia. From Paul S. C. Taçon, "Australia," in *Handbook of Rock Art Research,* **ed. David S. Whitley (Walnut Creek, CA: AltaMira Press, 2001); and itself adapted from Robert Layton,** *Australian Rock Art: A New Synthesis* **(Cambridge: Cambridge University Press, 1992).**

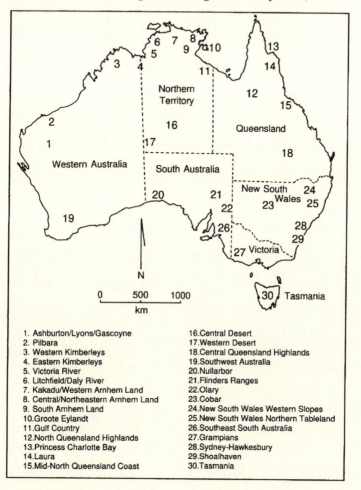

1. Ashburton/Lyons/Gascoyne	16.Central Desert
2. Pilbara	17.Western Desert
3. Western Kimberleys	18.Central Queensland Highlands
4. Eastern Kimberleys	19.Southwest Australia
5. Victoria River	20.Nullarbor
6. Litchfield/Daly River	21.Flinders Ranges
7. Kakadu/Western Arnhem Land	22.Olary
8. Central/Northeastern Arnhem Land	23.Cobar
9. South Arnhem Land	24.New South Wales Western Slopes
10.Groote Eylandt	25.New South Wales Northern Tableland
11.Gulf Country	26.Southeast South Australia
12.North Queensland Highlands	27.Grampians
13.Princess Charlotte Bay	28.Sydney-Hawkesbury
14.Laura	29.Shoalhaven
15.Mid-North Queensland Coast	30.Tasmania

many hundreds of years ago and has therefore only survived in a small and fragmentary proportion. Unfortunately, and alarmingly so, Australian rock art is also fading and eroding. A case in point is the most famous single panel in all Australian rock art, the group of polychrome paintings at Nourlangie in Kakadu National Park.[1] Painted in the 1960s, the paintings are now visibly degraded, despite a considered effort at conservation. At Nourlangie, and at many other sites, there can be seen, behind the most recent paintings, traces of their predecessors. So the signs are that some or much Australian rock art will not survive in the very long term; instead, it was perpetuated by repainting older images or creating new paintings which took the place of those that perished. Where Aboriginal people no longer paint—and that is in most of Australia—a corresponding diminution in rock art is now taking place.

A third reason for the quantity of rock art is the most instructive and the least explored. It follows from the particular relation between Aboriginal people and their land, captured in English in the word *country*. Your country is the region where you were born, where your parents and kin came from, where you belong, the place to which you have affinity. Country and attitudes to country are central to the profoundly different attitudes among Aboriginals and European immigrants who now occupy Australia. Rock art is an important expression of attitudes toward country, and part of the social processes by which those attitudes are created and maintained. Because those attitudes are so important, and because they have much in common right across Australia, it is not surprising that rock art is widely found throughout the country.

Australian Aboriginal attitudes toward landscape have something in common with those of other peoples in other places, especially other hunter-gatherers. There is an important and understudied correspondence here between social forms, attitudes toward land and the wider world, and rock art. Regions rich in rock art traditions are often populated by hunter-gatherers. Some herding, pastoralist, and agricultural peoples also produce rock art, but it is largely absent from urban societies like our own, where profoundly different views of land prevail, and we have different ways of marking it. Australia, a continent of hunter-gatherers, duly has a large corpus of great rock art.

INFORMED METHODS AND FORMAL METHODS

A key concern—many archeologists think *the* key concern—in rock art research is its meaning. We often (and perhaps with too much confidence) assume that we know what rock art images represent—human beings, animals, bird tracks, fish, boomerangs, spear-throwers. But what do those physical things mean? Archeologists, following the anthropologists, have been much influenced by structuralist semiotics, which states that there is no simple, consistent, or necessary relationship between the form a symbol takes and what it stands for. Like most strong generalizations, this is far from being the full truth, and insofar as it is true, it is unhelpful. However, it usefully draws attention to those precious instances where we *do* know the relation between the sign and the signified. Australian rock art has a unique importance for providing us with a direct record of its meaning. By contrast, the rock art of ancient Europe is an extremely elusive phenomenon, as we have no access to the native knowledge behind it, perhaps not even to any transformed memories of it in later periods. Classical writers make no reference to rock art, and the few scraps of information we have from medieval times stem from ignorant outsiders like ourselves, who were trying to make sense of the puzzling and already ancient things they saw.

It is useful, then, to distinguish between the two circumstances under which we study rock art. Where we are fortunate, we have some guide or glimpse as to the structure of meaning, of what stands for what and why it was produced; that is, we are privileged in having some access to insider knowledge, which we can work from and with using *informed methods*. When we have no reliable information, we can work only with the images themselves and their contexts, using *formal methods* to determine immanent or implied meaning. Since the images and what we know of their context are always available to us as sources of information, *formal methods* of interpretation can always be employed. And in some lucky cases, both *informed methods* and *formal methods* can be applied together.[2]

The ethnographic and ethnohistoric sources which make informed methods possible are, by their nature, located in that time and place where the direct record is placed. Perhaps, if local information can be extended to other places and times, we may see how both the form and the meaning of rock art may have changed over time—concerns of special interest in those regions of Australia where long-time continuity for rock art can be demonstrated.

The rest of this chapter summarizes three case studies in which the research balance moves from informed methods toward formal methods.

THE STORY OF THE LIGHTNING BROTHERS AND THEIR PAINTING AT YIWARLALAY: FROM PRESENT INTO THE RECENT PAST BY INFORMED METHODS

The Aboriginal communities of tropical north Australia are divided into distinct clans and language groups. Many of the groups are small in number—reduced by disease and depopulation after the European impact. But in the past also, it seems, they were not very large, yet this not-large region has more languages than nearly any other on earth. Much of the knowledge of country is specific to a group; yet, at the same time, much is common in the stories told by different groups.

The Wardaman people are one of the northern groups. Their traditional territory extends from near the modern town of Katherine along the modern highway that runs to the Victoria River and, beyond that, to Western Australia. This is cattle country now, divided into huge stations where semiwild cattle are annually rounded up and the surplus stock shipped out. Yiwarlalay, a place which is now on Delamere cattle station, is a most important place for Wardaman people as the spot where key events in one of their defining stories took place and where the rock art is both evidence for and memory of these events.[3]

This part of Wardaman country is gentle in relief, undulating sandy ridges and dips, all covered with eucalyptus woodland. The trees grow thin and rangy, well spaced, and only to a certain height; then the termites gnaw their tunnels through them, and the trees by degrees die back and perish. Between the trees, long grass grows green and tall in the rains of the monsoon season, dries back yellow and stiff in the dry season. Amongst endless kilometers of grass woodland, Yiwarlalay is not easy to find if you don't know where to look. Then, at a certain distance in the approach, the top starts to rise above the trees of a great flat-topped sandstone crag in orange-red and black, with sheer cliffs on each side. This is Yiwarlalay.

There are several rock art panels at Yiwarlalay. The best-known and the most impressive has two great images of striped figures, one a little taller than the other. These are the Lightning Brothers, and this is their story as Wardaman elders tell it:

There were two brothers. The older of the two was called Jabirringi; he was the smaller. The younger was called Yagjagbula; though the younger, he was much taller and more handsome. Jabirringi was married to a woman, Garnayanda. The two brothers and the woman camped together. One day, Jabirringi went out hunting alone. When he returned to camp from his hunting, he discovered his younger brother seducing his wife. So the brothers fought. They fought with such force and violence that they created lightning in the sky. The lightning, striking down from the sky on to the great rock, hit it with such a blow that it split into two. The frogs *(jabarlng)* came up from the south to watch the battle between the brothers. So did the rain *(wiyan)* who was going through the country on its way to another special place in Wardaman country, Yingalarri water-hole. Distracted by the fighting, the rain went instead to Yiwarlalay. At the same time the Rainbow Serpent, Gorrondolmi, flashed his forked tongue at the rain; this was a warning that the rain should not go on to Yingalarri. So Wiyan the rain "sat down" and there became the Water Rock, Nganalanjarri. The brothers' famous fight at last came to an end when Yagjagbula, the younger brother, knocked the head-dress off the older brother Jabirringi with his boomerang. And then the brothers painted themselves on to the wall, where we see them today.

And so today, on the wall of Yiwarlalay, there are indeed representations of the two brothers, one larger than the other, as the story tells. Both are painted in strong stripes of, primarily, red and white. At other important sites in Wardaman country there are other large striped figures, some on the face of it also following a human form as the Brothers do. Often, but not always, they come in pairs. Generally, they are executed in some combination of red and/or yellow, alternating with and outlined by white. This is a characteristic way of representing Beings from Wardaman Dreaming stories. Photographs and written records from last century show how the Yiwarlalay figures have changed a little, both by their weathering and by their being repainted or retouched during the 1930s. According to Wardaman tradition, this does not alter the defining essentials of the images: these are the Lightning Brothers *as they painted themselves* on to the rock—just as other important Beings in Wardaman mythology, such as the Black-Headed Python, painted themselves on other rock sites in order to create an enduring image of themselves. The records made at different times of the Lightning Brothers story indicate that for decades it has remained constant. The version I give here is a summary of the one I have heard from Wardaman elders on the spot in the late 1990s (the wording above is partly adapted from that published by Flood and David[4]).

The wonderfully detailed story of the Lightning Brothers illustrates the richness of Aboriginal knowledge at its fullest. One should underline that it is not a generalized account of a motif, as Christian sources can explain what meaning there is in the image of Jesus on the cross; rather, it is a *specific* record of *specific* events, which take place at a *certain* place, and of which the record is set at that *very* place. Characteristically, one element in the story explains singular features of that place; so, the story is also an account of how the great rock at Yiwarlalay came to have the form it has. Notice also that in this Aboriginal knowledge the images were made in place by the ancient Beings themselves. Western knowledge, with its different frames of reference, does not easily conceive of rock paintings being made other than by human means. Western knowledge also treats chronology as a fundamental, and a first concern will be: what age are the figures? Wardaman knowledge recognizes paintings as having come about in three different ways: some paintings were made by the ancestral Beings, some paintings were made by Wardaman people, and some paintings were made by other peoples. But it does not see these as chronological units, or expect some neat ordering by which these three kinds of image-creating will fall into a simple sequence.

Archeological researchers, working with and alongside Wardaman elders and acknowledging their different way of thinking, address chronology in their own terms. A first strand of evidence is the record of the Lightning Brothers images at Yiwarlalay, and of the story of the Brothers, some decades ago in the Western record. A second is the results of archeological excavation at Yiwarlalay. A distinct horizon rich in ocher pigment, at a certain dated depth in the strata below the painted surface, might have been made at the time when painting began there on the scale we see on the painted surface today. This would set the story of the Lightning Brothers, or a comparable story illustrated by similar grand imagery, as having been told at and about Yiwarlalay for at least several hundred years in the past.

THE STORY OF THE RAINBOW SERPENT, AND ITS IMAGES IN WESTERN ARNHEM LAND PAINTING: FROM PRESENT INTO A FURTHER PAST BY INFORMED METHODS AND THEN BY FORMAL METHODS

Other stories in Wardaman country, as noted above, concern the Black-Headed Python, who painted himself on the rock at various places as he passed through Wardaman country, and created distinct and distinctive features in the landscape. Stories of a great serpent as a creator being (now generally known in English as the Rainbow Serpent; see Figure 2) are

Figure 2
Archaic Rainbow Serpent of characteristic form. Drawing after a painting in Western Arnhem Land. From Christopher Chippindale, Benjamin Smith, and Paul S. C. Taçon, "Visions of Dynamic Power," *Cambridge Archaeological Journal* **10 (2000).**

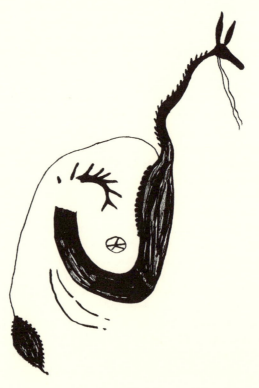

widespread throughout tropical north Australia. One of these serpents, Gorrondolmi, is central to the story of events at Yingalarri, as sketched above. Today and in recent times, Rainbow Serpents are not painted as simple snakes but as composite creatures.[5] Rainbow Serpents have the thick body of a muscular snake, like those of the python family, but this is combined with the head of another creature, often a large or powerful one—a large wallaby, a crocodile, even a water buffalo. And Rainbow Serpents have special tails, not like those of everyday snakes. Sometimes they have other features, such as arms or trailing lines from the head or neck, which real-world snakes do not possess. Other elements combined with the Rainbow Serpent include water lilies, for Rainbow Serpents are particularly associated with water holes.

So the Rainbow Serpent is a fairly unambiguous subject as painted today on bark or paper, and as represented in rock art. Aboriginal people in Arnhem Land are certainly confident in their identification of both recent and old images of Rainbow Serpents on the rock-art surfaces, and as archeologists we share that confidence. There also exist pictures of snakes, but consistently these have the traits of snakes alone, rather than the composite shapes of Rainbow Serpents. Again we can share the Aboriginals' confidence in distinguishing depictions of snakes from those of Rainbow Serpents.

Because of its distinctive form, the Rainbow Serpent in recent rock art is easy to recognize and one can see how its form has changed over time by reference to a well-understood relative chronology[6] and to the fairly well-based absolute chronology of rock art in Western Arnhem Land,[7] a well-studied region with many hundreds of rock-painting sites and many thousands of images. Its rock-art sequence is marked by distinctive changes both in subject and in the manners by which those subjects are depicted. Across a period of many hundreds of years we can identify Rainbow Serpent depictions, that is, images of which the central component is a snake, or snakelike body, combined with other characteristics such as heads of other animals, limbs, and singular tails which no real snake possesses. All these aspects are consistent with the way Rainbow Serpents are painted in later times.

Another striking element is the existence of two distinct types of tails to the Rainbow Serpents: one type has a tail as a single spike, the other a tail that has several radiating spikes. Sometimes Rainbow Serpents occur in pairs, one of each tail type. We wonder if these traits match the gender of Rainbow Serpents, one type male, the other female. Rainbow Serpents in the modern stories are of both genders. The earliest of the Rainbow Serpent images are distinctive and remarkably consistent in their forms and attributes; it is as if the image of the Rainbow Serpent had a more fixed form than it came to possess later. And these early Rainbow Serpents are in a well-recognized manner of painting which we think can be coupled with a distinct chronological period, about 4,000 to 6,000 years ago. These early images have a distinctive head, but no shoulder or broadening where the neck blends into the body. Instead, the body simply swells into a fatter zone, and then tapers into the start of the tail. The head has ragged ears on top, then tapers into a long snout, which drops sharply as if the Rainbow Serpent were pressing its snout down toward its tummy. Also, strikingly, instead of tapering like the doggy nose of a wallaby, as is typical of marsupials, the snout is parallel-sided, and even swells out a little at its tip. When Meredith Wilson, Paul S. C. Taçon, and I were looking at these early Rainbow Serpents, we wondered what creature(s) those features might come from. Since reptiles—snakes, lizards, crocodiles, geckos—do not have ears, the creature could only be a mammal. But there were no legs, and the striking form of the body and of the head echoed no north Australian mammal. The combination of curved swelling body with long snout pressed down over the chest did remind us of one kind of creature, the sea horse family of fishes, and so did the curving tail tapering from the body. But fish don't have ears! However, the banded pipefish, a fish of the sea horse family known from inshore waters of the Arnhem Land coast, does have fleshy tufts trailing back from the head much as ears do; it is thought they provide camouflage for the fish in weed beds.

A formal analysis of these early Rainbow Serpent traits compared them with those of pipefish and other plausible animals that might have contributed to the form of the Rainbow Serpents; it led us to conclude that the pipefish contributed a large element to the form of Rainbow Serpents as painted then.[8] We believe also that other motifs, distinctive of the period and characteristically painted alongside early Rainbow Serpents, may be derived from marine subjects. Later in time, those other elements disappear, together with the fishlike element in Rainbow Serpents. Neither occur in or with the Rainbow Serpents as they are painted today.

As we saw in the story of the Lightning Brothers, the Rainbow Serpent plays an important role in Wardaman mythology. It is a powerful supernatural being that passed through the country, making and shaping its character, at that time when the world was put into order. In the modern stories, the Rainbow Serpent is strongly connected with water. Typically (but not always), the Rainbow Serpent is involved in making water holes as she travels across the country. Fresh water is precious in Australia, and the billabongs and water holes are important also in other ways: they are good camping places; they provide food—fish, water snakes, water lilies, water goannas, crocodiles—and attract other creatures—ducks, geese, water birds, wallabies—that are also good tucker. So it is not surprising that the stories about how water holes came into existence are central to Aboriginal society. But there is no suggestion in present-day knowledge that the Rainbow Serpent is related to a little fish of the salty sea water, as seems to have been the case at the beginning.

The Lightning Brothers are an instance of a story associated with a special place and evident in the images at that place. We can follow the paintings at Yiwarlalay, and the stories related to them, several decades into the past; they may even be hundreds of years old. But we cannot trace them any further back in time. Nor can we make the same deduction from other large images of striped beings at other sites important in Wardaman knowledge. Although superficially similar in form to the Yiwarlalay paintings, they tell different stories, which do not involve the Lightning Brothers, or they are identified as beings that are not human at all.

Because the icon of the Rainbow Serpent is so distinctive in Arnhem Land painting, we can see how it extends several thousands of years into the past—but it does not go back forever. There seems to be a certain continuity across that period, but attributes of the Rainbow Serpents have also changed during that time. If the stories illustrated by the Rainbow Serpent pictures were closely linked to just what they depict, as they are today, then one can infer that the stories involving the Rainbow Serpent may have also decisively changed. The maritime element in the early Rainbow Serpent images has probably disappeared from later Rainbow Serpents in a changing environment, and the water places in the Rainbow Serpent stories are inland creeks and water holes.

THE DYNAMIC FIGURES OF WESTERN ARNHEM LAND PAINTING: INTO A FAR PAST BY FORMAL METHODS

As we have seen, learning about the Lightning Brothers and what happened at Yiwarlalay relies on *informed methods,* which depend on having access to Wardaman knowledge. In exploring images of the Rainbow Serpents, we began again with *informed methods* and drew on the knowledge of the Western Kunwinjku and Gunjeipni people. Having learned in that way to identify traits of the Rainbow Serpent which are distinctive enough to act as diagnostic pointers, we could extend into *formal methods;* that is, we learned to recognize Rainbow Serpents even when they take a rather different form. We were able to see how Rainbow Serpents have changed over time and, by extension, to sketch how the stories may have followed this transformation.

If the Rainbow Serpent extends back only to a certain period, then preceding phases of Arnhem Land art may belong in some sense to a different world of knowledge. Can we say anything about it? The changes in the form of the Rainbow Serpents caution us to expect something different, and so does the art. Although there are some strong elements of consistency and continuity in Western Arnhem Land art through its long sequence, there are also major changes. The most substantial shift in both subject matter and manner of depiction occurring between the time of the early Rainbow Serpents and a preceding era can be observed in the Dynamic Figures, named so by George Chaloupka because of the speedy energy with which these wonderfully elegant human figures run and tumble and interact.[9] The modern-day inhabitants of Arnhem Land refer to these old paintings as Mimi figures, made by former peoples who still occupy the land as spirits. They do not identify themselves with these thin beings living in cracks of the rocks, nor offer explanation of them in terms of their own knowledge. In short, the Dynamic Figures exist *beyond* informed knowledge. If we are to make sense of them, we have to take recourse to formal methods.

The work of David Lewis-Williams and colleagues in South Africa has, with reason, been an inspiration to researchers working on rock art in other regions. Starting with *informed methods,* that is, with the ethnographic and ethnohistoric sources concerning the knowledge of San peoples in southern Africa, he was able to look with fresh eyes at San rock paintings, images which before had been seen as naturalistic depictions of real-world subjects—animals, especially the eland, which is the greatest of the southern African antelope, and humans variously dressed, posed and busy about their hunting business. But, crucially, there were other images which could not be simple reproductions of a real natural world. Amongst these were therianthropes, beings which combined traits of humans and animals in a single being. The most famous of those Lewis-Williams identified—the one he calls the Rosetta Stone of his research—is at Game Pass Shelter in KwaZulu-Natal Province, South Africa. It is a picture of a human being with an eland head and eland feet, adjacent to and involved with a great dying eland. And in San knowledge, Lewis-Williams realized, a key element of experience is the visionary interaction in trance of San shamans with, especially, eland; in short, the Game Pass image is of the interaction of humans with eland in a visionary world of spiritual and ecstatic experience. From these initial insights, Lewis-Williams developed a dialectical dialogue between art and ethnographic knowledge, the former offering detailed images for which meaning was to be sought, the latter suggesting insights which might be manifest in the images.[10] Generalizing from the San example, Lewis-Williams and colleagues established a characteristic series of physical feelings and sensations, which shamans and humans experience in visionary transformations. So Lewis-Williams was able to generalize from the special case of San imagery, as understood through *informed methods,* to broader or even universal aspects to the imagery of visionary experience, that is, *formal methods* which could be explored for rock art of any place or time. The most developed case study, using those formal methods, is the explanation of elements in the Paleolithic cave art of Europe as imagery resulting from visionary experience.[11]

In our first field season together, in Western Arnhem Land, Benjamin Smith (then a newly graduated Ph.D. student and now head of the Rock Art Research Institute at the University of the Witwatersrand, South Africa, in succession to Lewis-Williams) and I looked together at previously reported rock art sites, some near the celebrated water hole of Djuwarr. We wondered whether his field experience with African rock art could also be applied to this Australian case. We looked with care at Dynamic Figures and noticed in them some traits reminiscent of visionary iconography as it is found in Southern Africa. One of us chanced to look at the rough back side of a large block at Djuwarr with a conspicuous painted panel on the other, smooth side. On the back, not noticed in earlier field-work, there was a fine painting in the unmistakable Dynamic manner: two standing figures adjacent and interacting, one a human figure, one a human with a kangaroo head—an animal-headed being (Figure 3).

On reviewing the range of imagery in the Dynamic Figures, we find in them a whole series of traits consistent with visionary iconography. There

Figure 3
Dynamic Figure group. Drawing after a painting in Western Arnhem Land. From Christopher Chippindale, Benjamin Smith, and Paul S. C. Taçon, "Visions of Dynamic Power," *Cambridge Archaeological Journal* **10 (2000).**

are therianthropes of various kinds, some with the head of a flying fox (fruit bat). These animal-headed beings carry dilly bags and spears, and they interact with humans. There are associations with fishes and birds, and there is a repeated element in the iconography, which again may suggest visionary metaphor. This element is a set of dots or dashes, which occur in many groups of Dynamic Figures, sometimes painted around the mouths of human figures (as if showing speech), or accompanying spears as if indicating their flight, or related to a wounded figure as if signifying blood, or associated with animal tracks as if to indicate their freshness. Explanations like these can make sense of each occurrence in a piecemeal way. But it would be more persuasive to see a single uniting factor in the dots, as an image which represents in a conventional way the sources of power associated with visionary experience.

In short, the distinctive characteristics of Dynamic Figures are consistent with visionary experience which, although having a biological and neurological basis, is experienced in different ways in different cultures. There is no single set of indicators for it, but rather a range of metaphors—being underwater or drowning (which would explain the fishes), rising above the earth (which would explain the birds and the flying foxes), or being stretched (which would explain the several Dynamic Figures which appear elongated), and so on. Although there are varied metaphors, and therefore varied imageries, that arise from visionary experience or are associated with it, there does not seem to be a single, distinctive, and unique set of traits in imagery which are *diagnostic* of visionary experience. On balance, in my view, the traits of Dynamic Figures are sufficiently distinctive and striking, and sufficiently consistent with its metaphors and experiences, so that visionary knowledge is likely to be a major part of the Dynamic imagery.

A special kind of knowledge in recent times in Arnhem Land is *clever men's business,* a form of benign sorcery. Many of its typical elements are elsewhere associated with visionary experience. Clever men can cure illness by extracting from the sufferer stones and objects, which they take out through the skin of their stomachs. They can travel distances by nonphysical means, to meet or consult other clever men who are at a far distance. Having established by formal means the likelihood of there being a visionary element to early Arnhem Land painting, we have looked with care at the informed sources, and duly found in recent knowledge that element, in clever men's skills and the business they do.

SUMMARY: AUSTRALIAN ROCK ART ON THE WORLD STAGE

In Australian rock art we can see how the country's indigenous population has been characterized both by stability and by change. The European immigrants' former view that Aborigines were primitives who had failed to evolve to a higher culture is now being countered by an emphasis on the green attitudes of indigenous Australians, as people who rightly resist the headlong and unsustainable fury of constant change which defines Western societies. What unites these seemingly opposing views is their defining Aborigines as an *unchanging* people. The Northern Territory rock art tells us a quite different story, one of a long sequence of transformations, in which some elements are stable over the long term, while others shift and change.

In this chapter, I have outlined some distinctive elements which make Australian rock art rather special and distinct from the rock art traditions of other regions and times, addressed elsewhere in the present volume. I have used three case studies to show a research approach facilitated by the rather special Australian circumstances. Australia is not only abundant in rock art, but also unusually rich in ethnohistoric and ethnographic knowledge extending into the very present, explaining why rock art was made and what it means. This provides us—better than in any other region of the world—with a solid base for what I called above an *informed* method of investigation, alongside the *formal* methods we everywhere struggle to improve. Australia also offers excellent circumstances for novel dating methods and establishing both *relative*[12] and *absolute* chronology.[13]

The combination of modern ethnographic insight with reasonably robust chronologies—elements present in all three case studies sketched here—facilitates the exploration of how much stability and how much change there may be in long-term patterns in rock art; so the key concerns of continuity and transformation in art and its imagery can be studied. In these and in varied other ways, the singular riches of Australian rock art give opportunities not often reached elsewhere.

ACKNOWLEDGMENTS

I thank my Aboriginal colleagues, whose country I have worked in, for access to sites, and my research colleagues, who worked with me on Australian and other rock art matters. I thank both for insights, teachings, companionship, and sharing my enjoyment of this great heritage.

NOTES

1. See George Chaloupka, *Burrunguy, Nourlangie Rock* (Darwin, NT: Northart, 1982); and Paul S. C. Taçon and Christopher Chippindale, "Najombolmi's People: From Rock Painting to National Icon," in *Histories Of Old Ages: Essays in Honour of Rhys Jones*, ed. Atholl Anderson, Ian Lilley, and Sue O'Connor (Canberra, ACT: Pandanus, Research School of Pacific and Asian Studies, Australian National University, 2001), 301–310.

2. For a further exploration of the issues see Paul S. C. Taçon and Christopher Chippindale. "Introduction: An Archaeology of Rock Art through Informed Methods and Formal Methods." In *The Archaeology Of Rock Art*, ed. Christopher Chippindale and Paul S. C. Taçon. Cambridge: Cambridge University Press, 1998: 1–10; George Nash and Christopher Chippindale, eds. *European Landscapes of Rock Art*. London: Routledge, 2000; Christopher Chippindale and George Nash, eds. *Pictures In Place: Looking At Rock Art In Its Landscape*. Cambridge: Cambridge University Press, 2003.

3. See Bruno David, Ian McNiven, Josephine Flood, and Robin Frost. "Yiwarlarlay 1: Archaeological Excavations at the Lightning Brothers Site, Delamere Station, Northern Territory." *Archaeology in Oceania* 25 (1990): 79–84.

4. See Josephine Flood and Bruno David. "Traditional Systems of Encoding Meaning in Wardaman Rock Art, Northern Territory, Australia." *Artefact* 17 (1994): 6–22.

5. See the paintings reproduced, for example, in Wally Caruana. *Aboriginal Art*. London: Thames and Hudson, 1993; and Christine Adrian Dyer, ed. *Kunwinjku Art From Injalak 1991–1992: The John W. Kluge Commission*. North Adelaide, SA: Museum Art International, 1994.

6. See Christopher Chippindale and Paul S. C. Taçon. "The Many Ways of Dating Arnhem Land Rock Art, North Australia." In *The Archaeology Of Rock Art*, ed. Christopher Chippindale and Paul S. C. Taçon. Cambridge: Cambridge University Press, 1998: 90–111.

7. See George Chaloupka. *Journey In Time: The World's Longest Continuing Art Tradition*. Chatswood, NSW: Reed, 1993.

8. Paul S. C. Taçon, Meredith Wilson, and Christopher Chippindale. "Birth of the Rainbow Serpent in Arnhem Land Rock Art and Oral History." *Archaeology in Oceania* 31 (1996): 103–124.

9. George Chaloupka. "Rock Paintings of the Dynamic Figures Style, Arnhem Land Plateau Region, Northern Territory, Australia." *Ars Praehistorica* 7–8 (1988–89): 329–337.

10. For this method in action see, for example, J. David Lewis-Williams. *The World of Man and the World of Spirit: An Interpretation of the Linton Rock Paintings*. Cape Town: South African Museum, 1988. Other examples and a discussion of consequent issues can be found in Geoffrey Blundell, Christopher Chippindale, and Benjamin Smith, eds. *Knowing And Seeing: Understanding Rock Art With And Without Ethnography*. In preparation.

11. A brief and early statement was given in J. David Lewis-Williams and Thomas A. Dowson. "The Signs of All Times: Entoptic Phenomena in Upper Paleolithic Art." *Current Anthropology* 29 (1988): 201–245. A fuller exposition is given in Jean Clottes and J. David Lewis-Williams. *The Shamans of Prehistory: Trance And Magic in the Painted Caves*. New York: Harry N. Abrams, 1998; and J. David Lewis-Williams. *The Mind in the Cave: Exploring Consciousness and Prehistoric Art*. London: Thames and Hudson, 2002. For a remarkable study, in the same spirit, of the celebrated Early Neolithic site of Çatalhöyük see J. David Lewis-Williams. "Constructing a Cosmos: Image, Power and Domestication at Çatalhöyük." In *Çatalhöyük Research Report* 2, ed. Ian Hodder. In press.

12. See Christopher Chippindale and Paul S. C. Taçon. "Two Old Painted Panels from Kakadu: Variation and Sequence in Arnhem Land Rock Art." In *Time And*

Space: Dating And Spatial Considerations In Rock Art Research (Papers Of Symposia F And E, Aura Congress Cairns 1992) ed. Jack Steinbring et al. Melbourne: Australian Rock Art Research Association. 1993: 32–56.

13. See R. Roberts, G. Walsh, A. Murray, J. Olley, R. Jones, M. Morwood, C. Tuniz, E. Lawson, M. Macphail, D. Bowdery and I. Naumann. "Luminescence Dating of Rock Art and Past Environments Using Mud-Wasp Nests in Northern Australia." *Nature* 387 (1997): 696–699; and D. Erle Nelson et al. *The Beeswax Art of Northern Australia.* Burnaby, BC: Simon Fraser University, Department of Archaeology, 2000.

Cyclical Nucleation and Sacred Space: Rock Art at the Center

Solveig A. Turpin

Two rock art enclaves in the arid lands of northern Mexico and the southwestern United States are used to test one step in a model that describes the transition from simple to complex societies. The Schaedelian model proposes a sequence that passes from dispersed foraging to cyclical nucleation to quasi sedentism, which may or may not lead to settled village life. At the core of this model is the shrine, or sacred space, around which the settlement pattern orbits. Two prehistoric societies provide support for the intermediate step in this model, demonstrating that aggregation coincided with the production of ritual art that sanctified natural features of the landscape. Thousands of petroglyphs surround distinctive geological formations on the eastern fringes of the Sierra Madre Oriental of northern Mexico, marking areas of diverse and accessible natural resources capable of supporting aggregations of people. Elaborate, monumental pictographs, produced by communal effort, were painted in the densely occupied rock shelters along the border between Mexico and the United States as part of a symbolic system generated to compensate for increased population density. Both areas demonstrate the relationship between cyclical nucleation and sacred space, as predicted in the Schaedelian model.

INTRODUCTION

The transition from egalitarian hunting and gathering to complex societies requires a series of structural transformations, whose material traces are often obscure and ambiguous, thus leaving both the underlying processes and their manifestations open to debate. Schaedel[1] has proposed an archeologically testable model that describes how hunters and gatherers move from dispersed foraging to cyclical nucleation to quasi sedentism, establishing the preconditions for a final step to sedentism that may or may not take place. At the core of Schaedel's model is the shrine, or sacred space, which forms the nucleus of the cyclical settlement pattern orbit and provides the most archeologically visible test of this hypothetical progression. By the time sedentism, village life, and later urbanism are firmly established, it is often difficult to find the nuclei of early settlement and especially the ephemeral early shrines. However, if Schaedel's model is valid, the roots and antecedents must lie in the patterned movements of hunting and gathering people and in the nodes of their scheduled or seasonal rounds. In the arid reaches of northern Mexico and southwestern Texas (Figure 1), two prehistoric hunting-and-gathering societies that never made the transition to sedentism provide examples of Schaedel's postulated relationship between cyclical nucleation and the emergence of sacred space, thus establishing support for that step in his model.

In both cases, aggregation is evidenced by dense concentrations of elaborate rock art which, by virtue of sheer size and complexity, imply group participation in the rituals that produced them. Although the two areas are

Figure 1
Map showing general location of the study areas, drafted by Carole Medlar.

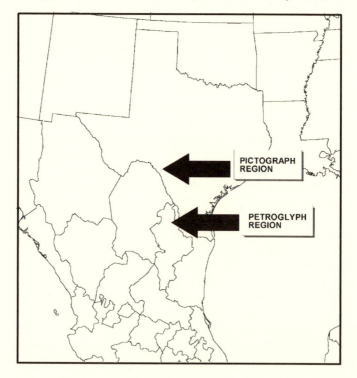

strikingly different in theme, style, technique, and medium, each is internally cohesive, thus defining the territory from which the pool of participants was drawn. In addition, both are exemplars of art generated by shamanistic religious systems, which rely upon altered states of consciousness and visionary experiences to unite the natural and supernatural landscapes. Unlike later art styles that are biographical, commemorative, or historical accounts of real events, the archaic styles are fraught with esoteric and hidden symbolism that can only be partially understood in the broad context of the history of religion[2] and the universality of the human nervous system.[3]

EXPLANATION OF TERMS

Hunting and gathering is used here to describe economies that were based completely on the exploitation of natural resources, although the emphasis should be reversed, since gathering was the mainstay of arid lands subsistence. Plants, and most specifically desert succulents, supplied the bulk of the diet as well as raw material for a fiber industry that fulfilled a myriad of other household needs. The people were nomadic in the sense that their seasonal or scheduled movements were influenced by the distribution of critical resources, primarily water and secondarily the maturation of plants and animals. Thus, some degree of dispersal was often necessary to avoid overtaxing the resource base, and aggregation was essential to the survival of a viable population.

Cyclical nucleation is a form of scheduled or seasonal aggregation that brings people together for a multitude of purposes, not the least of which are the selection of mates, the transfer of information, and the forging of social networks. At such times, leaders emerge from the egalitarian substrate, forming expedient or sequential hierarchies[4] that are inherently unstable or impermanent.[5] The new social order often relies on ritual as the information pathway that communicates and reifies its legitimacy. The ritual activity in turn contributes to the sanctification of nodes or centers of cyclical nucleation, defining sacred spaces or places that are recognized by the community and affect its physical and social configuration. The nodes then form the nucleus of a settlement strategy, which provides a framework for quasi sedentism with the shrine at the core of the emerging hamlet or village, either within the populated area or at the hub of smaller, more dispersed communities. Schaedel[6] defines quasi sedentism as a "phase of development within the food production process in which a society becomes sedentary without food production," often as a result of niche reduction or circumscription by natural or cultural forces. Another qualitatively different intermediate step is semisedentism, where horticulture or, in rare cases, natural abundance permit some residential stability on a seasonal basis. Sedentism, and the rise of complex societies, sees the replacement of rock art with ornamentation of a built environment, but many of the iconographic conventions or embedded meanings persist in altered form.

Shrines, or sacred spaces, cover such a broad spectrum of natural and artificial features that the definition here must focus on material remains that are archeologically recognizable.[7] Traditionally, sanctity or special powers are attributed to unusual or dramatic aspects of the landscape, such as mountains, springs, cliffs, or caves. However, the supernatural role of these landmarks remains speculative unless their special status is in some way physically marked or identified by oral tradition, ethnography, myth, or legend. The most visible means of imprinting a cultural stamp upon a natural feature is to paint on or incise images into a semipermanent medium, such as rock. Redundancy in theme and rule-bound iconography, in turn, identify images as ritual art that conveys information about the social condition while contributing to the consecration of these hallowed sites. Clearly, not all rock art is sacred nor are all shrines culturally modified, so their definition depends on discriminating variables such as context and content.

TEST CRITERIA

Two criteria must be met before Schaedel's model can be applied: (1) the settlement pattern must evidence seasonal or scheduled occupations of targeted locations by aggregated or relatively large populations; and (2) sacred space must have been marked by ritual activity that left archeologically visible traces, such as nonordinary architecture, art, or artifacts. Both these conditions are met by two prehistoric hunting-and-gathering populations who occupied relatively different ecological settings within the zone of aridity that characterizes northern Mexico and southwestern Texas. In both areas, ritual activity in the form of elaborate rock art bespeaks participation in a unified belief system that was also an organizing principle in the structure of these presumably egalitarian societies. Although executed in two different media, both petroglyphs and pictographs are the physical remains of rituals that define sacred space, creating the cores or nuclei around which the settlement pattern orbited. The first group of artists lived in the basin-and-range zone of Nuevo León and Coahuila; the second occupied both sides of the Rio Grande (or Río Bravo, as it is known in Mexico) in Coahuila and Texas, centering on the mouth of the Pecos River (Figure 1). Beyond their generalized adaptation to an exceedingly arid habitat, their commonality is expressed by their investiture of considerable effort in the production of elaborate, often monumental, rock art: in the Mexican case, petroglyphs, and in the Lower Pecos region, pictographs.

THE MEXICAN CASE

Along the fringes of the Sierra Madre Oriental, in the northern Mexican states of Nuevo León and Coahuila, a consistent relationship between large prehistoric open camps, petroglyphs, and alluvial fans at the constricted mouths of mountain valleys presents a good case for cyclical nucleation, ritual activity, and the emergence of shrines at aggregational nodes.[8] Somewhat to the west in Coahuila, Taylor[9] recognized that the juxtaposition of occupation sites and specific topographic features was environmentally determined, in large part to reconcile two most elemental needs: water and food. He used the term *tethered nomadism* to describe a system in which people were tied to isolated water sources from which they exploited the diverse vegetation of the *monte,* or valley slopes. As a consequence, in his model, population density remained low, cultural conservatism prevailed, and outside influences were minimized.

The distribution of sites in Nuevo León and eastern Coahuila is also hydrologically driven for many of the same reasons suggested by Taylor. Desertification of the region[10] has reduced the natural habitat to a barren wasteland, but pollen, phytoliths, gastropods, place names, and ethnohistoric accounts demonstrate a much more mesic environment during prehistory and early Colonial times than is in effect today.[11] The paucity of archeological research carried out in northeastern Mexico means that the full range of site types, their relative ages, and their distribution across the landscape remain relatively unknown. The sites under discussion here are an exception because the elaborate rock art was the focus of a government-funded survey that followed upon the work of Murray[12] and his colleagues.[13] Subsequently, extensive archeological research was undertaken at one of the largest sites, Boca de Potrerillos, in anticipation of its development as a cultural landmark.[14]

Archeologically, the large open petroglyph sites share three characteristics that are more consistent with Schaedel's model of cyclical nucleation and shrine formation than with Taylor's concept of dispersal and isolation: (1) site placement at the juncture of diverse ecological zones; (2) domestic evidence of aggregated or concentrated populations; and (3) sacred space established by the distinctive landforms and the abundant rock art. Exceptions include isolated petroglyph boulders that may have been hunting stations, open camps and rock shelters with occupational debris but no rock art, and pictograph sites that may belong to a different time and different people.

Physical Setting

Nuevo León and Coahuila are part of the great Mexican basin-and-range topographic zone, so named for high mountain basins isolated by the upthrust of the linear parallel mountain ranges that together make up the backbone of Mexico, the Sierra Madre. The eastern flanks of the Sierra are cut by canyons that are series of contiguous basins, encircled by rocky *cuestas*, or ridges, with constricted outlets that lead ever downward until the great plain of the Rio Grande Embayment is met. Although generally deficient in drinkable water, the canyons are configured so that precipitation coalesces in the bottom of the basins where it is channeled into streams or pools behind the natural dams created by the narrow *bocas*, or mouths. Ponding thus slows runoff and makes it available to humans, plants, and animals for a longer period of time.

The alluvial fans created by the transport of fine silt from the slopes provided extensive level, soft camp sites. The abutting slopes were littered with rocks that were the raw material for hearths, expedient tools, grinding slabs, and mobilary art, as well as the petroglyphs. The gravel beds at the base of the wide ravine contained other lithic raw material, such as silicified limestone, transported from upstream. The ponded water supported hydrophilic flora and fauna encircled by extensive grasslands; agave, yucca, and prickly pear grew on the rocky slopes, and the higher elevations were forested. The key element in the duration and frequency of occupation was rainfall. The sporadic precipitation and the small watersheds would have mandated strict attention to scheduling so that localized rainfall could be anticipated and exploited. Moderate rainfall was also the key to the preservation of the archeological record since the sediments carried downslope by runoff were capable of quickly burying intact hearths, complete with charcoal suitable for radiocarbon dating. The same factors that attracted prehistoric occupation were exploited in historic times by agricultural populations who planted subsistence crops on the alluvial fans. However, their methods were fairly primitive and caused little long-term damage to buried archeological deposits. Unfortunately, highway engineers noted the expediency of these graded crossings of the mountain ridges with much more disastrous effect (see Figure 2), often pushing aside petroglyph boulders and shattering others.

The dark side of nature was also a factor in the duration of occupation and the preservation of its remains. Raging torrents, often the result of hurricanes making landfall along the Gulf Coast, periodically ripped through the alluvial fans, cutting deep channels that scour to bedrock. The result is an inverse stratigraphy in which the older cultural deposits are now retained only on the fringes, at higher elevations than the more recent occupational debris left on the newly reforming fans. By virtue of their placement along the base and slopes of the ridges, the petroglyph boulders remained relatively secure, adding to the difficulty in assigning them to any particular time period or cultural levels.

A less tangible factor in the physical setting of these sites is the dramatic character of the topography. The upthrust ridges, with their characteristic V-formation (Figure 3), are highly visible landmarks and would presum-

Figure 2
The alluvial fans at the juncture of upthrust geological formations. Photo by
H. H. Eling, Jr.

ably figure as prominently in the mythic or sacred landscape. Murray[15] has noted the topographic potential for astronomical observations and alignments that may be reflected in the petroglyph assemblage, as well as the rudiments of a counting system similar to that of Mesoamerica (Figure 4). If true, the latter relationship would indicate contact if not familiarity with agricultural societies and emerging city-states far to the south; but again, the question of when and how is unanswerable at this time.

Evidence of Aggregated Populations

The domestic debris, which consists of hundreds of basin-shaped hearths, numerous grinding implements, stone tools, and a very few sherds of plain ceramics, demonstrates that people were drawn to these localized water sources and the more abundant vegetation that grew in the vicinity. The one site that has been subjected to intensive study, Boca de Potrerillos, has produced radiocarbon dates documenting a 7,800-year span of occupation that ended in 1958 when deep drilling of the aquifer began to substantially lower the local water table.[16] The stratigraphic sequence and the suite of dates reflect alternating periods of erosion and

Figure 3
The dramatic V-formation that usually signals concentrations of petroglyphs
and occupational debris. Photo by H. H. Eling, Jr.

Figure 4
Elaborate panel at Presa de la Mula. Drawing by Cristina Martínez.

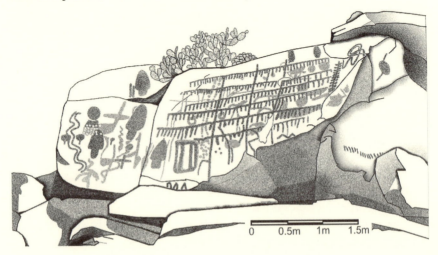

aggradation which would have affected the density, variety, and types of food sources available under any given climatic regime. Unfortunately, none of the radiocarbon dates could be directly related to any of the thousands of petroglyphs that encircle the site, although the iconography and technology are clearly prehistoric.

That some form of art was a part of the ideological system for at least 5,000 years was demonstrated by two types of incised sandstone pebbles, separated in time and space as well as by theme and technique.[17] The oldest style, dating to the period between 4,800 and 5,400 years ago, or 2,800 to 3,400 B.C.E., consisted of thin smoothed pieces of laminated sandstone deeply engraved with curvilinear designs. The central motif of a vulva-form was often elaborated into a butterfly or flower, suggesting some relationship to natural fecundity (Figure 5). The younger set was much simpler, marked by indecipherable shallow linear scratches. Subsequently, scores of similar stones of both types have been found in other locales by collectors, confirming their widespread distribution, typological uniformity, and probable symbolic importance to the local populace. Although the pebbles cannot be directly related to the larger petroglyph assemblage, they confirm that the practice of dinting and smoothing elaborate designs into stone was part of the local cultural trajectory more than five millennia ago.

Mortuary caves, replete with bundled burials encased in textiles and accompanied by funeral offerings, are another proxy measure of increased social complexity and aggregated populations. The most famous cemetery cave in Coahuila, Cueva de la Candelaria,[18] is the exemplar for the Mayrán complex, so named by Taylor to accommodate the material evidence of patterned mortuary behavior. Although contemporaneity with the petroglyphs cannot be confirmed by absolute dates, hafted knives found among the grave goods are portrayed in the rock art (see Figures 4 and 6), thus endowing both with ritual significance.

Figure 5
Incised pebbles from northern Coahuila. Drawing by David G. Robinson.

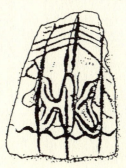

Figure 6
Boulder at Boca de Potrerillos. Photo by Solveig Turpin.

The Petroglyphs

At Boca de Potrerillos, and many other sites in similar settings, thousands of petroglyphs have been abraded into freestanding boulders (Figure 6) or exposed rock faces (Figure 4), thus sacralizing dramatic features of the landscape. In these sites, the focus was apparently the V-shaped clefts formed by upthrown *cuestas*, or ridges (Figures 2 and 3). Elsewhere, glyphs concentrate and consecrate unusual physiographic features, sometimes hills or rocky outcrops that rise above the flat plain. Any doubt about the enduring sanctity of these shrines is dispelled by Cerro Bola, where the Altar, a monumental petroglyph (Figure 7), lies at the base of a peyote-clad slope capped by three crosses. The Christian sanctuary on its summit is the destination of a Lenten pilgrimage of flagellants, which culminates with three penitents reenacting the Crucifixion. Scattered ashes show where the faithful have burned their sins as part of the redemptive process.

Presa de la Mula and Cerro Bola are exemplars of an iconography dom-

Figure 7
The Altar petroglyph at Cerro Bola. Drawing by Cristina Martínez.

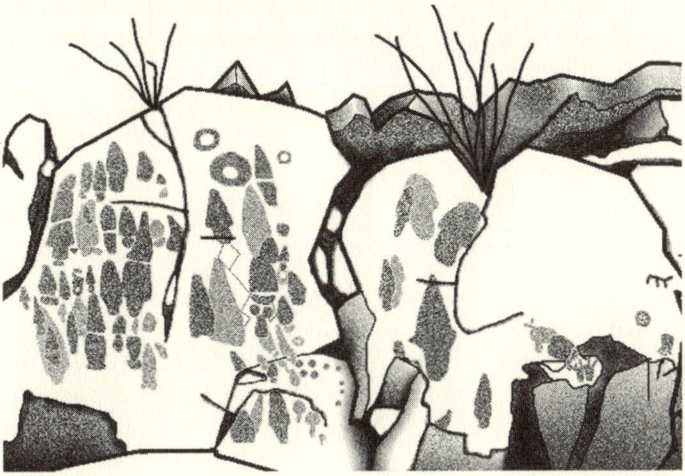

inated by redundant symbols (Figures 4 and 7). In both, hafted knives associated with an elaborate mortuary complex[19] suggest possible scarification or ritual blood-letting, a common element in Mesoamerican religion and one apparently embraced by the peripheral hunting-and-gathering people of Coahuila.[20] The general iconographic repertoire is much broader. Representational, but not necessarily realistic, designs include weapons, such as the hafted knives, spear throwers, and projectile points; human beings, either frontally posed or abstracted to foot prints and hand prints; and animals, which are usually reduced to antlers or tracks. The majority of the glyphs are abstract geometrics, whose forms are virtually universal and perhaps best explained in the context of recent theories on the neuropsychological response to altered states of consciousness. Variously called phosphenes, form constants, or entoptic phenomena, these nonrepresentational motifs are thought to mirror inner-eye experiences in a variety of stressful situations, ranging from migraine headaches to psychedelic visions. Native practitioners consistently record seeing specific classes of abstract designs while in an altered state of consciousness or trances associated with religious rites and ceremonies, regardless of their cultural or ethnic affiliation. Peyote is abundant in the vicinity of these sites and may have been used to induce a visionary experience, which was then translated into rock engravings, although similar effects can be achieved by any number of techniques, including sensory deprivation, rhythmic movements, starvation, and sleeplessness.

It is not necessary to invoke shamanistic or visionary sources to establish the ritual origin of the petroglyphs. The same designs are repeated within each site and from site to site, with varying proportions but very little innovation. Redundancy, repetition, and a standard rule-bound iconography are characteristics that identify ritual art[21] irrespective of the complexity of the society that produced it. In addition, like the pictographs discussed below, the Mexican glyphs are public art, open to view at all times, thus suggesting that their esoteric vocabulary served to inform the general populace.

Summary of the Mexican Case

Although springs and permanent water courses are rare in this region, the peculiarities of the local topography counteract the overall aridity by channeling sparse and sporadic rainfall into the basins, where it seeps downstream to pond at the restricted mouths of the canyons. Thus concentrated, the enhanced accessibility of water and its corollary biota provides the functional impetus for seasonal or scheduled use of specific locations largely conditioned by the timing of rainfall. Stratified, radiocarbon-dated domestic features and artifacts testify to the longevity of human occupation at these locales. Cyclical nucleation—people coming together for social reasons—was thus enabled by the physical proximity of essential resources; aggregated populations are represented by the density of domestic debris; and the shrine or sacred space is defined by the thousands of petroglyphs and their redundant iconography.

THE LOWER PECOS CASE

About 250 kilometers to the north, the Archaic hunters and gatherers who occupied the area around the mouth of the Pecos River some 3,000 to 4,000 years ago were so archeologically distinct from their contemporaries that an ethnic identity can be assumed. A finely honed adaptation to the semidesert environment revolved around the three major rivers that traverse the region: the Devils, the Pecos, and the Rio Grande. Here, the nodes of cyclical nucleation were rock shelters in the deeply entrenched canyons, overlooking the rivers or their tributaries (Figure 8). Like their more southerly neighbors, the Lower Pecos people were able to exploit diverse environmental zones from their sheltered habitations, but the medium that manifests their ritual art and performance is mural art, painted with mineral pigments derived from local sources. In rock shelters large and small, the Pecos River people painted monumental polychrome pictographs (Figure 9), whose restricted iconography and redundant themes mark them as ritual art,[22] created by communal investment and public display.

Figure 8
Black Cave. Photo by Solveig Turpin.

Physical Setting

A different set of physical constraints molded the settlement pattern of the Lower Pecos people. To the south, the northernmost outliers of the Sierra Madre rise abruptly from a waterless plain which extends almost to the Rio Grande. The mountains apparently presented a topographic and psychological barrier, which on rare occasions was penetrated by artists familiar with the thematic and iconographic conventions of the Pecos River style. On the northern front, rolling limestone hills flatten into expanses of shallow soils over limestone bedrock. They are dissected by entrenched tributaries, which deepen near the three major rivers whose confluences are now submerged by Amistad Reservoir. The natural shelter of caves and rock overhangs that line the canyons offered a protected environment for everyday life, and also contributed to the preservation of both domestic debris and the elaborate rock art. The sheer canyon walls were a major factor influencing the accessibility of resource zones created by the verticality of the topography. Despite shallow soils and limited water supplies, the desert succulents that flourished on the upland flats and rocky slopes provided most of the calories consumed by the Archaic people. The earth ovens used to process roots, bulbs, and any other edible plant parts are now reduced to mounds of burnt rock fringing the canyon and spilling down the slopes in front of dry rock shelters. The same plants

Figure 9
A section of one of the most famous Pecos River style pictographs. Segment of
a painting by Michael J. O'Brien. Courtesy of Michael J. O'Brien.

provided the raw materials from which mats, baskets, sandals, snares, nets, rope, and some clothing were woven. Vast exposures of ancient river gravel that cap many of the divides and line the stream courses provided a limitless supply of raw material for stone-tool manufacture.

The intermittent tributaries supported more mesic vegetation, such as oak groves favored by the white-tailed deer. It was the largest game animal for most of prehistory and ranks second only to the native mountain lion or puma in the hierarchy of the rock art bestiary, even though rabbits, squirrels, and rodents probably were more commonly caught and consumed. The floodplains now inundated by Lake Amistad afforded access to aquatic resources, represented in dry rock shelter deposits as fish bones, turtle carapaces, and mussel shells, as well as riverine vegetation and the animals it attracted. Here, too, were exotic stones transported from the mountainous regions, providing the local inhabitants with high-quality materials from distant sources.

Despite the characteristic aridity, then and now, abundant water, although of varying degrees of potability, is provided by the three permanent rivers: the saline Pecos, the muddy Rio Grande, and the clear spring-fed Devils. All three flow through the northern half of the region; there is no reliable source of water between the Rio Grande and the isolated springs in the mountain ranges to the south. The more influential variable, and the one that most affected the distribution of people across the landscape, was the replenishment of seasonal springs and casual water contained in natural cavities in the rocks (tinajas) that permitted free ranging in the upland environment. The pictographs in Pecos River style were produced during a period of increased aridity, which presumably encouraged the establishment of base camps along the permanent water sources supported by task-oriented forays into the uplands.[23]

Evidence of Aggregated Populations

The deeply stratified rock shelters were used by indigenous people over a period of about 10,000 years, beginning at the end of the Pleistocene and continuing into the late nineteenth century; but the well-honed desert adaptation, locally known as the Archaic period, extended from about 8,000 to 1,000 years before the present. The arid climate and the sheltered environment contribute to the preservation of normally perishable items, including skeletal remains, charcoal, fiber, wood, shell, and paint. Rock shelter excavations have produced ornamental river pebbles whose time depth equals or surpasses that of the incised stones of northern Mexico, but here the medium is paint, with the designs often replicating parts of the human body, such as eyes and female genitalia[24] (Figure 10). Bundled burials, some naturally mummified by aridity, are relatively common in dry rock shelter deposits, but natural sinkholes also served as convenient cemeteries.

The entire Archaic sequence is also represented by well-dated projectile point styles found in open camps, in the uplands and along the major rivers where many have been inundated or destroyed. In addition to rock shelters, typical Archaic site types are accumulations of burnt rock, the residue of hearths or earth ovens used to process desert succulents, and lithic scatters that represent all stages in the production of stone tools from the abundant chert sources.

Frequency counts of temporally diagnostic projectile points, radiocarbon dates, number of dated components, and mass of accumulated domestic debris peak in concert during two periods: between 3,000 and 4,000

Figure 10
Two painted pebbles with anthropomorphic elements from the Lower Pecos region. Drawing by Cristina Martínez.

years ago, during the Middle Archaic in the local sequence, and again between the time of Christ and 1,000 C.E., the latter portion of the Late Archaic period.[25] Here the emphasis is on the first peak, which correlates with the production of the majority of the extant pictographs, called the Pecos River style. Although rock art was produced by indigenous people until the time of European contact, only the Pecos River style clearly meets the criteria for ritual art based on its complexity, redundancy, communal involvement, and public display.

Like the open petroglyph sites of Nuevo León and Coahuila, the large rock shelters of the Lower Pecos were part of a dramatic landscape of mythic proportions (Figure 8). The huge overhangs would serve well as backdrops for staged performances, and canyon acoustics are such that the spoken word can often be heard over great distances. The paintings, however, depict a supernatural universe and the beings that inhabit it, thus sacralizing the shelter walls.

The Pictographs

The polychrome pictographs of the Pecos River style are monumental in scale and characterized by iconographic and thematic redundancy, which confirms their ritual function, whether in large site or small. The central figure is a towering anthropomorph, sometimes standing erect with raised hands, flourishing weapons, other times ascending, soaring, or flying horizontally (Figure 9). Several iconographic conventions are employed to illustrate the supernatural status of the focal character. The power of magical flight is conveyed by winged, soaring, or ascending figures, often emerging from faults or cracks in the bedrock.[26] Others rise or fall from circular motifs that signify the passage between the upper, middle, and lower tiers of the supernatural universe. The central figure is frequently surrounded by spirit guardians that look like miniature replicas of the main character, disembodied antlers, spear throwers, birds, and feathers, the latter as an abstracted metaphor for magical flight.

The shamanistic metamorphosis, especially the ability to assume animal form, is expressed by secondary characteristics such as antlers, claws, feathers, fur, and composites thereof.[27] The most powerful animal in the local bestiary, the mountain lion or puma, also dominates the rock art, often appearing in conflated human form, standing erect but with feline attributes, hence the nickname were-cougar (Figure 11). Other favored animals are deer, birds, rabbits, and serpents, but two powerful predators—bears and canines—are curiously missing in the Pecos River style.

The dangers experienced during the so-called little death of shamanistic trance are illustrated by inverted figures with down-flowing hair or, more infrequently, by skeletonizing (Figure 9). Less obvious is the concept of duality, which is encoded by placing animals in a subsidiary position, flanking a central composite human-animal figure, or by shadowing, layering two identical outlines so that one appears behind the other (Figure 9). The religious implications of the Pecos River style have been discussed in detail in several publications,[28] but less so the elements that are of critical importance here: its communal production during a hypothesized period of emerging social complexity.

Figure 11
Anthropomorphic mountain lion. Excerpt from drawing by David G. Robinson.

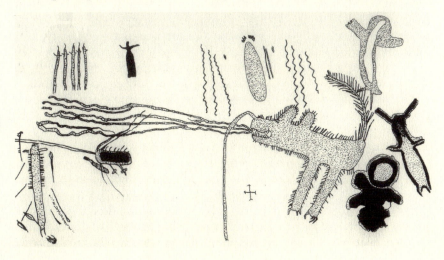

Communal involvement in the production of the art is suggested by the size of some of the paintings, which reach heights of six meters above the ground, and by the inaccessibility of others. These figures could not have been painted without the aid of scaffolds or ladders. Some of the more monumental pieces appear to have been outlined, perhaps by more skilled artists, with helpers filling in the interior. Other assistants may have contributed the labor required to gather and grind the mineral pigments, an act consistent with preparation for ceremonies to be enacted during aggregation. Large compressed cakes of pigment recovered from dry rock shelters demonstrate both an anticipated need and the means of fulfilling it, underscoring the planning and preparation that preceded the acts of creation. The recurring depiction of motifs not seen in nature, such as some of the fantastic or grotesque creatures found on shelter walls throughout the region, also indicates that the community at large understood and recognized the meaning of images which might be inscrutable outside the context of the belief system that conceived them.

The larger, more complex Pecos River style pictographs are public displays, sometimes visible from considerable distances. Isolated paintings do appear in smaller shelters, where their audience would perforce be limited and their function probably more personal, but the most elaborate compositions seem to have a performative character. The panels are notable for their size, coloration, and layers of overpainting. Superimposition provides clear evidence of sequential use of the same space, often to the point where the individual figures are obscured. It appears that the act of painting in this specific place was more important than the clarity of the artwork itself. The shelter wall had become sacred space, drawing from and contributing to the solemnity of the ceremonies performed within its bounds. It is perhaps noteworthy that the later indigenous styles, painted hundreds or thousands of years later, rarely desecrate or even overlap the more ancient works, suggesting their supernatural power was acknowledged for millennia after the passing of the artists.

Finally, territoriality, a corollary of population density, may be expressed in the rock art at various aggregation sites. Although all the Pecos River style pictographs convey a shamanistic worldview, differences in emphasis may reflect group affiliation within the larger society. For example, Panther Cave is so named for the many large felines or feline shamans, while Seminole Canyon is dominated by winged and antlered anthropomorphs found nowhere else. Rattlesnake Canyon has many rabbit-eared snake shamans, but no were-cougars, as though proprietary control of motifs was spatially segregated. In sites that are clearly not aggregation nodes, the highland Mexican anthropomorphs rarely wield weapons, as though the need for blatant power declined with distance from the heartland and the need to control desirable resources. Instead, a recurring motif that shows felines impaled upon a lance or long rod implies some disdain for the signature animal of the riverfront caves (Figure 12). Such expressions of territoriality would be consistent with the hypothesized population density and the principles of cyclical nucleation.

Summary of the Lower Pecos Case

Although three physical factors—climatic aridity, hydrology, and geology—obviously affected the distribution of people and their exploitation strategies, the emergence of a strongly regionalized cultural persona, verging on ethnicity and including the florescence of monumental art, can only be explained in a social context. The physical preconditions may have

Figure 12
Two versions of the impalement theme. Drawings by Deborah and Jennifer Cannon.

begun sometime around 5,000 years ago, when a regional trend toward aridity peaked.[29] Evidence for climatic change has been detected in pollen and macroflora studies, flood sequences, massive erosion episodes, and indirectly through a proliferation of processing and storage facilities for desert succulents, as well as through broadening of resource procurement strategies.[30] The key index markers for this period are highly distinctive contracting stem dart points, whose distribution is roughly the same as that of the Pecos River style pictographs. These projectile point styles are well fixed in time by their stratigraphic associations with radiocarbon dates, generated by decades of excavation in various dry rock shelters, and serve as chronological diagnostics for open sites where datable material is lacking. Thus, these stone tools are a proxy measure of site frequency and occupational intensity, especially since their period of popularity can be correlated with other environmental and cultural changes.[31] The physical evidence for regionalization then clearly defines an insular cultural area some 150 kilometers in diameter centering on the mouth of the Pecos River and extending south of the Rio Grande into the mountainous zone of northern Coahuila. The social response to environmental stimuli included a number of economic and social strategies, not the least of which were intensification of ritual, the production of monumental art, and the emergence of an ethnic identity.

Although increased aridity generally connotes decline in available resources, the proliferation of desert succulents provided a reliable although monotonous foodstuff that soon became the staple of the Lower Pecos diet. As the ephemeral water sources of the uplands evaporated, the bulk of the population was constrained to the major rivers with their permanent supply of fresh water. To accommodate this redistribution of settlement, procurement strategies shifted from collective foraging on a seasonal schedule to task-oriented groups that forayed into the dissected canyon-upland zone to exploit the flora and fauna and return them to the riverine camps. The result is an apparent contradiction since both a proliferation of upland camps and an intensification of rock-shelter or river-terrace occupations would occur simultaneously. Such an effect might be misconstrued as an increase in population, when in fact it is the result of concentrating a large percentage of the people in a smaller space for a longer period, specifically, population density instead of sheer numbers of people.

Increased population density, effected by this form of environmental conscription, incited the need for social controls, which were reified by ritual performances such as the production of monumental art.[32] Thus, for the duration of the need, the nomadic hunters and gatherers of the Lower Pecos Region adopted a nascent form of quasi sedentism, which included cyclical nucleation for ceremonial purposes and the delineation of sacred space by ritually produced art.

SUMMARY

Schaedel's[33] model of cyclical nucleation and quasi sedentism is derived from his decades of inquiry into the processes that led to urbanism and the rise of the state, especially in the Andes. However, the antecedents are best sought in hunting-and-gathering societies, where the key elements can still be detected archeologically. Two such prehistoric societies occupied different ecological zones within the arid lands of northeastern Mexico and southwestern Texas. The indigenous people of Nuevo León and Coahuila defined sacred space by incising thousands of abstract petroglyphs into boulders surrounding highly distinctive topographic features. These landmarks also served to identify abundant resource zones capable of supporting aggregated populations. The Archaic inhabitants of the Rio Grande, along the *frontera* between Coahuila and Texas, created a monumental art style to commemorate their religious and social beliefs during a period of emerging complexity, perhaps encouraged by an incipient form of quasi sedentism. In both cases, shrines or sacred places were established as one of the social mechanisms attendant on cyclical nucleation, thus fulfilling expectations derived from Schaedel's model.

ACKNOWLEDGMENTS

The thesis of this paper derived from many conversations with Dr. Richard P. Schaedel, who never formally explicated this model in print, but rather elaborated it in his graduate classes and in conversations with his colleagues, most especially Drs. Herbert H. Eling and David G. Robinson. The many illustrators who contributed to this paper are gratefully acknowledged: Cristina Martínez, David G. Robinson, Michael O'Brien, and Deborah and Jennifer Cannon.

NOTES

1. Richard P. Schaedel. "The Temporal Variants of Proto-State Societies." In *Alternative Pathways to Early State*, ed. Nikolay N. Kradin and Valeri A. Lynsha. Vladivostok: Dal'nauka, 1995: 47–53.

2. Mircea Eliade. *Shamanism: Archaic Techniques of Ecstasy*. New Jersey: Princeton University Press, 1972.

3. J. David Lewis-Williams and Thomas Dowson. "Signs of the Times: Entopic Phenomenon in Upper Paleolithic Art." *Current Anthropology* 29 (1988): 201–245.

4. Gregory A. Johnson: "Organizational Structure and Scalar Stress." In *Theory and Explanation in Archaeology*, ed. Colin Renfrew, Michael J. Rowlands, and Barbara Abbott Segraves. London: Academic Press, 1982: 402–403.

5. Margaret J. Conkey. "Ritual Communication, Social Elaboration, and the Variable Trajectories of Paleolithic Material Culture." In *Prehistoric Hunter-Gatherers: The Emergence of Social Complexity*, ed. T. Douglas Price and James A. Brown. New York: Academic Press, 1985: 300.

6. See Schaedel. "The Temporal Variants of Proto-State Societies." p. 48.

7. David Carmichael, Jane Hubert, Brian Reeves, and Audhild Schanche. *Sacred Sites, Sacred Places.* London: Routledge, 1994.

8. Stephen M. Carpenter. "Archaeology of the Upper Rio Salinas Basin." M.A. thesis, University of Texas at Austin, 1996.

9. Walter W. Taylor. "Tethered Nomadism and Water Territoriality: An Hypothesis." *Actas y Memorias del XXXV Congreso Internacional de Americanistas,* 1964: 197–203.

10. W. Breen Murray. "Environmental Impacts of Hyperutilization in a Semi-Arid Region: Monterrey's Search for Water." *El Norte* (Monterrey, Mexico) (7 July 1991).

11. Solveig A. Turpin, Herbert H. Eling, Jr. and Moisés Valadez Moreno. "From Marshland to Desert: The Late Prehistoric Environment of Boca de Potrerillos, Nuevo León, Mexico." *North American Archaeologist* 14:4 (1993): 305–323; *idem:* "The Archaic Environment of Boca de Potrerillos, Northeastern Mexico." *North American Archaeologist* 15:4 (1994): 331–357; *idem:* "Boca de Potrerillos, Nuevo León: Adaptación prehispánica a las áridas del noreste de México." In *Arqueologia del Occidente y Norte de México,* ed. Eduardo Williams and Phil C. Weigand. Zamora, Mexico: El Colegio de Michoacán, 1995: 177–224.

12. W. Breen Murray. "Rock Art and Site Environment at Boca de Potrerillos, Nuevo León, Mexico." *American Indian Rock Art* 7–8 (1982): 57–68.

13. Jon Olson. "Un sitio de petroglifos en el noreste de México." In *Boca de Potrerillos,* ed. Ernestina Lozano de Salas. Monterrey, Mexico: Universidad Autónoma de Nuevo León y Museo de Bernabe de las Casas, 1998: 55–123; María Guadalupe de Witt Sepúlveda and José Francisco Garza Corillo. "Arte rupestre en la sierra El Antrisco, Mina, Nuevo León." In *Boca de Potrerillos,* ed. Ernestina Lozano de Salas. Monterrey, Mexico: Universidad Autónoma de Nuevo León y Museo de Bernabe de las Casas, 1998: 35–47.

14. See Turpin et al. "Boca de Potrerillos, Nuevo León."

15. W. Breen Murray. "Calendric Petroglyphs of Northern Mexico." In *Archaeoastronomy in the New World,* ed. Anthony F. Aveni. Cambridge: Cambridge University Press, 1982: 195–204; *idem:* "Numerical Representations in North American Rock Art." In *Native American Mathematics,* ed. Michael E. Closs. Austin: University of Texas Press, 1986: 45–70; *idem: Arte rupestre de Nuevo León: Numeración prehistórica.* Monterrey, México: Archivo General del Estado, Cuadernos del Archivo 13 (1987).

16. See Turpin et al. "Boca de Potrerillos, Nuevo León."

17. Solveig A. Turpin, Herbert H. Eling, Jr., and Moises Valadez M. "The Mobiliary Art of Boca de Potrerillos." *Plains Anthropologist* 41:156 (1996): 105–116.

18. Luis Aveleyra de Anda, Manuel Maldonado-Koerdell, and Pablo Martínez del Río. *Cueva de la Candelaria.* México, D.F.: Memorias del Instituto Nacional de Antropología e Historia V, 1956; Walter W. Taylor. "Archaic Cultures Adjacent to the Northeastern Frontier of Mesoamerica." In *Handbook of Middle American Indians. Vol. 4: Archaeological Frontiers and External Connections,* ed. Gordon F. Eckholm and Gordon R. Willey. Austin, TX: University of Texas Press, 1966: 59–94.

19. See Aveleyra et al. *Cueva de la Candelaria:* 87–91; and Walter W. Taylor. "Archaic Cultures Adjacent to the Northeastern Frontier of Mesoamerica." In *Handbook of Middle American Indians. Vol. 4: Archaeological Frontiers and External*

Connections, ed. Gordon F. Eckholm and Gordon R. Willey. Austin: University of Texas Press, 1966: 59–94.

20. Solveig A. Turpin and Herbert H. Eling, Jr. *Cueva Pilote: Ritual Bloodletting Among the Prehistoric Hunters and Gatherers of Northern Coahuila, Mexico.* University of Texas at Austin: Institute of Latin American Studies and Saltillo, Coahuila: Instituto Nacional de Antropología e Historia, 1999.

21. See Conkey. "Ritual Communication, Social Elaboration, and the Variable Trajectories of Paleolithic Material Culture"; Christopher Donnan. *Moche Art and Iconography.* Los Angeles: University of California Latin American Studies 33, 1976: 5; John H. Rowe. "Form and Meaning in Chavin Art." In *Peruvian Archaeology,* ed. John Howland Rowe and Dorothy Menzel. Palo Alto, CA: Peek Publications, 1967: 78.

22. Forrest Kirkland and William W. Newcomb, Jr. *The Rock Art of Texas Indians.* Austin, TX: University of Texas Press, 1967; Solveig A. Turpin. "Speculations on the Age and Origin of the Pecos River Style." *American Indian Rock Art* 16 (1990): 99–122; *idem:* "Rock Art and Its Contribution to Hunter-Gather Archaeology: A Case Study from the Lower Pecos River Region of Southwest Texas and Northern Mexico." *Journal of Field Archaeology* 17:3 (1990): 263–281; *idem:* "The Were-Cougar Theme in Pecos River-Style Art and Its Implications for Traditional Archaeology." In *New Light on Old Art,* ed. David S. Whitley and Lawrence L. Loendorf. University of California at Los Angeles: Institute of Archaeology Monograph 36, 1994: 75–80; *idem:* "On a Wing and a Prayer: Flight Metaphors in Pecos River Art." In *Shamanism and Rock Art in North America,* ed. S. A. Turpin. San Antonio, TX: Rock Art Foundation, 1995: 73–102.

23. See Turpin. "Rock Art and Its Contribution to Hunter Gatherer Archaeology."

24. Mark L. Parsons. "Painted Pebbles." In *Ancient Texans,* ed. Harry J. Shafer. San Antonio, TX: Texas Monthly Press, 1986: 185.

25. See Turpin. "Speculations on the Age and Origin of the Pecos River Style."

26. See Turpin. "On a Wing and a Prayer: Flight Metaphors in Pecos River Art."

27. See Turpin. "The Were-Cougar Theme in Pecos River-Style Art and Its Implications for Traditional Archaeology."

28. See Kirkland and Newcomb. *The Rock Art of Texas Indians.*

29. Vaughn M Bryant. *Late Full-Glacial and Postglacial Pollen Analysis of Texas Sediments.* Ph.D. dissertation. The University of Texas at Austin, 1969.

30. Kenneth Brown. "Prehistoric Economics at Baker Cave: A Plan for Research." In *Papers on Lower Pecos Prehistory,* ed. S. A. Turpin. The University of Texas at Austin: Studies in Archeology 8 (1991): 87–140.

31. See Turpin. "Rock Art and Its Contribution to Hunter Gatherer Archaeology."

32. See Turpin. "Speculations on the Age and Origin of the Pecos River Style."

33. See Schaedel. "The Temporal Variants of Proto-State Societies."

Women in Prehistoric Art

Camilla Power

In this chapter I will first discuss women's role in the emergence of art. I will then show how this evolutionary approach can illuminate imagery of women in art from the European Upper Paleolithic and African Later Stone Age. Current Darwinian models argue that female strategies drove the earliest symbolic behavior. As brain sizes increased in *Homo heidelbergensis* and the immediate ancestors of *Homo sapiens* (specifically the period from 500 to 130,000 B.P.), so did reproductive stress on females. Evolutionary ecology predicts conflict between the sexes over investment in offspring. Once ovulation had been concealed in the human lineage, menstrual bleeding became the only good indicator of impending fertility. But while concealed ovulation withholds information from males about which females are fertile at any time, the salience of the menstrual signal undermines this effect, marking out imminently fertile females from pregnant or lactating ones. To resist male discrimination between cycling and noncycling females, coalitions of late archaic/early modern *Homo sapiens* women began cosmetically manipulating menstrual signals—sham menstruation. Collective, deceptive, and amplified use of red pigments as body paint confused information available to men about women's reproductive status, and effectively formed a preadaptation to ritual. This model predicts that the earliest art will be evidenced by a cosmetics industry, dominated by red pigments. The model offers further predictions in relation to the rock art record. Particularly I will address: (a) the focus on women's reproductive signals; (b) the importance of coalitions; (c) the link between women and game animals; and (d) the original signature of ritual power.

INTRODUCTION

From a Darwinian perspective, symbolism in general and art in particular present a puzzle. Evolutionary ecologists are concerned with calculating the costs and benefits of behavior. From this point of view, human engagement with the symbolic realm in elaborate ritual, religious, and artistic traditions appears inordinately costly. And for what end? In a world rife with competition for mates and resources, why would it be adaptive for an individual to expend time and energy trying to communicate her dreams and illusions? Why would it benefit others to bother with such unverifiable fantasies? What evolutionary process could have led human ancestors to waste so much time and energy on things that don't exist?

Given the late dating for any secure archeological evidence of art and symbolism, we can agree with Philip Chase that "there is no reason to believe symbolic culture was ever essential for survival."[1] Rather than an adaptation to environment, the extraordinary wastefulness of art may better be explained in terms of sexual or signal selection.[2] Here, I will use sexual selection theory to outline a model for the emergence of art and ritual. I aim to "employ theory to deduce the conditions under which particular social or behavioral forms will emerge or persist. This deduction must then be framed in testable (operational) terms, and compared with relevant observations."[3] The model should constrain what we expect to see as evidence of art and ritual in the archeological record, indicating correlatives of that evidence. If initial conditions can be specified with sufficient precision, it may be possible to make predictions which are testable against the ethnographic database of recently extant ritual and rock art traditions. Such testing is not a matter of appeal to particularist ethnographic precedents, projected back onto a patchy Pleistocene record. The model is theory-driven, constraining our expectation of the way symbolic systems emerge and are transmitted. If a narrative of symbolic cultural origins fails to offer parsimonious, predictive accounts of symbolic systems, it hardly amounts to a theory at all.

A DARWINIAN MODEL FOR THE EVOLUTION OF ART AND RITUAL

The model is succinctly stated: cosmetic and symbolic signaling arose as a strategic response by female coalitions to the reproductive stress experienced as a result of rapid encephalization in the late Middle Pleistocene. Males who were relatives of female coalition members would be included, whereas males who were potential or actual mates would be excluded from these coalitions. These outgroup males were the targets of the female coalitionary signals, which were designed to motivate them to produce high-energy foods for consumption by members of the coalition.

The basic premise of the model is the expectation of conflicting reproductive strategies between the sexes. Crudely put, for any sexually reproducing species, males and females get their genes into the next generation by different means. For mammals and especially primates, this involves lengthy periods of gestation and lactation requiring investment of considerable resources by females, while males are not necessarily committed to more than the energy needed to access and impregnate mates.[4] There will be differential trade-offs between the sexes over investment of energy in current offspring (parental effort) as against energy expended for producing future offspring (mating effort). In the case of human evolution, these trade-offs are likely to be especially critical because of the extraordinary energetic costs imposed on human mothers by encephalization.[5]

Critical to the reproductive success of females as they came under selection pressure for larger-brained offspring was extracting energy from new sources. The first major increase in brain size occurs with the appearance of early *Homo* more than two million years ago, culminating in *Homo ergaster*. These costs could have been offset by shifts to a high quality diet, allowing reduction of gut size;[6] increases in female body size;[7] and changes in life history variables, such as increased longevity, promoting grandmothering,[8] and secondary altriciality, slowing down maturation rates of the larger-brained offspring.[9] Investment by males may have been intermittent rather than systematic, and directed as mating effort towards cycling females, rather than pregnant/lactating females.[10] A period of more than a million years, from the Lower to early Middle Pleistocene, is characterized by stasis in relative brain size.[11] The accelerated encephalization rates of the late Middle Pleistocene brought increased reproductive costs, particularly to mothers in early stages of lactation. These steeply increasing costs of reproduction are likely to have driven major social and sexual behavioral changes.[12] Above all, those females who secured increased levels of investment provided by males would have enhanced their fitness.[13]

For females, sexual signals are the primary mechanisms for eliciting behavioral changes in males. Once signs of ovulation were phased out in human evolution, there still remained a highly visible signal giving information to males about imminent fertility. On Darwinian theoretical grounds we can expect that Pleistocene males would be very interested in knowing which female is menstruating, since that female is likely to be fertile within a short period. Males can be expected to compete to put effort—mating effort—into bonding with such a female if this is likely to improve their prospects of a fertile mating. This means that the menstrual signal is economically valuable, and it could be used by females to manipulate male behavior. In a natural fertility population with interbirth intervals of several years and long periods of lactation, a minority of the female population would be cycling at any one time. The menstrual signal does not enable a philanderer (i.e., a male who aims to find fertile females but avoids any further investment) to pinpoint a female's moment of fertility with accuracy, but it does allow a would-be philanderer to target a female who is likely to be fertile in the near future. This makes possible a type of philanderer strategy whereby a male locates a cycling female and directs mating effort toward her to gain fertile matings. But once she is pregnant or early in lactation, the philanderer is liable to desert her if another cycling female becomes available.

From the viewpoint of a pregnant or lactating female, a cycling female represents a threat, capable of diverting male investment away from her. What strategies can noncycling females develop to deal with this problem? We could expect to see noncycling females cooperating to prevent any cycling female from flaunting her menstrual signal. But there is an important reason why this is not going to be the most productive strategy from the viewpoint of noncycling females. Remember that the menstrual signal is economically valuable. It promotes male mating effort; males should compete to bond with menstrual females. Above all it is important for noncycling females to control access to the attractive cycling female, surrounding her and preventing any philanderer male from abducting her.

If they are able to do this (possibly with help of male kin), then they are in a position to use her attractions for their own benefit. Now, all the females can join in with the menstruant, borrowing her signal and amplifying it by use of blood-colored substances. This has the effect of broadcasting to potential male provisioners that there is an imminently fertile female in the vicinity, to mobilize male mating effort. But it also aims to deter males from discriminating between cycling and noncycling females.

This strategy of sham menstruation generates protosymbolic ritual coalitions. It is effective as long as noncycling females receive some of the benefits of male mating effort mobilized by the prospect of access to cycling females. It has an inbuilt reciprocity, since any fertile female alternates between cycling and not cycling. It also generates a basic sexual morality. Each time she menstruates, a female is put on the spot. Is she going to cheat on noncycling females, and use her attractions for short-term gain? Or will she cooperate in using her attractions for the benefit of a wider coalition? In cooperating, a cycling female offers a costly and reliable signal of commitment to a long-term alliance with noncycling members of the coalition. Once she herself is pregnant and subsequently lactating, she expects to receive reciprocal benefits, derived from the signals of other cycling members of the coalition.

Such a strategy of coalitionary cosmetics use offers the prototype for ritual in general, and puberty and initiation rites in particular. I argue that investor males came to sexually select such cosmetically decorated females because these females ritually displayed social alliances that were invaluable for the support of large-brained offspring.

Members of these cosmetically decorated coalitions had a strong interest in sharing and sustaining imaginary constructs. A full-blown symbolic repertoire would emerge as a result of the specific form of signaling used by females in their strategy of resisting male philanderers. The last thing that any female coalition wants is for a dominant male philanderer to grab the most attractive, cycling member(s) of the coalition. So they surround these menstruating females, creating a fence or picket line around them, drawing on the support of male kin, sons and brothers, in this protective strategy. It is in signaling "no access" that symbolism is born. If a female chimp signals (with her large estrous swelling) to a male chimp that she is ready to mate, she is communicating that she is the right species, the right sex, and that this is the right time for fertile mating. In the ritual resistance strategy of human females, we predict the precise opposite: signals communicating "we are the WRONG species, the WRONG sex, and this is the WRONG time (we're all menstruating which implies that soon it will be the right time)." Multimedia effects of song, dance, body paint, and ritual pantomime will be used to get that message across to outsider males who may initially be reluctant to comply. The result will be a collective repertoire of shared fantasy constructs, things that do not and cannot exist in the real world, but only in a symbolic realm—gods that are at the same time male and female, human and animal. The flag which highlights these constructs of ritual power will be red. Females in a taboo state of menstruation are as if transformed into animals and males, while their male kin inside the protective coalition also become animal and bloody, gender ambiguous, quasi female. During ritual action, perceptual categories are transcended by a signal of ritual power which reads "WRONG!"

PREDICTIONS FROM THE SHAM MENSTRUATION MODEL

The main prediction derived from the sham menstruation model is that the earliest evidence of ritual traditions in the archeological record will take the form of a cosmetics industry focused on red pigment. Male sexual selection for cosmetically decorated females should drive an explosive spread of such traditions, such processes of sexual selection reinforcing speciation of anatomically modern humans.[14] This first evidence for ritual should correlate with the first evidence for modern hunting and homebase behaviors. Since sham menstruation is a response to the stress of encephalization, the model would be falsified if significant pigment use were found prior to major increase in brain size, or only subsequent to cranial capacities maximizing. The onset is predicted in the period roughly from 500,000 to 100,000 B.P.

The model predicts that the first gods should be wrong species/sex metaphors linked with red or menstrual cosmetics. These signals establish taboos—rules about access or consumption—on the flesh of women and game animals. As women ritually identify themselves as animals, the blood of menstruating women becomes equated with the blood of hunted prey.[15]

EVIDENCE OF PIGMENT USE IN ARCHEOLOGY AND ETHNOGRAPHY

I do not intend to test all these predictions in this chapter, since some have been addressed in more detail elsewhere.[16] Here I briefly review the Middle Stone Age record of ocher use in sub-Saharan Africa and ethnohistorical accounts of Khoisan pigment use.

The Archeological Record of Pigment Use

The archeological record suggests that *Homo heidelbergensis* was the first human to use iron oxides. Ian Watts has comprehensively examined the geographic and temporal record of ocher use.[17] He finds that no claim for pigments associated with *Homo erectus* can be substantiated, and lists some dozen possible and definite cases of pigment use predating the Late Pleistocene worldwide.[18] Nearly all involve small assemblages, mostly single pieces, of ocher and hematite, a pure iron oxide producing red streak. While definitely striated pieces are found in Europe and Asia, the majority occurs in the Late Acheulean and early Middle Stone Age (MSA) in sub-Saharan Africa—within the past 300,000 years. To these cases can be added material from the Kapthurin Formation, Kenya,[19] and Twin Rivers, Zambia.[20] The Twin Rivers site probably illuminates the Acheulean–Middle Stone Age transition. More than 300 pieces of pigment have been recovered, largely specularite and hematite, dating between 270,000 and 170,000 B.P.[21]

Following these sporadic early occurrences, the records in Eurasia and Africa diverge. Between c. 220,000 and 100,000 B.P. no more ocher is reported in Eurasia. By contrast, in Africa there appears to be continuity to the end of the Middle Pleistocene.[22] The early Late Pleistocene (120,000 to 100,000 B.P.) sees an efflorescence of ocher use in southern Africa, which persists thereafter and is not matched outside Africa until the European Upper Paleolithic (UP). In the European Late Pleistocene, although there is some evidence of pigment use in the French Mousterian (with black manganese predominating over iron oxides), the major change occurs at the Middle/Upper Paleolithic boundary, associated with both Châtelperronian[23] and Aurignacian[24] industries, when red ocher becomes the focus. That is 50,000 to 60,000 years later than in Africa.

But is this material actually pigment? Some archeologists, resisting the implication of an early date for symbolic behavior, have proposed alternative hypotheses of metal oxides being used as a hide preservative or environmental protection. Watts decisively rejects these arguments, pointing out that such uses imply no selection for color—blacks and yellows should be equally useful.[25] Analyzing more than 4,000 pieces of potential pigment from 17 southern African MSA sites, Watts found that reds comprised 81.4 percent, with browns (including reddish-browns) and then yellows accounting for most of the rest; black was virtually absent.[26] Light and strong reds made up similar proportions of the sample which produced a streak, but when it came to modification, "MSA people were clearly selecting the most saturated shades of red."[27] Of 383 definitely ground specimens, 52 percent were strong reds, compared with 30 percent light reds. Forty-eight of these ground pieces were classified as crayons: "intensively utilized pieces where ground facets tended to converge to a point"[28] (Figure 1). Among these, color selection was even more pronounced, over 60 percent showing strong red streak. The shape of some of these pieces, with honed points and small facets, may have been produced by intensive grinding, but it is also possible that they could have

Figure 1
Middle Stone Age specularite crayon from Olieboompoort Bed 2, South Africa.
Photo by Ian Watts.

been applied to produce defined areas of color, design, or pattern on certain surfaces.

Watts concludes that ritual and symbolic uses for ocher were primary, with strong selection bias for qualities of redness and brilliance showing that ocher was used for visual signaling.[29] Recent excavations at Blombos Cave in South Africa have unearthed more than 8,000 pieces of ocher, many bearing signs of utilization, from MSA layers.[30] It is again material of saturated red and brown-red that appears most highly prized. At Blombos, two unequivocally engraved pieces of ocher bearing geometric representations have been dated to c. 76,000 b.p.[31]—twice as old as any comparable evidence for design in the European UP record.

The Ethnohistorical Record of Pigment Use in the Region

Most archeologists working on southern and Central African MSA sites interpret ocher as evidence for body painting and ritual activity.[32] They recognize that art on the body is likely to precede art in other media, but rarely offer any theoretical model of why these specific behaviors should emerge as part of the modern human repertoire. Ritual body art appears as a mere epiphenomenon of emergent human cognitive complexity.

Such an art-for-art's-sake argument cannot be satisfying from an evolutionary perspective because of the costs involved in procuring and processing materials. The sham menstruation hypothesis is the only Darwinian explanation for the presence of red ocher in African MSA sites, and its association with the earliest evidence of modern human occupation of the Middle East, Australia, and Europe. Rather than appeal weakly to ethnographic analogy, here the expectations of the sham menstruation model are assessed against ethnohistorical accounts of Khoisan pigment use. Do female reproductive or economic strategies underlie ritual usage? Do women advertise their imminent fertility, particularly in coalitions? And is it women who spend most time and effort getting and preparing ocher? If it were men, then the sham menstruation model would be undermined.

The Khoisan value bright red and brilliant pigments most highly,[33] especially hematite and specularite, but where mineral pigments were scarce, "red dye woods (particularly *Pterocarpus angolensis*) were held in similar esteem."[34] People selected these materials by the same criteria as identified for the MSA, and traveled long distances to obtain them. Historically and cross-culturally in southern Africa, women have "played a major role in the quarrying of earth pigments."[35] If procurement of pigments was predominantly a female task, it was even more so when it came to processing.[36]

In Ju/'hoan (!Kung) oral narratives, one metaphor for impending ritual action was the sound of women pounding red ocher in camp.[37] In various groups, ritual injunctions governed pigment procurement and processing. Overwhelmingly, Khoisan peoples used red pigment in ritual contexts, especially menarcheal observances.[38] A /Xam female initiate, on emergence from seclusion, would present the women of the band with lumps of hematite for decorating their faces and cloaks and also for adorning the young men to protect them when out hunting,[39] as did the Ju/'hoan maiden.[40] Ritualization of ocher use at menstruation among herder groups was at least as elaborate. For Khoisan generally, redness and brilliance signaled supernatural potency, overlapping with a range of cosmological concepts revolving around rain, fertility, hunting luck, horned antelope, the moon, death, and the trickster.[41] It appears that menarcheal ritual provides a template for other rituals of transition, including first-kills, marriage, and death. I argue below that it provides the metaphor for the movement to the other world involved in trance death. The preoccupation of /Xam narratives with the dire consequences of violation of proper menarcheal observances confirms that no other ritual context is so vital to reproduction of the Khoisan cosmos, affecting the fertility of women, the land and the game, and success in the hunt.

Even where no specific ritual contexts are mentioned, use of cosmetics may be directly linked to women's fertility cycles. Fischer[42] noted that Khoisan in Namibia painted their faces with red iron oxides at "the time of menstruation." In default of the desired hematite, women used other substances such as soot mixed with fat as cosmetics. Wilhelm[43] writes that !Kung women when menstruating would smear their inner thighs with fat of a large antelope, and paint soot around their eyes. A menstruating !Kung woman would also cut a tonsure in the hair of her youngest child and paint that with fat and soot—as if advertising her imminent fertility after lactational amenorrhea.

THE SIGNATURE OF RITUAL POWER IN ROCK ART

The archeological and ethnohistorical records of pigment use in southern Africa appear consistent with predictions of the sham menstruation model. The primary signature of ritual power is expected to take the form of wrong species/sex metamorphosis coupled with the flow of blood. I now consider how the model may be used as a key to interpretation of rock art in the region, again drawing on ethnographic data to inform the argument.

The most renowned of Khoisan initiation practices is the Eland Bull dance, the climax of a girl's first menstruation ceremony. Prevalent in the Kalahari, this dance or its close equivalent probably belonged to Southern groups as well. A painting at Fulton's Rock in the Drakensberg Mountains has been interpreted as representing the dance (Figure 2).[44]

Figure 2
Fulton's Rock, Drakensberg, Natal. After Lewis-Williams, *Believing and Seeing* (London: Academic Press, 1981), 42. Courtesy of the Rock Art Research Institute, University of Witwatersrand.

A Ju/'hoan initiate lies under a cloak inside a seclusion hut. The new maiden is created an adult when the women of the band dance, pretending to be eland.[45] In costume for the dance, women remove their rear aprons, tying strings of ostrich eggshell beads to hang down between their bare buttocks "simulating the tail of the Eland."[46] Heinz reports similar costume for the !Xõ.[47] Such exposure is considered highly erotic, men being banished to a distance to protect themselves and their hunting weapons.[48] In typical Ju/'hoan or Nharo practice, an older man, or possibly two—in the grand-relative category to the maiden—may join the dance wearing horns as "bulls."[49] The dance mimics the rutting behavior of eland, especially in the climax when the women move their buttocks violently from side to side, causing the tails of ostrich eggshell beads to lash to and fro. In imitating mating behavior of female eland, the dancing women are clearly signaling wrong species. Do they also play at wrong sex? Men do not always wield the horns. There are accounts of Ju/'hoan[50] and !Xõ[51] women dancing without men, while among the Kua, the name used by Valiente-Noailles for G/wi and G//ana groups, it is women who perform as eland bulls.[52]

Who really is the Eland Bull? Part of the ambiguity here lies in the eland's own liminal characteristics. Alone among the antelopes hunted by the Ju/'hoansi, the male eland is fatter than the female. !Kun/obe, an old Ju/'hoan woman, told Lewis-Williams: "The Eland Bull dance is danced because the eland is a good thing and has much fat. And the girl is also a good thing and she is all fat; therefore they are called the same thing."[53]

This identity of the Ju/'hoan girl with the Eland Bull, marked by androgyny and fatness, is prescribed during seclusion through language use and taboo: her menstruation is *eland sickness*; she must use special respect terms for eland; and she must not eat eland meat. On her emergence, the identity is ritually enacted: she is painted in ocher with an antelope mask and anointed with eland fat; as she comes out she must keep her eyes down, so that the eland will not see the stalking hunter.[54] Similar injunctions were placed on /Xam, !Xõ, and Kua maidens. Merely by looking up, the /Xam girl could make the game wild.[55]

The fat of the girl and the Eland Bull embody the fat of the land. The Ju/'hoan girl receives the Eland Bull dance, according to !Kun/obe, "so that she won't be thin ... she won't be very hungry ... all will go well with the land and the rain will fall."[56] The Kua dance as eland "because the eland is the biggest antelope, and has a big croup, giving the idea of fertility and body development."[57] The desirable fatness of the buttocks, associated with eland and emphatically signaled by women performers during the eland dance, carries connotations of eroticism combined with ritual respect and avoidance. Lewis-Williams[58] and Solomon[59] discuss examples in rock art of rear-end views of female eland in mating posture or female therianthropes—human females with large buttocks and eland heads. The /Xam respect word for eland is translated by Lewis-Williams as "when it lashes its tail."[60] A probable equivalent of the respect word used by a Ju/'hoan girl during puberty ritual, it evokes the characteristic signal of the mating female eland, imitated by the women eland dancers.

Since his early interpretation of the Fulton's Rock painting as a puberty dance, Lewis-Williams has altered his view to argue that the image refers to trance experience and healing. Anne Solomon has vigorously defended the position that initiation ritual is an important referent of Khoisan rock art.[61] I strongly support that view. Several specific features of the Fulton's Rock image indicate that it depicts a Drakensberg version of the eland dance. There is emphasis on the characteristic posture of dancers bending

over and baring round female buttocks with swinging tails attached toward the figure inside the hut. The inner ring of dancers is dominated by
women, with two figures of uncertain sex, but probably male, carrying
sticks as horns. Such a structure, with women on the inside and all definite
male figures distanced toward the periphery, in association with their
hunting weapons, recalls the context of female initiation rather than a
healing dance. In addition, a number of males have bars across the penis,
indicative of the strong sexual taboos in place on such an occasion.

The marginal position of the hunting weapons refers to a paradox of
the menarcheal girl's power. Contact with her blood threatens hunters and
the efficacy of their arrow poison,[62] yet if her potency is harnessed through
proper ritual observance, the new maiden will bring "the benefits of, specifically, 'fatness,' rain and successful hunting."[63] This effect of the girl's
potency on future hunting is channeled in the Fulton's Rock painting by
the game shaman (seated right) who points a finger of power at the giant
eland summoned by the women's dance.

Not only does the girl share the eland's power, standing "between
this world and the spirit world,"[64] but in Kalahari tradition she also acts
out as a hunter—further illustration of wrong sex. A Ju/'hoan metaphor
for first menstruation is: "She has shot an eland!"[65] Among the !Xõ, on
the last day of seclusion, a gemsbok-skin shield is hung at the back of the
menstrual hut and the maiden is helped to shoot it with arrows by the
mistress of ceremonies.[66]

Evidence from Drakensberg paintings suggests that the Maluti Bushmen played out a similar drama at female initiation. Solomon identifies a
series of gender-anomalous images holding bows and arrows as representing initiate girls.[67] Characteristic features include thighs spread wide
apart and, besides possession of weaponry, ambiguous genitalia with central emphasis on large, red blobs of potency between the thighs. Equipped
as hunters, the Drakensberg images have animal heads, or are linked to
game animals by lines of power. Each has a penis *and* blob of menstrual
potency, appearing double-sexed. The figures may also bear reference to
the rain, with patterns of stripes and dots on Figures 3a and 3c, and a
special cap on the head in Figure 3b. In Kalahari initiation tradition for
both sexes, special precautions surround initiates in relation to the rains.
Caps must be worn to ward off the sun or until the rain breaks.[68] A Kua
girl must cover herself if it rains "so that her body's smell cannot reach
the rain, lest the lightning might kill people."[69] This closely recalls /Xam
narratives of the great Rain being !Khwa whose terrible wrath is aroused
by any violation of menarcheal observance, and who is attracted by "the
odour of the girl."[70] Such power of thunder, lightning, and whirlwind is
conceptualized as male,[71] while soft, gentle female rain is not mentioned
in puberty lore.[72]

Interpreted through the wrong species/sex model of the primary sig-

Figure 3
Double-sexed, spread-legged figures from Drakensberg, Natal: (a) Willcox's
Shelter; (b) Sorceror's Rock; (c) Orange River. After Patricia Vinnicombe, *People*
of the Eland **(Pietermaritzburg: University of Natal Press, 1976), 160.**

nature of ritual power, these enigmatic figures are seen as emblems of ritual potency or taboo. Just as the peculiarly fat and female Eland Bull serves to unite opposites in initiation ceremony, these images signal ritual potency through the metaphor of the female initiate whose attributes are paradoxically male.

FATNESS, TRANCE, AND MENSTRUAL POTENCY

In line with their shamanist theory of rock art, Lewis-Williams and Dowson read the Willcox's shelter figure (Figure 3a) as "hallucinatory," deriving from the spirit world of trance experience. Faced with the artist's exaggerated emphasis on the genital region, they choose to ignore it, pointing out "the ears, whiskers and dots."[73] Lewis-Williams' radical and illuminating hypothesis of Bushman art as the depiction of trance experience has led to an unfortunate bandwagon effect, whereby every paradoxical or enigmatic image is simply ascribed to a general category of hallucination. We are in danger of losing explanatory power, where an interpretation based in initiation ritual allows greater insight into specific details. Given the central importance of menstrual potency in Bushman ideology, ritual, and narrative of initiation, resistance to seeing portrayal of that metaphor of power in rock art is surprising. This defers to our own culture's deep-seated taboos, but obstructs our understanding of Bushman cosmology and its representation.

To attempt to counterpose trance to initiation in this imagery is to miss a fundamental aspect of Khoisan representation of supernatural potency. Whether belonging to a healer or to a menarcheal girl, it is the same potency. The experience of one may be rendered in terms of the experience of the other, conflating the world of trance with the body of the menarcheal maiden. Gender ritual provides an organizing principle of the cosmos, a template for movement to the other world. This unity of power is beautifully expressed in Megan Biesele's discussion of a Ju/'hoan narrative:

When /Asa N!a'an told her story about G!kon//'amdima's heart turning into a steenbok, I asked her how it happened that a human heart could become an animal. Her answer made . . . clear something that all the metaphors had pointed to, that womanly power and manly power and the power of shamans, of n/omkxaosi, are really one power . . . /Asa N!a'an said, 'Her heart left G!kon//'amdima's back through her n//ao spot and became a steenbok, and that was the first meat.'[74]

In the idiom of healing, potency boils and rises up the spine to emerge at the back of the healer's neck as trance is achieved. Here, it is used to describe metamorphosis of woman into meat, most often a metaphor associated with hunting and initiation. While the menarcheal maiden is herself the eland wounded with arrow poison, depiction of the dying eland in southern Bushman rock art was a "powerful metaphor of the trancing medicine man."[75] In the paintings, trance death is constructed as transformation into the wrong species combined with the flowing of blood.

Within the gender conventions of Bushman art, the fat, round bellies of Figure 3a and 3c strongly connote female, but it is this quality of fatness that identifies the initiate with the androgynous eland. By contrast, the slender shape of Figure 3b suggests a male initiate, a first-kill hunter, who displays menstrual potency since he would be treated ritually as if a menstruant.[76] These double-sexed Drakensberg images belong to a much larger set of more or less detailed spread-legged figures found from the Cape to Tanzania. The age of the Drakensberg paintings cannot be reliably estimated,[77] but Maluti Bushmen persisted in the region to the end of the nineteenth century. Zimbabwean Later Stone Age paintings are likewise difficult to date, but with the Bushmen long since driven from the area, Peter Garlake suggests a probable range of 10,000 to 2,000 B.P.,[78] some evidence pointing to even earlier dates. Highly characteristic of these Matapo Hills paintings are obese, female figures with exaggerated flows between the legs. They carry as their prime emblem a crescent symbol.[79] Appearing in pairs, the women may have manes of hair which only otherwise appear on hunters (Figure 4).

Garlake documents these dramatic figures in *The Hunter's Vision*[80] without mentioning menstruation or referring to any ethnography of Khoisan initiation. In his Ph.D. thesis he discusses the possibility that the flows refer to menstruation, but rejects it on the grounds that Khoisan rituals connected with menstruation do not involve trance.[81] Hence, by adopting the trance hypothesis as his premise, Garlake can only see trance. The swollen stomachs of the figures, he argues, connote activation and expansion of potency similar to the Ju/'hoan concept of *n/om*.[82] I see nothing wrong with that idea, but only ask: Why are females in a condition of potency regularly shown with genital flows? This leads us back to the *n/om* potency of the girl at menarche.

In Figure 5, the large, round body, full of potency, holds up a distinctive crescent shape (only partly visible here). From between her legs, great rainbows of blood arch up to pass between the horns of two large ante-

Figure 4
Obese female pair with crescent, manes, and stream of potency, Mutoko, Zimbabwe. After Garlake, *The Painted Caves* (Harare: Modus Publications, 1987), 51.

Figure 5
Obese female with streams of potency and crescent (partly visible) linked to horned antelope, Mutoko, Zimbabwe. After Garlake, *The Hunter's Vision* (London: British Museum Press, 1995), 88.

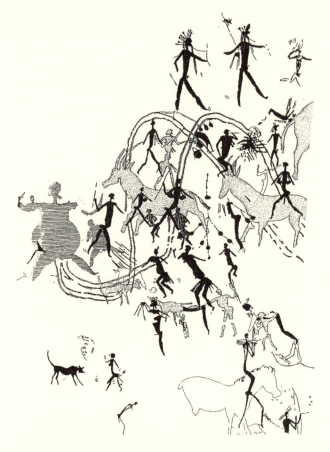

lope. Extreme caution is needed in comparing material from the Drakensberg. But it is worth observing the similarity of structure between this figure and the Sorceror's Rock image (Figure 3b), which has red lines of potency extending from the figure to nearby rhebok. The red blob of potency between the legs of Figure 3b may correspond to the potent fatness in Figure 5. The crescent symbol supports an interpretation of the Mutoko panel in terms of initiation. Lunar periodicity, and specifically the appearance of new moon, is central to Khoisan ideology of hunting and initiation.[83] Just as in Ju/'hoan conception, the initiate girl brings benefits of fatness, rain, and good hunting, so in Figure 5, the maiden at menarche, identified with the new moon, is linked through lines of potency to the great horned antelope, which may themselves refer to seasonal rains.

Such swollen-bellied figures can also be anatomically male.[84] After puzzling over the way "the imagery transcends designations of gender," Garlake suggests these figures are "in a sense androgynous. This may be one of the sources of their power."[85] He compares this to the ideology connected with the fat male eland, the fundamental metaphor of initiation.

The Mutoko panel (Figure 5) also has superimposed referents to trance, notably the male figures with nosebleeds striding over the arches of blood. Immediately juxtaposed on the left hand side of this panel is a prostrate male figure pierced with arrows,[86] which can certainly be interpreted as referring to a stage of trance when the trancer has been shot with "arrows of n/om."[87] There are a number of instances of small figures, with diagnostics of trance such as nose-bleeding, depicted clambering along bloodlines of potency emanating from fat women.[88] Figures 6a and 6b make abundantly clear the equivalence in Khoisan conception of menstrual and trance potency as means of moving to the other world.

In the Wedza panel (Figure 6a), a large-bellied figure with antelope ears[89] produces a zig-zag flow on which tiny figures float and crawl, upward and downward. Similar movement between worlds is portrayed in the Marondera image (Figure 6b), where a group of women watch a recumbent figure lying at the bottom of a rectilinear ladder to the sky. Several small figures near the foot of the ladder appear caught in the process of transformation as they approach and move upward. Near the top, the straight lines lead into a curvilinear snake in whose folds figures tumble and are lost. The snake has similar large ears to the Wedza female and a female figure with a stick in close attendance.

Snakes are among the key symbols that motivate overlap and conflation of the ideologies surrounding trance and initiation. Also prominent in both fields is the symbolism of arrows, which are shot into trance dancers. Menarcheal maidens, as we have seen, possess arrows, and their blood is conceptually linked to arrow poison.[90] Transmission of potency via bodily fluids—noseblood, menstrual blood, sweat, and amniotic fluids[91]—is featured in both trance and menarcheal ritual. An allied concept shared in both arenas is synchrony, whether rhythmical synchrony of the dance or physiological synchrony of bleeding. All these—snakes, arrows, flow, and synchrony—are regularly represented in Khoisan rock art. The same concept of wrong species metamorphosis with blood flow underlies both initiation and trance. One other power which links trance and initiation experience is the trickster, or lesser god. Custodian of the arrows of trance medicine, this being also governs initiation observances.[92]

Finally, further afield than Zimbabwe, there is more evidence for parallel representation of trance and initiatory experience. Figure 7 shows a famous but sadly faded panel from Kisese 2, near Kolo in Tanzania.

The round belly of a spread-legged figure on the left is echoed by motifs of concentric circles. Extraordinarily elaborate and finely drawn, these

Figure 6
Movement between worlds conflating trance and menstruation: (a) Wedza, Zimbabwe; (b) Marondera, Zimbabwe. After Garlake, *The Hunter's Vision* (London: British Museum Press, 1995), 87, 131.

a)   b)

may be seen as entoptic images, while another spread-legged figure appears on the edge at the right. Figure 8, from Thawe near Kolo, shows another small but elaborate spread-legged figure, with significant entoptic imagery enveloping the head. Juxtaposed on the right is a large figure whose elongation probably refers to trance. The two figures appear by themselves on the rockface.

These and many other such deliberate juxtapositions suggest that artists producing imagery derived from the neurophysiological experience of trance sought to appropriate cultural constructions of potency embedded in initiatory, particularly menarcheal, ritual. Equations were being drawn

Figure 7
**Spread-legged figures with concentric circles, Kisese, Tanzania. After Mary Lea-
key,** *Africa's Vanishing Rock Art: The Rock Paintings of Tanzania* **(London: Ham-
ish Hamilton, 1983), 102–103.**

between two modes of access to the spirit world, two manifestations of
the same potency.

CAN WRONG SPECIES/SEX APPLY TO THE
EUROPEAN UPPER PALEOLITHIC RECORD?

While there is no space here for any systematic analysis, several prevalent themes and motifs in the European Upper Paleolithic record suggest
that the model of the original signature of ritual power described here
could be used as a tool for interpretation. In particular, it may elucidate
the focus on women's reproductive signals or periodicity, the relationship
of women and game animals, and imagery of women's coalitions.

Anthropomorphic and therianthropic constructs—by definition, wrong
species—are found in the earliest European traditions of painting and
sculpture, notably the lion-headed statuette from Hohlenstein-Stadel
(c. 33,000 B.P.), and the half-bison, half-human figure from Chauvet Cave
of roughly similar date.[93] From the same period come the Aurignacian

Figure 8
Spread-legged figure next to elongated trancer, Thawe, Tanzania. Photo by Elena Mouriki.

vulva images found in the Dordogne as rock engravings. These abstract and geometric female signs may be grouped together or be seen in association with animals.[94]

Among more than 200 female figurines of the Gravettian period (c. 29,000 to 20,000 B.P.), from West and especially Central and East Europe, a number show significant focus on dress.[95] Including such famous examples as the Venus of Willendorf and the Venus of Lespugue, these have a variety of special ornaments—caps and head-dresses, bandeaux, belts, skirts, and jewelry. Soffer and colleagues argue that these "transcendent cultural facts carved into stone, ivory and bone"[96] display the prestige items of a highly valued textile industry. The selective iconography of these widespread figurine traditions highlights signifiers of women's ritual and perhaps reproductive status. In the case of some Ukrainian figures, from Kostenki and Avdeevo (Figure 9a), and more recent examples from Mezin (Figure 9c), the stylization leads to an extraordinary degree of gender ambiguity. Evidently female decorated bodies become overtly phallic. An abstract ivory figurine with breasts from Dolní Věstonice (Figure 9b) also falls into this category. This bears engraved marks, which in Alexander Marshack's analysis may fit a lunar tradition of notation.[97]

The renowned Gravettian sculpted relief at Laussel of a woman holding a bison horn shows no evidence of wrong sex or species, beyond the emblematic connection with the bison. But it is hard to resist comparing this icon (Figure 10a) to Figure 5 above, from the Zimbabwe tradition. In both images, a large-bodied, potent female holds up a crescent shape. In the

Figure 9
Female figurines with overt phallic form: (a) Kostenki and Avdeevo. After Marianna Gvozdover, "The Typology of Female Figurines of the Kostenki Paleolithic Culture," *Soviet Anthropology and Archaeology* **27, no. 4 (1989), Fig. 8; (b) Dolní Věstonice. After Marshack,** *The Roots of Civilisation* **(London: Weidenfeld and Nicolson, 1972), 290; (c) Mezin. After I. G. Šovkopljas,** *Mezinskaja stojanka* **(Kiev, 1965).**

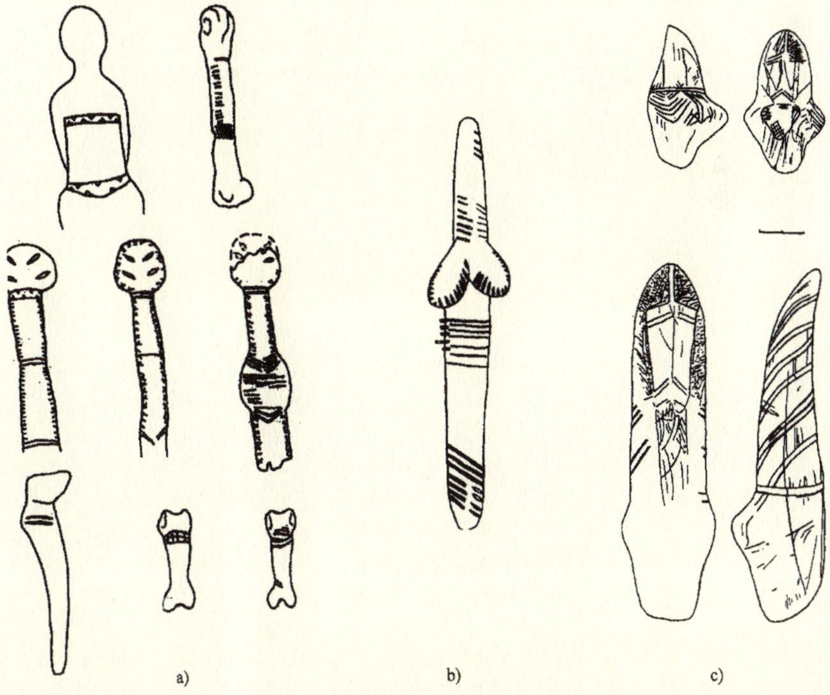

a)   b)   c)

Zimbabwe case, with the prominent flow, this appears to relate to ideology of initiation, connected to game animals and lunar periodicity. The Laussel figure has been ochered, the horn being notched with 13 marks—probably a lunar reference.[98]

Leroi-Gourhan collected together several examples from the Franco-Cantabrian Upper Paleolithic associating women with bison (Figure 10).[99] These suggest transformation and identification of females with bison, resembling the identification of Khoisan initiate girls with the Eland. Notable is the sequence of metamorphosis from woman to bison from Pech-Merle (Figure 10b). Again, the interpretation could be either in terms of trance or initiation. Pech-Merle has one of two examples in the region of an arrow-pierced male figure, seen in conjunction with a geometric which is possibly a spread-legged image.[100] The engraved bone from Isturitz (Figure 10c) makes a direct equation between a female with an arrow wound in the thigh on one side and a bison with arrow wounds to the body on the other.

In later Magdalenian traditions, iconography of women shows increasing schematization, whether in sculpture or engraving on stone plaquettes. Two lines may be sufficient to render a female silhouette—one vertical stroke attached to a looped shape for the buttocks.[101] Where the

Figure 10
Women identified with bison: (a) Laussel; (b) Pech-Merle; (c) Isturitz. After Leroi-Gourhan, *L'Art pariétal* (Grenoble: Millon, 1992), 158.

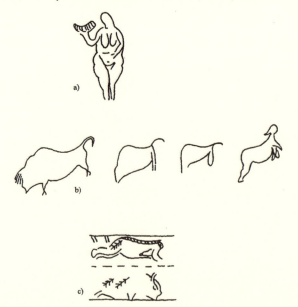

loop is reversed, similar to the form of a "P," Marshack considers this to represent pregnancy, with the bulge in front rather than behind.[102] An engraved horse with flowing wound in its hindquarters at Les Trois-Frères has superimposed upon it a line of 14 "P" figures (Figure 11). The figure has been redrawn on a number of occasions.

Portable limestone plaquettes from Gönnersdorf in Germany and Lalinde in France show numbers of schematized female figures in dance formation.[103] In his microscopic analysis of female imagery from Gönnersdorf, Lalinde, and Mezin, among other sites, Marshack demonstrates that vulvas, vaginas, and buttocks were repeatedly overmarked, presumably on different ritual occasions.[104] On the Lalinde plaquette (see detail, Figure 12), women are linked by lines running between the deeply gouged powerpoints of their vulvas. It is tempting to read this in terms of ritualized menstrual synchrony.

In numerous articles, Marshack has discussed Paleolithic symbol systems as "time-factored." He has documented lunar notation systems and illustrated the repeated marking of female sexual images, often through use of red ocher. Yet, he has been reticent on the subject of menstruation. Ethnography of hunting peoples the world over shows that lunar and menstrual periodicity is critical in governing hunting success.[105] Menstruation provides a natural body metaphor for cosmic periodicity and renewal. But the evolutionary model of sham menstruation enables us to understand why shared, periodic blood flow came to symbolize ritual solidarity and taboo. The strategies of female coalitions, symbolically

Figure 11
Horse with flowing wound and superimposed line of female figures, Les Trois-Frères. After H. Begouën and H. Breuil, *Les Cavernes du Volp. Trois Frères, Tuc d'Audoubert* **(Paris: Arts et Métiers Graphiques, 1958).**

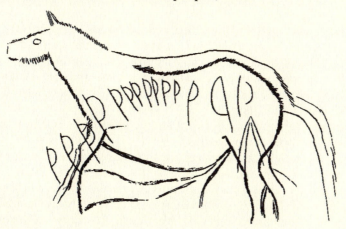

Figure 12
Detail of heavily overmarked female figures, Lalinde (Dordogne). Photo © Alexander Marshack.

linked by potent flows and identified with wounded game animals, haunt a large subset of Upper Paleolithic images. Such strategies relate to real problems of hunter-gatherer social organization, including such familiar features of the ethnographic record as the gendered division of labor, bride service, initiation, and taboos surrounding menstruation, hunting, and meat. Cognitive models based in the neurophysiology of shamanic experience may be valid and relevant for the production of the art but do not inform us about social contexts.

If these female images of power are showing us the earliest gods, it is also likely that such imagery of periodic ritual potency was at some stage appropriated by ritual collectives of men. Attempts to reconstruct Upper Paleolithic sexual politics should be treated cautiously and examined in contexts of particular ecologies. In Aboriginal Australian cultures, initiated men substantiate claims to ritual power through rock art and ritual enactment of the story of how synchronously menstruating sisters conjured up the Rainbow Snake.[106] By subincizing their penises, male initiates usurp the ability to menstruate collectively. Acknowledging that they have stolen what belongs to women, initiated men of Arnhem Land now turn the ideology of menstrual potency against women themselves.[107]

CONCLUSION

Drawing on principles of evolutionary ecology, I have outlined a testable model for the emergence of symbolic culture. The sham menstruation hypothesis argues that as they came under increasing pressure from encephalization, coalitions of evolving modern human females began to cosmetically manipulate their reproductive (menstrual) signals to motivate male labor. The model offers predictions testable across the disciplines of paleontology, archeology, and ethnography. It provides the only Darwinian explanation for the presence of red ocher in early modern human industries throughout Africa, the Middle East, Australia, and Eurasia.

Women's strategy of ritual resistance generates symbolic constructs of wrong species/sex in conjunction with cosmetic menstrual flow. I examine the record of Khoisan rock art in the light of this model, alongside ethnography of Khoisan initiation. I extend the argument to aspects of the European Upper Paleolithic record. While powerful, the shamanic interpretation of rock art neglects questions about social organization and gender relations because of its cognitive focus. In Khoisan conception, experiences of trance and initiation are not counterposed but regularly conflated, with artists producing entoptic imagery while appropriating the grammar of gender ritual. We need models that raise questions about the social conditions leading to elaboration of religious experience. Other primates lack such collectively imagined otherworlds, which can emerge only given certain uniquely human forms of social life.

NOTES

1. Philip G. Chase. "On Symbols and the Palaeolithic." *Current Anthropology* 35:5 (December 1994): 627.

2. Amotz Zahavi and Avishag Zahavi. *The Handicap Principle.* New York and Oxford: Oxford University Press, 1997.

3. Eric Alden Smith. *Inujjuamiut Foraging Strategies.* New York: Aldine de Gruyter, 1991: 8.

4. Robert L. Trivers. "Parental Investment and Sexual Selection." In *Sexual Selection and the Descent of Man 1871–1971*, ed. Bernard Campbell. Chicago: Aldine, 1972: 136–179.

5. Robert Foley and Phyllis Lee. "Ecology and Energetics of Encephalization

in Hominid Evolution." *Philosophical Transactions of the Royal Society, London* 334 (1991): 223–232.

6. Leslie C. Aiello and Peter Wheeler. "The Expensive Tissue Hypothesis: The Brain and the Digestive System in Human and Primate Evolution." *Current Anthropology* 36 (1995): 199–221.

7. Henry M. McHenry. "Sexual Dimorphism in Fossil Hominids and its Socioecological Implications." In *The Archaeology of Human Ancestry*, ed. James Steele and Stephen Shennan. London: Routledge, 1996: 91–109.

8. James F. O'Connell, Kristen Hawkes, and Nicholas G. Blurton Jones. "Grandmothering and the Evolution of *Homo erectus*." *Journal of Human Evolution* 36 (1999): 461–85.

9. Foley and Lee. "Ecology and Energetics of Encephalization."

10. Camilla Power and Leslie C. Aiello. "Female Proto-symbolic Strategies." In *Women in Human Evolution*, ed. Lori D. Hager. New York and London: Routledge, 1997: 153–171.

11. Christopher B. Ruff, Erik Trinkaus, and Trenton W. Holliday. "Body Mass and Encephalization in Pleistocene *Homo*." *Nature* 387 (8 May 1997): 173–176.

12. Robert Foley and Phyllis Lee. "Finite Social Space and the Evolution of Human Social Behaviour." In *The Archaeology of Human Ancestry*, ed. James Steele and Stephen Shennan. London: Routledge, 1996: 63–64.

13. Frank Marlowe. "Male Contribution to Diet and Female Reproductive Success Among Foragers." *Current Anthropology* 42 (2001): 755–760.

14. Camilla Power. "Beauty Magic: The Origins of Art." In *The Evolution of Culture*, ed. Robin Dunbar, Chris Knight, and Camilla Power. Edinburgh: Edinburgh University Press, 1999: 100–101.

15. Chris Knight, Camilla Power, and Ian Watts. "The Human Symbolic Revolution: A Darwinian Account." *Cambridge Archaeological Journal* 5:1 (1995): 82.

16. Ian Watts. "The Origin of Symbolic Culture." In *The Evolution of Culture*, ed. Robin Dunbar, Chris Knight, and Camilla Power. Edinburgh: Edinburgh University Press, 1999: 113–146.

17. Ibid.

18. Ibid., p. 122.

19. Sally McBrearty. "The Archaeology of the Kapthurin Formation." In *Late Cenozoic Environments and Hominid Evolution: A Tribute to Bill Bishop*, ed. Peter Andrews and Peter Banham. London: Geological Society, 1999: 143–156.

20. Lawrence S. Barham. *The Middle Stone Age of Zambia, South-central Africa*. Bristol: Western Academic and Specialist Press, 2001. See also Barham, this volume.

21. Lawrence S. Barham. "Systematic Pigment Use in the Middle Pleistocene of South-central Africa." *Current Anthropology* 43:1 (February 2002): 188.

22. See Watts. "The Origin of Symbolic Culture," p. 122; Barham: "Systematic Pigment Use in the Middle Pleistocene"; J. Desmond Clark and K. Brown: "The Twin Rivers Kopje, Zambia: Stratigraphy, Fauna, and Artifact Assemblages from the 1954 and 1956 Excavations." *Journal of Archaeological Science* 28 (2001): 305–330.

23. C. Couraud. "Les Pigments des grottes d'Arcy-sur-Cure (Yonne)." *Gallia Préhistoire* 33 (1991): 17–52.

24. Randall White. "Comment on Bednarik's 'Concept-mediated Marking in the Lower Palaeolithic.' " *Current Anthropology* 36 (1995): 623–625.

25. Watts. "The Origin of Symbolic Culture," p. 121.

26. Ibid., pp. 126–127.

27. Ibid.

28. Ibid.

29. Ibid., p. 128.

30. Christopher S. Henshilwood, Judith C. Sealy, Royden Yates, K. Cruz-Uribe, P. Goldberg, F. E. Grine, Richard G. Klein, C. Poggenpoel, K. van Niekerk, and Ian Watts. "Blombos Cave, Southern Cape, South Africa: Preliminary Report on the 1992–1999 Excavations of the Middle Stone Age Levels." *Journal of Archaeological Science* 28:4 (April 2001): 421–448.

31. Christopher S. Henshilwood, Francesco d'Errico, Royden Yates, Zenobia Jacobs, Chantal Tribolo, Geoff A. T. Duller, Norbert Mercier, Judith C. Sealy, Helene Valladas, Ian Watts, and Ann G. Wintle. "Emergence of Modern Human Behavior: Middle Stone Age Engravings from South Africa." *Science* 295 (February 15 2002): 1278–1280.

32. See Hilary J. Deacon. "Two Late Pleistocene-Holocene Archaeological Depositories from the Southern Cape, South Africa." *South African Archaeological Bulletin* 50 (1995): 128; J. Desmond Clark. "The Middle Stone Age of East Africa and the Beginnings of Regional Identity." *Journal of World Prehistory* 2:3 (1988): 299; Barham, this volume.

33. See Wilhelm H. I. Bleek and Lucy C. Lloyd. *Specimens of Bushman Folklore.* London: Allen, 1911: 377–379; and J. David Lewis-Williams and Megan Biesele. "Eland Hunting Rituals Among the Northern and Southern San Groups: Striking Similarities." *Africa* 48 (1978): 117–134.

34. Watts. "The Origin of Symbolic Culture," p. 133, and see references.

35. Ibid.

36. Ibid., p. 134, and see references.

37. Megan Biesele. *Women Like Meat.* Johannesburg: Witwatersrand University Press, 1993: 163, 196.

38. Watts. "The Origin of Symbolic Culture," p. 134.

39. Roger L. Hewitt. *Structure, Meaning and Ritual in the Narratives of the Southern San* Hamburg: Buske, 1986: 281.

40. J. David Lewis-Williams. *Believing and Seeing. Symbolic Meanings in Southern San Rock Paintings.* London: Academic Press, 1981: 51.

41. Camilla Power and Ian Watts. "The Woman with the Zebra's Penis: Gender, Mutability and Performance." *Journal of the Royal Anthropological Institute (N. S.)* 3:3 (September 1997): 546.

42. Eugen Fischer. *Die Rehobother Bastards.* Jena: Fischer, 1913: 259.

43. J. H. Wilhelm. "Die !Kung Buschleute." *Jahrbuch des Museums für Völkerkunde zu Leipzig* 12 (1954): 118.

44. See Lewis-Williams. *Believing and Seeing,* pp. 41–53; and Anne Solomon. "Rock Art in Southern Africa." *Scientific American,* November 1996: 89.

45. Lewis-Williams. *Believing and Seeing,* p. 62.

46. Nicholas M. England. *Music Among the Zu/'wã-si and Related Peoples of Namibia, Angola and Botswana.* New York and London: Garland, 1995: 274.

47. Hans-Joachim Heinz. *The Social Organisation of the !Kõ Bushmen.* M.A. Thesis, University of South Africa, 1966: 123.

48. England. *Music Among the Zu/'wã-si,* p. 266.

49. Alan Barnard. "Sex Roles Among the Nharo Bushmen of Botswana." *Africa* 50 (1980): 117–118.

50. Lewis-Williams. *Believing and Seeing*, p. 45.

51. Heinz. *The Social Organisation of the !Kō Bushmen*, p. 124.

52. Carlos Valiente-Noailles. *The Kúa: Life and Soul of the Central Kalahari Bushman*. Rotterdam and Brookfield: Balkema, 1993: 95–96.

53. Lewis-Williams. *Believing and Seeing*, p. 48.

54. Power and Watts. "The Woman with the Zebra's Penis," p. 543, and see references.

55. Hewitt. *Structure, Meaning and Ritual*, p. 285.

56. Lewis-Williams. *Believing and Seeing*, p. 50.

57. Valiente-Noailles. *The Kúa*, p. 96.

58. Lewis-Williams. *Believing and Seeing*, pp. 46–47.

59. Anne Solomon. "Gender, Representation and Power in San Ethnography and Rock Art." *Journal of Anthropological Archaeology* 11 (1992): 313–312.

60. Lewis-Williams. *Believing and Seeing*, p. 46.

61. Solomon. " Gender, Representation and Power," pp. 291–329; Anne Solomon: " 'Mythic Women': A Study in Variability in San Rock Art and Narrative." In *Contested Images: Diversity in Southern African Rock Art Research*, ed. Thomas Dowson and J. David Lewis-Williams. Johannesburg: Witwatersrand University Press, 1994: 331–371; Anne Solomon. " 'Mythic Women': A Response to Humphreys." *South African Archaeological Bulletin* 51 (1996): 33–35.

62. Power and Watts. "The Woman with the Zebra's Penis," p. 542.

63. Lewis-Williams. *Believing and Seeing*, p. 52.

64. Thomas Dowson, cited in J. David Lewis-Williams. *Discovering Southern African Rock Art*. Cape Town: Philip, 1990: 80.

65. Lewis-Williams. *Believing and Seeing*, p. 51.

66. Heinz. *The Social Organisation of the !Kō Bushmen*, p. 122.

67. Solomon. " Gender, Representation and Power," pp. 313–314.

68. Valiente-Noailles. *The Kúa*, p. 97; and Heinz. *The Social Organisation of the !Kō Bushmen*, p. 124.

69. Valiente-Noailles. *The Kúa*, p. 97.

70. Hewitt. *Structure, Meaning and Ritual*, p. 285.

71. Power and Watts. "The Woman with the Zebra's Penis," pp. 545–546.

72. Hewitt. *Structure, Meaning and Ritual*, p. 284.

73. J. David Lewis-Williams and Thomas Dowson. *Images of Power: Understanding Bushman Rock Art*. Johannesburg: Southern Book Publishers, 1989: 173.

74. Biesele. *Women Like Meat*, p. 202.

75. Lewis-Williams. *Believing and Seeing*, p. 91.

76. Power and Watts. "The Woman with the Zebra's Penis," p. 547.

77. Aron Mazel. "Rock Art and Natal Drakensberg Hunter-gatherer History: A Reply to Dowson." *Antiquity* 67 (1993): 889–892.

78. Peter Garlake. *The Painted Caves: An Introduction to the Prehistoric Rock Art of Zimbabwe*. Harare: Modus Publications, 1987: 5.

79. Peter Garlake. *The Hunter's Vision: The Prehistoric Art of Zimbabwe*. London: British Museum Press, 1995: 87.

80. Garlake. *The Hunter's Vision*, pp. 85–89.

81. Peter Garlake. *Rock Art in Zimbabwe*. Ph.D. Thesis, University of London, 1993.

82. Garlake. *The Hunter's Vision*, p. 86.

83. Power and Watts. "The Woman with the Zebra's Penis," pp. 544–545.

84. Garlake. *The Hunter's Vision*, p. 85.

85. Garlake. *Rock Art in Zimbabwe*, p. 262.

86. Garlake. *The Hunter's Vision*, p. 130, fig. 155.

87. Richard Katz. *Boiling Energy. Community Healing Among the Kalahari Kung.* Cambridge, MA: Harvard University Press, 1982: 46.

88. See, for example, Garlake. *The Hunter's Vision*, p. 90, fig. 101.

89. They are called hare-headed beings in Leo Frobenius: *Madsimu Dsangara.* Berlin: Atlantis, 1931: 21.

90. Power and Watts. "The Woman with the Zebra's Penis," pp. 542, 544.

91. Thomas N. Huffman "The Trance Hypothesis and the Rock Art of Zimbabwe." *South African Archaeological Society Goodwin Series* 4 (1983): 49–53.

92. Mathias Guenther. *Tricksters and Trancer: Bushman Religion and Society.* Bloomington, IN: Indiana University Press, 1999: 112–113.

93. Jean Clottes and J. David Lewis-Williams. *The Shamans of Prehistory: Trance and Magic in the Painted Caves*. New York: Abrams, 1998: 45, figs. 41–42.

94. Gerhard Bosinski. *Homo Sapiens*. Paris: Éditions Errance, 1990: 73, 76.

95. Olga Soffer, James Adovasio, and D. C. Hyland. "The 'Venus' Figurines: Textiles, Basketry, Gender, and Status in the Upper Palaeolithic." *Current Anthropology* 41:4 (August–October 2000): 517.

96. Soffer, Adovasio, and Hyland. "The 'Venus' Figurines," p. 524.

97. Alexander Marshack. *The Roots of Civilisation*. London: Weidenfeld and Nicolson, 1972: 290.

98. Marshack. *The Roots of Civilisation*, p. 335, n. 17.

99. André Leroi-Gourhan. *L'Art pariétal: Langage de la préhistoire*. Grenoble: Millon, 1992: 158.

100. Bosinski. *Homo Sapiens*, p. 141.

101. Marshack. *The Roots of Civilisation*, p. 309.

102. Marshack. *The Roots of Civilisation*, p. 327.

103. Bosinski. *Homo Sapiens*, p. 232–234.

104. Alexander Marshack. "An Innovative Analytical Technology: A Discussion of Its Present and Potential Use." *Rock Art Research* (1991): 37–59; and "The Female Image: A 'Time-factored' Symbol. A Study in Style and Aspect of Image Use in the Upper Palaeolithic." *Proceedings of the Prehistoric Society* 57:1 (1991): 17–31.

105. Chris Knight. *Blood Relations. Menstruation and the Origins of Culture*. New Haven and London: Yale University Press, 1991: 327–416.

106. Ibid., pp. 449–479.

107. Ibid., p. 479.

Art in Human Evolution

Lawrence S. Barham

Rock art is a relatively recent phenomenon in human development, or so it seems. The current consensus among archeologists links the evolution of the modern mind with that of language, and we see both expressed in the first cave art of 30,000 years ago. A small but growing body of evidence from Africa points to an early development of art, in the form of body ornamentation, as a new medium for communication in addition to language. The evidence is indirect and takes the form of the use of mineral pigments associated with changes in tool-making technology and the settlement of previously uninhabited regions of central Africa. These combined developments may mark the beginning of cooperative social groups based on a shared identity developed through language and reinforced by visual signals. The signals survive in the form of pigments and the first regionally distinctive style of stone tools. The settlement of the Congo basin 300,000 years ago may be the signature of identity-conscious social groups expanding into new territories with the aid of language, art, and technology. This package of behaviors would give later anatomically modern humans the adaptive flexibility to colonize the Old World and replace indigenous populations, including Neanderthals in Europe. The emergence of cave art 30,000 years ago is an elaboration of a long-held capacity to use visual symbols in the face of environmental and social challenges.

INTRODUCTION

Did art play a formative role in the development of modern human behavior? For most archeologists, the answer is a resounding yes. Elaborate cave art in Europe, Africa, and Australia, created by anatomically modern humans about 30,000 years ago and later, is the colorful evidence.

But what if art in the form of image making actually emerged as early as 300,000 years ago? And what if it appeared first in Africa, with a species called *Homo heidelbergensis,* which predates modern humans? This is a relatively daring proposition for an archeologist to make, yet there is evidence, albeit indirect, to suggest that long before the first paintings were made at Chauvet Cave, art had been integral to the evolution of human behavior.

Archeologists have at their disposal more than 2.5 million years of human prehistory from which to distill, and attempt to explain, broad patterns of behavioral change. Art, in the form of cave paintings and portable, shaped objects, appears first in Europe and very late in this picture, fewer than 40,000 years ago, long after the modern human form had evolved. That, at least, is the consensus as expressed in most undergraduate textbooks and one that has underpinned academic debate for more than a decade. But recent discoveries in Africa now pose a concerted challenge to all tenets of that prevailing view. The African archeological record is forcing us to reconsider our preconceptions about what early art looked like, why it might have been made, and by which species.

In south-central and eastern Africa, indirect evidence for image-making survives in the form of pigments found in archeological sites, many transported some distance and showing evidence of scraping, rubbing, or grinding. The collecting and processing of pigments is assumed to have been largely for decorative purposes rather than for more prosaic uses, such as tanning hides. At these same sites there is also evidence of innovation in stone tool-making.[1] Taken together, the appearance of these pigments with new, geographically distinctive ways of tool-making may mark the development of social groups whose members shared a sense of belonging based on an agreed set of symbols in the form of language and images. Art arguably played a central role in forming and maintaining a sense of a group identity beyond basic kinship, something it still does today. The formation of highly cooperative social groups has evolutionary implications, especially for increased survival, and particularly for females with offspring.

If there was a big bang in human cognitive and social evolution, it took place not 30,000 years ago with cave painting in Europe, but long before, with the emergence of symbol-using *Homo heidelbergensis* between 400,000 and 300,000 years ago. The African record is unique in the story it tells about the behavior and biology of this species. Only in Africa do we see the continuous use of pigments as part of the social lives of hunter-gatherers from 300,000 years ago to the historic present. And only in Africa is there an unbroken evolutionary sequence from premodern to fully anatomically modern humans, *Homo sapiens sapiens.* Image making, it seems, was part of the coevolution of the behavior and biology of our immediate ancestors and of our own species. The relatively late florescence of cave art in the

Upper Paleolithic of Europe was an elaboration of an existing capacity to use symbols. Art in the form of body adornment was part of the behavioral repertoire of the modern humans who 40,000 years ago colonized Europe, a continent that was already inhabited by another species of human, *Homo neanderthalensis.* The human ability to form, maintain, and assert group identities based on shared ideas and images may have facilitated the extinction of Neanderthals and contributed to the success of our species as a global colonizer. This is not to say that Neanderthals lacked a capacity for symbol use or did not use pigments to signal identity on occasion, but rather that they did not use these behaviors as systematically and effectively as our ancestors.

DEFINING ART

Before looking at the archeological evidence for the emergence of the human capacity to make and use images, we need a working definition of art that applies cross-culturally and across time. Dictionary definitions of art refer typically to human skill, and the application of skill and imagination to activities, including painting and architecture. Older dictionaries often include a sense of aesthetics and beauty in their definitions of art. From an anthropological perspective, we now recognize that these concepts and activities are far from universal and reflect a Western tradition of thinking about art and the specialized role of artists in society.[2] We must also ask: who sets the standards and judges what is skillful or aesthetically pleasing? The Dada movement in the early decades of the twentieth century challenged Western preconceptions about the place of skill and beauty in art, and that challenge continues unabated.

The great individuality and freedom of expression that typifies contemporary Western art would not be acceptable in small-scale hunter-gatherer societies such as those of the Bushmen of the Kalahari or the Aborigines of Arnhem Land, northern Australia. Among these communities, the role of art and of artists is not to challenge conventions or to express individual angst, but to communicate the shared beliefs and values that give the group, and individuals within the group, an identity. There is room for individual expression in these societies, but within the bounds of what is considered acceptable variation, beyond which means communication is impaired. Art, and especially bodily adornment, plays a central role in rituals that mark changes in the status of individuals, such as the shift from child to adult, single to married couple, and living being to ancestor. These rites of passage are found in all kinds of societies, not just among hunter-gatherers, and provide a public context for transmitting complex information.[3] We shall return to this concept later, but first a working definition of art is needed that is applicable to the archeological record. Robert Bednarik, a specialist in the study of Australian rock art, describes art as "the medium conveying awareness of a perceived reality to the sensory perception of other humans."[4] This includes the media of music and dance, which are often overlooked by archeologists, for the obvious reason that they rarely leave enduring traces. What this definition does offer is a value-free concept of art that recognizes the communicative function of imagery and actions.

Art transmits and objectifies symbols through images, sound, and movement. Even if painted images or body decorations no longer survive, the medium for their expression may do so in the form of mineral pigments. The close link between images, their symbolic potential, and the humble stuff of paint is the key to unlocking an impasse in the archeological record—did the capacity to make images exist much before the earliest surviving cave paintings?

AN ARCHEOLOGICAL CONUNDRUM

Archeologists recognize several thresholds in the long sweep of prehistory which demarcate changes in technology or other behaviors that have made a lasting impact. These include the first stone tool–using ancestors 2.6 million years ago in Africa, the dispersal of early humans from Africa into Asia and Europe some time after 2.0 million years ago, innovations in tool technology at approximately 1.5 million and 300,000 years ago, the evolution of anatomically modern humans (Homo sapiens) about 160,000 years ago in Africa, the settlement of Australia by modern humans about 60,000 years ago, and the settlement of Europe by modern humans about 40,000 years ago. These early modern Europeans were also the first people to produce imagery that survives in the form of beadwork and cave paintings. They also contributed, in one way or another, to the extinction of the indigenous Neanderthals, who disappeared shortly after 30,000 years ago. The development of farming and the later rise of states took place just yesterday in this framework—after 10,000 years ago. This condensed timeline masks debate about dates, places, processes of change, and the significance of these thresholds, but these developments are the bedrock of current archeological teaching and research.

The appearance of art is central to arguments about the emergence of the modern mind with its capacity to use symbols in the form of language, objects, and images to communicate complex and abstract concepts.[5] To paraphrase Descartes, "I paint, therefore I am." For many archeologists, the cave art of western Europe is the only unambiguous evidence for the evolution of symbol use.[6] The prevailing model of a European origin of art has its vocal critics who point to examples of marked, drilled, or shaped objects from Australasia, Europe, and Africa that arguably reflect a capacity to use external symbols (they are not purely functional items) and which predate the cave art of France and Spain by tens of thousands of years.[7] Such finds are typically isolated occurrences, separated in space and time from each other. Their sporadic distribution can be explained by the vagaries of preservation, which have left us with a palimpsest of the extent and true antiquity of symbol use.

This challenge to the Eurocentric orthodoxy is a spoiler argument that draws on disparate examples of images or humanly modified objects that predate the appearance of European cave art. The underlying weakness of this approach is twofold. The majority of the modified bone objects thought to be evidence of early deliberate marking and shaping have been shown to be naturally modified[8] or remain to be examined closely by independent researchers. Notable exceptions, such as an incised igneous pebble in human form dated to more than 230,000 B.P. from Berekhat Ram, Israel, draw attention to the long gaps in time between first appearances of supposed symbolic objects and later undoubted symbols. In the case of Berekhat Ram, human figures in stone are not found again in the archeological record of the Near East until 14,000 years ago, almost 20,000 years after people had been carving images of humans and animals in western Europe. Archeologists are loathe to accept negative evidence as data and the lack of continuity between first appearances and later symbol use undermines the challenge to the European orthodoxy. We assume that once symbols are expressed in material form, the advantages of this method of communication are so great that there is no going back.

You cannot easily change the cognitive capacity for making symbols; it is part of our evolutionary and genetic inheritance.[9] Symbols are with us for good or ill, but we can change their content, appearance, and rules of usage. Perhaps in the Near East the accepted medium for making human figurines changed after 230,000 B.P. from stone to wood or some other perishable substance, or the human form was no longer an agreed-upon image for communication. But this is pure speculation in the absence of evidence. Without more such figurines from the same time and place, we cannot say that the capacity for symbol use had developed fully in the form we recognize today. Symbols as used by modern humans are infinitely flexible in form and meaning and these features are culturally determined through consensus. Meaning has to be agreed upon and shared between individuals; otherwise, there is no common ground for understanding. Symbols are inherently arbitrary,[10] just like the letters and words on this page, but because you, the reader, and I, the writer, share an understanding of written English, these images are intelligible, even if my argument is incoherent. These words also enable me to communicate abstract concepts in my absence, because you are familiar with the conventions of representing sounds and meanings as letters, words, sentences, and so on. Symbols resonate with meaning across physical distance and time so long as the shared codes are understood.

Archeologists studying European rock art soon realized that certain images were repeated, such as horse and bison, and that these images were selected from a potentially broad range of animals in the landscape. The art of the show caves of Lascaux or Altamira was not the product of random doodling but a structured form of communication. Just what the images meant to their makers and viewers we can never know because the shared codes are lost. David Lewis-Williams' trance hypothesis[11] offers some possibility of recovering the social contexts in which the images were made, but not their meanings. In contrast, the lone Berekhat Ram figurine offers little hope of reconstructing the social context of its use beyond the generalities of time, place, and method of manufacture. This figurine is typical of the isolated examples of art cited by proponents of an early evolution of the human capacity to make and use symbols.

Communication based on symbols involves much repetition of images, or in the case of music and dance, the conventionalized use of sound and actions. Some redundancy seems to be essential to get a message across. When, then, do multiple examples of images in bone, stone, and paint first appear? For most archeologists the answer lies with the rock art of Upper Paleolithic Europe. The oldest known images are dated to 32,000 B.P. and are associated with an industry of the early part of the Upper Paleolithic known as the Aurignacian. Although human fossils are rare for the very earliest phases, we must assume that the makers of Aurignacian stone tools were *Homo sapiens*. They had first entered continental Europe about 40,000 years ago, probably from the Near East,[12] and had then spread westward during a brief warm interval of the last glacial cycle. They may have encountered the indigenous population of Neanderthals at various points en route, but there is no direct evidence for interaction between the two species. Neanderthal extinction was not sudden, and some populations retained footholds in parts of Europe, such as southern Spain and what is now Croatia, for the next 10,000 years.[13] A worsening climate after 38,000 B.P., combined with less developed social networks than those of the Aurignacian moderns, and only limited use of symbols for information exchange, may have contributed to the demise of *Homo neanderthalensis*.[14] We know that Neanderthals did not make art in the conventional sense of paintings and carvings, but they seem to have had a capacity for symbolic thought as reflected in their differing burial customs[15] and in the sporadic use of pigments. They may have adopted bead making from their Aurignacian neighbors, but the evidence for acculturation or other forms of interaction is minimal and highly controversial.[16] The Aurignacians clearly valued personal adornment as a form of communication, perhaps signaling the social status of the wearer and simultaneously membership of a group. Their sites often contain large quantities of drilled mammoth ivory beads and pendants in contrast to the rarity of beads in contemporary Neanderthal sites. Body ornamentation precedes the painting and engraving of caves by several millennia.

At Chauvet Cave in the Ardèche region of southeastern France, accomplished paintings of bison, giant deer, horse, cow, and woolly rhinoceros have been directly dated to between 32,000 and 30,000 B.P.[17] There are two other painted caves in France with similar images that have been dated to roughly this period. At the same time, Aurignacian peoples in southwestern Germany were also carving mammoth ivory to create portable images of mammoths, lion, and horse. There is a common theme in the painted and portable art of the Aurignacian which is geographically and temporally restricted.[18] These images are clearly symbols. Their consistency in content, context, and style reflects the shared codes understood by their makers and viewers.

The art of the Aurginacian, beadwork included, represents the earliest undoubted evidence for symbol use in the archeological record. In Africa, the site of the Apollo 11 cave in Namibia has produced seven slabs painted with animal images from deposits dated to 27,000 B.P. These are the earliest representational paintings on this continent. Engraved images on stone and bone, however, are considerably older. Ongoing excavations at Blombos Cave on the southern Cape coast have revealed a remarkable collection of engraved pieces of hematite or red ocher with criss-cross geometric designs and incised bone pieces all dated to greater than 70,000 years ago.[19] So far, the Blombos assemblage is unique in the region and for skeptics it is another example of an isolated occurrence of imagery that serves to highlight the disjuncture between the art of the Upper Paleolithic and all preceding attempts at symbol use.

The apparently late emergence of cave art sits uneasily with the fossil record, which shows that anatomically modern humans had evolved by 160,000 years ago in Africa.[20] The large brain we all have is even older, having developed its current average of 1,400 cubic centimeters between 600,000 and 300,000 years ago. A large brain comes with hidden evolutionary costs for the mother, the infant, and other members of a social group.[21] Compared with other primates, human infants have disproportionately big heads at birth to accommodate a brain that will grow rapidly in the first year of life.[22] As well as making childbirth hazardous for the mother, the large human brain creates a long period of dependency of the infant on the mother, and others, for food and protection. Symbol-based communication would have been a considerable adaptive asset in the development of cooperative behaviors for supporting females with children and for maintaining cohesion through a shared identity. Among contemporary hunter-gatherers, male provisioning of offspring does increase female fertility, even if done indirectly through the group sharing of nutritious foods, such as meat and honey.[23] Put simply, the more a male provides by way of food, the more children a woman can bear and raise over the course of her reproductive life. The male provisioning of meat may be at the root of the ubiquitous nuclear family found among hunter-gatherers today, and the equally widespread division of labor between the sexes. There is vigorous debate about the strength of the link between meat and marriage among modern foragers,[24] but if this ethnographic model can be applied to the distant past, it gives us a social and demographic context for explaining the emergence of symbol use.

A MODEL FOR THE EVOLUTION OF ART

Anthropologists, philosophers, and psychologists have long debated whether some aspects of human behavior are so widely distributed in space and time that they can be considered as universal to our species. The concept of behavioral universals remains controversial, but in the context of the evolution of symbol use, and by implication, art, there are some general observations that enable us to bridge the gap between the cave art of the Aurignacian and the much earlier evolution of the modern brain. The editor of the journal *Current Anthropology* has distilled the following universals of social behavior:

- recognition of others as distinct individuals;
- recognition that individuals are born into and live in distinct bounded groups; and
- recognition that the individual life comes to an end.[25]

These are not exclusively human traits, but only humans use symbols to recognize these attributes of social life. Our complex language plays a central role in the act of representing others, their actions, and their state of being through symbols. We also use rituals based on symbols to mark a change of state, such as the transition from child to adult. No other animal does this. Steven Pinker argues that there are 300 universals that define modern humans and that these are genetically based as a result of having been part of our evolution for some time.[26] His list includes body art, suggesting that we cannot help but paint ourselves.

Anthropologists are more cautious in their assessments of the impact of nature over nurture, and, on the whole, place culture in the driving seat of human behavioral development. Early in the history of the discipline, the social anthropologist Arnold Van Gennep observed in *The Rites of Passage* that all societies hold rites of passage to mark the major transitions in the life history of an individual from birth, puberty, and marriage to death. These rites serve to unify and maintain communities at times of change and reinforce a sense of belonging to a social group larger than the immediate family. For the participants, these rites often create what Van Gennep calls a liminal state, in which the normal social status of the individual is suspended and they are in limbo between a past and future status. For archeologists, the value of Gennep's observations lies in their association with material objects and sometimes special places in the landscape. Rites of passage often involve personal adornment, feasting, dancing, and music as well as burials, sometimes with offerings as grave goods.

The physical symbols used to mark individuals are either organic (e.g., blood, leaves, feathers, shells) or inorganic (e.g., mineral pigments), but the chances of organic symbols surviving in the archeological record are remote. Among the Mbuti Pygmies of the Congo basin, for example, the transition to puberty among girls is signaled by vegetable- and clay-based body paints and by the painting of bark cloth skirts with vegetable dyes.[27] Neither set of symbols would leave an archeological signature. Occasionally, the marking of death by deliberate burial survives, as do grave goods as in the case of the Upper Paleolithic burials at Sungir, near Moscow, some 24,000 years ago. Here, the bodies of three individuals have been found: two children buried head to head and one elderly adult male in a separate grave. All three were adorned with thousands of drilled mammoth ivory beads, among other offerings. Similarly adorned burials occur across northern Europe at this time and are part of a regional pattern of behavior linked to this rite of passage.[28] But rich burials like these are the exception, with the archeological record before the Upper Paleolithic largely bereft of examples.

COLORING THE PAST

Although almost no objects linked to symbol use are likely to survive, there is one category of material that may just be the key to inferring the presence of a symbolic capacity long before the Upper Paleolithic. Mineral pigments such as hematite (iron oxide), limonite (iron hydroxide), and manganese dioxide are unlikely to be altered in the archeological record except under unusual local conditions of high temperature, pressure, and acidity.[29] As the color-giving constituents to the red, yellow, and black paints found in many Upper Paleolithic caves, they survive on walls where they are protected from running water, frost, or bacterial activity. Hematite in its many forms is common worldwide and was used by prehistoric artists in both the Old and New World. In powdered form, these iron minerals are also the most widely used sources of the colors red, purple, and yellow in body paints. From an archeological perspective, evidence for pigment use may survive as stains in the soil, on tools such as grinding stones, or simply as pieces of the minerals on sites where they were processed and used. The presence of pigment in the archeological record can offer indirect evidence for the existence of ritual and symbol use before 40,000 B.P. To draw such an inference involves some sleight of mind to bridge the gap between certainty (i.e., cave art = symbol use) and persuasive probability (pigment alone). Archeologists looking at mineral pigments have two sources of information with which to interpret their data; the one is ethnographic and the other contextual.

Before looking at these sources of data, some mention must be made of alternative, more functional, interpretations of the use of pigment. The argument for a symbolic value placed on pigment has been countered by claims for the use of iron minerals as hide preservatives,[30] as medicines,[31] as an ingredient of sunblock creams and insect repellent,[32] and as a constituent of glues used in hafting stone tools.[33] The use of hematite in curing and preserving hides is the most commonly cited functional alternative and as such has received considerable critical evaluation.[34] In brief, the ethnographic support for this option comes largely from Australia, but a close reading of these reports shows that ocher, mixed with grease, was invariably applied in the final stages of preparation of the skin. The grease kept the skin soft and waterproof while the ocher gave color to the finished garments. The use of ocher as a tanning agent was not common. Most hunter-gatherers in temperate and tropical environments employed organic substances such as brains, urine, bark, marrow, or vegetable oils. The archeological evidence for the use of ocher in hide processing comes from a few Upper Paleolithic and Mesolithic assemblages in Europe, which show staining on scrapers and other tools that may have been used in processing skins.[35] Sediments stained with ocher have also been interpreted as indirect evidence of ocher-colored skins that once covered dwellings. These inferences rely in part on the equivocal ethnographic data from Australia and elsewhere for the application of ocher and grease to hides. The same combination of grease and ocher is reported in sunblocks and insect repellents applied to the body and hair. The aesthetic value of ocher can be separated from the efficacy of grease, given its well-known protective properties.

Ethnographic observations of pigment use among contemporary hunter-gatherers have been used to make compelling arguments for symbolic content in cases where direct continuity can be seen between the archeological record and the present. In Australia, the first settlers (*Homo sapiens*) who arrived about 60,000 years ago used hematite (in burials and at living sites) and there is an unbroken record of pigment use to the present.[36] Sources of hematite in central Australia that were quarried 32,000 years ago are still being used today to paint bodies, objects, and rock surfaces with images of ritual, mythological, and clan significance.[37] Yellow ocher (limonite), white clay, and charcoal complete the range of colors used across the continent for rock art and adornment of bodies and objects. Red ocher (hematite) in particular was widely seen as representing human blood in ritual contexts.[38] Rock art is at least 20,000 years old and the tradition of painting continues today with the same range of colors being used, but the content and style of the imagery has changed over time.[39] The association of the earliest evidence of pigment use with the act of burial combined with the regular and widespread use of pigment over 60,000 years strengthens the analogical argument for early Australians possessing the capacity to create and use symbols. That capacity combined with the use of language enabled the first settlers to plan and work co-operatively in making the sea crossing necessary to reach Australia from the Asian mainland.[40]

The oldest evidence of continuous pigment use comes from sub-Saharan Africa, but here the ethnographic record is less extensive because of the restricted distribution of hunter-gatherers who have long competed for land and resources with farmers, herders, and European settlers. In southern Africa, the ancestors of the Kalahari Bushmen probably lived in the region at least 120,000 years ago based on fossil and genetic evidence.[41] But pigment use as part of Bushman symbolic culture can only be extended with certainty to 27,000 B.P. in the form of the painted slabs at Apollo 11 cave, Namibia. The tradition of painting on rock surfaces continued to the late nineteenth century, from which fragmented historical accounts survive of the painters, their beliefs, and rituals that gave the art meaning.[42] Pigment is still used for body painting among the few remaining Bushmen of the Kalahari in the context of rites of passage and other ceremonies central to the well-being of the group.[43] As we review the archeological record before the ethnographic present, the link between meaning and images grows tenuous and the emphasis necessarily shifts to the search for evidence of symbol use rather than its meanings. That search takes us back 300,000 years, making the archeological record of southern Africa unique in its longevity of pigment use.

The equation of pigments with symbol use cannot simply be assumed—it has to be demonstrated, especially for the very earliest evidence, which occurs in association with another species that is not *Homo sapiens*. The earliest evidence for the regular use of pigments comes from two sites dated to approximately 300,000 B.P. (Figure 1). The first is a collapsed cave on top of Twin Rivers hill, Zambia, that contained deposits dated between older than 400,000 and 170,000 years ago.[44] Hundreds of pieces of pigment were found in the cave sediments spanning this period, and perhaps thousands more were unintentionally discarded in an earlier excavation at the site in the 1950s.[45] An iron-stained grinding stone (Figure 2) was geochemically analyzed and shown to have been used to process a crystalline form of hematite that produces a distinctive, sparkling purple streak. Other colors were used at Twin Rivers, including red, yellow, black, and maybe pink—the latter found in local iron-rich sandstones (extensive yellow stains were noted in the deposits in the 1950s excavation). All these materials had to be brought to the hilltop from different sources, which means that the selection of colors was intentional. If the purpose was purely utilitarian and based on the iron content of the minerals, then the

Figure 1
Map showing the location of Twin Rivers cave, Zambia, and the Kapthurin Formation, Kenya.

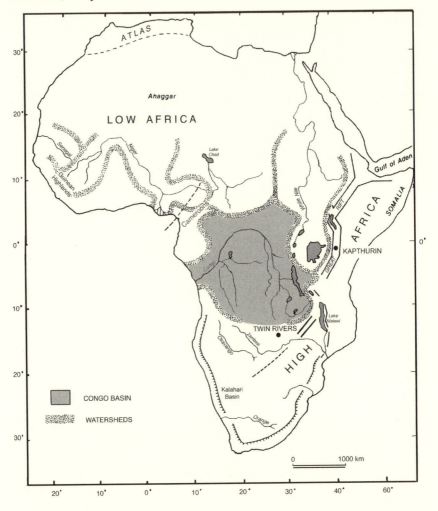

occupants of Twin Rivers behaved irrationally and chose the hardest of the available materials and one which needed processing by grinding.

The selection of purple, red, and yellow may have been made on the visibility of these colors against the background of a woodland environment in which greens and browns predominate. If pigments were meant to be signals as well as symbols, then the range of colors at Twin Rivers, with the exception of black, would be highly visible on skin of most any hue. Color vision has deep evolutionary roots in our primate ancestry,

Figure 2
A grinding stone from Twin Rivers cave, Zambia, dated to 300,000 years ago.

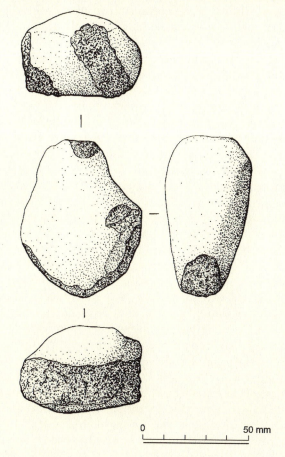

0   50 mm

with the detection of red and yellow being particularly well developed, presumably to detect ripe fruits and young leaves against a green background.[46]

From deposits near Lake Baringo, Kenya, comes the second site with evidence of early pigment use from the time range of Twin Rivers. A surface site with more than 70 pieces of pigment and grinding stones has been excavated from the Kapthurin Formation and dated to about 300,000 years ago.[47] Twin Rivers and the Lake Baringo site together represent a small sample on which to base claims of regular and widespread pigment use, but they are the only well-dated sites from this period. (Others are known with similar stone tool types and with pigments but they remain undated.) More importantly for the argument that the capacity for symbol

use had evolved by 300,000 B.P., both sites are associated with a fundamental technological shift in the way tools were made that appears to
have its origin in Africa. The development of hafted tool technology took
place at this time with flakes and blades being made for attaching to han-
dles and shafts. Large hand-held tools, which had been made for more
than one million years (Acheulean industry), now disappear from the
African archeological record. The advent of hafting made an evolutionary
impact by increasing the amount of force that could be applied to cutting
and scraping edges and at the same time reducing the risk of injury and
infection to the tool user. Stone-tipped spears would also have increased
the effectiveness of hunting and improved the security and quality of diet
for groups of cooperative hunters and their large-brained dependants.
Marlowe argues that the development of effective hunting tools enabled
males to provide a surplus of food for provisioning females. Thus began
the division of labor, which characterizes hunter-gatherer societies to this
day: "With increased foraging efficiency, males may have gained more by
targeting foods different from those females acquired since their trade
value would have been greater, resulting in a sexual division in labour."[48]
The shift from hand-held tools to those made of multiple working parts
is apparently unrelated to the evolution of art, but the two behavioral
changes occur in concert with, and arguably in support of, the expansion
of our brain size to modern levels. A complex feedback loop existed between biology and behavior, of which the use of symbols was an integral
component among some central and east African populations.

Symbols are adaptive in that they enable collections of unrelated individuals to act cohesively because of a shared sense of belonging to an
identifiable group. They facilitate the creation of oppositions between us
and them that include and exclude at the same time. The impact of symbol
use (and language) in these initial stages may be difficult to detect archeologically because of its transitory forms of expression. But as well as
pigments and technological change at 300,000 B.P., there is another indirect
indicator of something new in the human behavioral repertoire. In central
Africa the first regionally distinctive archeological culture or industry appears at this time. The Lupemban industry is identifiable by its unique
artifacts, in particular a long, thin lance-like point (Figure 3) which is
restricted in distribution to the Congo basin and its margins. The makers
of Lupemban tools were the first people to settle what is now the tropical
forest belt of central Africa. The region had been uninhabited previously
and, even today, life in the rain forest is difficult for hunter-gatherers because of the inaccessibility of some basic nutrients, especially carbohy-
drates.[49] It is tempting to see in the Lupemban the emergence of a regional
style of tool-making that was not only functional, but one that communicated a sense of shared identity to its makers and acted as a warning
sign to others. The use of pigments in symbol-charged contexts, such as

Figure 3
A lance-like stone point of the Lupemban industry.

0 ⌞ ⌟ 50 mm

rites of passage, would have consolidated Lupemban communities as co-operative groups and contributed to their successful colonization of the Congo basin. This is admittedly a speculative model, but it animates and integrates fundamental changes in human behavior and biology that oc-curred nearly simultaneously. To ignore or minimize the contribution of the symbolic domain, whether in the form of language or image-making, would be intellectually irresponsible.

Pigments remain a part of the archeological record of southern Africa for the following 300,000 years, during which there are changing patterns of color preference and presumably in the social contexts of use. The range of colors found at Twin Rivers gives way to the selection of bright reds after 120,000 years ago[50] and the modification of hematite by drilling, notching, and incising as in the case of Blombos cave. Powers (this volume) draws on ethnographic analogy to suggest a link between red pigment, blood symbolism, and the formation of female coalitions to ensure male participation in the provisioning of mothers and their large-brained infants with high quality food, namely meat. The exclusive use of pigments by females is archeologically invisible and the ethnographic record shows us that both men and women used pigments, including hematite. Among extant African hunter-gatherers, farmers, and herders, body painting is carried out in the context of rites of passage such as coming of age, marriage, and death but also to attract a mate of either sex, when communicating with the supernatural, and in preparation for conflict between groups.[51] As an aside, we still mark our bodies for some of the same reasons. The revival of tattooing and body piercing in recent years has its parallels with creating an identity and attracting like-minded mates. Lipstick and nail polish are other obvious examples of how we paint ourselves to appeal to others. Signaling group membership and allegiance is still of importance (just go to any football match), and perhaps even more so in a highly fragmented society with few common social bonds. The universal attributes of social life outlined above are very much with us as they were 300,000 years ago in Africa.

THE BIG QUESTIONS

If there was a cognitive big bang early in the African record, then we are faced with the fundamental questions of why it took place about 300,000 B.P., not before, and why such a long interval separates the first pigment use and the first cave paintings, which appear about 30,000 years ago. Both answers may be related to the effects of population pressures. Stephen Shennan has modeled demographic shifts for the last 100,000 years and sees a close correlation between population rise and the emergence of modern human culture 50,000 to 40,000 years ago, the currently accepted date for behavioral modernity.[52] He makes a more general observation that technological innovations often go hand in hand with an increase in population, thus enhancing the adaptive fitness of the group. Small bands of 20 or fewer people, such as a hunter-gatherer band of four or five families, offer fewer channels for the transmission of innovations from one generation to the next. They also contain fewer people to make innovations, apply them, and act as models for others to compare the results between existing and new ideas. As the size of the interacting group increases from 20 to 100 individuals, there are more potential innovators, and people to observe and learn from, who are not one's own parents. The rate of transmission of helpful innovations increases markedly as does the group's ability to respond to pressures from the environment, including competing groups of humans. And, of course, successful innovations can enable a population to grow, which has ramifications for the transmission of innovations and adaptive fitness.

The settlement of the Congo basin happened as a consequence of the innovations in the Lupemban tool kit, which enabled these hunter-gatherers to extract protein and energy from a previously inaccessible environment. We have no idea what size Lupemban social groups may have been—the kinds of sites that might give this information, such as base camps, have not been found. In the absence of concrete data we can only speculate that the communal threshold of 20 or more people was crossed by this time. Language enables humans to live in large social groups and maintain close tabs on the emotional states of others without having to resort to the time-consuming practice of social grooming used by other primates for this purpose.[53] It may not be possible to untangle the chicken-and-egg relationship between brain size, language, technology, and group size, but these variables all seem to have come together by 300,000 B.P. in parts of Africa. The close ties between language and symbol use allow us to add symbol-based behaviors to the equation. Archeologists now need to concentrate on the period between 400,000 and 300,000 B.P. to identify the links between climate change, shifts in biogeography, and the consequences for the distribution of human populations. There may well have been places, such as southeastern Africa, where population pressures rose as a consequence of climate change. The Kalahari desert spread as far north as the equator during the height of glacial periods, which had profound effects on the distribution of plants, animals, and humans across southern Africa.[54] One such long, dry interval began just before 300,000 B.P. (oxygen isotope stage 8) and lasted 50,000 years. The timing coincides closely with the innovations of the Lupemban, the extensive use of pigments at Twin Rivers, and the spread of humans into the Congo basin. The human species involved in these developments was large-brained *Homo heidelbergensis*, the direct ancestor of *Homo sapiens* in Africa.

The long interval between the appearance of pigment use in the archeological record and the first evidence of cave painting poses a challenge to the argument that fully modern symbolic behaviors had developed much earlier than the Upper Paleolithic. For some, this gap is illusory. Cave art simply would not survive much beyond 40,000 years because of weathering in temperate climates.[55] Alternatively, if cave art is genuinely no more than 32,000 years old, then another explanation is needed. The social anthropologist Mary Douglas has, unintentionally, provided a model for describing the social conditions which could promote the development of cave art and at the same time describe the long preamble of pigment use in the archeological record. Douglas argues that the form of ritual and use of symbols in a society closely mirrors its social structure. A fluid social structure is reflected in loosely organized rituals; conversely, a highly structured society is reflected by prescribed rituals and use of symbols. Put simply, the more a society is structured, the richer the art will be. From an evolutionary perspective, the appearance of European cave art reflects a shift from fluid to more structured belief systems and arguably took place under the stimulus of population pressure in certain favored regions or from competition between Neanderthals and modern humans. Demographic changes may also explain the development of cave art in Africa and Australia, but that argument is not developed here.

In *Natural Symbols: Explorations in Cosmology,* Douglas begins her analysis of the social constraints on the expression of symbols with the premise: "If ritual is taken to be a form of restricted code, and if the condition for a restricted code to emerge is that the members of a group should know one another so well that they share a common backcloth of assumptions which never need to be made explicit, then tribes may well vary on this basis."[56] To illustrate and analyze the sources of variation, she applies a grid/group analysis (Figure 4). This form of structural analysis classifies societies and aspects of cultures according to degrees of social

Figure 4
Mary Douglas's grid/group classification of societies based on separate axes.

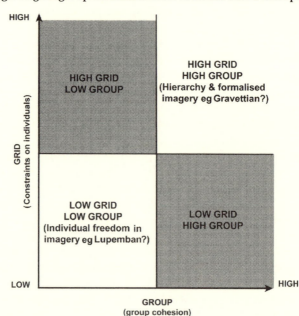

cohesion in a group and the constraints on decision-making imposed by the society on individuals. The grid axis marks a continuum from high individual freedom to act within personal beliefs to the opposite extreme of low freedom because of socially controlled decision-making. The group axis charts the extent of group cohesion from low to high, with the involvement of the individual within the group ranging from loosely to highly defined by social norms. Douglas points to military organizations as examples of high grid/high group institutions that demand extreme conformity from their members. At the opposite extreme, the individual or group who actively resists dominant social pressures to conform would be low grid/low group, such as travelers or gypsies. The latter may have their own rule-bound behaviors, but they are not those of the wider community.

If we link art, including bodily adornment, to ritual and thereby social structure, the grid/group analysis gives us a model for classifying prehistoric cultures. In societies with low grid and low group pressures there are few rules governing rituals and the imagery is free to vary between individuals. In societies with clear hierarchies (high grid) and strong sense of cohesion (high group) the imagery will be formalized with little room for variation. Between these extremes are societies with relative equality between individuals (low grid) and clear group identity (high group). The ritual imagery in this case will be defined and shared by the group with room for individual expression. The combination of a hierarchical society (high grid) with low social cohesion (low group) is rare among most hunter-gatherer societies, but where it occurs, such as among the Nootka of British Columbia, the imagery associated with ceremonies is complex and symbols of rank are displayed on these occasions and in daily dress. By contrast, the Mbuti pygmies of the Ituri forest, Democratic Republic of Congo, are low grid and low group. Mbuti women paint designs on bark cloth and on their bodies for ceremonies and coming of age rituals. The designs vary greatly between individuals, though they are almost always geometric in form and symbolize natural or cultural themes.[57] The body paint is wiped away and the bark cloth garments are not kept. This is ephemeral art produced for the occasion and not for reverence or display of status. Mbuti ceremonies are loosely structured in time and place of performance, and the roles of individuals are not specified. From an archeological perspective, this type of ritual and its imagery are unlikely to leave any lasting physical signature. Even the pigments they use to produce the colors red, yellow, and blue-black are transitory vegetable dyes. The impermanence of Mbuti beliefs is a sobering reminder that the archeological record is a poor reflection of much of human behavior. By comparison with Mbuti material culture, the Lupemban peoples have left us a colorful legacy.

RETURNING TO EUROPE

Looking afresh at the archeological record from the perspective of the grid/group analysis, it seems that until 40,000 years ago most societies were low grid/low group or some variant that did not produce highly formalized imagery which survives. Of course, we can never know what use was made of organic materials, such as wood or bone, as media for expression. The Aurignacian does represent something new with its ivory and shell beadwork and subsequent cave art. The earliest cave art with its underlying themes of large and dangerous animals is relatively stylized, and, in the case of Chauvet cave, the placement of images within the cave itself is highly structured by color (e.g., red images are separated from black) and content (e.g., bears separate from lions). In terms of Douglas's analysis, the individuals in this society shared a set of restricted codes and were themselves restricted in what could be portrayed and where. We could classify these Aurignacian peoples as either low grid/high group or high grid/high group, but there is little evidence for a social hierarchy. This only appears in the Gravettian period (c. 26,000 to 24,000 B.P.) with its spectacularly rich burials, such as Sungir and Paviland Cave, Wales.[58] To explain the apparently abrupt development of extensive body decoration and painted and portable art, we need to return in part to Shennan's ideas on population growth.

The initial Aurignacian colonists of Europe were behaviorally and anatomically modern humans who brought with them a long pedigree of symbol use in social contexts. They not only entered a continent inhabited by another human species, the Neanderthals, but these early modern humans also faced the challenges of a glacial landscape. *Homo sapiens* evolved as a tropical African species; to survive and thrive in the high latitudes of Europe they capitalized on their capacity to innovate and to use symbols within and between groups. The maintenance of long-distance social ties in widely dispersed and highly mobile bands of hunter-gatherers would have been critical to ensure the flow of information about resources and mates. Personal adornment presumably played a role in these networks, perhaps as objects of exchange or as signals of group identity. Bone and antler objects also seem to have been used to store information in the form of tally marks.[59] The initial pioneering phase of colonization appears to have been rapid and was followed by a settling-in period during which populations grew and cave art emerged in parts of France and Spain.

In southwestern France, the Aurignacians coexisted with Neanderthals during the period between 38,000 and 32,000 B.P.[60] Evidence for their direct interaction is highly disputed, but it is clear that the elaboration of Aurignacian symbol use from body art to cave art takes place at this time. The presence of Neanderthals may have been the stimulus for the consolidation of the modern human ability to mobilize groups of people to act as a cohesive whole in the face of adversity. It seems that Aurignacians engaged in the human universal of recognizing individuals as living in socially bounded groups. They reinforced that recognition through the signaling of membership (body ornamentation) and later by marking the landscape with corporate symbols (rock art). Douglas was aware that some causal link might exist between population pressure and high levels of social order and constraint on individuals, but cautioned that "these can be as easily absent in dense as in sparse populations."[61] Instead, she argued that "economic expansion and restriction turn out to be much more significant variables,"[62] with stricter social control exercised under conditions of perceived contraction of resources. The ethnographic record of historic hunter-gatherers in Papua New Guinea neatly illustrates the correlation between resource availability, demographic structure, social order, and complexity of visual art.[63] Those who relied on the hunting of unpredictable terrestrial and arboreal game were typically highly mobile, had low population densities, were politically egalitarian, and had a simple ritual life with few forms of art other than body decoration, singing, and dancing. These societies would be classified as low grid/low group, like the Mbuti of the Ituri Forest. At the other end of the demographic spectrum were communities that depended on rich marine foods and supported sedentary, dense populations that were socially stratified and practiced complex rituals associated with elaborate visual arts, including carved wooden structures. The similarities with the high grid/high group Nootka are uncanny.

The Aurignacian settlers of glacial Europe entered an unfamiliar landscape that was already inhabited in part by Neanderthals. These newcomers may have responded to such uncertainties by creating tighter social controls and encouraging group cohesion through shared imagery. Neanderthals seem to have lacked that capacity to mobilize social controls, which may have been a factor in their extinction shortly after 30,000 B.P. Their lack of art, or more precisely their limited use of their ability to express a shared perception of reality to others using media other than language, seems to have been a genuine handicap in the evolutionary stakes. The rock art of France and Spain becomes a significant feature of the landscape after the extinction of the Neanderthals, but the processes underlying its development are the same as those that lead the Aurignacians to adorn themselves.

Demographic pressure and uncertainty of resource stability continued to play a formative role. The climatic downturn that affected Europe beginning about 26,000 to 24,000 years ago placed ever-greater pressures on resource-rich environments.[64] Northern Spain and southwestern France were favored with relatively abundant animal and plant foods, including salmon, and the northern European plains supported large herbivores, such as mammoth, bison, and horse. Competition for these resources increased as populations expanded following the initial colonization phase and became intimately familiar with the most productive areas of the landscape. Declining temperatures and the expansion of ice sheets on the northern fringe and on mountain ranges would have begun to squeeze populations as the distribution of animals and plants shifted. Under these combined pressures, we might expect to see social changes underway that reflected increasing constraints on individuality in favor of group cohesion. The elaborate burials of select adults and children across Europe during the Gravettian may echo an increasingly stratified social order with some individuals in positions of inherited authority.

SUMMARY

This chapter has taken what may be, for some, an uncomfortable and unfashionable view of the role of art in human evolution. The capacity to communicate through images, as well by sound, was and remains central to the behaviors that make us recognizably human. Art is a medium for expressing and developing a sense of self within the context of a larger social unit. It also plays a central role in the construction and maintenance of group identities, which provide common ground for acting as a unity rather than as a collection of disparate individuals. Cooperative behaviors, initially involving males and females in the feeding and care of large-brained infants, emerged about 500,000 years ago. By 300,000 B.P., the first indirect evidence for symbol use appears in central and east Africa. A threshold in human cognitive evolution was crossed with the emergence of a symbol-using species, one which also made new kinds of tools and settled previously uninhabited environments and continents. The behavioral consequences of the evolution of symbolic culture were slow to materialize after this initial burst of activity, and for many archeologists the appearance of rock art is the only direct evidence of material symbols in action. But the florescence of cave art in Europe and later in Africa and Australia had its roots in the long prelude of pigment use in Africa. The capacity to create symbols in forms other than language began with *Homo heidelbergensis* and was maintained and elaborated by its direct descendant, *Homo sapiens,* who evolved 160,000 years ago in Africa.

As populations grew in size, the transmission of cultural information between generations quickened and more tangible signs of symbol use surface in the archeological record. The engraved blocks of pigment at Blombos Cave 70,000 years ago are a local signal that a population threshold had been crossed. In the context of population growth and increased competition for resources, art and ritual may have become more structured to enhance group cohesion at times of stress. This appears to be the pattern observed among some contemporary communities that are highly mobile and it provides a model for explaining the relatively abrupt appearance of cave art. The first modern humans to colonize Europe and Australia carried with them a long tradition of symbol use that initially arose in Africa. In the context of Europe, the symbolic heritage of the immigrants contributed to their success in settling the continent and hastened the extinction of indigenous Neanderthals. The colonizers used beads as signals of social identity and later cave art and portable images to consolidate ownership and a sense of belonging to places in the landscape.

Art in the traditional Western sense of the creation of aesthetically pleasing images, and in its many contemporary manifestations, still echoes the ancestral roles of giving a sense of identity to the viewer and maker, creating a sense of shared community—though now restricted to a small cognoscenti—and ultimately of communicating a perception of the world around us to another human being. Once the genie of shared imagery had been let loose, we became an altogether different kind of social animal, one that could harness the power of cooperative ventures to create and destroy on a scale not known in nature.

I end this chapter with a quote from an old, but still active, British artist who encapsulates the essence of my argument: "Fashions change, but you only have to see children on the beach drawing in the sand with their fingers and wanting to make colour to realise that painting is part of our development."[65]

ACKNOWLEDGMENTS

My thanks to Günter Berghaus for the invitation to present these ideas in a public forum and now in print. Paul Pettitt read an early draft of this chapter and his critical comments are much appreciated. The research in Zambia on which my argument is based was supported by the British Academy, the L.S.B. Leakey Foundation, the National Geographic Society, and the Prehistoric Society.

NOTES

1. See Lawrence Barham. "Systematic Pigment Use in the Middle Pleistocene of South-Central Africa." *Current Anthropology* 43 (2002): 181–190.

2. See Robert Layton. *The Anthropology of Art*, 2nd ed. Cambridge: Cambridge University Press, 1992.

3. See the classical study of Arnold Van Gennep. *The Rites of Passage*. Chicago: University of Chicago Press, 1960.

4. Robert Bednarik. "Proposed Glossary of Rock Art Research." *AURA Newsletter* 2000: 8.

5. See J. David Lewis-Williams. *The Mind in the Cave and the Origins of Human Consciousness*. London: Thames and Hudson, 2002.

6. See, for example, Richard Klein. "Archaeology and the Evolution of Human Behavior." *Evolutionary Anthropology* 9 (2000): 17–36.

7. See, for example, Robert Bednarik. "Concept-mediated Marking in the Lower Palaeolithic." *Current Anthropology* 36 (1995): 605–634.

8. Francesco d'Errico and Paola Villa. "Hole and Grooves: The Contribution of Microscopy and Taphonomy to the Problem of Art Origins." *Journal of Human Evolution* 33 (1997): 1–31.

9. Terrence Deacon. *The Symbolic Species: The Co-evolution of Language and the Human Brain.* London: Penguin Books, 1997.

10. Mary LeCron Foster. *The Life of Symbols.* Boulder, CO: Westview Press, 1990.

11. See Jean Clottes and J. David Lewis-Williams. *The Shamans of Prehistor: Trance and Magic in the Painted Caves.* New York: Abrams, 1998; and Lewis-Williams' recent study, *The Mind in the Cave.* London: Thames and Hudson, 2002.

12. See Ofer Bar-Yosef. "The Upper Paleolithic Revolution." *Annual Reviews of Anthropology* 31 (2002): 363–393.

13. Paul Mellars. "The Neanderthal Problem Continued." *Current Anthropology* 40 (1999): 341–350.

14. See William Davies. "A Very Model of a Modern Human Industry: New Perspectives on the Origins and Spread of the Aurignacian in Europe." *Proceedings of the Prehistoric Society* 67 (2001): 195–217.

15. See Paul Pettitt. "The Neanderthal Dead: Exploring Mortuary Variability in Middle Palaeolithic Eurasia." *Before Farming: The Archaeology of Old World Hunter-gatherers* 1 (2002): 1–19.

16. Randall White. "Personal Ornaments from the Grotte du Renne at Arcy-sur-Cure." *Athena Review* 2 (2001): 41–46.

17. Helène Valladas, Jean Clottes, J.-M. Geneste, M. A. Garcia, M. Arnold, H. Cachier, and N. Tisnérat-Laborde. "Palaeolithic Paintings: Evolution of Prehistoric Cave Art." *Nature* 413 (2001): 479.

18. Jean Clottes. "Thematic Changes in Upper Palaeolithic Art: The View from Grotte Chauvet." *Antiquity* 70 (268): 276–288.

19. See Francesco D'Errico, Christopher Henshilwood, and Peter Nilssen. "An Engraved Bone Fragment from c. 70,000-Year-Old Middle Stone Age Levels at Blombos Cave, South Africa: Implications for the Origins of Symbolism and Language." *Antiquity* 75 (2001): 309–318; Christopher S. Henshilwood, Francesco d'Errico, Royden Yates, Zenobia Jacobs, Chantal Tribolo, Geoff A. T. Duller, Norbert Mercier, Judith C. Sealy, Hélène Valladas, Ian Watts, and Ann G. Wintle. "Emergence of Modern Human Behaviour: Middle Stone Age Engravings from South Africa." *Science* 295:5558 (15 February 2002): 1278–1280.

20. See Tim D. White, Berhane Asfaw, David DeGusta, Henry Gilbert, Gary D. Richards, Gen Suwa, and F. Clark Howell. "Pleistocene *Homo sapiens* from Middle Awash, Ethiopia." *Nature* 423 (12 June 2003): 742–747.

21. See Powers, this volume.

22. Sarah Blaffer Hrdy. *Mother Nature: Natural Selection and the Female of the Species.* London: Chatto and Windus, 1999.

23. Frank Marlowe. "Male Contribution to Diet and Female Reproductive Success among Foragers." *Current Anthropology* 42 (2001): 755–760.

24. See, for example, Kristen Hawkes, James F. O'Connell, and Nicholas Blurton

Jones. "Hunting and Nuclear Families: Some Lessons form the Hadza about Men's Work." *Current Anthropology* 42 (2001): 681–709.

25. Benjamin Orlove. "Editorial: The Evolution of Symbolic Capacities and Human Society." *Current Anthropology* 42 (2001): i–iii.

26. Steven Pinker. *The Blank Slate: The Modern Denial of Human Nature*. London: Lane, 2002.

27. Colin Turnbull. *The Forest People*. London: Chatto and Windus, 1961.

28. Stephen Aldhouse-Green, ed. *Paviland Cave and the "Red Lady": A Definitive Report*. Bristol: Western Academic and Specialist Press, 2000.

29. R. J. King. "Minerals Explained 30: Hematite." *Geology Today*, July–August 2000: 158–160.

30. Lawrence Keeley. *Experimental Determination of Stone Tool Uses: A Microwear Analysis*. Chicago, IL: University of Chicago Press, 1980.

31. J. Velo. "Ochre as Medicine: A Suggestion for the Interpretation of the Archaeological Record." *Current Anthropology* 25 (1984): 674.

32. William J. Sollas. *Ancient Hunters and Their Modern Representatives*, 3rd ed. London: MacMillan, 1924: 277.

33. For example, Stanley Ambrose. "Chronology of the Later Stone Age and Food Production in East Africa." *Journal of Archaeological Science* 25 (1998): 377–392.

34. See Christopher Knight, Camilla Power, and Ian Watts. "The Human Symbolic Revolution: A Darwinian Account." *Cambridge Archaeological Journal* 5 (1995): 75–114; Camilla Power and Ian Watts. "Female Strategies and Collective Behaviour: The Archaeology of Earliest *Homo sapiens*." In *The Archaeology of Human Ancestry: Power, Sex and Tradition*, ed. James Steele and Stephen Shennan. London: Routledge, 1996: 306–330.

35. S. Phillibert. "L'Ocre et le traitement des peaux: Révision d'une conception traditionelle par l'analyse fonctionelle des grattoirs ocrés de la Balma Margineda (Andorre). *L'Anthropologie* 98 (1994): 447–453.

36. Josephine Flood. "Culture in Early Aboriginal Australia." *Cambridge Archaeological Journal* 6 (1996): 6–36.

37. See M.A. Smith, B. Frankhauser, and M. Jercher. "The Changing Provenance of Red Ochre at Puritjarra Rock Shelter, Central Australia: Late Pleistocene to Present." *Proceedings of the Prehistoric Society* 64 (1998): 275–292.

38. Rhys Jones. "Gun-gugaliya rrawai: Place, Ochre and Death. A Perspective from Aboriginal Australia." In *Paviland Cave and the "Red Lady,"* Aldhouse-Green. pp. 247–264.

39. See Chippindale, this volume.

40. Iain Davidson, and William Noble. "Why the First Colonisation of the Australian Region Is the Earliest Evidence of Modern Human Behaviour." *Archaeology in Oceania* 27 (1992): 113–119.

41. R. Kittles and O. Y. Keita. "Interpreting African Genetic Diversity." *African Archaeological Review* 16 (1999): 87–91.

42. See Lewis-Williams, this volume.

43. Roger L. Hewitt. *Structure, Meaning and Ritual in the Narratives of the Southern San*. Hamburg: Buske, 1986.

44. Lawrence Barham, ed. *The Middle Stone Age of Zambia, South Central Africa*. Bristol: Western Academic and Specialist Press, 2000.

45. Barham. "Systematic Pigment Use."

46. D. Osorio and M. Vorobyev. "Color-vision as an Adaptation to Frugivory in Primates." *Proceedings of the Royal Society of London B* 263 (1996): 593–599.

47. Sally McBrearty. "The Middle Pleistocene of East Africa." In *Human Roots: Africa and Asia in the Middle Pleistocene,* ed. Lawrence Barham and Kate Robson-Brown. Bristol: Western Academic and Specialist Press, 2001: 81–98.

48. "Male Contribution to Diet," p. 759.

49. Barham: *The Middle Stone Age of Zambia, South Central Africa.*

50. Ian Watts. "Ochre in the Middle Stone Age of Southern Africa: Ritualised Display or Hide Preservative?" *South African Archaeological Review* 57 (2002): 1–14.

51. Carol Beckwith and Angela Fisher. *African Ceremonies.* Noew York: Abrams, 1999.

52. "Demography and Cultural Innovation: A Model and its Implications for the Emergence of Modern Human Culture." *Cambridge Archaeological Journal* 11 (2001): 5–16.

53. Robin Dunbar. "Neocortex Size as a Constraint on Group Size in Primates." *Journal of Human Evolution* 20 (1992): 469–493.

54. Barham. *The Middle Stone Age of Zambia.*

55. Bednarik. "Concept Mediated Marking."

56. Mary Douglas. *Natural Symbols: Explorations in Cosmology,* London: Barrie and Jenkins, 1973: 78.

57. Georges Meurant and Robert Farris Thompson. *Mbuti Design: Paintings by Pygmy Women of the Ituri Forest.* London: Thames and Hudson, 1995.

58. Aldhouse-Green. "Paviland Cave."

59. Davies. "A Very Model of an Industry."

60. Pettitt. Personal communication.

61. Douglas. *Natural Symbols,* p. 130.

62. Ibid., p. 130

63. Paul Roscoe. "The Hunters and Gatherers of New Guinea." *Current Anthropology* 43 (2002): 153–162.

64. See Clive Gamble. *The Palaeolithic Societies of Europe.* Cambridge: Cambridge University Press, 1999.

65. Wilhemina Barns-Graham in Hilly Janes "Return of the OBAs." *The Observer Magazine,* 4 November 2001: 40–45; quotation from p. 43.

Paleoperformance: Investigating the Human Use of Caves in the Upper Paleolithic

Yann-Pierre Montelle

This chapter is dedicated to the memory of John E. Pfeiffer.

Based on discrete lines of archeological evidence, the author believes that the deep caves of Southern France and Northern Spain were used primarily as loci for initiatory procedures in the Upper Paleolithic (c. 35,000 to 8,000 B.C.). To support this point of view, the author introduces the concept of Paleoperformance as a means to reconstruct performative behavioral patterns based on archeological remains. The author endorses the use of ethnographic analogy as a valid methodological process to investigate the human use of caves in the Upper Paleolithic. While acknowledging the multifunctional nature of a deep cave and the variety of supporting evidence, the author presents one such function based on a specific line of evidence centered primarily around the sound-making artifacts found in many Upper-Paleolithic locations. In light of this, initiatory procedures will be shown to offer a series of structural characteristics, which help articulate the following hypothesis: throughout the 25,000-year span of the Upper Paleolithic, the decorated deep caves functioned as cultural containers where liminal[1] activities were performed and systematized and esoteric knowledge was archived.

INTRODUCTION

According to archeological evidence, the so-called cavemen rarely lived inside caves. Admittedly, there are a few exceptions[2] where hearths and traces of economic activities have been found in caves. But for the overwhelming majority of cases, occupation was restricted to open-air rock-shelters and the mouth of caves. Furthermore, it has been established that hominids lived in or near the caves' openings for thousands of years before exploring their tantalizing subterranean depth.

In the cave, cognitive processes have been either intentionally recorded or unintentionally imprinted. The traces left behind point toward behavioral patterns by which humans in the Upper Paleolithic lived. As a cultural reservoir, the cave was a place where myths were generated and recorded. The cave functioned as a book in which specific facets of cognition were encoded in the forms of mnemonics on the cave wall. It served as a classroom where specific hunting techniques were taught in the safety of the subterranean environment. It was also used for healing purposes, where the shaman transcribed his or her diagnostic on the cave wall. It was a sanctuary, where increase ceremonies were performed. It was a place where initiated men returned to receive higher a degree of esoteric knowledge and expertise. More to the point, the cave was used as a ceremonial locus, where individuals submitted to the ordeals of initiation. Ultimately, the cave, as reservoir, was a container for human activities of a pedagogical and initiatory nature.

THE HUMAN USE OF CAVES IN THE UPPER PALEOLITHIC

In his monograph, *Beyond the Bounds of History* (1949), Henri Breuil presents a collage of 31 scenes from the Stone Age, each accompanied by an illustration "showing the stages of development of Fossil Man and his civilizations."[3] Breuil displays a colorful prehistoric theater where exotic hominids share the stage harmoniously with the animal world.

For example, Scene 25 has as its title *The Sanctuary of Trois Frères at Montesqieu-Avantès (Ariège)*. Breuil's narrative transports us into the Reindeer Age, when men ventured deep into the uncharted galleries of subterranean caverns, where they left imprints of their peregrinations as far as 1,650 meters from the entrance. Along the narrow corridors are the traces (engravings) of many passages which, according to Breuil, "makes it clear that the actors in these ceremonies passed that way, perhaps shouting or singing in such a fashion that the initiates would think the cries supernatural."[4] This spatial appropriation is signaled by identifiable markings on the cave wall. Were these engravings a manifestation of territorial concerns? Apparently, Ice Age populations resided at the mouth of the cave and not in the dark galleries. The latter were reserved for tribal initiation ceremonies and fertility rites. While cold winds gusted across the landscape, the caves offered a relatively warm and dry environment (approximately 11 degrees Celsius, or 52 degrees Fahrenheit). Breuil is unequivocal: Winter was the chosen season for tribal initiation. In the deep galleries, young initiates would be instructed about their societal obligations and the tribal traditions. For the occasion, secrets were revealed in carefully choreographed mask-dances and invocations of spirits. The initiate would learn the spiritual skills to cope with demons and to increase the game by willed multiplication. In Breuil's illustration, the initiates seem to be mesmerized by the ritual performance, center stage, of an impersonation of the well-known engraving of a man-bison playing a musical bow (also interpreted as a nose flute), a mythical ancestor in Breuil's terminology. Scene 25 ends with resonating screams from a hidden sorcerer accompanied by the roaring sound of a bullroarer announcing transformation for a group of anxious initiates.

Such ceremonies, according to Breuil, took place in the cave of the *Trois Frères* for thousands of years. It is my intention to assess the feasibility of Breuil's approach by discussing some of the evidence that supports the existence of such performative events in the Upper Paleolithic.

A BRIEF DISCUSSION OF ANALOGY

To assess the human use of caves in the Upper Paleolithic, recent researchers have relied almost exclusively on empirical processes. Few have expanded their investigations beyond the quantitative analysis of artifacts and archeological remains. The leap toward a more theoretical (and therefore speculative) ground seems to be, in many cases, considered either futile or unscientific. Borrowing Lewis-Williams's terminology, the empiricists operate under the false assumption that their investigations are, if nothing else, objective. Although there has been a healthy debate on the dyad objectivity/subjectivity in the discipline of anthropology, this is often deemed to be irrelevant to the field of prehistory. In fact, no matter how far removed from the evidence the researcher might be, his or her reading will always be subjected to a series of inherent constraints ranging from the researcher's level of expertise to his or her awareness of all the possible relationships between the evidence and the context.

Lewis-Williams writes that the Upper Paleolithic "must not be homogenized into a replica of any single ethnographically observed society: Multiple analogies and interpretations will be required to build up a multi-component mosaic that fits the highly diverse empirical evidence of Upper-Palaeolithic art."[5] Perhaps the most criticized methodology in the field of prehistory has been the use of analogy to recontextualize archeological remains. While it is undeniable that an artifact in context will generate a set of reliable premises, the problem seems to lie in the notion of conclusion. In many of the arguments against the use of analogy it is assumed that analogical reasoning is systematically conclusive.[6] It is true that in the field of prehistory there is a historical precedent for an interpretive discourse where analogies were indeed conclusive, but the hermeneutic excesses of these pioneers have opened a way toward understanding life in prehistoric times. In their footsteps, I wish to rehabilitate analogy as a grounded investigative component for the prehistoric discourse. Ethnographic relevance (rather than the classic accumulation of ethnographic precedents) is an adequate analytical framework for analogical reasoning.[7] I will approach analogy as an analytical tool to project into the past a set of societal aspects drawn from relevant ethnographic sources.

PALEOPERFORMANCE

Although suspiciously dramatic, Breuil's description of the human activities, which possibly took place in the cave of Les Trois Frères during the Upper-Paleolithic period, does not seem so farfetched after all. His narrative is substantiated by sound archeological evidence. Breuil's effort to reconstruct the initiatory procedures that may have taken place in this particular cave (and in many others) is commendable. Of course, critics might point out a myriad of inaccuracies in Breuil's account and a variety of iconographic elements that do not belong there. But a close examination of Breuil's approach reveals a complex bricolage of evidence. His intention is clear—to demonstrate that human use of caves was primarily initiatory in nature. Breuil's hypothesis is as relevant as any other formulated since then. But what is lacking in his approach is a methodological framework to establish the performative nature of these ceremonies. Still, his carefully manufactured mise-en-scène opens the door to another perspective—a behavioral point of view, which I have termed Paleoperformance.

In an attempt to answer the question "What is Paleoperformance?" I offer the following definition: Paleoperformance refers to a set of restored human behaviors from the Paleolithic based on recovered artifacts, which offer material evidence for activities that are both intentional and liminal. The liminal, or marginal, nature of these intended activities places them somewhat at odds with the empirical expectations inherent to archeological investigations. Paleoperformance offers a dynamic approach to archeological remains by focusing primarily on the reconstruction of potential cultural activities and the inherent performative, kinetic patterns associated to the products of these activities. I wish to establish Paleoperformance as a genuine part of the Upper-Paleolithic investigation, even though its field of research is as marginal as the liminal activities it investigates.

Looking at the archeological evidence from the Upper Paleolithic, one recurring characteristic is the *intentional* nature of many of these remains. It is undeniable that the manufacturing aspect of an artifact is inherently intentional. For example, the technological lineage between a Lower-Paleolithic chopper and a modern table knife is a testament to intentional improvement of what was once an accidental innovation. To develop this analogy further, I wish to show that the manufacturing aspect of an artifact is also inherently performative. The *chaîne opératoire* associated with the manufacture and use of a chopper or a knife can be reconstructed into a series of precise kinetic patterns that are restored every time the tool needs to be reproduced or utilized. These restored behaviors are the *sine qua non* conditions for an efficient use of the tools, and their systematization a mnemonic guarantee for their persistence beyond the stage of innovation. By approaching prehistoric material culture in terms of performance and intention, the artifacts cease to be inert fossils, but are projected back into a dynamic recontextualization.

Perhaps the most convincing argument for performative and intentional behavior comes from the realm of acoustics. Researchers have speculated on the relationship between points of high resonance and imagery, and have discovered that Upper-Paleolithic humans were sensitive to such acoustics and made their choice of paths based on carefully mapped sonic routes. The consequences of a performative and intentional action can be identified by two correlated phenomena: effect and affect. Effect and affect were, seemingly, two specific concerns for the prehistoric individual. But why would these two phenomena be of concern for cave users? To address this question, we need to approach the cave as a locus for initiatory activities designed to fulfill a variety of discrete functions. These include the storage of exoteric and esoteric knowledge as well as the learning of skills during initiatory procedures.

Throughout this chapter, I will consider initiation to be a performative behavior characterized by the following features:

- it involves an initiate whose ordeal anticipates the presence or absence of a potential observer;
- the initiate is processed through staged ordeals;
- the initiate's ordeal is transformative and psychologically destabilizing;
- the initiate's actions are imbued with a high degree of intentionality;
- the initiate is carefully maintained within a frame of anticipated behavioral patterns: restored behavior; and
- staged effects are used to emphasize the process of alienation for the initiate.

These manufactured effects for the staged ordeals affect the initiate to such a degree that the anxious individual is quickly conditioned and easily manipulated. This is a behavioral constant, which also provides a paradigmatic skeleton for Paleoperformance.

INITIATION CEREMONIES

The notion that caves served as repositories for social impulses of the art-for-art's-sake variety quickly collapses under the weight of the evidence for intentionality in the Upper Paleolithic. The caves acted as cultural reservoirs, where the organization of space resulted in a complex articulation of iconographic and archeological remains. Ultimately, the intention seems to have been to inform and initiate, at variable degrees, selected youths in order to fulfill social requirements.

Initiation is performative, that is, it expands the social activities on the margins of the necessary. Arguably, it is on these margins that performances such as music and dance find their roots as well as their societal validation.

It seems reasonable that our ancestors would have used every possible device, including singing and dancing, to help get the message across. There is evidence for this, both in the caves themselves and in the customs of present-day hunter-gatherers. Singing and dancing also may be accompanied by the low-throaty growl of bullroarers—carved boards twirled on cords. Such performances are pure theater.[8]

The following schema (Figure 1), borrowed from Van Gennep's seminal work, *The Rites of Passage* (1960), offers a workable format for analyzing initiation. It begins with the initiate's traumatic separation from the social structure (and the mother); the initiate is then monitored through an unfamiliar environment (a cave, for example) for an undetermined period of time (hours, days, months perhaps). This is followed by a reintegration into the social structure (often marked by a complete abandonment of the mother figure). The collective expects the subject to stabilize and behave in accordance with the social norms incumbent to his or her new status.

A preliminary classification of initiation, based on data collected from eHRAF's (Electronic Human Resource Area File) Collection of Ethnography,[9] is offered here in order to simplify what would otherwise be a complex discussion. It is important to note that all the initiations described in eHRAF show distinct variability and regional differences in forms and contents in terms of initiatory procedures. To avoid a trivial homogenizing of a complex notion such as initiation, the author will offer no narrowly prescriptive definitions. However, the recurrence of paradigms across the

Figure 1
Initiatory procedure inspired by Van Gennep tripartite structure.

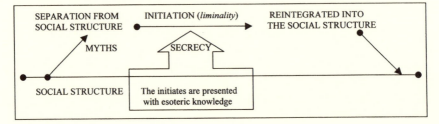

95 hunter-gatherer cultures investigated offers a sound analytical frame. For our purpose, I have isolated the following four patterns:

- seclusion (anxiety)
- ordeals (affirmation of subordination)
- secrecy (revelation and deception)
- esoteric knowledge (skills and status)

The seclusion of the initiates is a traumatic time of separation. It generates a high degree of anxiety among the initiates. This liminal stage varies considerably in length and location. Pfeiffer argues that

the more I have investigated the caves, the more obvious and elaborate and systematic the planning appears to me. It involved three stages: 1) leading the uninitiated through eerie and difficult route, a kind of obstacle course to soften them up to indoctrination; 2) catching and holding their attention with shocking and frightening displays; 3) finally, using every trick to imprint information intact and indelibly in memory.[10]

In many cases, terrified initiates are brutalized and humiliated in a series of planned interventions by the initiators. This period of seclusion is often equated to a symbolic death. The initiates develop psychotic behaviors, which are channeled through a series of voluntary ordeals and punishments. The fear of abandonment by the mother is, perhaps, one of the most studied psychotic manifestations proper to initiation rites.[11] The anxiety provoked by the forced separation of the initiate from his mother is the essence of initiation. To a large extent, the mise-en-scène of the initiation depends on the successful exploitation of this psychological phenomenon. Places for initiatory procedures are usually selected for their dramatic character. Alienated from the habitual, the initiate becomes a liminal presence: an absence.

To orchestrate a successful initiation, the initiators regiment the initiates with terrorizing behavior and brutal attacks. The initiate is surrounded by an unsettling atmosphere of danger and submits passively to aggression. It is important for the initiates to perform without complaint and with subordination. The initiate's ambiguous liminal status marks the unstable crossing of a threshold where boundaries are indicated by bloodstained trials. This threshold is a space where initiates demonstrate their fitness (physical and psychological) and their determination to belong to the collective. The expected total submission to an extreme form of authority and punishment marks the initiates' acceptance of the established authority. It is important to note that initiates are "at various stages of physical maturity; moreover, in many societies the rites are held well before, or after, the age of physical maturation."[12] Despite some noticeable age difference, initiates seem to be processed through the same degree of ordeals and expected to show the same level of obedience. It is not uncommon for initiates to lose their lives during initiation.

Hunter-gatherer initiations are often constructed around a secret. The semantic of initiation is a playful and deceptive discourse in which men's frustrations are shrouded in layers of secrecy and their factual lies are forbidden to women and children. The deceptive tactics used by the male cults bring initiation one step closer to the premeditated and fictitious world of performance.

If it were only a question of revealing a fabricated secret, initiation would have quickly been absorbed into other societal venues. Beyond the brutality and deception, initiation offers another aspect which is key to our understanding of initiatory procedures (and the human use of caves in the Upper Paleolithic). The diffusion of esoteric knowledge (tribal lore) during initiation is a well-established fact.[13] For our purpose, it is important to note that this esoteric knowledge is usually orally transmitted but in many cases can also be supported by visual mnemonics. The amount of information dispensed to initiates is contained into segmented and inconspicuous mnemonics associated with graphic patterns or simple images. The degree of revelation determines the degree of knowledge gathered by the initiates. Upon reaggregation, the initiates are systematically inducted into some preempted social roles. According to Gilbert Herdt, "the creators of cosmology and initiatory rites have almost certainly been those who had access to the innermost kernel of then-prevailing esoteric knowledge—which they modify and elaborate in ways that cumulate across generations."[14] This accumulation of cognition has, I will argue, left visible traces on the cave walls and floors.

ARCHITECTONICS AND ACOUSTICS

If the human use of caves was primarily initiatory, then it is our task to find archeological remains that will support this hypothesis. The potential archeological evidences are of three types:

- direct evidence: surface material remains, such as hearth, footprints, fossil images, engraved portable artifacts, hand-held lamps, and lithic material;
- indirect evidence: excavated material with a determined spatial and/or temporal link with the archeological remains under investigation;
- analogous evidence: comprehensive analysis of material evidence or behavioral evidence using parallels from ethnography, sociology, and psychology, among others.

The difficulty of finding archeological evidence to support my hypothesis lies in the fact that the majority of cave floors have been excavated to such an extent (and in such a way) that their reconstruction will always suffer from an unavoidable state of incompleteness. For this reason alone, the recontextualization of artifacts and behavior will always be biased and subjective. However, by analyzing the morphological and archeological components, such as architectonics (principles of architecture), acoustics (sound), and sound-producing artifacts, a great deal of information can be gathered and behavioral reconstructions can be attempted. Indeed, in the unfamiliar landscape of a deep cave, the senses are challenged and a series of behavioral responses can be expected. I would suggest that sensorial defamiliarization and anticipated behavioral responses would be instrumental in the process of indoctrination.

The rock formations, the dripping or flowing water, the utter blackness, the often total silence, the change in temperature, the loss of sense of direction in the sometimes labyrinthine passages, and the fear of being abandoned, lost and alone in the dark must all have combined to prepare apprehensive initiates for anything and make them vulnerable for indoctrination.[15]

If visibility was of concern for prehistoric individuals, so was audibility. Caves offer a great deal of variation in their ability to reflect sound.[16] Recent research into cave acoustics has confirmed the notion that pictorial manifestations were often situated in places with noticeably good acoustics. In other words, the use of the cave architecture depended on both scopic and sonic values. Arguably, Paleolithic initiators were well aware of the auditory and visual potentials, and, I might add, exploited these architectonic features to instill specific psychological stages in the initiates. Again, it is possible to assume that different routes were intentionally designed to reveal different levels of information according to the initiatory stages or individual status. Approaching the systematization of knowledge in terms of routes helps us understand why we find so many blank spaces between zones of minor or intense activity. These were calculated interruptions[17] manufactured to isolate specific areas allocated to discrete initiatory stages.

To resume, my research suggests that the cave was a cultural reservoir, where information was strategically laid out along pedagogical routes for the initiates. This inclination for staged sound would suggest that there is a potential for the use of sound-producing artifacts in the deep caves. Musical instruments as means of transformation emerged well before the human use of caves.

There is some evidence that a proclivity for making musical sounds and using musical effects started during the Mousterian, developed and flourished during the Solutrean and later, combining rhythm, sound, image, and symbol in order to create an emotional impact on the participants or the audience in some kind of ritual ceremony.[18]

LINES OF EVIDENCE: SOUND-PRODUCING ARTIFACTS

The following review of most of the known archeological evidence for sound-making devices in the Upper Paleolithic should help confirm the notion that these instruments might have been used (in conjunction with iconographic manifestations) during initiatory procedures performed in deep caves throughout the Upper Paleolithic. The question I wish to tackle is: What sort of archeological remains would sound-producing behavior, in the context of initiation in the Upper Paleolithic, leave behind?

The acoustic environment in the Upper Paleolithic determined the evolutionary task to recognize and index the spectrum of natural sounds and to manufacture distinct acoustic signals in order to channel modes of communication (and deception) that contrasted sharply with the sonic background. It is undeniable that man's first instrument was his voice. But the human voice is limited in terms of sound production. So, in order to expand the voice's tonal pitch and range, artificial means had to be developed. After experimenting with rudimentary tools (hands, plant stems, etc.), humans began to manufacture more complex instruments such as whistles and flutes (aerophones). If the voluntary clapping of hands is the mark of rhythmic kinetic, it must also be the precursor for the struck, scraped, or plucked instruments, such as Upper-Paleolithic lithophones and musical scrapers (idiophones).

It is important to note that the perspective we have on the origin of sound-producing artifact is inescapably biased by the simple fact that instruments made of perishable media, such as reed, wood, horn, and skin, are not present in the archeological record. No recognizable, intelligible transcription of musical scores has survived, thus limiting this discussion to typology. Paleolithic aerophones and idiophones have been found in varying degrees of preservation,[19] and interesting experiments have been made to reconstruct the sounds of the Upper Paleolithic.[20] (See Figure 2.) In the following section, I shall review the types of archeological remains which have been identified as "musical instruments" by ethnomusicologists and archeologists.

Recent work by Ian Cross, Ezra Zubrow, and Frank Cowan on what they have termed *lithoacoustics* has brought the study of the origins of repeatable sounds (music) beyond theoretical speculations and into the concrete realm of experimentation. Although this is still work-in-progress, it has already produced well-grounded hypotheses. To tackle the question, "What traces would musical behaviors leave behind?" they reviewed the available evidence for musical behavior in the archeological record and

Figure 2
Lithophone from Réseau Clastres (Ariège). Redrawn from Xavier Boutillon and Dauvois Michel, "Caractérisation acoustique des grottes ornées paléolithique et de leurs lithophones naturels," in *La Pluridisciplinarité en archéologie musicale: IVe rencontres internationales d'archéologie musicale de l'ICTM. Saint-Germain-en-Laye, 8–12 Octobre 1990*, eds. Catherine Homo-Lechner and Annie Bélis (Paris: Éditions de la Maison des Sciences de l'Homme, 1994), 229.

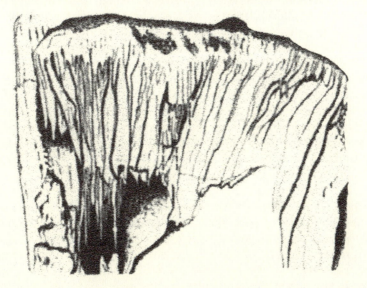

decided that the most suitable protomusical form to investigate was the percussive, rhythmic, and disharmonic sound produced by the skillful process of flint knapping (lithophonic). They concluded that the sounds generated by striking two blades together could be classified as musical, and that, archeologically speaking, it was possible to identify specific-to-the-experiment marks, which they found on lithic material from the Upper Paleolithic. The unambiguous nature of the evidence supports the notion that some lithic materials were used, among other functions, as sound-producing devices.[21]

From hand clapping to blade knapping, a noticeable evolutionary development has taken place: one hand supports while the other strikes. This innovative gesture must have generated a spectrum of technological innovations and undoubtedly helped increase the level of skills in the Paleolithic. One remarkable manifestation of this kinetic shift is a natural sound-making device called a lithophone that archeologists believe to have been employed to make sounds. Lya Dams defines a lithophone as "a natural limestone or calcite configuration which has been subjected to percussion by striking, in order to obtain musical vibrations."[22] Such limestone and calcite configurations showing human traces are found in many caves in association with remains from the Solutrean and the Magdalenian: Nerja (Malaga, Spain), Roucadour (Thémines, Lot), Cougnac (Gourdon, Lot), Pech-Merles (Cabrerets, Lot), Escoural (Portugal), Les Fieux (Miers, Lot), Gargas (Haute-Garonne), Le Portel (Ariège), Réseau Clastres (Ariège), Trois-Frères (Ariège), and Bédeilhac (Ariège).

Lithophones offer a wide range of tones and may have been played simultaneously, offering a rich sonic dialogue. One remarkable archeological characteristic about these lithophones is the series of red and black signs painted on their surfaces. It seems too random to be a system of annotation, but it recurs often enough to be considered some kind of mnemonic aid. This distinct sonic spacialization supports the notion of a sonic route; indeed these so-called signs might have been used as an efficient way to map the cave acoustically using a mnemonic index that could have been understood by specific individuals. Perhaps, the lithophones were marked thus to provide tonal information to potential users. With the lithophone, the cave becomes an effective sound box, a very potent agent of transformation for the initiates.

To diversify the spectrum of sound, the Upper-Paleolithic population must have experimented with all sorts of media, of which only a small sample survived. Carved in durable material, the scrapers seem to have survived as a portable sound device throughout the Upper Paleolithic. They probably originated from multifunctional tools, which Australian Aboriginals are still manufacturing today (a boomerang for example). These friction-based rhythmic instruments generate a distinct sound by running a hard stick or bone up and down over the grooves (see Figure 3). The sounds of these scrapers in a cave are very effective and systematically reconfigure the soundscape into an anxiety-producing environment. They are found on a wide range of utilitarian objects, such as spears and harpoons, dating from the Aurignacian to the Magdalenian periods.

The process of grooving these bone implements could have very easily led to a complete perforation of the material, and thus to a very powerful set of sound-producing instruments (see Figure 4). Indeed, evidence re-

Figure 3
Musical scraper from Pekarná (Moravia). Redrawn from Michel Dauvois, "Les témoins sonores paléolithique," in *La Pluridisciplinarité en archéologie musicale*, eds. Catherine Homo-Lechner and Annie Bélis, 173.

Figure 4
Whistle from Aurignac (Haute-Garonne). Redrawn from Michel Dauvois, "Les témoins sonores paléolithique," in *La Pluridisciplinarité en archéologie musicale*, eds. Catherine Homo-Lechner and Annie Bélis, 159.

flects this transition and Upper-Paleolithic craftsmen introduced the bone-made whistle into their instrumental kit, known today as aerophones. The conceptual triad of an air strip blown through the lips, a bevel (the tip), and a resonator (the hollow bone) marks an important milestone in the understanding of acoustics in the Upper Paleolithic. Archeological evidence shows that Paleolithic populations have consistently manufactured a vast quantity of whistles.[23] By partially concealing the hole with the finger, the whistle-blower can produce a wide spectrum of distinct (and repeatable) sounds. These sound-producing artifacts have a particularly interesting range of frequency—between 1,500 and 4,000 Hertz. This particular range of frequency is easily detectable from the surrounding acoustic environment and is also a very effective simulation of reindeer calls.[24]

Tests have been conducted using reconstructed bone whistles from the Upper Paleolithic and hunting whistles from present-day Mackenzie Indians in Northwest Canada.[25] Both whistles provoke a state of curiosity in reindeers. After scanning the landscape to find the sound source, the reindeer will approach the hunter, somewhat mesmerized. Repeated blowing of the whistle provokes a state of relaxation, followed by a complete loss of the defense mechanism. The reindeer lies on the ground in a complete state of trust and allows the hunter to strike. This phenomenon of rupturing the natural soundscape with artificial tones, forcing the listener (animal and human) to stop, scan, and anticipate another sound manifestation, would have been well-known to prehistoric humans. In terms of initiation, this potential to sonically prompt initiates into action was another effective way to raise anxieties and provoke the loss of rational responses.

At the Mousterian site of *La Quina* (Les Gardes, Charente), archeologists have excavated a hybrid whistle with two holes, probably used to introduce initiates to esoteric hunting skills. From this object to the concept of a flute may only be only a small step, yet it was a giant leap in terms of sonic effectiveness (see Figure 5). As it happened, the sound spectrum was further expanded when the ulnas (cubitus) of eagles and vultures were intentionally perforated in naturally hollowed bone tubes and converted into flutes.[26] Some of these have been found in archeological layers dating from the Mousterian to the Magdalenian, the best known stemming from Isturitz.[27] Despite its fragmentary state, it is complete enough to be reconstructed and tested for frequency and tones. Based on a series of acoustic analyses, Francesco d'Errico and his collaborators concluded that

- the holes drilled into the bone were purposefully situated so as to produce melodic continuity;
- the length of the flute seems to have been predetermined to correspond to precise acoustic expectations; and
- small notches seem to have helped the flute maker in determining length and positioning of the holes.

For our purpose, I wish to emphasize that the flute produces a wide spectrum of artificial sounds, which, I believe, was crucial for creating a sonic environment conducive to transformation (neurological, psychological, and physiological) in the cave.

Flutes have been used in rites of initiation worldwide. New Guinea offers the best analogy.[28] Gilbert Herdt writes about the ceremonies in the mountain-dwelling Sambia tribe, who regard flutes as an embodiment of mystical spirits (demons). The flutes are long hollow tubes and have no lateral stops to control pitch, and the interval between the notes is too wide for harmonic sequences. This structural handicap is overcome by pairing flutes and playing repetitive, antiphonal tunes.[29] For the Sambia, the flutes are, in most cases, the revelation of the initiation.

Except for learning that the flutes are sounded by men rather than by spirit-being voices, the initiates are not told much more about them at the time, a very strong

Figure 5
Perigordian Flute from Isturitz (Pyrénées-Atlantique). Redrawn from Dominique Buisson, "Les Flutes paléolithique d'Isturitz," in *La Pluridisciplinarité en archéologie musicale*, eds. Catherine Homo-Lechner and Annie Bélis, 269.

injunction is placed, however, on revealing their nature or exposing them to women or the uninitiated . . . "You must never play with them in the village. If . . . two of you play the flutes in front of children you will be killed."[30]

The flutes are heard but not seen by noninitiates. The mystical nature of the unseen phenomenon allows the initiates to terrorize the noninitiates. This point is important as it might help explain the recurring phenomenon of small sanctuaries in Upper-Paleolithic caves, which seem to have hosted transient passages entirely different from those that took place in the large halls. In other words, the hall was secular and visited indiscriminately, while the so-called sanctuaries were sacred loci reserved for initiation. Here, again, the sound of instruments used in the initiation may have been heard, but not necessarily seen. By projecting the kind of secrecy surrounding the instruments in New Guinea today into the Upper Paleolithic, we begin to see a confirmation of intentionally manufactured effective affects and affected effects. If indeed these bone flutes were used in a cave, they would have made a tremendous and unquestionable impact on potential initiates.

Pfeiffer writes that "instruments resembling bull-roarers . . . have been found in the caves, and one can only imagine how that unearthly noise would sound deep in the earth, bouncing and rebounding off the walls of natural echo chambers."[31] Carved in reindeer antler or mammoth ivory, the bullroarer (see Figure 6) has been the sound-making instrument best fitted to produce the low-pitched sound used in initiations. Indeed, the bullroarer is present in the Upper Paleolithic as well as in many historical hunter-gatherer societies (Africa, the Americas, Australia, Melanesia). The bullroarer in its apparent simplicity is actually kinetically challenging. Indeed, two distinct gestures are required to produce the necessary double rotation.

The bullroarer is necessarily foliated and symmetrical. The velocity and size of the bullroarer will determine its tone, an increase in frequency on the ascending half of the circular motion, and a characteristic and impressive roaring on the descending portion. The gyration is irregular and

Figure 6
Magdalenian bullroarer from Grotte de La Roche, Lalinde (Dordogne). Redrawn from Michel Dauvois, "Les témoins sonores paléolithique," 171.

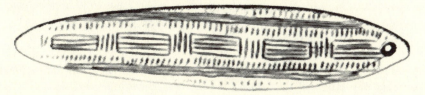

produces noticeable variations, which can be used to anthropomorphize the sound-making device. The faster the gyration the higher the frequency. The bullroarer seemed to have been associated to the bison and the auroch, in that they all emit characteristically low-frequency sounds. The sound of bullroarers in a cave is highly effective.[32] They could easily induce neurological responses in the initiates and would have undoubtedly contributed to their conditioning.

These sonic reproductions have been more remarkable in an underground location, plunged in permanent darkness, amidst particular spatial acoustics, where the softest sound takes on a more astonishing depth than anywhere else. To this end, the "Salon noir" in the cave of Niaux (Ariège) provides a kind of natural amphitheater with an exceptional acoustic due to its considerable height. The bullroarer's rotative motion provides the listener with an astonishing aerial feeling of verticality and spatialization for the "flying" sound. When the gallery is tighter, the sonic presence becomes closer, and this can be experienced in the caves of Trois-Frères and Le Portel.[33]

In central Australia, these instruments are called *churinga* or *tjurunga*, and Baldwin Spencer described their effect thus:

Women and children believe that the noise made by twirling the bullroarer is the voice of a great spirit that comes to carry off the boy during initiation and in no case is a woman allowed to see one. This belief, held by the women and children, is apparently widely spread over the whole of Central and Northern Australia and was probably, at one time, universal in its distribution amongst Australian tribes. It is equally true that the youths are, everywhere and always, at the time of initiation, told that the noise is not the voice of a spirit but is made by the bullroarer. They are also warned that on no account must they speak of it to the women and children.[34]

This quote reveals several aspects inherent to sound-making devices used in the context of initiation. The bullroarer embodies a demonic figure whose predilection is to visit initiates unannounced and to terrorize women with shrill and piercing sounds. It is also associated with the rumbling of thunder or the characteristic roar of strong wind. A third and important association is with male genitals (a flatulent phallus[35]). The bullroarer, like the flute in New Guinea, is kept secret and hidden from the noninitiates. In most cases, secrecy is meant to protect the circumcised initiate from the polluting gaze of noninitiates. And like the flutes in New Guinea, the noninitiates are prohibited from seeing the bullroarers. If beheld by noninitiates or shown intentionally by a man to a woman or infant, the punishment is death to all. As already observed, the notion of revelation is as universal as the prohibitions *vis-à-vis* noninitiates. The sound of the bullroarer symbolizes a layer of esoteric knowledge, which can only be revealed during initiation. What is revealed to the initiates is the deceptive aspect of the initiatory procedure: a secret that there is no secret, no demons, but only a mechanically produced sound. Through this initiatory procedure, the initiate is induced to the art of deception.

The last point I wish to make relates to the potential relationship between the parietal imagery and the sound-producing artifacts. As already mentioned, there seems to be a correlation between zones of iconographic manifestations and points of high resonance. The selection of acoustically suited loci for these images implies a complex planning procedure. This highly developed understanding of the caves' architectonics *confirms* the notion that these places were arbitrarily selected for specific activities and were also approached as cultural reservoirs where mnemonics were archived in formulaic layers. Who were the recipients of this exoteric and esoteric knowledge? How was the archived information transmitted? It is my belief that by gathering all the available lines of evidence we begin to see a faint, but nonetheless informative, behavioral outline.

By articulating three obviously related givens, such as acoustics, sound-producing artifacts, and parietal imagery, the cave becomes the receptacle for specific cultural activities, which have been consistently situated on the margins for the past 35,000 years. There seemed to have been a continuous desire among waves of human cultures throughout (pre)history to contain the unfathomable, the transient, and the altered into secret places. The parietal images in the deep caves were intentionally situated in places where access could be controlled. The revelation of these hidden images was only possible after varying degrees of physical ordeals. By associating the potential effectiveness of revealed images with the mind-altering sounds from sound-making devices, the cave becomes a very effective locus for initiation. In this anxiety-ridden environment, initiates' psychosomatic responses and conditioning could have been carefully monitored. In a group or alone, the transient passage of initiates in specific locations in the caves would have certainly been punctuated by very potent effects. The impact of a revealed image of a zoomorphic configuration with the low roaring of a bullroarer would persist in the initiate's memory. The next step would be to reveal the knowledge contained in the image or the mechanical nature of the bullroarer—in other words to initiate the individual (perhaps at varying degrees) to the core of the belief system which maintained the community as a unified whole.

CONCLUSION

Breuil's narrative was an attempt to reconstruct a past that fit into the expectations of an audience thirsty for exotic primitivism. But behind Breuil's ethnocentric façade is a key concept which was discarded too quickly by his successors: the cave as a place for ordeals, as a reservoir of esoteric knowledge, as a site of transformation where secrets were revealed to anxious initiates.

Ethnographic models of initiation derived from cross-cultural research contribute to a better understanding of the human use of caves in the Upper Paleolithic. By drawing an analogy with contemporary hunter-gatherer societies, we begin to observe a cultural constant, which survived for thousands of years. I am speaking here of the social necessity to mark life cycles and to initiate individuals to esoteric tribal lore. My discussion has been an attempt to emphasize the performative components inherent to these cultural practices. Ordeals require a prepared set of effects, which are manufactured to influence the individual both physically and psychologically. The premeditated and intentional nature of these procedures requires expertise and skills which do not necessarily belong to a collective's continuum of production. In other words, these ceremonies operated on the margins, and it was on this narrow path in between two worlds that the initiates proceeded with anxiety and fear.

The conditioning of the initiates is a vast subject matter; suffice it to state that initiation requires predetermined formulas that are the domain of experts in deception. These deceptive formulas are designed to create a certain degree of alteration and to emphasize the alienation factor—a traumatic (and dramatic) separation with the habitual. To manufacture this separation with the habitual, the initiators use a variety of techniques. For the purpose of our discussion, I have singled out one transformative phenomenon—acoustics. Changing the soundscape by means of sound-making devices turns the cave into a mesmerizing and terrifying environment. One can easily hypothesize that the revelation of these sound-producing artifacts was, very much like in Papua New Guinea, accompanied by threats and secrecy.

This hypothesis can be substantiated by looking at the cave's architectonics, specifically, the spatial systematization of knowledge by means of existing morphological and topographical configurations. Approached morphologically, the cave becomes a container where anthropogenic traces follow a predictable architectonic logic. The cave presented many opportunities for iconographic manifestations, but despite that plurality of potentially workable surfaces only specific places were selected. I firmly believe, as do some other prehistorians, that the organization of images according to architectonic particularities attests to a well-planned mise-en-scène.[36] Thus, the cave provided a locus where information could be archived according to conventions primarily based on the spaces' suitability for iconographic manifestations, collective gatherings, or individual seclusion.

The selection of specific places might have been a more complex process than expected. Indeed, as I have already mentioned, there seemed to have been an acoustic component for the choice of suitable wall surfaces. The

Paleolithic population appears to have had a well-established knowledge in the physics of sound. The dyad image/sound emerges as an empirical fact, to which I should like to add a third element: the sound-making device. Indeed, it is difficult to imagine that sound-producing artifacts were not used to transform the spatial characteristics of a cave. Therefore, the triad image/sound/instrument is offered here as another performative approach for the understanding of Upper-Paleolithic caves that draws on initiatory procedures in contemporary hunter-gatherer societies. This highly choreographed societal behavior on the margin of the habitual is what I define as Paleoperformance.

But is it really a new approach? Of course, the concept of the cave as a locus for initiation has been suggested before. But the notion that prehistoric remains can be methodically reconstructed may now avail itself of a methodology developed in the discipline of performance studies, where human behavior is the primary object of study, along with marginal social practice, and fieldwork in the participant observation mode.[37] In Figure 7, I have summarized the main fields currently under investigation. Linking these areas and their evidence offers a methodology that will contribute to the establishment of Paleoperformance as a genuine approach for our understanding of the human use of caves in the Upper Paleolithic.

I am convinced that, without incorporating the behavioral component into our interpretations, our understanding of prehistoric caves and their iconographic manifestations will always remain in the limited realm of the quantitative. Numbers are important, but the gestures behind the artifacts are also fundamental; fortunately, the one does not exclude the other. By comparing some contemporary initiatory procedures with the available archeological evidence from the Upper Paleolithic, I hope to have shown that not only was the cave a liminal locus for marginal activities, but that these activities were intentionally so, as well as highly performative, and, as Pfeiffer argued, "pure theater."[38]

Figure 7
Thematic structure connecting various evidence to Paleoperformances.

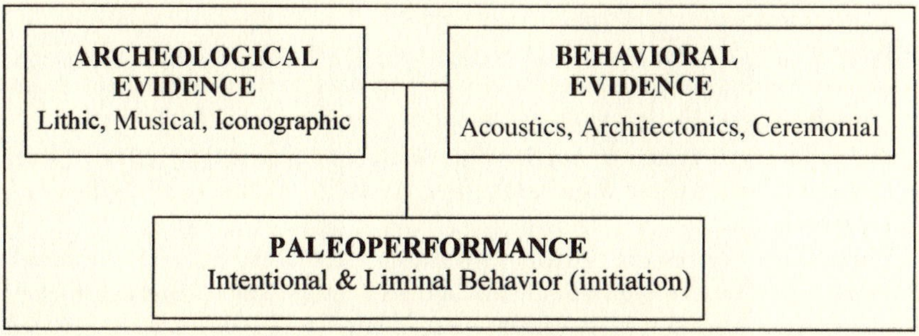

NOTES

1. From the Latin *limen,* meaning threshold or margin.

2. See, for example, Paul G. Bahn. *The Cambridge Illustrated History of Prehistoric Art.* Cambridge: Cambridge University Press, 1998.

3. Henri Breuil. *Beyond the Bounds of History.* London: Gawthorn, 1949: 16.

4. Breuil. *Beyond the Bounds of History,* p. 83.

5. J. David Lewis-Williams. "Rock Art and Ritual: Southern Africa and Beyond." In *Arte paleolítico,* ed. Teresa Chapa Brunet and Mario Menéndez Fernández. Madrid: Editorial Complutense, 1994: 277–289; quotation from p. 284.

6. See Henri Breuil. *Quatre Cents siècle d'art pariétal.* Paris: Presse de la Sapho, 1952; Salomon Reinach. "L'Art et la magie: A propos des peintures et des gravures de l'Age du Renne." *L'Anthropologie* 14 (1903): 257–266; Weston La Barre. *The Ghost Dance: The Origins of Religion.* New York: Dell, 1970.

7. See J. David Lewis-Williams. "Wrestling with Analogy: A Problem in Upper Palaeolithic Art Research." *Proceedings of the Prehistoric Society* 57 (1991): 149–162.

8. John E. Pfeiffer. *The Creative Explosion: An Inquiry into the Origins of Art and Religion.* New York: Harper & Row, 1982: 41–42.

9. http://www.yale.edu/hraf.

10. Pfeiffer. *The Creative Explosion,* p. 39.

11. See Giza Roheim. *The Eternal Ones of the Dream: A Psychoanalytic Interpretation of Australian Myth and Rituals.* New York: International Universities Press, 1945.

12. See Jean S. La Fontaine. *Initiation.* Manchester: Manchester University Press, 1985: 26.

13. See Roheim. *The Eternal Ones of the Dream;* Bruno Bettelheim. *Symbolic Wounds: Puberty Rites and the Envious Male.* New York: Collier Books, 1962; Audrey I. Richards. *Chisungu: A Girl's Initiation Ceremony among the Memba of Zambia.* London: Tavistock, 1956; Max Gluckman. "Les Rites de passage." In *Essays on the Ritual of Social Relations,* ed. Max Gluckman. Manchester: Manchester University Press, 1962: 1–52; Michael R. Allen. *Male Cults and Secret Initiations in Melanesia.* Melbourne: Melbourne University Press, 1967; Victor Turner. *The Ritual Process: Structure and Anti-structure.* New York: De Gruyter, 1969; Joan Bamberger. "Myth of Matriarchy: Why Men Rule in Primitive Society." In *Woman, Culture, and Society,* ed. Michelle Zimbalist Rosaldo and Louise Lamphere. Stanford: Stanford University Press, 1974: 263–280; La Fontaine. *Initiation;* Chris Knight. *Blood Relations: Menstruation and the Origins of Culture.* New Haven, CT: Yale University Press, 1991.

14. Gilbert H. Herdt. *Male Initiation in Papua New Guinea.* London: Transaction Publishers, 1982: 39.

15. Paul G. Bahn. "Dancing in the Dark: Probing the Phenomenon of Pleistocene Cave Art." In *Human Use of Caves,* ed. Clive Bonsall and Christopher Tolan-Smith. Oxford: Archaeopress: 35–37; quotation from p. 36.

16. See Steven J. Waller. "Sound Reflection as an Explanation for the Content and Context of Rock Art." *Rock Art Research* 10 (1993): 91–101; and "Taphonomic Considerations of Rock Art Acoustics." *Rock Art Research* 11 (1994): 120–121; Iégor Reznikoff. "Dimension sonore des grottes ornées." *Bulletin de la Société Préhistorique Française* 85 (1988): 238–246; and Michel Dauvois. "Sons et musique paléolithique." *Les Dossiers de l'Archéologie* 142 (1989): 2–11.

17. See Marc Groenen. *Ombre et lumière dans l'art des grottes*. Bruxelles: Université Libre de Bruxelles, Centre de Recherche et d'Études Technologiques des Arts Plastiques, 1997.

18. Lya Dams. "Palaeolithic Lithophones: Descriptions and Comparisons." *Oxford Journal of Archaeology* 4 (1985): 31–46; quotation from p. 45.

19. See Michel Dauvois. "Instruments sonores et musicaux préhistoriques." In *Préhistoire de la Musique*. Nemours: Musée de Préhistoire d'Ile-de-France, 2002: 33–45; Marcel Otte. "Regards sur la musique paléolithique." *News 95—Symposium 3A: Rock Art and Musiarchaeology*. <http://www.News95/NEWS95/3a/otte/otte.htm> (2002).

20. The result of his investigation can be found at <http://www.soundcenter.it/>.

21. To learn more about this very interesting work-in-progress, consult the following Web sites: <http://www.mus.cam.ac.uk/~ic108/lithoacoustics/#heading2> and <http://www.mus.cam.ac.uk/ic108/lithoacoustics/BAR2002/BARpreprint.html>.

22. Dams. "Palaeolithic Lithophones," p. 31.

23. See Dauvois. "Instruments sonores et musicaux préhistoriques."

24. See Dauvois. "Sons et musique paléolithique."

25. See Michel Dauvois and Xavier Boutillon. "Études acoustiques au Réseau Clastres: Salle des peintures et lithophones naturels." *Préhistoire Ariégoise* 45 (1990): 175–186.

26. See Dauvois and Boutillon. "Études acoustiques au Réseau Clastres"; Dominique Buisson. "Les Flutes paléolithiques d'Isturitz (Pyrénées-Atlantiques)." *Bulletin de la Société Française* 87 (1990): 420–433; Cècile Mourer-Chauviré and Gilbert Fages. "La Flute en os d'oiseau de la grotte sépulcrale de Veyreau (Aveyron) et inventaire des flutes préhistoriques d'Europe." *Mémoires de la Société Préhistorique Française* 16 (1983): 95–103; Francesco D'Errico, Paola Villa, Ana Llona Pinto, Rosa Idarraga Ruiz. "A Middle Paleolithic Origin of Music? Using Cave-bear Bone Accumulations to Assess the Divje Babe I Bone Flute." *Antiquity* 72 (1998): 65–79; Brago Kunej and Ivan Turk. "New Perspectives on the Beginnings of Music: Archaeological and Musical Analysis of a Middle Paleolithic Bone 'Flute.' " Nils L. Wallin, Björn Merker, and Steven Brown, eds. *The Origins of Music*. Cambridge, MA: MIT Press, 2000: 235–268.

27. Buisson. "Les Flutes paléolithiques d'Isturitz."

28. See Gilbert H. Herdt. *Guardians of the Flutes*. Vol. 1: *Idioms of Masculinity*. Chicago, IL: The University of Chicago Press, 1981; and idem, *Male Initiation in Papua New Guinea*; Yoichi Yamada. *Songs of Spirits: An Ethnography of Sounds in a Papua New Guinea Society*. Apwitihire: Institute of Papua New Guinea Studies, 1997; K.E. Read. "Nama Cult of the Central Highlands, New Guinea." *Oceania* 23 (1952): 1–25; Gregory Bateson. *Naven*. Stanford, CA: Stanford University Press, 1936.

29. See Yamada. *Songs of Spirits*, pp. 241–253.

30. Philip L. Newman and David J. Boyd. "The Making of Men: Ritual and Meaning in Awa Male Initiation" in *Rituals of Manhood*. Berkeley, CA: University of California Press, 1982: 263.

31. John E. Pfeiffer. "Was Europe's Fabulous Cave Art the Start of the Information Age?" *Smithsonian* 11:3 (1980): 90–13.

32. Walter Maioli, personal communication. Also Michel Dauvois. "Sons et musique paléolithique," p. 10.

33. Dauvois and Boutillon. "Études acoustiques au Réseau Clastres," p. 180.

34. Baldwin Spencer. *Native Tribes of the Northern Territory of Australia*. London: Macmillan, 1914: 211.

35. For a comprehensive discussion on the sexual nature of the bullroarer see Alan Dundes. "A Psychoanalytic Study of the Bullroarer." *Man* 11 (1976): 220–238.

36. See Groenen. *Ombre et lumière dans l'art des grottes*.

37. See Richard Schechner. *Performance Studies: An Introduction*. London and New York: Routledge, 2002.

38. See Pfeiffer. *The Creative Explosion*.

Rock Art and Rock Sites as Indicators of Prehistoric Theater and Ritual Performances

Jon Nygaard

This chapter seeks to address the question of what may have been the functions of rock art in the prehistory of Scandinavia. In the early part of the twentieth century, prehistoric rock art was interpreted as an element of ritual. Then it was understood as a kind of visual art in prehistory. In this chapter I shall interpret at least some rock art sites or rocks as indicators of performances in prehistory and the pictures and signs on the rocks as scenarios for ritual or dramatic performances. In my understanding, rock art sites were not public places and were not seen by large audiences, as were the monumental art of later periods, the decorations of public squares, or the objects displayed in art galleries. Rock art, or at least some rock art sites, formed part of the secret art of performers, shamans, or ritual specialists in prehistoric times. Understood in this way, rock art may not have been art at all. What we experience as rock *art* might have been an element of ritual. Accordingly, the rock or the rocks, the site and the landscape were as important, or even more important, than the figures on the rock face.

IS NORTHERN SCANDINAVIAN ROCK ART A RELIC OF PREHISTORIC THEATER?

In the early part of the twentieth century, scholars stressed the ritual and cultic functions of rock art,[1] both for arctic hunter-gatherers' carvings in the earliest Stone Age,[2] and southern agriculturalists' carvings in the later Bronze Age.[3] Very little further research has been undertaken in the second half of the twentieth century.[4] But over the last 10 years, we have seen a new trend in the interpretation of the northern rock carvings.[5] Several scholars have rejected the older hunting-magic thesis and have pointed out that the animals represented on the panels were not commonly part of a Stone Age diet. Excavations have revealed that people were mainly eating cod, herring, pollack, or cranberries, but none of these are to be seen on rock carvings. Therefore, they argue, the figures could not have been part of a ritual or cult designed to secure the means of subsistence; rather, the individual figures and the compositions as a whole were symbolic expressions of an artistic nature. Irregularities, which previously were interpreted as errors, defects, or misunderstandings, are now viewed as conscious expressions of prehistoric masters. Imperfections are seen to be as important as perfect images, and either of these features are interpreted as intentional stylistic traits, even when figures are superimposed on each other despite the fact that there is more than enough space around them. Panels and the motives on them are described as works of art, just as if they were displayed in a prehistoric art gallery. Some scholars have even regarded rock carvings as expressions of individual artists; and some archeologists in their descriptions of rock art borrow phrases from art history or art criticism, such as elegant, in pure style, clumsy, and immature.

In this chapter I will suggest that rock art figures are not ordinary pictures with artistic value in themselves. In my interpretation they are holy scriptures, or better, scripts for holy performances. Seen in this light, they offer instructions on how to survive, how to behave, and how to carry out a perilous hunt for food, how to conduct the ritual of the magic hunt or the ceremonies that foster the fertility of the earth. Carving the patterns of the ritual into the rock surface guaranteed that they could be repeated in just the same holy manner from year to year and be passed on from generation to generation (see Figure 1).

In my view, the place or the location is of great significance.[6] The carvings are not engravings as such, but holy incisions in a holy place, which might have been in use for hundreds or even thousands of years. The figures were carved on top of each other or inside each other, because new clans or tribes, who made the new figures, did not see the older figures any longer, or they may have intentionally erased a figure that represented the power of an other or earlier group.

The figures were not connected to the quotidian life, but to the supernatural realm. Therefore, we do not find representations of daily foodstuff that was in ample supply, but rather of big and strong animals, which served as guardian spirits or *totems*. A totem is an animal to identify with, but not to serve as food. Even if killed by accident, it may not be eaten, except in periods of great need, as is demonstrated in the Sámi and Finno-Ugric bear hunt rituals.[7] When embarking on a dangerous hunt or fishing journey, the men require protection by means of magic ritual. It was not dangerous to fish cod; but to catch a halibut was a perilous affair, not to

Figure 1
Lökeberg, Tanum, Sweden. From John Coles, *Images of the Past: A Guide to the Rock Carvings and Other Ancient Monuments of Northern Bohuslän* (Uddevalla: Bohusläns Museum, 1990).

mention killer whales *(orca)* or elk, which were important for the survival of the clan.

As regards the agrarian carvings, traditional interpretations relate the orientation of the panels to the surrounding fields and treat them as an integral part of peasant culture.[8] A new generation of archeologists cast doubts on this view and claimed that the ground around the panels was unsuitable for Bronze Age husbandry. Many of these supposed fields are sea sediments turned into heavy clay soil; consequently, we must suppose that Bronze Age agriculture would have taken place in lighter soil further up the hillsides.[9] The problem, however, is that all agrarian carvings (as in the Bohuslän and Østfold-area of western Sweden and southeastern Norway) are to be found in areas that do not contain any arable hillsides and are full of heavy clay and hard granite rocks. One must therefore assume that the rock-art panels in these regions indicated an effort to overcome economic problems and to master difficult ecological conditions.

Rock art has to be seen as a durable expression of a historical development, which defies our conventional understanding based on circumstantial evidence. In my interpretation of rock art and rock-art sites, I follow the Swedish professor of prehistory, Mats Malmer,[10] who emphasized that simple, functionalist explanations must be found for the prehistoric sites, and only if they are not forthcoming, then other explanations, such as religious and ritualistic purposes, may be acceptable. I, like other Norwegian scholars, suggest[11] that the rock art of Scandinavia could be regarded as a relic of prehistoric performances, and I will accordingly interpret the sites based on a concept of theater, theatricality, or performance. But whereas their interpretation has been largely based on agrarian carvings, I will derive my evidence from the much older hunter-gatherers' carvings of northern Scandinavia. And like Malmer,[12] I shall emphasize that although most early forms of theater cannot be reconstructed because of lack of evidence, we are actually in a better position with regard to Neolithic than to Bronze or Iron Age periods.

Traditionally, the origin of theater is believed to have developed from collective hunting magic and totemistic rites[13] or from shamanism.[14] Frazer[15] and the Cambridge School of Anthropology suggested that in later agrarian times, fertility rites[16] and death ceremonies[17] added further layers and features. For none of these theories do we have any hard evidence. We do not even have material testimony for the early stages of the Dionysian theatre in Athens. The texts that are purported to be tragedies of Aeschylus, Sophocles, or Euripides are in fact reconstructions based on much younger, rewritten versions of the texts used in the actual performances in Athens. Most of the theories of the origin of theater can therefore be rejected as speculations with no reliable substance. But rock art and rock art sites provide us with some hard evidence for theater and the performing arts in prehistory.

STORSTEINEN: A SPECIAL INTERPRETATION OF A SPECIAL ROCK ART ROCK

In the early 1970s, a rock art site was discovered almost by miracle in Alta in northernmost Norway. A large boulder was just about to be blown up, as it occupied a large space behind a newly built house, which the owners wanted to turn into a garden. During a final examination of the boulder before igniting the dynamite, the blaster saw some strange figures on its surface. The archeologist Knut Helskog[18] then registered more than 560 figures distributed over the 64-square-meter surface on the top of the boulder (Figures 2 and 3). These were more than had until then been recorded in the whole of northern Norway. The discovery led to further searches for rock-art sites, and within a few years archeologists discovered the largest rock art area in northern Europe. Consequently, in 1985, the Alta site was registered on the UNESCO World Heritage List.

Alta was already well known to Scandinavian scholars of prehistory. The Komsa culture, probably the oldest settlement in northern Europe, had been excavated in Alta in 1925 to 1936.[19] Nevertheless, the discovery of the boulder, which came to be known as *Storsteinen* ("the large boulder"), radically challenged the traditional interpretation of Norwegian prehistory and recent opinions on rock art. According to Helskog, layers upon layers of figures on top of Storsteinen had been created over a period lasting some 2,500 years, from 4,200 B.C. until 1,700 B.C. The oldest figure to be distinguished on the rock, a full size and naturalistic silhouette of a reindeer, may actually have been made as early as 9,000 or even 10,000 B.C. If this is the case, then Storsteinen has to be regarded as one of the oldest rock-art sites in Norway, if not Europe.

The rock art of Alta, on the seventieth degree of northern altitude, is more than 2,000 years older than Tanum in western Sweden, on the fifty-eighth degree, and 4,000 years older than the sites in Val Camonica in northern Italy, on the forty-sixth degree. The figures of Storsteinen challenged the established understanding of the early immigration to Norway from continental Europe. It also questioned the common view of prehis-

Figure 2
Storsteinen, Alta. Detail of a photograph of 1882 taken by Karl Krafft, now in the possession of Alta Museum.

Figure 3
Storsteinen, Alta. From Knut Helskog, *Helleristningene i Alta: Spor etter ritualer*
og dagligliv i Finnmarks forhistorie **(Alta: Alta Museum, 1988).**

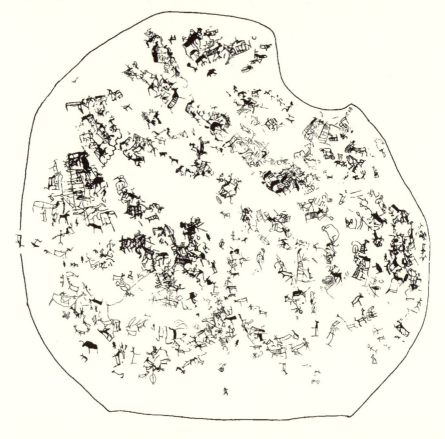

toric Norway, and of the Arctic region in general, as a cold, dark area
inhabited only by primitive hunters. Storsteinen and the other rock art
sites in Alta are indications of rather advanced societies in prehistoric
northern Scandinavia, for which, at present, we do not have any parallel
anywhere in Europe.

If we want to reach an understanding of the rock art at Storsteinen, we
need to ask ourselves why all the figures are situated on top of the boulder.
Helskog suggests that this was so because there are no other suitable rocks
in the area.[20] First of all, this is not correct, as just some hundred meters
away there is a small mountain. Secondly, and more important, the sides
of the Storsteinen rock itself, ranging in height from 2 to 4 meters, would
have offered a suitable surface for the incision of other figures. Whereas
the figures on top were visible only to those who managed to climb the

steep sides, side panels would have made the art accessible to the community at large. And even for the person(s) on top of the boulder the figures would have been difficult to distinguish, given their superimpositions and varying states of decay. This is why they were not recognized until 30 years ago.

It does not make much sense to treat the figures of Storsteinen as an expression of the visual arts. It was much more likely that they were the focus of a ritual conducted in the spectacular amphitheater naturally formed by the Bossekop Bay moraine in the Alta Fjord, facing the mountain Halde, known by the indigenous peoples of the region, the Sámi, as "the holy mountain." The shape of the boulder, with its flat top and steep sides, is unusual (see Figure 2). The front is marked by waves, which indicates that for a very long period it lay at a waterfront and then, for more than 10,000 years, above sea level. It is easy to see Storsteinen as a stage for ritual performances. The images on top of the boulder can be understood as indicators for the actions, movements, songs, or dances to be carried out there. As the figures cannot be seen by others, they may also have contained secret information for the performer(s). The similarities between the figures on Storsteinen and those on the drums of Sámi shamans (Figures 3 and 4) have been pointed out by other scholars.[21] The shaman's way of drumming, by moving the hammer in certain patterns over the drum and telling or singing the myths and rituals associated with the figures, provides a parallel to the arrangement of the figures at Storsteinen. It is therefore possible to regard Storsteinen as a stage and the figures as scripts for the action. In the following section, I shall examine this contention and provide evidence in support of it.

ROCK ART AND ROCKS AS AN EXPRESSION OF SHAMANIC VISION QUESTS

David S. Whitley has given a convincing interpretation of rock art as a reflection of shamanic rituals.[22] Inspired by Lewis-Williams's studies,[23] he has concerned himself with interpreting entoptic symbols and patterns in rock art, but has not considered to the same degree the rocks, boulders, or caves as structures for the vision quest.[24] His findings are largely derived from rock-art sites in far western North America, in southern California, and especially in the Coso Range. Although positioned at the opposite end of the world, the sites in far northern Europe offer many parallels and similarities. Eliade, in his analysis of shamanism, established a series of common elements to be found in the indigenous religions of North Eurasia and North America.[25] Hultkrantz has underlined the similarities between shamanism among north European Sámi and northwest American Shoshoni,[26] who have been the natives of the Great Basin from Coso in California to the Bighorn Basin and Dinwoody in Wyoming.

Figure 4
Decorated shaman drum or runebomme. Tromsø Museum.

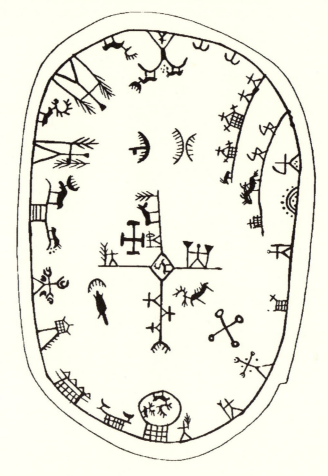

Whitley's interpretation of rock art is based on the general principles of shamanism and especially the process of becoming a shaman, which among the Shoshoni as well as Sámi was not primarily the result of a shamanic calling or a spontaneous trance. Rather, a young person might decide him- or herself to become a shaman. After many years of training, including periods of fasting and praying, the shaman would retreat to a secluded spot for a vision quest. If her or his preparation was adequate and s/he was considered worthy, s/he could then, according to Whitley,[27] enter the supernatural realm through trance and contact the spirits in the form of a vision. This vision was then painted in the form of entoptic lines and patterns on the rock surface, which take the shape of dots, grids, zigzags, spirals, or concentric circles.

Shamans of far western North America sought places for their vision quests where they could enter into contact with the spirit world. Caves, rocks, springs, lakes, and streams were believed to be portals to the sacred realm. Similar belief patterns and site preferences can be found among the Sámi, whose favorite cult places are underneath stones, under or beside large boulders, in a hollow between two stones, in a crevice between blocks of stones or in the crevice of a cleft boulder, between two solid stones, or on the top of solid stones.[28] Both in northern Norway and Jämtland in western Sweden, cleft boulders, which were split by lightning, were believed to possess a special power. Sámi sacrificial sites are also generally associated with lakes and rivers.[29] Before the supplicant advances to the rock art site, s/he takes a bath to cleanse her- or himself in the nearest creek or lake. This led Hultkrantz to establish a relation between water and the sacred rock art site[30] in a manner that resembles the general rules of the Shoshoni vision quest.

Whitley describes in detail a series of rock art panels in southern California,[31] but only occasionally refers to the vision quest site, the rock or the piles of rocks, and he hardly ever pays any attention to the surrounding landscape. The only significant exception is the Mockingbird Canyon site in Riverside County, where he analyzes three different rock-art panels. One is dominated by zigzag and diamond-chain motifs. Whitley interprets these motifs on two boulders on either side of a small stream as being related to girls' puberty ceremonies. The other panel displays a wide range of motifs painted in polychrome on a rock-shelter ceiling. Whitley interprets this to be shamanic art. He also mentions a so-called bedrock mortar, or cupules, in front of one of the boulders. He concludes that

Mockingbird Canyon, then, illustrates a pattern that is relatively common in southwestern California: puberty sites on open boulders and shamans' sites in less accessible and less visible caves and rock shelters. In either case, the site might be immediately within villages, or close nearby, yet a fundamental distinction pertained: The puberty sites resulted from public rituals and thus are easily visible, whereas the shaman's ritual activities were private and avoided by the general village populace, even when occurring in the midst of the village themselves.[32]

This pattern is also to be found at other rock art sites in southern California, like Hospital Rock, in Sequoia National Park, and Tulare Painted Rock, in Tule River Indian Reservation, but Whitley does not make any mention of it. At these sites we have the painted shelter for the shaman and standing boulders with cupules in front. At Morteros Village, in Anza-Borrego Desert Park, the large split boulder and the series of cupules, or mortars, are impressive, but the pictograph is just a very small panel near the ground on the backside of a large boulder with a smaller boulder alongside but not touching it. Whitley mentions that the smaller boulder has a series of cupules in it and a bedrock mortar on a horizontal rock nearby.[33] Whitley does not discuss it any further, but his description indicates that the pictographs are not the most important element at this supposed rock-art site. The boulders and the characteristic combination of rocks seem to be as important, or even more important, than the pictographs on the rocks. At the vision quest sites, which Whitley describes in Little Petroglyph Canyon in Coso, no pictographs are mentioned.[34] In a reference to Loendorf, Whitley also underlines that in other parts of North America "seemingly insignificant piles of rocks found in unusual locations," such as "circular or horseshoe shaped rock piles," are known "to have served as vision quest structures."[35]

Based on Whitley's descriptions we can conclude that pictographs might be a part of a vision quest, but they are not a necessary condition for the choice of a vision quest site. The important elements are the characteristic shapes and patterns of the rocks, which, like split boulders, can actually reveal shaman's shelters neglected by archeologists. In northern Norway such structures are obvious at the Stone Age village at Mortensnes in Varanger. At Savtso near Alta, a still-remaining shaman's shelter is the only witness of the close-by Stone Age village that was totally destroyed by the building of a hydroelectric power plant in the early 1980s.[36]

Californian rock art was produced over a very long period of time. The oldest Coso rock art might be as old as 16,500 years,[37] and the youngest might have been made fewer than 200 years ago. At many sites in California, local folk tales contain references to the makers of rock art, or link the rock art to historical shamans. In northern Europe, the period of rock art ended at least 1,500 to 2,000 years ago. In this area, no links to the present day may help us identify the makers or to understand the meaning of rock art. Vision quest sites, on the other hand, have been used over a much longer period of time, especially in the Sámi regions of Scandinavia. Several local folk tales explain split boulders as shelters for people during snowstorms. Even far outside of what is now regarded as Sámi territory, split boulders, such as the *Lappesteinen* (the Sámi Rock) at the mountain plateau Hardangervidda in central southern Norway, or the *Postmannshidleren* (the Postman's Rock) in Ølen in southwestern Norway, are linked to Sámi shamans and vision quests through local tales. These describe how apprentice shamans had to endure hardship, seek out a split boulder in a cold winter storm, and stay inside it during the storm.

Although it is possible to identify rocks as shamans' vision quest sites, these are usually remote and isolated structures far away from places of human habitation. Therefore, they cannot have functioned as sites for public performances. If we are looking for ritual sites with a public component, we have to look elsewhere.

GJØSTEIN: AN ENVIRONMENT FOR THEATER AND FOR ENVIRONMENTAL THEATER

At Gjøstein near Voss in western Norway (see Figure 5), the elements described by Whitley at Mockingbird Canyon are repeated in a far more impressive way. Voss was populated at least 7,000 years ago and is situated between the two longest fjords in Norway, Sognefjord and Hardangerfjord, and at north-south and west-east crossroads. At the entrance to Voss from the north, and along the path of a main prehistoric route, there are three sets of boulders, all decorated with carved circles and spirals, which according to Whitley are typical entoptic patterns. The local name is important: the prefix *gjø-* means "fatten" and is associated with *gjødsel* (manure or fertilizer). A proper translation should therefore be "Fertility Rocks." The rocks are oriented along the path from northeast to southwest. Entering from the north, the first of the Gjøstein rocks is a huge, standing boulder, locally called *Klipe* or "the Rock." The next rock is actually two split boulders on either side of the path, called *Porten* or "the Gate." The third is an enormous, almost perfectly cubic boulder, *Ringsteinen* or "the Circle Rock" (Figure 4).

Using Whitley and Hultkrantz's typology of shamanic sites, we can

Figure 5
Gjøstein, Voss. Photo by Jon Nygaard.

identify and read three stages of ritual action or performance in these three rocks. The first standing boulder or pillar may have been a place of preparation, for cleaning and purifying the initiant. In the Californian sites, there are often cupules in front of the pillars and these are interpreted as mortars for grinding acorn. This interpretation is not convincing. Acorn was a basic food for the native population of California. One should therefore find many mortars all over California and not just a few in front of boulders in rather remote areas. In Norway, locals still associate standing boulders like *Transteinen* at Mortensnes with sacrifice of cod-liver or fish oil. The cupules or cup holes of the Californian sites are therefore more likely to have had a ritual function and may have served as cups for oil, water, ointments, perfumes, or even drugs in the shaman's preparation for his or her journey. Until recently, the cupules in Sweden were filled with fat and wax and used in a manner that was similar to candles in Catholic services. The second set of split boulders at Gjøstein, "the Gate," has all the elements of a vision quest structure or shelter. Here the shaman supplicant went through his or her trial before going through the gate and performing a ritual or dance in the holy area of the "Circle Rock."

The three phases in the dramaturgy of a vision quest or a shaman's initiation ceremony correspond to three stages in the scenography, or environmental setting, of ritual performance: to prepare for the trial or quest in front of the pillar; to perform the quest in the split rock and enter through the gate; to be reborn or resurrected as a shaman on top of the cubic boulder. If this is the proper relation between the ritual and the environment where it is performed, then it would be hard to find these elements arranged in this very same manner even in rocky landscapes. This may have been the reason why shamans of the Great Basin region traveled over long distances to find a site for their vision quests. Dinwoody in Wyoming or Coso in California were particular spots where shamans could obtain particular spirit helpers or special supernatural powers associated with the given location.[38] To perform their ritual in the correct manner, they needed the right environment with the right elements for their performance. If a landscape had only a few rocks, or if an established ritual environment lost its supernatural power, the ritual performance could no longer be carried out. In this case, a space had to be fitted out with the same elements and in the same manner as those to be found in the natural environment. Such ritual sites may have functioned in a manner that was akin to Richard Schechner's concepts of "environmental theater."[39]

Large boulders can frequently be found along the edges of glaciers from the last Ice Age, as in the foothills of the Sierra Nevada in California or along the moraines and Ice Age deposits in northern Scandinavia. In regions without large boulders, their function seems to have been replaced by circles of stones. A dozen circular sacrificial sites are found in northernmost Norway[40] in areas north or south of Ice Age moraines (Figure 6).

Almost all circles are situated by the sea, lakes, or rivers, and half of them have a cairn in the middle. This pattern is similar to the reconstructed *orchaistra* in the Dionysian theater in Athens, with the altar or cairn of Dionysus at its center.

If stone circles can be associated with ritual performances and be interpreted as transformed spaces erected after the pattern of natural environments with boulders, we might have an explanation for the elements and pattern of the great stone circles of Britain and France. The best known of these is Stonehenge in Wiltshire, United Kingdom. Stonehenge was probably erected in three phases from about 3,500 B.C. until 1,500 B.C. This means that Stonehenge as a construction or totally transformed space is at least some 700 hundred years younger than the found space of Storsteinen in Alta. Both sites have been in use over a comparable period of more than 2,000 years.

STONEHENGE: AN EXAMPLE OF A TOTALLY TRANSFORMED SPACE FOR RITUAL PERFORMANCES?

On the Salisbury Plain, in the area around Stonehenge, no large boulders can be found today. All those that may have existed there were prob-

Figure 6
Ritual stone circle in Biekkanoaivve, northernmost Norway. From Ørnulf Vorren, "Circular Sacrificial Sites and Their Function," in *Saami Pre-Christian Religion*, eds. Luise Bäckman and Åke Hultkrantz (Stockholm: Almquist & Wiksell International, 1985).

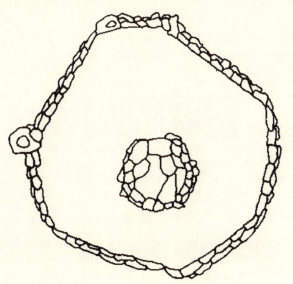

ably used for the construction of Stonehenge, and others may have been transported to the site from far away. Boulders were most probably a limited resource; therefore, the construction of a sacred site had to concentrate on essential elements, which made these all the more important. Three characteristic elements are to be distinguished, both at Stonehenge and most other stone circles in England, Ireland, and Brittany. First, there is an outlier, or pillar, stone at a distance from the real site, known at Stonehenge as the Heel Stone; or the King Stone at the Rollright Stones site in Oxfordshire; or as Long Meg at the Long Meg and Her Daughters site in Cumbria. Secondly, there is a gate or entrance. At Stonehenge the entrance can now only be seen as an opening in the ditch surrounding the site. Other sites, however, still have a distinct entrance or dolmen portal, like the Whispering Knights at the Rollright Stones (Figure 7). Thirdly, in the central structure itself, many sites have cairns inside. But no stone circles in Britain and Ireland, except Stonehenge, had lintels on top. Here, all 35 lintels were held in place by means of a projecting knob on the stone and a hollowed pit in the lintel. To ensure complete stability, the top of each pillar was chamfered like a shallow box, within which the bottom of the lintel rested. Where lintel lay against lintel, they were held in place by the tongue-and-groove method. The V-shaped projection at the end of one lintel was jutting neatly into the V-shaped cavity at the end of its partner stone.[41] This highly elaborate construction had to have a certain reason. A common explanation has been that Stonehenge is an astronomical structure and the Heel Stone may have been a marker for the midsummer sunrise and of the northern moonrise (see Figure 8). But why should the people of the Bronze Age need to mark the sunrise or moonrise? And if

Figure 7
The Rollight Stones. From William Camden, *Britain* (London, 1610).

Figure 8
Plan of Stonehenge. From Aubrey Burl, *Great Stone Circles* (New Haven and London: Yale University Press, 1999).

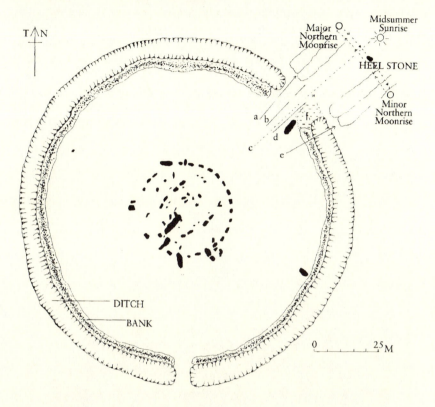

Stonehenge was really an astronomical center, why was the position of the marker stones so crudely oriented, when the lintels themselves were so precisely constructed? There is no doubt that the most characteristic and important elements in Stonehenge were the lintels. The crucial question is therefore: what may have been the purpose of the lintels?

Stonehenge and other stone circles were assembly places at times of festivals and seasonal gatherings right until the nineteenth century.[42] If in historic times they served for theatrical or other festivities, may they also have done so in prehistory? The circular shape of the earlier wall around Stonehenge has great similarities with the so-called Cornish Rounds in Cornwall. The origins of these structures are still debated, and the extent to which they were used for performance is uncertain. In this context, however, they may be interpreted as a local continuation of the tradition of the stone circles. The best known representation of a medieval Theater-in-the-Round is in the stage plan preserved in the manuscript of *The Castle of Perseverance* (1425), from East Anglia. It is related to a specific type of religious drama and represented a quite unusual configuration at the time, with an outer ring with a castle as an elevated construction in its center (Figure 9). The same principles might have been used at Stonehenge. The important action took place on an elevated construction, that is, on top of the lintels. The same principle of getting high above the ground may have applied to the large boulder stages of Storsteinen and Gjøstein. To move such solid boulders, or imitating them as solid structures, would have been impossible in prehistory. Replacing them with a construction as can be found in Stonehenge is actually a very elegant solution with similar effect. In the development of theater structures from prehistoric to modern

Figure 9
The Castle of Perseverance.

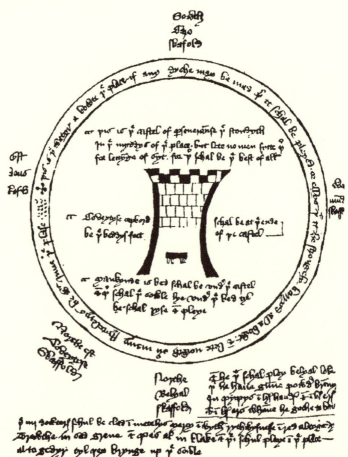

times, we can understand Stonehenge to be a link between the solid, natural boulder serving as a stage, and the wooden circular constructions with elevated stages in the medieval and Early Modern periods.

If Stonehenge was a site for ritual performances and not a solar alignment, the order and succession of the elements could not be seen from the central structure, but only from the outside (i.e., from the outlier). A wall surrounds the sacred area and to get in there one would need to be considered worthy of it. The outlier (the Heel Stone) is the first, preparatory station. The Slaughter Stone is the next station, as a horizontally placed stone for cleaning and preparing the person before he or she enters the holy circle. The final structure at Stonehenge is formed by the lintels, used for the resurrection. The orientation of the ritual performed at Stonehenge is therefore not toward the northeast, the sunrise or moonrise, but like the succession of stations at Gjøstein from the northeast toward the southwest. The southern gate at Stonehenge, and at many other stone circles, is not another entrance, but the exit, where the reborn performer disappears after the ritual. Therefore, the exit gates of the stone circles are small and seldom, if ever, in alignment with the entrance.

NARSJØ: THE DRAMATIC RITUAL AND THE DRAMA OF THE RITUAL LANDSCAPE

Large constructions such as Stonehenge provide evidence of the importance of ritual performances held in Neolithic Europe. The reason for the structures might not have been to *observe* the sun—an important element in most prehistoric cultures—but to perform magic rituals *for* the sun (see Figure 10). Fertility rites and magic ceremonies were performed at different times of the year, at different places, and under different conditions. Among their common elements and traits one can find again and again the myths of the descent into the underworld, of the dying hero who is reborn or resurrected. We know the drama from shamanic vision quests, the initiation rituals, and Christian religion.[43]

The general principles of this ritual drama can be found in many different parts of the world, but each culture has adapted it to local conditions. The ritual drama can either take place in transformed spaces, such as Stonehenge, or in found spaces, such as Storsteinen and Gjøstein. These latter sites are marked by pictographs, which associates them with ritual actions. In other sites these may be lacking, but here the landscape throws certain rocks, or piles of rocks, into relief and turns them into ritual stages on which the sun becomes a ritual actor.

Even sites without precise alignment as defined by astronomy are, in a certain way, related to the sun through religion, myth, or cosmology. Sun and sacred mountains have been basic elements of orientation for Native Americans. To decide on the axis of the world, a shaman faces the rising

Figure 10
Narsjø. Photo by Jon Nygaard.

sun, and the rising sun decides the most important direction in the ritual landscape at winter solstice, when the sun is at its lowest and therefore most accessible for the shaman to attain his or her power. Loendorf has associated the rock art in Finnegan Cave in Montana with the Winter Spirit Dance, performed at winter solstice before the shaman ascends to heaven on the rays of the sun.[44] The Winter Spirit Dance might offer an explanation for Storsteinen and Amtmannsnes (Figure 11), another site in Alta. Both are situated far north of the Arctic Circle, and by midwinter the sun disappears for several weeks. Thus, the return of the sun is very important, both as a donor of fertility and as a dispenser of magic power. In Norway, the sun's disappearance by midwinter can also be experienced in particular areas south of the Arctic Circle, where, for a longer or shorter period, the sun will not shine into the fjords and valleys because it is screened off by surrounding mountains. Landscapes where this phenomenon is distinct, and where we also have the three important rock structures like the pillar, the split boulder, and at least the boulder with the characteristic stage, may also have been sites for ritual performances associated with the death and rebirth of the sun, or with the shaman's Winter Spirit Dance carried out before the sun re-emerges at winter solstice.

If the unfolding ritual drama was marked by the three stages of the sun rising, disappearing, and rising again, then we may find that the site and

Figure 11
Amtmannsnes II, Alta. From Knut Helskog, *Helleristningene i Alta: Spor etter* *ritualer og dagligliv i Finnmarks forhistorie* **(Alta: Alta museum, 1988).**

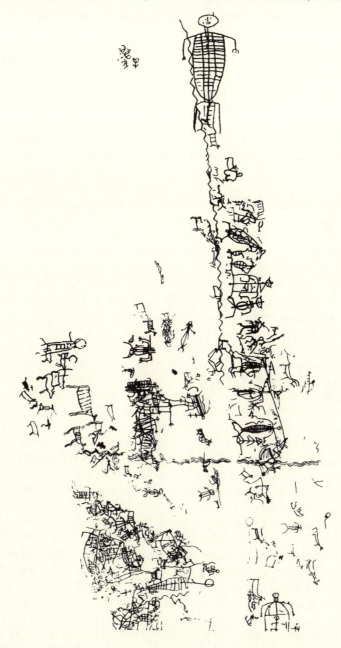

the landscape, and not rock art, were the determining forces in the ritual. A ritual landscape might therefore fill in some missing rock-art links, as in central Scandinavia, where Stone Age settlements are indicating long-lasting contacts between the populations of coastal and mountain areas. For instance, the hunter-gatherer rock art on the eastern side of the Trond-heim fjord, at the Atlantic coast, and in Jämtland, in inland Sweden, differ from the hunter-gatherer rock art at Nämforsen near the Swedish eastern (Baltic) coast. This has been used as an argument for the existence of close contacts between the Trondheim fjord area and Jämtland/Härjedalen.[45] In both districts, several large rock art sites, as well as large Stone Age settle-ments, have been found,[46] but no rock art has been discovered between these two sites, thus creating a missing link of about 150 kilometers.

Rock art is often distributed along old hunter-gatherer trails between the coast or fjords and interior mountain ranges, like Gjøstein at Voss. In historic times, important routes between the Trondheim fjord and Sweden led through the valleys of Stjørdal and Verdal north of Trondheim. One of them was known in historic times as *Kopparleden* ("the Copper Trail"). From the seventeenth century until the end of the nineteenth century, this was the main route between Trondheim fjord and Sweden and is by far the shortest connection between Trondheim and central Sweden. If in pre-history there existed a link between Trondheim fjord and Jämtland, it is also to be found along Kopparleden. This is an area of large Ice Age boul-ders and moraines, and the two largest river systems of Scandinavia have both their sources in this area. The landscape represents the crossing of the two dominant zones of the circumpolar region, the *taiga* and the *tun-dra*. This is still the region of the native southern Sámi. Almost midway on the route from west to east lies Lake Narsjø (Figure 12). To the south is a larger mountain (Sålekinna, 1,595 meters high). In the moraine land-scape around the lake there are several characteristic boulders. At mid-winter, the sun rises just to the southeast of the mountain and disappears almost immediately afterward behind the mountain. For about two hours, the lake and the landscape around it lie in the shadow of the mountain, before the sun again rises southwest of the mountain (Figure 10) and then shines brightly for another hour until it sets behind the next mountain.

All the important elements of the ritual landscape are present in the Narsjø area. The purest water, the pillars, the split boulders, the narrow passages between the boulders, and the stages. At two distinct sites around the lake, all the three basic types of ritual rocks are represented. All are facing southwest to the rerising sun, or in the same direction as both the boulders at Gjøstein and the structure of Stonehenge. If Stone Age shamans of central Scandinavia were searching for a space for their ritual performances of a Winter Spirit Dance, they could hardly have found a more perfect place for it. They certainly could not have missed it,

Figure 12
Scandinavia 6,500 B.C.

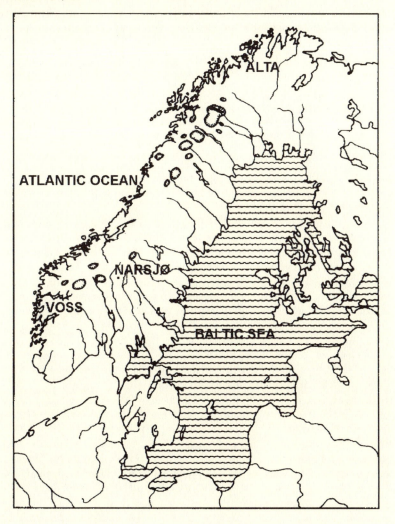

as it lay in the middle of their trail. Several Stone Age settlements are located and excavated in the area. As a ritual landscape, the Narsjø area is comparable with Dinwoody Lake and Ring Lake in the Wind River-area in Wyoming, and might have held the same importance as a ritual center.

I am not claiming here that any individual rock may have served as a site for ritual performances in prehistory. I am not even suggesting that the combination of three particular rocks—the pillar, the gate, and the stage—were by necessity sites for ritual performances. Like Malmer,[47] I should like to underline the importance of the surrounding landscape as a natural scenery for the stage. Secondly, it serves as an amphitheatrical setting allowing the action to be clearly visible for many spectators from afar.

NOTES

1. See A[nton] W[ilhelm] Brøgger. "Elg og ren paa helleristninger i det nordlige Norge." *Naturen* 30:12 (1906): 356–360; Gustaf Hallström. "Nordskandinaviska hällristningar I." *Fornvännen* 2 (1907): 161–176, and "Nordskandinaviska hällristningar III." *Fornvännen* 4 (1909): 140–148.

2. See Gutorm Gjessing's studies *Arktiske helleristninger i Nord-Norge.* Oslo: Aschehoug, 1932, and *Nordenfjelske ristninger og malninger av den arktiske gruppe.* Oslo: Aschehoug, 1936, published as part of Institutt for sammenlignende kulturforskning, series B, vols. 21 and 30.

3. See especially Oscar Almgren. *Hällristningar och kultbruk.* Stockholm: Kungl. Vitterhets Historie och Antikvitets Akademien, 1927.

4. As an exception one might mention Anders Hagen. "Regionindeling, særpreg og kontakt i bergkunsten." *Arkeologi i norr* 3 (1990 [i.e., 1992]): 19–30.

5. In Norway, this new trend is represented by Anders Hagen. *Bergkunst: Jegerfolkets helleristninger og malinger i norsk steinalder.* Oslo: Cappelen 1976; Anders Hesjedal. *Helleristninger som tegn og tekst: En analyse av veideristninger i Nordland og Troms.* Tromsø: Universitetet i Tromsø, Institutt for samfunnsvitenskap, 1994; and Hein Bjartmar Bjerck. *Bergbildene på Leiknes.* Bodø: Nordland fylkeskommune, 1993. In Germany, a similar approach was taken by Dietrich Evers in *Felsbilder arktischer Jägerkulturen des steinzeitlichen Skandinaviens.* Stuttgart: Steiner, 1988; and *Felsbilder: Botschaften der Vorzeit.* Leipzig: Urania, 1991.

6. In this I follow Poul Simonsen. "The Magic Picture: Used Once or More Times?" In *Words and Objects. Towards a Dialogue between Archeology and History of Religion,* ed. Gro Steinsland. Oslo: Norwegian University Press, 1986: 197–211; Kalle Sognnes. "Ritual Landscapes: Towards a Reinterpretation of Stone Age Rock Art in Trøndelag, Norway." *Norwegian Archaeological Review* 27 (1994): 29–50; and especially Mats P. Malmer. "Aspects of Neolithic Ritual Sites"; Steinsland. *Words and Objects:* 91–110. The relation between rock art and its landscape has also been underlined in recent international studies, such as Richard Bradley. *Rock Art and the Prehistory of Atlantic Europe: Signing the Land.* London: Routledge, 1997; Peter J. Ucko and Layton, Robert, eds. *The Archaeology and Anthropology of Landscape: Shaping Your Landscape.* London: Routledge, 1999; George Nashe. *Signifying Place and Space: World Perspectives of Rock Art and Landscape.* Oxford: Archaeopress, 2000; Christopher Chippindale and George Nash, eds. *Pictures in Place: Looking at Rock Art in Its Landscape.* Cambridge: Cambridge University Press, 2002.

7. See Lauri Honko. *The Great Bear: A Thematic Anthology of Oral Poetry in Finno-Ugrian Languages.* Helsinki: Suomalaisen kirjallisuuden seura, 1993.

8. This is emphasized by Sverre Marstrander in *Østfolds jordbruksristninger.* Oslo: Universitetsforlaget, 1963; and *Helleristningsfeltene i Gjerpen.* Skien: Sætrykk av Årbok for Telemark, 1969.

9. See Steinar Moe and Einar Østmo. *Norske helleristninger.* Exh. cat. Gjøvik: Olympic Arena, 1994: 20.

10. See Malmer. "Aspects of Neolithic Ritual Sites," p. 91.

11. See Hans Midbøe. "Helleristninger og kultspill: Nye funn fra Trøndelag." *Det kgl. Norske Videnskabers Selskabs Forhandlinger* 14 (1969): 80–90; Kristin Lyhmann. "Båten—Nordens eldste scene." *Spillerom* 3 (1988): 5–9; Kristin Lyhmann. "Førkristne kilder til teater i Østfold." *Spillerom* 1–2 (1992): 4–7; Kristin Lyhmann. "Det kvinnelige i fruktbarhetskulten i førhistorisk tid." In *HUN: En antologi om kunnskap fra kvinners liv,* ed. Gjertrud Sæter. Oslo: Spillerom, 1996: 23–46.

12. See Malmer. "Aspects of Neolithic Ritual Sites," p. 92.

13. See George Thomson. *Aeschylus and Athens: A Study in the Social Origins of Drama.* 3rd ed. London: Lawrence & Wishart, 1966; and Oscar Eberle. *Centalora: Leben, Glauben, Tanz und Theater der Urvölker.* Olten: Walter, 1955.

14. See E. T. Kirby. *Ur-Drama: The Origins of Theatre.* New York: New York University Press, 1975.

15. See James George Frazer. *The Golden Bough: A Study in Magic and Religion,* London: Macmillan, 1922.

16. See Gilbert Murray. *The Five Stages of Greek Religion.* Garden City, NY: Doubleday, 1951; Gilbert Murray. "Excursus on the Ritual Forms Preserved in Greek Tragedy"; Jane Ellen Harrison. *Themis: A Study of the Social Origins of Greek Religion.* New York: Merlin Press, 1963; Gilbert Murray. "Foreword." In *Thespis: Ritual, Myth, and Drama in the Ancient Near East,* Theodor H. Gaster. New York: The Norton Library, 1977; Jane Ellen Harrison. *Ancient Art and Ritual.* London: Williams and Norgate, 1913; Francis Macdonald Cornford. *The Origin of Attic Comedy.* London: Arnold, 1914; Arthur W. Pickard-Cambridge. *Dithyramb, Tragedy, and Comedy.* Oxford: Clarendon Press, 1962.

17. See William Ridgeway. *The Origin of Tragedy, with Special Reference to the Greek Tragedians.* Cambridge: Cambridge University Press, 1910; William Ridgeway. *The Drama and Dramatic Dances of Non-European Races in Special Reference to the Origin of Greek Tragedy.* Cambridge: Cambridge University Press, 1915.

18. Knut Helskog. *Helleristningene i Alta: Spor etter ritualer og dagligliv i Finnmarks forhistorie.* Alta: Alta Museum, 1988.

19. Johs Bøe and Anders Nummedal. *Le Finnmarkien: Les origines de la civilisation dans l'extrême-nord de l'Europe.* Oslo: Aschehoug, 1936.

20. Helskog. *Helleristningene i Alta,* p. 64.

21. See for example Arvid Sveen. *Helleristninger, Jiepmaluokta, Hjemmeluft, Alta.* Alta: Alta Museum, 1996.

22. See the following of Whitley's writings: "Shamanism and Rock Art in Far Western North America." *Cambridge Archaeological Journal* 2 (1992): 89–113; "Shamanism, Natural Modeling and the Rock Art of Far Western North American Hunter-Gatherers." In *Shamanism and Rock Art in North America,* ed. Solveig A. Turpin. San Antonio, TX: Rock Art Foundation, 1994: 1–44; *A Guide to Rock Art Sites: Southern California and Southern Nevada.* Missoula, MT: Mountain Press, 1996; "History and Prehistory of the Coso Range: The Native American Past on the Western Edge of the Great Basin." In *Coso Rock Art. A New Perspective,* ed. Elva Younkin. Ridgecrest, CA: Maturango Press, 1998: 29–68; "Meaning & Metaphor in the Coso Petroglyphs: Understanding Great Basin Rock Art." Younkin: *Coso Rock Art,* pp. 109–174; and *Following the Shaman's Path: A Walking Guide to Little*

Petroglyph Canyon Coso Range, California. Ridgecrest, CA: Maturango Museum, 1998.

23. See, in particular, *Believing and Seeing: Symbolic Meanings in Southern San Rock Paintings.* London: Academic Press, 1981; *The Rock Art of Southern Africa.* Cambridge: Cambridge University Press, 1983; *New Approaches to Southern African Rock Art.* Cape Town: South African Archaeological Society, 1983; *Images of Power: Understanding Bushman Rock Art.* Johannesburg: Southern Book Publishers, 1989; *Discovering Southern African Rock Art.* Cape Town: Philip, 1990.

24. See Whitley. "Meaning and Metaphor in the Coso Petroglyphs," p. 112.

25. Mircea Eliade. *Shamanism: Archaic Techniques of Ecstasy.* New York: Bollingen Foundation, 1964.

26. Åke Hultkrantz. *Native Religions of North America: The Power of Visions and Fertility.* San Francisco, CA: Harper and Row, 1987.

27. Whitely. *Southern California and Southern Nevada.*

28. See Inger Zacrisson. "New Archaeological Finds from the Territory of the Southern Saamis." In *Sami Pre-Christian Religion,* ed. Louise Bäckman and Åke Hultkrantz. Stockholm: Almqvist & Wiksell, 1985: 83–99; Rolf Kjellström. "Piles of Bones, Cult-places or Something Else?" In *Sami Pre-Christian Religion,* Bäckman and Hultkrantz. pp. 115–120.

29. See Ørnulf Vorren. "Circular Sacrificial Sites and Their Function." Bäckman and Hultkrantz: *Sami Pre-Christian Religion,* pp. 69–81; and Ørnulf Vorren and Hans Kr. Eriksen. *Samiske offerplasser i Varanger.* Stonglandseidet: Nordkalott, 1993.

30. Hultkrantz. *Native Religions of North America.*

31. Whitley. *Southern California and Southern Nevada.*

32. Ibid., p. 183.

33. Ibid., p. 104.

34. Whitley. *Following the Shaman's Path,* pp. 27–28.

35. Whitley. "Meaning and Metaphor in the Coso Petroglyphs," p. 112.

36. See Jon Nygaard. "Teater som uttrykk for kultur og identitet hos arktiske urfolk." *Spillerom* 1–4 (1998): 1–132; quotation from p. 93.

37. According to Ronald I. Dorn. "Age Determination of the Coso Rock Art." Younkin: *Coso Rock Art,* p. 80.

38. Whitley. *Southern California and Southern Nevada,* p. 9.

39. See Richard Schechner. *Environmental Theatre.* New York: Hawthorne Books, 1973.

40. Vorren. "Circular Sacrificial Sites and Their Function."

41. Aubrey Burl. *Great Stone Circles.* New Haven, CT: Yale University Press, 1999: 151.

42. Ibid., p. 161.

43. See the chapter "The Bridge and the 'Difficult Passage'" in Eliade's classic volume on shamanism, in which the passage through a narrow and dangerous conduit is described as a common element of initiation rites.

44. Julie E. Francis and Lawrence L. Loendorf. *Ancient Visions: Petroglyphs and Pictographs from the Wind River and Bighorn Country, Wyoming and Montana.* Salt Lake City, UT: University of Utah Press, 2002.

45. See Gustaf Hallström. *Monumental Art of Northern Europe from the Stone Age.* 2 vols. Stockholm: Thule, 1938.

46. In the Trondheim fjord area, the rock-art sites of Hell, Leirfall, Evenhus,

Bardal, and Bøla are among the largest and best known in Norway. In Jämtland and Härjedalen several rock art sites are situated close to the Norwegian border: in Jämtland, the rock carvings of Glösa and Gärdesån and the rock carvings and Stone Age settlements of Ånnsjön; in Härjedalen, the largest site of rock paintings in Sweden, Flatruet.

47. Malmer. "Aspects of Neolithic Ritual Sites," p. 107.

European Modernism and the Arts of Prehistory

Roger Cardinal

Cet art si près de nous semble abolir le temps.
[Our response to this art is so direct that we lose all idea of time.]
    Georges Bataille, *Lascaux ou la Naissance de l'art* (1955), 47

The call of the shaman which can be discerned in modern art
is a call to take wing beyond the familiar look and sound of things.
    Michael Tucker, *Dreaming with Open Eyes* (1992), 99

In twentieth-century Europe, a fast-growing interest in the arts of prehistoric times may be seen to coincide with the flowering of the early avant-garde. Discoveries at such sites as Altamira, Niaux, Trois-Frères, Lascaux, and Rouffignac brought the imagery of our distant ancestors before a widening audience, making it a popular point of reference in discussions of the creative impulse. In France especially, the association of prehistoric artistry with deep and perennial human needs was articulated in Georges Bataille's influential book *Lascaux* (1955). Several specific links may be drawn between prehistoric styles and primitivist works of recent times. In the case of the sculptors Brancusi, Giacometti, and Henry Moore, Cycladic borrowings are well attested. In 1949 there emerged in Spain a short-lived School of Altamira, whose adherents included Joan Miró and the Englishman Haydn Stubbing, an adept of hand-painting. The French painter Tal Coat pioneered an abstract idiom inspired by nonrepresentational marks in the Franco-Cantabrian caves. The interplay of trace and texture in the work of *art informel* artists like Fautrier, Dubuffet, and Michaux reflects tacit affinities with archaic markmaking. Although its direct impact cannot be measured precisely, the suffused influence of the prehistoric example may be deemed a key factor in the evolution of artistic Modernism.

INTRODUCTION

In Europe, the formal study of the arts of prehistory dates back at least to the early nineteenth century. However, it was not until the twentieth century that a wider public began to enjoy the privilege of access to prehistoric masterworks. This was an age marked by an astonishing sequence of archeological discoveries, including those of hitherto unknown sites like Font-de-Gaume (1901), Trois-Frères (1914), Val Camonica (1914), Pech-Merle (1922), Tassili n'Ajjer (1933), Lascaux (1940), Addaura (1953), Cosquer (1991), and Chauvet (1994), as well as those of hitherto ignored aspects of known sites, such as Niaux (1906) and Rouffignac (1956). The great Altamira cave had in fact been found in 1868 and explored by Sanz de Sautuola in 1879, yet, given that it was largely ignored until 1902, it was effectively in the early twentieth century that it entered art history.

Thanks to a telling conjuncture of cultural developments, the same century saw an unprecedented series of highly adventurous innovations within the arts of the Western world. Although the avant-garde groups and movements of European Modernism manifested themselves in different ways in different times and places, they did share one general ambition, which was to break with the enshrined doctrines and orthodoxies of the nineteenth century and to experiment with entirely fresh techniques and subject matters. One of the ways in which early Modernists deliberately sought to reinvigorate art was to jettison their academic training and to seek inspiration from what were then considered marginal arts, specifically tribal art (the art of so-called primitives from outside Europe), along with the creative expressions of a range of disregarded European subcultures: the art of untrained peasants, of autodidact outsiders, of the insane, of mediums, of naives, of prisoners, of children, and of anonymous graffitists, as well as the lowly print iconography of popular culture. I propose to add prehistoric art to this list of seductive alternatives along the margins of the Fine Art orthodoxy of metropolitan Europe.[1]

A coordinated history of the impact upon modern art of all these non-accredited and (at the time) largely despised art forms remains to be written. In the meantime, a succession of pioneering academic studies appeared during the 1990s that examine the impact upon Modernism of popular culture, outsider art, and child art.[2] Yet by far the most attractive territory for researchers has been Primitivism, in the sense of the role played by tribal art in the development of modern Western art.[3] Scholars have attended closely to the styles of such Western artists as Picasso, Brancusi, Klee, Kirchner, Giacometti, and Moore and delineated their indebtedness to tribal sources, whether through overt copying or quotation, through circumspect mimicry or stylistic allusion, or through less overt modalities of expression which pay homage not only to the styles, themes, and motifs, but also to the approaches and beliefs of non-European creators.[4]

By contrast, the no less fascinating topic of the impact of prehistoric art upon modern art remains largely unexplored. It is a strong hunch of mine that twentieth-century artists could not possibly have been ignorant of the arts of prehistory, and indeed that they frequently leave clues as to their awareness of their distant predecessors. What is frustrating to observe is that, at the present time, there is only a limited supply of uncontested facts with which to buttress my conjectures.[5] True, a monograph on an individual modern artist will occasionally refer to his or her receptivity to prehistoric work; and here and there, one finds mention of specific readings, even of visits to museums or archeological sites. But few scholars have ventured into this domain, and there is precious little in the way of an inventory of documented facts. Furthermore, few artists seem to have breathed more than a word about the stimulus which prehistoric art affords; indeed, I discern a symptomatic reticence on the subject, as if an avowal of any debt to such remote antecedents were somehow unseemly. Or is it that the subject is somehow so momentous as to instill caution?

I dare say there are obvious reasons why studies of Primitivism have privileged tribal over prehistoric art. One is that it is relatively hard to make contact with authentic examples of prehistoric art. In the early twentieth century, a wide range of tribal objects were becoming available for purchase through the long established trading circuits of colonialism and the metropolitan outlets of commercial galleries and auction-houses. Conversely, most outstanding examples of prehistoric art simply cannot be moved: to view the great murals of Altamira and Lascaux, the rock art of the Alps or Karelia, or the megaliths of Carnac and Callanish, it has always been necessary to make long and sometimes arduous cross-country journeys. True, there are specimens of Paleolithic *art mobilier* in the archeological museums of the West, yet these are in effect permanently immobilized, scarcely ever leaving their showcases. Moreover, unlike tribal artifacts, prehistoric carvings have rarely been displayed *as artworks* in art galleries. Whereas modern artists loved to hang tribal masks on the walls of their studios, it was rarely possible for them to collect prehistoric art otherwise than in the mediated form of the replica.[6]

It is nevertheless my contention that prehistoric art should be cited along with other marginal arts as a contributory or corroborative factor in the historical development of Modernism. There is evidence that some artists did succeed in getting to key places like Altamira and Lascaux. And, above all, there is the fact that, in a cultural epoch saluted by Walter Benjamin as uniquely shaped by the swift mechanical reproduction and transmission of pictures, it was always possible for curiosity to be aroused by the images of prehistoric works from around the world. Illustrated books such as Hugo Obermaier's *Der Mensch der Vorzeit* (1911), Salomon Reinach's *Répertoire de l'art quaternaire* (1913), and Maurice Burkitt's *Prehistory* (1921) testify to the early development of a market for such imagery, a market which was to expand greatly during the second half of the century. Most pertinently, the imaging of painted figures from Altamira and Lascaux became so widespread in the later period as to establish those remote renderings of leaping bulls and horses as integral to twentieth-century culture at large. I can, for instance, recall reproductions of details from the Lascaux murals hanging in the corridors of my London school in the 1950s; nowadays, motifs from the caves are entirely commonplace on tourist brochures, on stamps, and in other popular contexts.

There must, I insist, be some signs of a response to such familiar material on the part of the artists of the century. What follows represents a preliminary outline of instances which support this conjecture.

TRACING THE PREHISTORIC IN MODERN ART

It should be remembered that prehistoric art-making encompasses a great variety of styles, from the florid naturalism of the Upper Paleolithic to the intellectual schematization of the Neolithic and Bronze ages. Throughout prehistory, the representation of objects in the real world— above all, animals and human beings—was a matter of expressive realism modified by schematization, ornamentation, and abstraction. The surviving examples of Paleolithic portable art exhibit patterns of intermittent mimeticism and striking distortion. An apparently unique model of aesthetic expression arises in the context of megalithic sites and ritual landscaping. Yet this lack of uniformity need not rule out the possibility that many aspects of prehistoric styles find their echo in the modern period.

Within the sculptural domain, a number of prehistoric antecedents can be confidently linked to the experimentation of the twentieth-century avant-garde. Early in the century, the Romanian sculptor Constantin Brancusi (1876–1957) pioneered a reductionist approach in which elemental form eclipses almost all trace of realistic allusion. His *Sculpture for the Blind* (1916) was undoubtedly inspired by archaic and primitive art, and in particular by Cycladic art, in the sense of those severe schematizations of female figures and heads produced more than 4,000 years ago in the Aegean islands of the Cyclades. These statuettes, carved in semitransparent marble, had been circulating since the discovery of Early Cycladic burial sites in the late nineteenth century. Their formal purity seems to incarnate an uncanny modernity: they are well known to have fascinated other sculptors, such as Henry Moore and Alberto Giacometti, for whom the aesthetic principle of reduction to essentials was paramount.

The successive findings of Paleolithic stone or ivory carvings of female figures through the late nineteenth and early twentieth centuries led to the recognition of a distinct prehistoric genre known as Venus figurines. Finds bunched within the first quarter of the century are: the *Sireuil Venus* (1900), the *Willendorf Venus* (1908), the *Laussel Venus*, also known as the

Dame à la corne (1910s), the *Lespugue Venus* (1922), and the *Savignano Venus* (1925). Since we know so little about the purposes of such carvings, it goes without saying that to dub each a Venus introduces a potentially mislead-ing assimilation to the Western Classical tradition.[7] It would seem futile to draw a comparison between, say, the prehistoric nude figure called *Venus impudica* (found at Laugerie-Basse) and the Hellenistic *Venus de Milo* of the late second century B.C. And yet there could be a point in juxta-posing *Venus impudica* with an important bronze by the Swiss sculptor Alberto Giacometti (1901–1966) entitled *Walking Woman* (1932–1934). In either case, the figure lacks a head and has a declivity in the chest; each possesses a slender, naked torso, with legs apparently in motion or on the verge of taking a step. Despite the fact that the originals are very different in scale, the juxtaposition of photographic reproductions is sufficiently telling to prompt the sense of some sort of convergence. Certainly the comparison throws light upon the intentions of the twentieth-century art-ist, who is clearly not concerned with invoking the sensuous beauty of a graceful Classical nude; rather Giacometti seems to want to engage with a more robust and perhaps magical embodiment of some elemental force.[8]

Another sculptor in this vein is Hans Arp (1886–1966), whose marble carvings of nonspecific biomorphic shapes are often highly reminiscent of Cycladic heads. In the 1950s, Arp produced a cycle of *Torsos*, slender half-abstracted figures in white marble which bear a marked resemblance to the Venus figures of prehistory; in 1956 he named a similar bronze sculp-ture *Venus of Meudon*, as if deliberately to spell out this association.[9] It may be noted that one of Arp's first critics, Carl Einstein, rhapsodized about the artist's biomorphic and cosmological vision, which in his view "reit-erates the rites of a prehistoric childhood."[10]

There seems no doubt that the small river-stone carvings executed from 1948 onward by the Hungarian photographer and part-time sculptor Bras-saï (1899–1984) were made with prehistoric antecedents in mind; the artist himself ratifies this in so many words, alluding to the Venus motif and emphasizing his concern with sculpture designed to be held in the hand.[11] When some two dozen of these pieces were shown at the Hayward Gal-lery in London in 2001, in a retrospective otherwise dominated by the artist's photographs, the showcase had, at first glance, all the air of an archeological display. Here one might hesitate to characterize the nature of the artist's response: are these modest works to be seen as a legitimate homage to the originals, a Modernist's salute to the remote past? Or are they relatively worthless, little more than successful pastiches with no original expressive content?[12]

Although there is a long tradition of making on-site drawings of pre-historic imagery—the Abbé Breuil being the outstanding exponent—these have always tended to be documentary rather than strictly artistic in spirit. And where modern art is concerned, there seem to be very few drawings inspired by prehistoric work. One might suppose that an alert artist encountering the compositions at Altamira or Niaux would be moved to take out pencil and sketch pad. Yet the few examples of such sketching which I have found were prompted not by calls to actual sites but by visits to museums, and, above all, illustrations in books and magazines. A compulsive sketch-maker throughout his career, Giacometti accumulated copies of a gamut of archaic and primitive works; many were inspired by his visits to the Louvre and the Musée d'Ethnographie du Trocadéro, with their collections of Egyptian, African, Oceanic, and Pre-Columbian work. Among these are several sketches of prehistoric figurines from the Cyclades.[13]

Henry Moore (1898–1986) was also an inveterate draftsman, and began his career as a forthright avant-garde experimenter by dint of sketching in the British Museum, where he frequented the diverse and well-stocked displays of tribal and archaic art (including Egyptian and Assyrian art), as well as the sections devoted to Cycladic art. Moore's personal library included some key specialist publications, and his sketches from printed sources include a powerful copy of the *Grimaldi Venus* and quite faithful renderings of Norwegian Neolithic engravings. A more fanciful drawing of 1934 entitled *Two Animals* depicts two horned creatures and, though not a literal copy of a prehistoric image, may have been a response to one of the Paleolithic sites he visited in that year: for once, it is a documented fact that, on a motoring holiday in Spain and France, Moore went inside the decorated caves at Altamira and Font-de-Gaume. One or two of his sculptural pieces carry strong echoes of prehistoric antecedents, such as the small sculpture *Horse* (1978), which has some resemblance to the carved horses of Vogelherd (Germany) or Les Espélugues (France). It is in keeping with Moore's passion for setting up his sculptures in the open air that he should have loved Stonehenge, which he first experienced in 1921 on a memorable visit by moonlight. The motif of the massive monolith became a stock element in Moore's mature sculptural repertoire, while the specific affinity with Stonehenge was celebrated in a cycle of dark lithographs entitled *Stonehenge Suite* (1971–1973).

Paul Klee (1879–1940) was a well known cultural plunderer who set no limits upon the sources of his inspiration, exhibiting a voracious interest in tribal art, psychotic art, child art, folk art, and other marginal expressions. His appropriation of such miscellaneous material was conducted with an unusually strong sense of priority, such that the original scarcely ever survives as an unaltered replica, but tends to be converted into an equivalent about whose overall tonality one is tempted to comment that it has become perfectly Klee-like. In other words, even in his spontaneous sketches, Klee's work is never a matter of mechanical transposition: it is always a matter of metamorphosis. Hence, parallels between his work and the arts of prehistory remain putative, a matter of intuition or subjective opinion. One rare instance of critical certainty might be a watercolor of 1917 which bears the title *Landscape with Prehistoric Animals*. However, its indebtedness to any prehistoric model is unclear, its main contents being some thick zigzag shapes and a few skeletal birds scrawled in a vaguely childlike manner. One might be tempted to compare at least one of these birds to the schematic bird-on-a-stick which is a key feature of the famous Well Scene at Lascaux (which I shall mention again later), were it not that the Lascaux image only became public some three decades later. (Of course, this does not preclude Klee's having noted some alternative prehistoric source.) Rather more convincing support for my thesis is offered by what might be called the Neolithic air of many of the late paintings, produced during Klee's final illness. These exploit a lexicon of diagrammatic motifs representing animal and human figures, along with geometric or abstract cyphers. This is an idiom which flourishes in the transitional zone *in between* iconic figuration and purely conceptual markings, that is to say, between picture-making and a primitive form of glyph-making. Similar ensembles of iconic and symbolic signs are typical of the Neolithic incisions found at such rock sites as Monte Bego and Val Camonica.[14]

Pablo Picasso (1881–1973) adds momentum to my inquiry in his oft-reported comment about the paintings in the cave at Altamira: "None of us is capable of painting like this."[15] It is well known that, early in his career, Picasso visited the Louvre and the Trocadéro ethnographic museum and that elements of early Greek, Egyptian, and Iberian art as well as of African tribal art played their part in that extraordinary cavalcade of contrasting styles which was Picasso's way of proving himself the most protean of Modernists. To establish an argument for the direct impact of prehistoric art would be difficult here, since Picasso's fluency and self-assurance were stronger than anyone's and thus quite likely to have deleted all overt traces. Did Picasso ever visit Altamira?[16] And if Picasso did see prehistoric art up close, what revelations could we expect to find in his work immediately after? My sense is that, as with Klee, the notion of influence needs to be most rigorously qualified or, to put it another way, rather than expect direct replications, we must look out for subtle reconfigurations. The Minotaur who dominates Picasso's interwar sketches and lithographs might seem an obvious link with the Altamira bulls: for even if Picasso never visited the actual cave, its imagery was certainly well known to him. Yet the connection is weakened when we reflect that bulls and bullfighting were in any event part and parcel of Picasso's Spanish culture; further, the Minotaur was not a bull as such but a bull-headed man, undoubtedly derived from Classical mythology. What might be a more plausible line of argument is that Picasso was espousing a thematic corpus—fearsomeness, magnificence, virile potency—embodied in the motif of the bull, and that any debt to Altamira has filtered through into a generalized, semiarticulate resonance or echo. This is exactly the point which William Rubin makes about Picasso's response to African tribal art: "More important, however, than any visible borrowings was Picasso's sense of tribal objects as charged with intense emotion, with a magical force capable of deeply affecting us."[17] In other words, the prehistoric model may have impressed itself most potently upon the modern artist at an affective level which eludes direct vision, rather than at the visible level of compositional or stylistic features. This somewhat guarded observation may indeed be all-important in this problematic domain.

The English artist Newton Haydn ("Tony") Stubbing (1921–1983) left England in 1947 for Spain, where he became a charter member of the so-called School of Altamira. This was an association established following a congress of artists, writers, and art historians held in 1949 at Santillana del Mar, near the Altamira site. The group was named by the sculptor Angel Ferrant and led by the painter Mathias Goeritz; other members included the critic Eduardo Westerdahl, the ceramicist Llorens Artigas, and the artists Eduardo Saura, Willi Baumeister, and Joan Miró. The school survived for only a couple of years, though it managed to publish a journal called *Bisonte*. If no common style emerged, there was a collective ideological commitment to venerating the Magdalenian epoch as a source of renewal. Robert Hobbs suggests that many of the group's members were "influenced by surrealism and found the caves a wonderful metaphor for the inner pathways of the mind."[18] As for Stubbing, he went on in 1954 to develop a characteristic technique of hand-painting. Mimicking the handprints he had seen on the walls at Altamira, and especially at nearby El Castillo, he produced dense, semiabstract ensembles using oil paint pressed onto the canvas with his bare hands.[19]

The Surrealist painter and sculptor Joan Miró (1893–1983) was also a member of the School of Altamira. During his Paris years, he had developed an assured repertoire of dancing symbols which bear comparison with the crowded Mesolithic pictographs of the Spanish Levant, found at sites such as Minateda and Albarracín, as well as with the stark Neolithic schematizations of the Monte Bego, although I have no evidence of direct or indirect contact. Some of Miró's later oils cultivate the superimposition of separate design elements, a feature of some overcrowded cave art, as in for instance the 1951 canvas *The Glare of the Sun Wounding the Late Star*. When Miró was commissioned to produce a large ceramic mural for the UNESCO building in Paris, he is known to have made a return visit to Altamira in 1957 with his collaborator Llorens Artigas, ostensibly to gain inspiration for the work. However, despite this clear evidence of a purposeful dialogue with primordial expressions, I discern no obvious impact on the resulting mural, which simply repeats the mannerisms of Miró's signature style. Hence there is little practical support for Raymond Queneau's bright idea of calling Miró "le poète préhistorique," beyond the occasional gnomic remark in Miró's recorded interviews about the connection between anonymity and universality.[20]

A more decisive example is that of the French painter and printmaker Pierre Tal Coat (1905–1985), who in the late 1930s developed a keen interest in prehistoric art and the ideas of the Abbé Breuil. In 1940, he moved for a while to Aix en Provence and befriended the painter André Masson (1896–1987), who in the mid-1920s, as a participant in Paris Surrealism, had pioneered automatic drawing. Both artists now cultivated an art of spontaneous gestural markings, typically in black ink on white paper. Masson's work was vehement and dense, whereas Tal Coat's etchings done in 1946–1947 and labeled *Profil sous l'eau* (Underwater Profile) consist of the minimal outlines of an indeterminate figure; were it not that they were inspired by the vision of his wife half-hidden beneath a waterfall, they might be thought to foreshadow the elliptical renderings of mammoths which Louis-René Nougier would discover at Rouffignac in 1956. In 1949 Tal Coat made a number of sketches in dark inks which depict a galloping horse, much in the manner of the leaping horses of Lascaux, whose imagery was by then widely familiar. It is known that the artist visited the Dordogne in 1955, seeking out Lascaux as well as other sites in the Les Eyzies region. By the late 1960s he had begun producing aquatints and ink sketches at his studio in Saint Prex by Lake Geneva, some of which carry suggestions of the nonrepresentational marks often found in the Paleolithic sites of Northern Spain. Charles Wentinck engineers a telling encounter by placing a diptych by Tal Coat entitled *Signs* (1965) opposite a detail from a mural at El Castillo: their common elements are some roughly parallel rows of large dots or blobs, and long semicurved parallel lines with transverse lines at right angles. Regarding the prehistoric marks, commentators have conjectured that their geometric shapes represent huts or houses; Wentinck indicates that in all probability Tal Coat's marks constitute a purely abstract or aesthetic statement.[21] My own sense of the matter is that, poised as they are between replicating a prehistoric style and reinventing it within a Modernist mode of lyrical abstraction, these *Signs* reveal Tal Coat as one of the most persuasive mediators between the primordial and the modern.

The painter and printmaker Jean Dubuffet (1901–1985) represents a classic case of modern Primitivism. Dubuffet's work reflects an idiosyncratic allegiance to the most downtrodden modalities of art-making: the popular art of North Africa, child art, anonymous graffiti, and the art of incarcerated lunatics and other mavericks. Dubuffet's pioneering collection of *Art brut* comprised a high proportion of pictures shaped from unkempt materials by untutored hands: he was drawn to the roughly configured wooden wall of a prison cell chiseled with a sharpened spoon by the interned Clément Fraisse and the black finger-paintings of the psychotic Louis Soutter. Among Dubuffet's own early work in the immediate postwar years was a set of portraits of friends produced by scoring dark expanses of impasto with the sharp end of a brush. Charles Wentinck juxtaposes one of these gaunt caricatures, *Michel Tapié Soleil* (1946), with a face hammered from a rock-face at the Paleolithic site of Marsoulas in the Pyrenees.[22] The two caricatural faces seem to form a natural pair, yet the connection may be no more than accidental, given that Dubuffet enjoyed a more immediate source of inspiration, namely the anonymous graffiti scratched into the ravaged walls of wartime Paris. Many were still in the process of being recorded by Brassaï, who had published photos of graffiti in the Surrealist magazine *Minotaure* as early as 1933, positing a continuity between the prehistoric cave wall and the modern factory wall.[23] His subsequent album *Graffiti* (1961) collates dozens of photos of faces, figures, and crude symbols, gouged into often crumbling brickwork. Their combination of bold incision and unpolished surface is certainly reminiscent both of Paleolithic and Neolithic scratch marks, although this could doubtless be said of graffiti from other periods of history.[24]

It is nonetheless the case that the postwar art of France was dominated by *abstraction lyrique*—otherwise known as *art informel*—which favored inchoate textures and vehement gestural attacks on the vertical surface, characteristics which fit nicely with the popular myth of the prehistoric artist engaging with a rough wall in the half-dark, albeit ignoring the robust thematics of cave art. The postwar painting of Jean Fautrier (1898–1964) merits attention for its characteristic use of unguent impasto and vigorous stabbing and scoring lines, which could be said to suggest the quasi expressionistic urgency popularly attributed to the Lascaux artists. Fautrier's career took a dramatic turn in 1943 when, living clandestinely in the grounds of a mental asylum on the outskirts of Paris, he painted the series *Otages* (Hostages), a cycle of scarcely decipherable human heads. The legend is that these ravaged images were inspired by the sounds of torture which Fautrier heard while working by night in a studio next to a forest used by the Gestapo for summary executions. First exhibited in 1945, these works may be seen as representative of a widespread contemporary preoccupation with themes of anguish and mutilation: it may not be far-fetched to tie these in with Georges Bataille's reading of prehistoric art as an engagement with themes of mortality, transgression, and violence, of which more below.

Fautrier's *Otages* foreshadow the cult of the *informel* in artists like Wols, Camille Bryen, and Henri Michaux (1899–1980), each of whom experimented with impromptu markings, or traces, which are at once dynamic and indecipherable. Certain pages of Michaux's textless book *Mouvements* (1950) consist of virtuoso splashes and lunges of black ink which suggest dancing or stricken human figures. These quasi ideogrammatic signs seem to hark back to certain Mesolithic configurations, such as those at Minateda and Valltorta Gorge in eastern Spain, although the analogy only really comes alive if one views the latter in their transcribed and printed form, whereby matt ocher brushstrokes upon limestone are converted into vivid black blotches upon the white page.

In the 1950s and 1960s, the Belgian artist Christian Dotremont (1922–1979) developed an idiom of ill-legible (or downright illegible) calligraphies which he dubbed *logogrammes*. Dotremont had studied Viking art in Denmark and later traveled in Lapland, where it seems highly probable he would have come across Neolithic rock art. Dotremont was an associate of Asger Jorn (1914–1973), a Danish artist with a passion for Nordic stone inscriptions who also worked on Danish prehistoric art with the archaeologist P. V. Glob. Both Dotremont and Jorn were members of the international COBRA group, which made no secret of its enthusiasm for tribal art, popular art, and child art.

Among the common denominators in these bewildering eruptions of creativity are: a commitment to spontaneous gestural markmaking, a vehement treatment of the picture surface, and a tacit association of the unprogrammed gesture with some sort of universality of expression. The tally of such characteristics is hardly definite proof that prehistoric art served as a conscious point of reference for all these artists; what I would suggest, nonetheless, is that it is appropriate to mention it as an eloquent, if semiocculted, presence within the contemporary Zeitgeist.

What I am beginning to articulate here is the notion of a tacit acknowledgment of prehistoric antecedents among modern artists active, especially in France, in the years following the second World War. My guess is that the discovery of the Lascaux cave in 1940, and especially its opening to the public in 1948, were significant stimuli, coinciding as they did with the contemporary desire for a fresh start and a neo-Primitivism tied to the marginal arts of graffiti, tribal art, and child art. The emergence of *abstraction lyrique*, or *art informel*, in the years following, running more or less in tandem with the upsurge of Abstract Expressionism in North America, is, I would suggest, no mere coincidence.

To put the point more emphatically, my hunch is that the popularization of Lascaux in contemporary newspapers and magazines released some significant cultural tremors, establishing in effect a myth of Lascaux which affected artists like Tal Coat, Fautrier, Dubuffet, and others. In this context, Georges Bataille (1897–1962) may be seen as an important mediating influence. The Swiss publisher Albert Skira asked the writer to compose a text to accompany a fine set of color prints taken in the caves by the photographers Hans Hinz and Claudio Emmer, and Bataille seems to have leaped at the chance to situate Lascaux as a supreme example of human creativity.

At this time, the Lascaux murals were still thought to be among the earliest ever artistic productions, dating back to the Aurignacian period (or early Upper Paleolithic); in the popular imagination, the painters of

Lascaux *were* the first artists.[25] Thus Bataille was only echoing popular cliché when he held forth about "the miracle of Lascaux" and "the birth of art."[26] However, it particularly suited Bataille's private ideology to reject the conventional view that it was Classical Greek art which prefigured modernity, and to project the glamorous alternative image of *Homo sapiens sapiens* springing into conscious being at Lascaux, wrenching himself out of his prehuman or animal condition, and blazing his new identity upon the cave walls.[27]

It is true that Bataille retails expert analyses drawn from Abbé Breuil and others; yet his major emphasis is on the art as a stupendous and epoch-making expression. What interests him is the combination of erotic and metaphysical impulses in the Lascaux imagery, brought to a head in the controversial Well Scene, with its disemboweled bison and rigid shaman.[28] In a later disquisition upon the centrality of eroticism in all human cultures, *L'Érotisme* (1957), Bataille ties the erotic urge to man's desperate awareness of death and the need for interdicts, transgression, and sacrifice. Most pertinent to my argument are the book's eclectic illustrations, a parade of worldwide sacred art, including the Lascaux Well Scene, bull-headed shamans from Trois-Frères, and a Mesolithic battle-scene from Morella la Vella in the Spanish Levant. There is something of the hit-and-miss approach to this eclecticism, but my point is that Bataille was very much of his time in placing such references on the cultural agenda.

One of the most original and long-lasting avant-garde movements of the last decades of the twentieth century has been Land Art, manifested in earthworks, stone installations, and other interventions in the landscape. Much of this work is expressly associated with the ritual stone sites of the Neolithic. The English artist Richard Long (b. 1945) has traveled alone to remote parts of Britain like Dartmoor as well as to the Himalaya and Andes mountains, producing ritualistic stone patterns—circles, spirals, straight lines—and documenting them in photographs. There is little doubt that many Land Art activities are in tune with a certain corpus of conjectures regarding the placement and cosmological purpose of prehistoric sites, popularized in the writings of authors like Alfred Watkins and Guy Underwood.[29]

A related category is the landscape art of painters who directly portray prehistoric monuments in their work, such as the Englishman Paul Nash (1889–1946), who in the 1930s painted Silbury Hill, Maiden Castle, and the Men-an-Tol stone in Cornwall, stylizing their forms and thereby guiding them into the orbit of his semimystical landscape vision, much as had been done a century before by Romantic artists like Constable (who painted Stonehenge) and Friedrich (who painted the *Heidenhügel* or Neolithic tombs of the Baltic coastal lands). Another modern English artist, Ewen Henderson (1935–2000), drew and painted such sites as the Ring of Brodgar on Orkney and the Long Meg Stone in Northumbria. All of this points to a general twentieth-century concern to revive the lost meaning of ancient sites, converting old stones into symbols of a lost spirituality, if not a latent patriotism. Hints of a mystical ideology may be inferred from Jacquetta Hawkes's popular book on the geology of Britain, *A Land* (1953), where she evokes the persistent "shadowy hieroglyphs" which are the chambered tombs and mounds of prehistoric cultures, while in the same breath praising Henry Moore for the "tautness of surface" he derives from the hard, fossil-bearing Liassic stones.[30]

Finally, there is the question of shamanism. During the latter half of the twentieth century, the scientific investigation of prehistoric art was propelled more and more compellingly by the thesis that its meanings were inseparable from the circumstances of its production and in particular the physiological and mental state of its practitioners. Within ethnographic studies, close examination of the practices of extant or more recently extinct tribal cultures, in such regions as Lapland, Siberia, North America, southern Africa, and Australia, had nourished the paradigm of the global prominence of shamanism. Despite the risks of fanciful projection, a further ambit of comparison was drawn between these tribal cultures and the cultures of prehistory, thereby establishing a strong case for seeing the prehistoric arts in terms of shamanic beliefs and practices. Researchers such as Thomas Dowson and David Lewis-Williams have established a neuropsychological model of the creative process which indicates a close link between ecstatic trances, usually self-induced, and the depiction of spiritual beings, typically figured as animals. A key figure in all primitive societies, the shaman is thus seen as the archetype of the visionary healer and artist. The literature on this topic has thrived on the visual corroboration of certain classic images, such as the stag-headed man at Trois-Frères, the stiff, entranced male in the Well Scene from Lascaux, and the disembodied face of the Sorcerer or Magus of Monte Bego.

The ultimate stitch in the fabric of correspondences would be to connect this model of the artist-shaman of prehistory with that of the modern art-maker. In his eclectic study *Dreaming with Open Eyes,* Michael Tucker confers shamanic status upon a very wide range of twentieth-century creators, including Van Gogh, Edvard Munch, Joan Miró, Antoni Tàpies, Frans Widerberg, Alan Davie, Meret Oppenheim, Barbara Hepworth, Leonora Carrington, and Joseph Beuys, not to mention poets such as Hugo Ball and Kenneth White, and the jazz musicians Cecil Taylor and Jan Gabarek.[31] Tucker's freewheeling argument draws support from the writings of Mircea Eliade, Joseph Campbell, and Gaston Bachelard, while invoking Lucien Lévy-Bruhl's concept of *participation mystique* alongside Erich Neumann's equation of creativity with the state of possession. A skein of recurrent motifs—shamanic possession, animism, the spiritual journey, the metamorphosis, the absorption within the sacred—color Tucker's account of entranced art-making and imply the continuity of the creative vocation across time, implicitly linking the modern artist to his prehistoric ancestor. What Tucker does not do is to attempt to show any visual resemblance between the shamanic imagery of prehistory and that of modern times. But how could he? The disparateness of the Modernists he has chosen rules out the possibility of consistently eloquent juxtapositions. Essentially, his argument is about the ubiquity of archetypal themes and spiritual states, rather than of recurrent attributes of style.

GAUGING THE IMPACT OF PREHISTORIC ART

The above outline does no more than gesture toward a field of research that remains to be properly explored. Yet despite the paucity of facts, I think a number of useful signposts have been set out. One thing is clear: a straightforward conception of influence is of little use, for there are hardly any irrefutable indications that art made thousands of years ago has exercised an unmediated and unqualified impact upon sensibilities conditioned by modern culture. The occasional cherished anecdote about a Moore or a Miró entering a prehistoric cave may bring color to the narrative and lend credence to the idea of an elective affinity between the modern and the primordial artist; yet there still remains the problem of just how to measure the actual impact of the prehistoric example, once it is recognized that the Modernist in question is, first, intent upon absorbing that impact within his or her personal style, and is, second, subject to any number of simultaneous influences or temptations, including those of other marginal arts like graffiti, and not forgetting those of other avant-gardists. It has also to be said that the serendipity of the telling juxtaposition—the "hey presto!" of the art historian—is hardly a very reliable research tool, since even the most seductive visual correspondence may be falsifiable.

We are, I think, on fairly firm ground when we consider the relevance to Modernism of certain specific styles from prehistory: we can be quite sure that Cycladic art did affect Brancusi and Moore (though, as ever, not in isolation), while the semiabstracted ideograms of the Neolithic can legitimately be seen as antecedents for Klee. (Again, they are by no means an exclusive source.) The dynamism of Paleolithic cave art may be deemed to have a kinship with the bodily or gestural expressions of a Stubbing, a Tal Coat, a Dubuffet, a Fautrier, although the only truly explicit sign here is the handprint. Perhaps the truth of the matter is that the genuine reception and assimilation of a marginal art must entail translation and reconfiguration, processes which inevitably delete the traces of indebtedness. Another way of envisaging the situation could be to say that revealing moments of empathetic contact with prehistoric art need not lead to literal borrowings at all; rather, an illuminating encounter with Otherness may be a stimulus to the Modernist's self-recognition, obliquely enabling or corroborating a risky step forward in an unprecedented direction.

Over and above these observations concerning contact and perceptible response, my intuition tells me that there may be a further dimension which is notoriously at odds with scholarly protocol. It would seem that the modern artists' empathy with those working at the very dawn of art must rest on a distinctive propensity for imaginative projection. This propensity may well be inherent in their very nature as creative spirits, but the fact that few are able or willing to analyze it makes it something very difficult to introduce into the intellectual discussion. I believe, nevertheless, that it is fundamental. What Guy Davenport calls the "renaissance of the archaic"[32] in modern times seems to me to embrace a neo-Romantic or Edenic hankering for a unique point of origin, along with a truly modern rebellion against the stark facts of contemporary history, as much as against the constraints of artistic conformism. The much discussed alienation in modern civilization could be what sets off a reflex of yearning for timeless values, for a continuity of human understanding, confirmed in acts of markmaking which blaze across the firmament of history just as they transcend the individual. Notions of spirituality and the sense of the sacred begin to impress themselves on the discussion. What did the prehistoric artist have in mind, exactly? Perhaps, after all, the handprint is the central clue, for this sign of human presence must surely represent a decisive link across the millennia, its unaltered and ever familiar shape making it the ultimate universal symbol. Miró and Michaux were not alone in expressing the desire to shake off the subjectivity of gesture and accede to an atemporal space of essential forms, an elemental realm in which some have recognized Jung's collective unconscious or the matrix of racial memory. Perhaps Primitivism at large could be said to partake of this effort of self-transcendence through daring acts of exposure to Otherness, while the magical or shamanic spirit which Tucker sees as permeating Modernism chimes in not only with the theories that link shamanism to prehistoric art but also with recent scientific research concerning the creative function of trance-states. What remains fraught about investigating the dialogue of the modern and the primordial is nothing less than the terrifying prospect of laying bare the very secret of the art-making impulse itself.

NOTES

1. A survey of these marginal arts is offered in my chapter "Marginalia" in *Marginalia: Perspectives on Outsider Art*, Ans van Berkum et al. Zwolle: Museum De Stadshof, 2001: 51–75.

2. See Kirk Varnedoe and Adam Gopnik. *High and Low: Modern Art and Popular Culture*. New York: Museum of Modern Art, 1990; Maurice Tuchman and Carol S.

Eliel. *Parallel Visions: Modern Artists and Outsider Art.* Exhibition catalog. Princeton, NJ: Princeton University Press, 1992; and Jonathan Fineberg. *The Innocent Eye: Children's Art and the Modern Artist.* Princeton, NJ: Princeton University Press, 1997.

3. At one time, the term *primitive art* frequently encompassed both the arts of prehistory and the more recent arts of non-European tribal peoples. Nowadays, its application is restricted more or less exclusively to the latter, albeit partisans of tribal art have contested the appropriateness of applying the term to what they rightly see as sophisticated and complex works. As for the term *Primitivism*, it is a commonplace in scholarly discussions to apologize for any hint of deprecation or racism by placing it in quotation marks. By now, though, Primitivism has the status of a technical term relating to a distinct phenomenon within art history. See *The Concept of the Primitive*, ed. Ashley Montagu. New York: The Free Press, 1968.

4. A large exhibition on the topic of Primitivism was held in New York in 1984, its weighty catalog of comparative essays testifying to the legitimacy of Primitivism as an elective terrain for the modern art historian. See *"Primitivism" in 20th-Century Art: Affinity of the Tribal and Modern*, ed. William S. Rubin. New York: Museum of Modern Art, 1984. Robert Goldwater's classic 1938 study, *Primitivism in Modern Painting* (reissued in 1967 in a revised form as *Primitivism in Modern Art*), offered a broader panorama by taking account of Orientalist influences in the Romantic period and the twentieth-century interest in child art, folk art, and psychotic art. A more recent survey is Colin Rhodes. *Primitivism and Modern Art.* London: Thames & Hudson, 1994.

5. Among the more helpful publications I have come across are the catalog to the 1949 exhibition at London's Institute of Contemporary Art, entitled *40,000 Years of Modern Art*, and Lucy R. Lippard's fertile and thought-provoking *Overlay* of 1983, which draws parallels between prehistoric earthworks and late twentieth-century Land Art. Guy Davenport offers a brief but stimulating essay, "The Symbol of the Archaic." In *The Geography of the Imagination*. London: Picador, 1984: 16–29. Colin Renfrew's *The Cycladic Spirit: Masterpieces from the Nicholas P. Goulandris Collection*. New York: Abrams, 1991, has a thoughtful chapter on the perception of Cycladic art through the lens of modern taste. Though his is not a very probing account, credit must go to Charles Wentinck for offering suggestive visual evidence of borrowings, or at least of affinities, in his *Modern and Primitive Art.* Oxford: Phaidon Press, 1974.

6. The Surrealist painter and professional anthropologist Desmond Morris recently auctioned off his fine collection of ceramics from Archaic Cyprus, whose glyphic sign-system he had examined in his 1985 book, *The Art of Ancient Cyprus,* Oxford: Phaidon Press, 1985.

7. Paul Bahn points out that the term *Venus* was first used by the Marquis de Vibraye in the 1860s in reference to the *Venus impudica* found at Laugerie-Basse in about 1864, and that Édouard Piette later adopted it as a generic reference to the corpulent female figurines typical of the Paleolithic. See Paul Bahn and Jean Vertut. *Journey through the Ice Age.* London: Weidenfeld and Nicolson, 1997: 160.

8. As the first life-size female figures made by Giacometti, *Walking Woman* and its successor *The Invisible Object* (1934) constitute a turning-point in his production. Commentators have ascribed other sources of inspiration to these pieces, notably upright princess figures from Ancient Egypt.

9. Meudon was the name of the Paris suburb where Arp lived from 1927. In

fact, Arp's *Venus* is about five feet tall, many times larger than the hand-held statuettes of the Paleolithic.

10. "Arp répète dans ses œuvres les rites d'une enfance préhistorique." Carl Einstein. "L'Enfance néolithique." *Documents* 8 (1930): 35–43; quotation from p. 43. In the previous issue of this magazine, edited by Georges Bataille, Bataille had published his own "L'Art primitif."

11. See Brassaï. "Sculptures." In *Brassaï: "No Ordinary Eyes,"* ed. Alain Sayag and Annick Lionel-Marie. London: Thames & Hudson, 2000: 200.

12. Charles Wentinck offers the seductive juxtaposition of a Paleolithic female figurine carved in a dark soapstone, and known as the *Trasimeno Venus*, with Brassaï's *Black Venus* (undated), noting that the latter also carries echoes of the schematic style of Cycladic sculpture. See Wentinck. *Modern and Primitive Art*, figures 27a and 27b.

13. The catalog *Alberto Giacometti: Le Dessin à l'œuvre*, Paris: Centre Pompidou, 2001, reproduces the artist's copies of Cycladic statuettes from the British Museum (pp. 84 and 115), dated 1922–1927 and 1937, respectively, as well as a 1929 sketch (p. 78) of the *Laussel Venus* (discovered in the 1910s). It is perfectly possible that each of these sketches was based upon a magazine illustration.

14. The French poet and critic Claude Roy (1915–1997), author of books on archaic and tribal art, has argued of the markings at Naquane in the Val Camonica that they represent the final stage of a progression from iconic representation to abstract symbolism, such glyphs, or ideograms, falling just short of becoming actual writing. See his "Naquane, ou la signification des signes." In *Naquane: Découverte d'un pays et d'une civilisation*, Fulvio Roiter, Claude Roy, and Emmanuel Anati. Éditions Clairefontaine, Lausanne, 1966: 9–21.

15. Although many publications cite this statement, none I have seen actually gives an original source for it.

16. One tale is that he clambered into the cave after the Abbé Breuil to watch him copying the bulls on the cave ceiling. The anecdote is mentioned by Guy Davenport in "The Symbol of the Archaic," p. 21, but I have yet to see it corroborated.

17. Rubin. *"Primitivism" in 20th Century Art*, vol. 1: 268.

18. Robert Hobbs. "Haydn Stubbing: School of Altamira." *N. H. (Tony) Stubbing Retrospective*. Exhibition catalog. London: England & Co, 2000: 22–24; quotation from p. 22.

19. In fact, the majority of the hand prints at El Castillo are stenciled outlines produced by puffing or spraying pigment around the hand. In the 1980s and 1990s, the British artist Richard Long produced several large works made by slapping mud from the River Avon onto a wall with his bare hands. Stubbing was forced to discontinue his hand-painting in the late 1960s because of a suspected allergy to oil paint.

20. See Raymond Queneau. "Miró ou le poète préhistorique." *Bâtons, chiffres et lettres*. Paris: Gallimard, 1965: 305–316. Queneau's title is reminiscent of that of Carl Einstein's essay on Hans Arp, "L'Enfance néolithique." Miró's observations on art are in *Joan Miró. Selected Writings and Interviews*, ed. Margit Rowell. London: Thames & Hudson, 1987.

21. See Wentinck. *Modern and Primitive Art*, figures 33a and 33b.

22. See Wentinck, figures 31a and 31b. Another parallel might be drawn between

the obese *Willendorf Venus* (discovered in Austria in 1908) and the outrageously corpulent female nudes of Dubuffet's *Corps de dames* series (1950–1951). Interestingly, it was Picasso who owned a copy of the *Lespugue Venus*, an intriguing ivory figurine found in 1922.

23. See Brassaï. "Du mur des cavernes au mur des usines." *Minotaure* 3–4 (1933): 6–7; translated as "From Cave Wall to Factory Wall" in *Brassaï: "No Ordinary Eyes,"* Sayag and Lionel-Marie, p. 292.

24. It may be noted that as early as 1910, Georges-Henri Luquet, author of studies of prehistoric art, tribal art, and child art, wrote an article about prehistoric imagery, seen in the light of modern graffiti. See his article "Sur les caractères des figures humaines dans l'art paléolithique." *L'Anthropologie* 21 (1910): 409–423.

25. Radiocarbon dating, pioneered only in the 1950s, would assign to the Lascaux murals a putative date of no earlier than 20,000 B.C. The discovery in the 1990s of the magnificent caves of Cosquer and Chauvet finally exposed the myth of Lascaux as the birthplace of art, for their novel compositions date back at least 10,000 years earlier! Of course, it is too early to tell what impact these designs may be exerting upon the art of our own epoch.

26. That telling phrase "the birth of art" appears in Bataille's title, but had been used earlier in, for instance, Virgilio Ghilardoni's less well known book, *Naissance de l'Art*. Lausanne: La Guilde du Livre, 1948. Doubtless this was not the first time the idea had been put forward, though it is revealing to witness Ghilardoni's dramatic crystallization of the notion of a primordial creative moment: "L'art, tout l'art du monde, est né avec la première pierre taillée sortie des mains du chasseur préhistorique." [Art, the whole of world art, was born when the first carved stone sprang from the hands of the prehistoric hunter.] (p. 8). Ghilardoni expounds the theme of artistic universalism and provides an erudite conspectus of prehistoric and tribal art, with plates ranging from Aurignacian figurines to Oceanic masks.

27. It may be surmised that postwar France was particularly receptive to such flamboyant readings. The near-coincidence of the Fall of France in June 1940 and the discovery of Lascaux in September of that year points to the emergence of Lascaux as an icon of self-determination in the Resistance and post-Liberation years.

28. In 1952, the Resistance poet René Char (1907–1988) published a set of four short poems under the general title "Lascaux." Conveying both horror and fascination, they focus upon the Well Scene, the frieze of black deer, the enigmatic two-horned beast dubbed the Unicorn, and the young horse with the vaporous mane. Elisabeth Bosch suggests that Char might have discussed Lascaux with Bataille, who was working on his famous book at the time. See Elisabeth Bosch. "René Char, Georges Bataille et Lascaux." In *Lectures de René Char*, ed. Tineke Kingma-Eijgendaal and Paul J. Smith. Amsterdam: Rodopi, 1990: 98–117.

29. In *Overlay*, Lucy Lippard acknowledges a widespread nostalgia for distant cultures and examines the ritualism of Land Art, focusing largely on American practitioners like Carl André, Robert Smithson, Michelle Stuart, and Bill Vazan.

30. See Jacquetta Hawkes. *A Land*. London: Cresset Press, 1953: 185–186. Moore contributed two color plates to this book, implying the continuity of his sculptural vision with the forms of the British landscape.

31. Michael Tucker. *Dreaming with Open Eyes: The Shamanic Spirit in Twentieth Century Art and Culture*. San Francisco, CA: Aquarian/Harper, 1992.

32. See Guy Davenport. "The Symbol of the Archaic," p. 20.

Selective Bibliography

Compiled by Günter Berghaus

This bibliography lists publications predominantly of recent date, and some important studies from the late nineteenth and early twentieth centuries. Coverage is worldwide, although the profusion of studies dedicated to the classic regions of France and Spain means also that this bibliography has a strong European bias. I have, on the whole, omitted books dedicated to individual sites, as inclusion of such studies would have inflated this list to an unacceptable size. However, given the historic role and the important dating issues involved with some sites such as Altamira, Lascaux, Rouffignac, Niaux, Cosquer, Cougnac, Gargas, Pergouset, and Pech Merle, some exceptions had to be made to this general rule.

PERIODICALS

Adoranten: Årsskrift för Scandinavian Society for Prehistoric Art. Underslös: Tanums Hällristningsmuseum, 1978ff.

American Indian Rock Art. El Paso, TX: Archaeological Society, 1975ff.

Ars praehistorica. Anuario internacional de arte prehistórico. Sabadell/Barcelona: Editorial AUSA, 1982–1989.

Bollettino del Centro Camuno di Studi Preistorici. Capo di Ponte: Centro Camuno di Studi Preistorici, 1964/65ff.

Canadian Rock Art Research Association Newsletter. Saskatoon (Saskatchewan): Canadian Rock Art Research Association, 1973ff.

Contribuciones al estudio del arte rupestre sudamericano. La Paz: SIARB, 1987ff.

IPEK: Jahrbuch für prähistorische und ethnographische Kunst = Annual Review of Prehistoric and Ethnographical Art = Annuaire d'art préhistorique et ethnographique. Berlin and New York: De Gruyter, 1925–1977.

Jahrbuch der Gesellschaft für Vergleichende Felsbildforschung. Graz, 1977ff.

International Newsletter on Rock Art: I.N.O.R.A., Foix: C.A.R (Comité International d'Art Rupestre/International Committee on Rock Art); Union Internationale des Sciences Préhistoriques et Protohistoriques (U.I.S.P.P. Commission 9: Art Préhistorique)/International Union of Prehistoric and Protohistoric Sciences. Commission 9; Association Pour le Rayonnement de l'Art Pariétal Européen, 1992ff.

Mitteilungen der ANISA. Gröbming: ANISA [Verein für die Erforschung und Erhaltung der Altertümer, im Speziellen der Felsbilder in den Österreichischen Alpen; Verein für Alpine Felsbild- und Siedlungsforschung], 1980ff.

Pictogram. Parkhurst: Southern African Rock Art Research Association, 1987ff.

La Pictura: Rock Art Symposium Newsletter. Whittier, CA: Rock Art Symposium, 1974ff.

La Pintura: American Rock Art Research Association Newsletter. El Toro, CA: American Rock Art Research Association, 1974ff.

Rock Art Papers. San Diego, CA: San Diego Museum of Man, 1983ff. [Published as part of *San Diego Museum Papers* vol. 16 ff.]

Rock Art Quarterly. Winnepeg: Rock Art Association of Canada, 1990ff.

Rock Art Research: The Journal of the Australian Rock Art Research Association (AURA). Melbourne: Archaeological Publications, 1984ff.

Travaux de L'Institut d'Art Préhistorique de la Faculté des Lettres et Sciences Humaines, Université de Toulouse–Le Mirail. Toulouse: L'Institut, 1958–1991.

BOOKS AND ESSAYS

A arte em Lepenski Vir. Exh. cat. Lisboa: Galeria de Exposiçoes Temporárias, 1986; Lisboa: Coelho Dias, 1986.

Abélanet, Jean. *Signes sans paroles: Cent siècles d'art rupestre en Europe occidentale.* Paris: Hachette, 1986.

Abramova, Zoia Aleksandrovna. *L'Art paléolithique d'Europe orientale et de Sibérie.* Grenoble: Millon, 1995.

———. *Paleoliticheskoye iskusstvo na territoriyi SSSR.* Leningrad: Izdatel'stvo Akademii nauk SSSR, 1962; Engl. ed. "Palaeolithic Art in the USSR." *Arctic Anthropology* 4:2 (1967): 1–179; *Palaeolithic Art in the U.S.S.R.* Madison, WI: University of Wisconsin Press, 1967.

———. *Izobrazheniia cheloveka v paleoliticheskom iskusstve Evrazii.* Leningrad: Nauka [Leningradskoe otdelenie], 1966.

Abramova, Zoia Aleksandrovna and Paolo Graziosi, eds. *Les Courants stylistiques dans l'art mobilier au paléolithique supérieur: [IXe Congrés Union Internationale des Sciences Préhistoriques et Protohistoriques (U.I.S.P.P.)] Colloque XIV: Nice, vendredi 17 septembre [1976].* Paris: Centre National de la Recherche Scientifique, 1976.

Acanfora, Maria Ornella. *Pittura dell'età preistorica.* Milano: Società Editrice Libraria, 1960.

Acosta Martínez, Pilar. *Representaciones de ídolos en la pintura rupestre esquemática española.* Madrid: Librería Científica del Consejo Superior de Investigaciones Científicas, 1967.

———. *La pintura rupestre esquemática en España.* Salamanca: Universidad de Salamanca, 1968.

Actas del VIII simposium internacional de arte rupestre americano: Museo del Hombre Dominicano, 8–13 de junio de 1987, Santo Domingo, D.N., República Dominicana = Proceedings of the VIII International Symposium of American Rock Art: June 8–13, 1987, Museo del Hombre Dominicano, Santo Domingo, D.N., Dominican Republic. Santo Domingo: El Museo, 1987 [i.e., 1988].

Adam, J. C.. *Reconnaissance de rupestres dans l'Ahnet, Sahara algérien.* Paris: Harmattan, 1992.

Adam, Karl Dietrich and Renate Kurz. *Eiszeitkunst im süddeutschen Raum.* Stuttgart: Theiss, 1980.

Adán Alvarez, Gema Elvira, et al. *Deesses: Imatges femenines de la Mediterrània de la prehistòria al món romà = Diosas: Imágenes femeninas del Mediterráneo de la prehistoria al mundo romano = Goddesses: Mediterranean Female Images from Prehistoric Times to the Roman Period.* Exh. cat. Barcelona: Museu d'Història de la Ciutat, 2000.

Ageorges, Véronique and Henri de Saint-Blaquant. *Lascaux et son temps.* Paris: Casterman, 1989.

Aguilar, Nelson, ed. *Mostra do Redescobrimento. Arte: Evolução ou revolução? A primeira descoberta da América = Art: Evolution or Revolution? The First Discovery of the Americas.* Exh. cat. São Paulo: Parque Ibirapuera, 2000. São Paulo: Fundação Bienal de São Paulo, 2000.

Airvaux, Jean. *L'Art préhistorique du Poitou-Charentes: Sculptures et gravures des temps glaciaires.* Paris: Maison des Roches, 2001.

Alcalde del Río, Hermilio. *Las pinturas y grabados de los cavernas prehistóricas de la provincia de Santander: Altamira, Covalanas, Hornos de la Peña, Castillo.* Santander: Blanchard y Arce, 1906.

Alcalde del Río, Hermilio, Henri Breuil, and Lorenzo Sierra. *Les Cavernes de la région cantabrique (Espagne).* Monaco: Chêne, 1911.

Aldunate del Solar, Carlos, José Berenguer Rodríguez, and Victoria Castro Rojas, eds. *Estudios en arte rupestre: Primeras Jornadas de Arte y Arqueología. El arte rupestre en Chile, Santiago 16 al 19 de 1983.* Santiago de Chile: Museo Chileno de Arte Precolombino, 1985.

Aldunate del Solar, Carlos and Francisco Gallardo Ibánez, eds. *Arte rupestre en los Andes de Capricornio.* Santiago de Chile: Banco Santiago, 1999.

Alfaro de Lanzone, Lidia Carlota *Miscelánea de arte rupestre de la República Argentina.* Barcelona: Diputación Provincial de Barcelona, Instituto de Prehistoria y Arqueología; New York: Wenner Gren Foundation for Anthropological Research, 1979.

Alland, Alexander. *The Artistic Animal: An Inquiry into the Biological Roots of Art.* Garden City, NY: Anchor Books, 1977.

Almagro Basch, Martin. *Altamira, cumbre del arte prehistórico.* Madrid: Instituto Español de Antropologia Aplicada, 1968.

Almagro Basch, Martin and Antonio García y Bellido. *Arte prehistórico.* Madrid, Editorial Plus-Ultra, 1947.

Almagro Basch, Martín and Martín Almagro Gorbea. *Estudios de arte rupestre nubio.* Vol.1: *Yacimientos situados en la orilla oriental del Nilo, entre Nag Kolorodna y Kars Ibrim (Nubia egipcia).* Madrid: Ministerio de Asuntos Exteriores. Dirección General de Relaciones Culturales, 1968.

Almagro Basch, Martín and Miguel Ángel García Guinea, eds. *Santander Sympo-*

*sium: Actas del symposium internacional de arte rupestre, Santander-Asturias, 14
al 20 de Septiembre 1970.* Santander: Museo de Prehistoria, and Madrid: Librería Científica del Consejo Superior de Investigaciones Científicas, 1972.

Almgren, Oscar. *Nordische Felszeichnungen als religiöse Urkunden.* Frankfurt am Main: Diesterweg, 1934.

Alonso Tejada, Ana and Alexandre Grimal. *Investigaciones sobre arte rupestre prehistórico en las Sierras Albacetenses: El Cerro Barbatón.* Albacete: Instituto de Estudios Albacetenses de la Excma. Diputación de Albacete, 1996.

Altamira Symposium: Actas del symposium internacional sobre arte prehistórico celebrado en conmemoración del primer centenario del descubrimiento de las pinturas de Altamira (1879–1979). Madrid: Ministerio de Cultura, Dirección General de Bellas Artes, Archivos y Bibliotecas, Subdirección General de Arqueologia, 1981.

Altuna, Jesús. *Las figuras rupestres paleolíticas de la cueva de Altxerri (Guipuzcoa).* San Sebastian: Sociedad de Ciencias Naturales Aranzadi, 1976.

———. "On the Relationship between Archaeo-faunas and Parietal Art in the Caves of the Cantabrian Region." In *Animals and Archaeology: Hunters and their Prey,* ed. Juliet Clutton-Brock and Caroline Grigson. Vol. 1. Oxford: British Archaeological Reports, 1983: 227–238.

———. "La relacion fauna consumida—fauna representada en el Paleolítico Superior cantábrico." *Arte paleolítico,* ed. Teresa Chapa Brunet and Mario Menéndez Fernández. Madrid: Editorial Complutense, 1994: 303–312.

Altuna, Jesús, Amelia Baldeon Inigo, and Koro Mariezkurrena. *Ekain und Altxerri bei San Sebastian: Zwei altsteinzeitliche Bilderhöhlen im spanischen Baskenland.* Sigmaringen: Thorbecke, 1996; French ed. *L'Art des cavernes en Pays basque, Ekain et Altxerri.* Paris: Seuil, 1997.

Anati, Ariela Fradkin and Thomas King, eds. *Who's Who in Rock Art: A World Directory of Specialists, Scholars and Technicians in Rock Art;* 2nd ed. Capo di Ponte: Edizioni del Centro, 1996.

Anati, Emmanuel. *La Civilisation du Val Camonica.* Paris: Arthaud, 1960; Engl. ed. *Camonica Valley: A Depiction of Village Life in the Alps from Neolithic Times to the Birth of Christ, As Revealed by Thousands of Newly Found Rock Carvings.* New York: Knopf, 1961.

———. *Rock-art in Central Arabia.* 4 vols. Louvain: Institut Orientaliste, 1968–1974.

———. *Arte rupestre nelle regioni occidentali della penisola Iberica.* Capo di Ponte: Edizioni del Centro, 1968.

———. *Arte preistorica in Valtellina.* Capo di Ponte: Edizioni del Centro, 1968.

———. *Origini della civiltà camuna.* Capo di Ponte: Edizioni del Centro, 1968; 2nd ed. 1974.

———. *Arte preistorica in Anatolia.* Capo di Ponte: Edizioni del Centro, 1972.

———. *Evoluzione e stile nell'arte rupestre camuna.* Capo de Ponte: Edizioni del Centro, 1975; Engl. ed. *Evolution and Style in Camunian Rock Art.* Capo de Ponte: Edizioni del Centro, 1976.

———. *Metodi di rilevamento e di analisi dell'arte rupestre.* 2nd ed. Capo di Ponte: Edizioni del Centro, 1976.

———. "The Origins of Art." *Museum* 23 (1981): 200–210.

———. *Valcamonica: 10.000 anni di storia.* 2nd ed. Capo di Ponte: Edizioni del Centro, 1982.

————. "The State of Research in Rock Art." *Bollettino del Centro Camuno di Studi Preistorici* 21 (1984): 13–56.

————. "État de la recherche sur l'art rupestre: Rapport mondial." *L'Anthropologie* 90 (1986): 783–800.

————. *The Plaza Sites of Har Karkom = I siti a plaza di Har Karkom.* Capo di Ponte: Edizioni del Centro, 1987.

————. *Le origini e il problema dell'homo religiosus.* Milano: Jaca Book-Massimo, 1989; French ed. *Origines et le problème de l'homo religiosus.* Paris: Desclée, 1992.

————. *Origini dell'arte e della concettualità.* Milano: Jaca Book, 1989; French ed. *Origines de l'art.* Paris: Albin Michel, 1989.

————. *Le origini della Valtellina e della Valchiavenna: Contributi di storia sociale dalla preistoria all'alto medioevo.* Sondrio: Centro Culturale e Sociale "Don Minzoni," 1989.

————. *Le radici della cultura.* Milano: Jaca Book, 1992; French ed. *Les Racines de la culture.* Capo di Ponte: Edizioni del Centro, 1995.

————. *Rock Art: The State of Research. Archetypes, Constants and Universal Paradigms.* Colombo: ICOMOS, 1993.

————. *World Rock Art: The Primordial Language.* Capo di Ponte: Edizioni del Centro, 1993.

————. *Il linguaggio delle pietre: Valcamonica, una storia per l'Europa.* Capo di Ponte: Edizioni del Centro, 1994.

————. *La religione delle origini.* Capo di Ponte: Edizioni del Centro, 1995.

————. *Il museo immaginario della preistoria: L'arte rupestre nel mondo.* Milano: Jaca Book, 1995.

————. "The Art of Beginnings." *Diogenes* 47:1 (#185) (1999): 5–16.

Anati, Emmanuel, ed. *Symposium international d'art préhistorique: Valcamonica, 23–28 Septembre 1968.* Capo di Ponte: Edizioni del Centro, 1970.

————. *Symposium international sur les religions de la préhistoire: Valcamonica, 18–23 Septembre 1972.* Capo di Ponte: Edizioni del Centro, 1975.

————. *The Intellectual Expression of Prehistoric Man: Art and Religion: Acts of the Valcamonica Symposium 1979.* Capo di Ponte: Edizioni del Centro, 1983.

Anderson, Irene. *Rock Paintings and Petroglyphs of South and Central Africa, 1959–1970: A Bibliography.* Johannesburg: University of Witwatersrand, Department of Bibliography, Librarianship and Typography, 1971.

Anderson, Richard L. *Art in Primitive Societies.* Englewood Cliffs, NJ: Prentice-Hall, 1979; 2nd ed. *Art in Small-scale Societies.* Englewood Cliffs, NJ: Prentice-Hall, 1989.

Angel, Myron. *The Painted Rock of California: La piedra pintada. A Legend.* San Luis Obispo, CA: Padre Productions, 1979.

Aparicio Pérez, José and Julián San Valero Aparisi. *El primer arte valenciano.* Vol. 1: *El arte parpallones.* Valencia: Instituto Valenciano para el Estudio y Protección del Patrimonio Histórico-Artístico y Arqueológico, 1983.

Aparicio Pérez, José, Vicente Meseguer Folch, and Federico Rubio Gomis. *El primer arte Valenciano.* Vol. 2: *"El arte rupestre levantino".* Valencia: Instituto Valenciano para el Estudio y Protección del Patrimonio Histórico-Artístico y Arqueológico, 1982.

Aparicio Pérez, José, Antonio Beltrán Martínez, and J. de D. Boronat Soler. *Nuevas pinturas rupestres en la Comunidad Valenciana*. 2 vols. Valencia: Academia de Cultura Valencia, 1988.

Apellániz, Juan María. *El arte prehistórico del País Vasco y sus vecinos*. Bilbao: Desclée de Brouwer, 1982.

———. *Modelo de análisis de la autoría en el arte figurativo del paleolítico*. Bilbao: Universidad de Deusto, 1991.

———. *La abstracción en el arte figurativo del paleolítico: Análisis del componente abstracto en la figuración naturalista del grafismo paleolítico*. Bilbao: Universidad de Deusto, 2001.

Apellániz, Juan María and Félix Calvo Gómez. *La forma del arte paleolítico y la estadística: Análisis de la forma del arte figurativo paleolítico y su tratamiento estadístico*. Bilbao: Universidad de Deusto, 1999.

Appenzeller, Tim. "Art: Evolution or Revolution?" *Science* 282:5393 (20 November 1998): 1451–1454.

Arbore-Popescu, Grigore, Andrei Alekseev, and Jurij Piotrovskij, eds. *Siberia: Gli uomini dei fiumi ghiacciati*. Exh. cat. Trieste: Scuderie del Castello di Miramare, 2001. Milano: Electa, 2001.

Arcà, Andrea and Angelo Fossati, eds. *Sui sentieri dell'arte rupestre: Le rocce incise delle Alpi. Storia, ricerche, escursioni*. Torino: CDA, 1995.

Archer, William George and Robert Melville, eds. *40,000 Years of Modern Art: A Comparison of Primitive and Modern*. Exh. cat. London: Institute of Contemporary Arts, 1948–1949.

L'Art des cavernes: Atlas des grottes ornées paléolithiques françaises. Paris: Ministère de la Culture, Direction du Patrimoine, Sous-direction de l'Archéologie. Imprimerie Nationale, 1984.

L'art esquematic. Exh. cat. Cocentaina, Palau Comtlal, 2000. Concentaina: Centre d'Estudis Contestans, 2000.

Art paleolític i postpaleolític: Recull de les conferències donades al Museu Arqueològic de Barcelona els anys 1988 i 1989. Barcelona: Museu Arqueològic; Diputació de Barcelona, [1992?].

Artamonov, Michail Illarionovich, ed. *The Dawn of Art: Palaeolithic, Neolithic, Bronze Age, and Iron Age Remains Found in the Territory of the Soviet Union. The Hermitage Collection*. Leningrad: Aurora Art Publishers, 1974.

Arte preistorica del Sahara. Exh. cat. Firenze: Museo Archeologico, 1986; Roma: DeLuca; Milano: Mondadori, 1986.

Arte rupestre del Sahara = Art rupestre du Sahara = Rock Art of Sahara. [News 95 International Rock Art Congress, Turin, 1995]. s.l.: Association des Amis de l'Art Rupestre Saharien, 1995.

El arte rupestre en Chile. Exh. cat. Santiago de Chile: Museo Chileno de Arte Precolombino, [1983?].

Arte rupestre en España. Special issue of *Revista de arqueología* 7 (April 1987). Madrid: Zugarto Ediciones, 1987.

Arutiunov, Sergej Aleksandrovic. "The Many Levels of the Problem of the Genesis of Art." *Soviet Anthropology and Anthropology* 16:3–4 (Winter-Spring 1977–78): 72–79.

Aumassip, Ginette. *Chronologies de l'Art rupestre saharien et nord africain*. Calvisson: Gandini, 1993.

Aumassip, Ginette, John Desmond Clark, and Fabrizio Mori, eds. *The Prehistory of*

Africa. International Congress of Prehistoric and Protohistoric Sciences (13th: 1996: Forlì, Italy). Colloquium XXIX: The Most Ancient Manifestations of Rock-Art in Africa and Their "Religiousness." Colloquium XXX: The Concept of the "Neolithic" in Africa, with Particular Reference to the Saharan Region. Forlì: A.B.A.C.O., 1996.

Australian Rock Art Heritage: A Bibliography from HERA. Canberra, ACT: Austrian Heritage Commission, 1988. Rev. ed. *Australian Rock Art.* Canberra, ACT: Austrian Government Publication Service, 1989; 2nd rev. ed. 1990.

Avant les Scythes: Préhistoire de l'art en U.R.S.S. Exh. cat. Paris: Grand Palais 1979. Paris: Éditions de la Réunion des Musées Nationaux, 1979.

Bahn, Paul G. "New Advances in the Field of Ice Age Art." In *Origins of Anatomically Modern Humans,* ed. Matthew H. Nitecki and Doris V. Nitecki. New York: Plenum Press, 1994. 121–132.

———. "No Sex Please, We're Aurignacians." *Rock Art Research* 3 (1986): 99–120.

———. "Lascaux: Composition or Accumulation?" *Zephyrus* 47 (1994): 3–13.

———. "Some New Developments in Ice Age Art." In *Arte paleolítico,* ed. Teresa Chapa Brunet and Mario Menéndez Fernández. Madrid: Editorial Complutense, 1994. 197–202.

———. "Membrane and Numb Brain: A Close Look at a Recent Claim for Shamanism in Palaeolithic Art." *Rock Art Research* 14 (1997): 62–68.

———. "Dancing in the Dark: Probing the Phenomenon of Pleistocene Cave Art." In *The Human Use of Caves,* ed. Clive Bonsall and Christopher Tolan-Smith. Oxford: Archaeopress, 1997. 35–37.

———. *The Cambridge Illustrated History of Prehistoric Art.* Cambridge: Cambridge University Press, 1998.

Bahn, Paul G. and Angelo Fossati, eds. *Rock Art Studies: News of the World I. Recent Developments in Rock Art Research. Acts of Symposium 14D at the NEWS95 World Rock Art Congress, Turin and Pinerolo, Italy.* Oxford: Oxbow, 1996.

Bahn, Paul G. and Andrée Rosenfeld, eds. *Rock Art and Prehistory: Papers Presented to Symposium G of the AURA Congress, Darwin 1988.* Oxford: Oxbow Books, 1991.

Bahn, Paul G. and Jean Vertut. *Images of the Ice Age.* New York: Facts on File, 1988; 2nd ed. *Journey Through the Ice Age.* London: Weidenfeld & Nicolson, 1997.

Balter, Michael. "New Light on the Oldest Stone Art." *Science* 283:5404 (12 February 1999): 920–922.

Bandaranayake, Senake. *The Rock and Wall Paintings of Sri Lanka.* Colombo: Lake House Bookshop, 1986.

Bandi, Hans-Georg. *L'Art préhistorique: Les cavernes. Le Levant espagnol. Les régions Artiques.* Fribourg: Office du Livre, [1955?].

Bandi, Hans-Georg, Henri Breuil, Lilo Berger-Kirchner, and Henri Lhote. *Die Steinzeit.* Baden-Baden: Holle, 1961; Engl. ed. *The Art of the Stone Age: Forty Thousand Years of Rock Art.* London: Methuen, 1961; French ed. *L'Age de pierre: Quarante millénaires d'art pariétal.* Paris: Michel, 1961; Spanish ed. *La edad de piedra.* Barcelona: Praxis, 1962.

Bandi, Hans-Georg, Walter Huber, Marc-Roland Sauter, and Beat Sitter, eds. *La Contribution de la zoologie et de l'éthologie à l'interprétation de l'art des peuples chasseurs préhistoriques: 3e Colloque de la Société Suisse des Sciences Humaines, 1979.* Fribourg: Éditions Universitaires, 1984.

Barandiarán Maestu, Ignacio. *Arte mueble del paleolítico cantábrico.* Zaragoza: Departamentos de Prehistoria y Arqueología de la Universidad, 1972.

Barandiarán, José Miguel de, Joaquin González Echegaray, and Julián San Valero Aparisi: *El hombre prehistórico y el arte rupestre en España.* Bilbao: Junta de Cultura de Vizcaya, 1962.

Barham, Lawrence S. *The Middle Stone Age of Zambia, South-central Africa.* Bristol: Western Academic and Specialist Press, 2000.

———. "Systematic Pigment Use in the Middle Pleistocene of South-central Africa." *Current Anthropology* 43:1 (February 2002): 181–190.

Barnard, Alan. "Modern Hunter-gatherers and Early Symbolic Culture." In *The Evolution of Culture: An Interdisciplinary View,* ed. Robin Dunbar, Chris Knight, and Camilla Power. New Brunswick, NJ: Rutgers University Press, 1999: 50–68.

Barnes, Francis Audrey. *Canyon Country Prehistoric Rock Art: An Illustrated Guide to Viewing, Understanding, and Appreciating the Rock Art of the Prehistoric Indian Cultures of Utah, the Great Basin and the General Four Corners Region.* Salt Lake City, UT: Wasatch Publishers, 1982.

Barrière, Claude. *L'Art pariétal de Rouffignac: La grotte aux cent mammouths.* Paris: Fondation Singer-Polignac & Picard, 1982.

Barrière, Claude and Ali Sahly. *L'Art pariétal de la Grotte de Gargas = Palaeolithic Art in the Grotte de Gargas.* Oxford: British Archaeological Reports, 1976.

Barton, C. Michael, Geoffrey A. Clark, and Allison E. Cohen. "Art as Information: Explaining Upper Palaeolithic Art in Western Europe." *World Archaeology* 26 (1994): 185–207.

Bassett, Stephen Townley. *Rock Paintings of South Africa.* Cape Town: Philip; London: Global, 2002.

Bataille, Georges. *La Peinture préhistorique: Lascaux ou la Naissance de l'art.* Lausanne: Skira, 1955; reprinted in Georges Bataille: *Œuvres complètes,* vol. 9 Paris: Gallimard, 1979; Engl. ed. *Lascaux, or The Birth of Art: Prehistoric Painting.* Lausanne: Skira, 1955; 2nd ed. *Prehistoric Painting: Lascaux or the Birth of Art.* London: Macmillan, 1980.

Battiss, Walter W. *Art in South Africa: The Amazing Bushman.* Pretoria: Red Fawn Press, 1939.

———. *The Artists of the Rocks.* Pretoria: Red Fawn Press, 1948.

Beck, Dunja. *Das Mittelpaläolithikum des Hohlenstein-Stadel und die Bärenhöhle im Lonetal.* Bonn: Habelt, 1999.

Beckensall, Stan. *British Prehistoric Rock Art.* Stroud, and Charleston/SC: Tempus, 1999.

Bednarik, Robert G. "Parietal Finger Markings in Europe and Australia." *Rock Art Research* 3 (1986): 30–61; 159–170.

———. "On Neuropsychology and Shamanism in Rock Art." *Current Anthropology* 31 (1990): 77–80.

———. "Rock Art as a Cultural Determinant." *Survey* 5–6 (1991–1992): 11–20.

———. "Palaeoart and Archaeological Myths." *Cambridge Archaeological Journal* 2 (1992): 27–57.

———. "European Palaeolithic Art: Typical or Exceptional?" *Oxford Journal of Archaeology* 12 (1993): 1–8.

———. " Oldest Dated Rock Art in the World." *International Newsletter of Rock Art* 4 (1993): 5–6.

———. "A Taphonomy of Palaeoart." *Antiquity* 68 (1994): 68–74.

———. "Concept-mediated Marking in the Lower Palaeolithic." *Current Anthropology* 36 (1995): 623–625.

———. "European Art: The Palaeolithic Legacy." *Cambridge Archaeological Journal* 7 (1997): 255–268.

———. "The Technology of Petroglyphs." *Rock Art Research* 15 (1998): 23–35.

———. *Rock Art Science: The Scientific Study of Palaeoart.* Turnhout: Brepols, 2001.

Bégouën, Henri. "The Magic Origin of Prehistoric Art." *Antiquity* 3 (1929): 5–19.

———. "A propos de l'idée de fécondité dans l'iconographie préhistorique." *Bulletin de la Société Préhistorique Française* 29 (1929): 197–199.

Bégouën, Henri and Henri Breuil. *Les Cavernes du Volp. Trois Frères, Tuc d'Audoubert.* Paris: Arts et Métiers Graphiques, 1958. Reprint Tucson, AZ: American Rock Art Research Association, 1999.

Behn, Friedrich. *Vorgeschichtliche Felsbilder in Karelien und West-Sibirien.* Berlin: Sächsische Akademie der Wissenschaften, Akademie-Verlag, 1950.

———. *Zur Problematik der Felsbilder.* Berlin: Sächsische Akademie der Wissenschaften, Akademie-Verlag, 1962.

Behn, Friedrich and Dominik Josef Wölfel. *L'Art préhistorique en Europe.* Paris: Payot, 1960; German ed. *Vorgeschichtliche Kunst in Europa.* Berlin: Ullstein, 1963; Spanish ed. *El arte prehistórico en Europa.* Bilbao: Moretón, 1967.

Beltrán Martínez, Antonio. *Arte rupestre levantino.* Zaragoza: Seminario de Prehistoria y Protohistoria, 1968.

———. *Arte rupestre levantino: Adiciones 1968–1978.* Zaragoza: Departamento de Prehistoria y Arqueología, 1979.

———. *Da cacciatori ad allevatori: L'arte rupestre del Levante spagnolo.* Milano: Jaca, 1980; Spanish ed. *De cazadores a pastores: El arte rupestre del Levante español.* Madrid: Encuentro, 1982; Engl. ed. *Rock Art of the Spanish Levant.* Cambridge: Cambridge University Press, 1982.

———. *Ensayo sobre el orígen y significación del arte prehistórico.* Zaragoza: Prensas Universitarias Zaragoza, 1989.

———. *Arte prehistórico en Aragón.* Zaragoza: Caja de Ahorros y Monte de Piedad de Zaragoza, Aragón y la Rioja, 1993.

———. *Arte prehistórico en la península ibérica.* Castelló: Diputació de Castelló, Servei d'Investigacions Arqueològiques i Prehistòriques, 1998.

Beltrán Martínez, Antonio, René Gailli, and Romain Robert: *La cueva de Niaux.* Zaragoza: Departamento de Prehistoria y Arqueología, 1973.

Beltrán Martínez, Antonio, ed. *Altamira. Fotografía, Pedro A. Saura Ramos.* Barcelona: Lunwerg, 1998; Engl. ed. *The Cave of Altamira. Photographs by Pedro A. Saura Ramos. With Essays by Matilde Múzquiz Pérez-Seoane et al.* New York: Abrams, 1999.

Benz-Zauner, Margareta. *Altamira: Höhlenmalerei der Steinzeit.* Exh. cat. München: Deutsches Museum, 1995.

Berenguer, Magín. *Prehistoric Man and His Art: The Caves of Ribadesella.* Park Ridge, NJ: Noyes Press, 1973.

———. *El arte prehistórico en la "Cueva Tito Bustillo" (Ribadesella-Asturias).* Madrid: Editorial Everest, 1985.

————. *Arte prehistórico en cuevas del norte de España, Asturias = Prehistoric Cave Art in Northern Spain, Asturias*. Ciudad de México: Frente de Afirmación Hispanista, 1994.

Bernaldo de Quirós, Federico and Victoria Cabrera Valdés. *El arte paleolítico en la cornisa cantábrica*. Madrid: Ministerio de Cultura, Dirección General de Bellas Artes, Archivos y Bibliotecas, 1982.

Bicknell, Clarence A. *The Prehistoric Rock Engravings in the Italian Maritime Alps*. Bordighera: Gibelli, 1902; 2nd ed. 1911.

————. *A Guide to the Prehistoric Rock Engravings in the Italian Maritime Alps*. Bordighera: Bessone, 1913.

Bicknell, Robin Scott. *Images from the Past: Rock Art: A Self-guided Tour of Petroglyphs and Pictographs of the American Southwest*. Tucson, AZ: Patrice Press, 2001.

Biedermann, Hans. *Lexikon der Felsbildkunst*. Graz: Verlag für Sammler, 1976.

————. *Höhlenkunst der Eiszeit: Wege zur Sinndeutung der ältesten Kunst Europas*. Köln: DuMont, 1984.

Blundell, Geoffrey, Christopher Chippindale, and Benjamin Smith, eds. *Knowing and Seeing: Understanding Rock Art With and Without Ethnography*. Forthcoming.

Bordes, François. "Sur l'usage probable de la peinture corporelle dans certaines tribus moustériennes." *Bulletin de la Société Préhistorique Française* 49 (1952): 169–171.

Bosinski, Gerhard. *Die Kunst der Eiszeit in Deutschland und in der Schweiz*. Bonn: Habelt, 1982.

Bosinski, Gerhard and Gisela Fischer. *Die Menschendarstellungen von Gönnersdorf der Ausgrabung von 1968*. Wiesbaden: Steiner, 1974.

————. *Mammut- und Pferdedarstellungen in Gönnersdorf*. Wiesbaden: Steiner, 1980.

Bosinksi, Gerhard, Francesco d'Errico, and Petra Schiller. *Die gravierten Frauendarstellungen von Gönnersdorf*. Stuttgart: Steiner, 2001.

Boucher de Perthes, Jacques. *Antiquités celtiques et antédiluviennes: Mémoire sur l'industrie primitive et les arts à leur origine*. 3 vol. Paris: Treuttel et Würtz, 1847–1864.

————. *De l'Homme antédiluvien et de ses œuvres*. Paris: Jung-Treuttel, 1860; 2nd ed. 1864.

Bourdier, Franck. *L'Art préhistoriques et ses essais d'interprétation*. Paris: Université de Paris, Palais de la Découverte, 1962.

Bower, John. "Rock Art: The Search for Meaning." *Quarterly Review of Archaeology* 9:2 (Summer 1988): 1–3.

Bradley, Richard. "Rock Art and the Perception of Landscape." *Cambridge Archaeological Journal* 1 (1991): 77–101.

————. *Rock Art and the Prehistory of Atlantic Europe: Signing the Land*. London: Routledge, 1997.

Brandl, Eric Joseph. *Australian Aboriginal Paintings in Western and Central Arnhem Land: Temporal Sequences and Elements of Style in Cadell River and Deaf Adder Creek Art*. Canberra, ACT: Australian Institute of Aboriginal Studies, 1973.

Brentjes, Burchard. *Fels- und Höhlenbilder Afrikas*. Leipzig: Koehler & Amelang, 1965; Engl. ed. *African Rock Art*. London: Dent, 1969.

Breuil, Henri. "L'Art à ses débuts: L'enfant, les primitifs." *Revue de Philosophie* 7 (1906): 162–178.

————. *L'Age des cavernes et roches ornées de France et d'Espagne*. Paris: Leroux, 1912. [Extrait de *Revue Archéologique* 4th series 19 (1912): 193–234.]

————. "Les Origines de l'art." *Journal de Psychologie* 22 (1925): 289–296.

————. "Les Origines de l'art decoratif." *Journal de Psychologie* 23 (1926): 364–375.

————. *Les Peintures rupestres schematiques de la peninsule iberique*. 4 vols. Lagny: Imprimerie de Lagny, 1933–1935.

————. *Œuvres d'art magdaléniennes de Lagerie basse (Dordogne)*. Paris: Hermann, 1936.

————. *Beyond the Bounds of History: Scenes from the Old Stone Age*. London: Gawthorn, 1949.

————. *Quatre Cents siècle d'art pariétal*. Paris: Presse de la Sapho, 1952; Engl. ed. *Four Hundred Centuries of Cave Art*. Montignac: Dordogne Centre d'Études et de Documentation Préhistoriques, 1952; 2nd ed. New York: Hacker Art Books, 1979.

————. *Les Roches peintes du Tassili-n-Ajjer d'après les relevés du Colonel Brenans*. Paris: Arts et Métiers Graphiques, 1954.

————. *Cave Drawings: An Exhibition of Drawings by the Abbé Breuil of Palaeolithic Paintings and Engravings*. London: Arts Council, 1954.

————. *The Rock Paintings of Southern Africa*. 6 vols. Paris: Trianon Press, et al. 1955–1975. Vol. l: *The White Lady of the Brandberg*. London: Trianon Press for the Abbé Breuil Trust, 1955; vol. 2: *Philipp Cave*. London: Abbé Breuil Publications, 1957; vol. 3: *Tsisab Ravine*. [Lisboa]: Calouste Gulbenkian Foundation through Trianon Press, 1959; vol. 4: *Anibib & Omandumba and Other Erongo Sites*. [Lisboa]: Calouste Gulbenkian Foundation through Trianon Press, 1960; vol. 5: *Southern Rhodesia: The District of Fort Victoria and other Sites*. Paris: Singer-Polignac Foundation through the Trianon Press, 1966; vol. 6: *The Sphinx and White Ghost Shelters and other Spitzkopje Sites*. Paris: Trianon Press, 1975.

[Festschrift Henri Breuil] *Hommage à M. l'abbé Henri Breuil [pour son quatre-vingtième anniversaire: Sa vie, son œuvre, bibliographie de ses travaux]*. Ed. by Raymond Lantier, Germaine Henri-Martin, et al. Paris: Henri-Martin: 1957.

Breuil, Henri and Mary E. Boyle. *Les Roches peintes de la Rhodesie du Sud: Les environs de Fort Victoria et d'autres sites*. Paris: Trianon, 1966.

Breuil, Henri and Raymond Lantier. *Les Hommes de la pierre ancienne*. Paris: Payot, 1959; 2nd ed. 1979; Engl. ed. *The Men of the Old Stone Age (Palaeolithic and Mesolithic)*. London: Harrap, 1965; 2nd ed. Westport, CN: Greenwood Press, 1980.

Breuil, Henri, Miles Crawford Burkitt, and Montagu Montagu-Pollock. *Rock Paintings of Southern Andalusia: A Description of a Neolithic and Copper Age Art Group*. Oxford: Clarendon Press, 1929.

Broby-Johansen, Rudolf. *Oldnordiske stenbilleder*. København: Gyldendal, 1967; 2nd rev. ed. 1973.

Brodrick, Alan Houghton. *Prehistoric Painting*. London: Avalon Press, 1948; Spanish ed. *La pintura prehistórica*. México: Fondo de Cultura Económica, 1975.

————. *Lascaux: A Commentary*. London: Lindsay Drummond, 1949.

————. *The Abbé Breuil, Prehistorian: A Biography*. London: Hutchinson, 1963; American ed. *Father of Prehistory: The Abbé Henri Breuil. His Life and Times*. New York: Morrow, 1963.

Brooks, Robert Romano Ravi and Vishnu S. Wakankar. *Stone Age Painting in India*. New Haven, CT: Yale University Press, 1976.

Brown, Gerard Baldwin. *The Art of the Cave Dweller: A Study of the Earliest Artistic Activities of Man*. London, Murray, 1928; 2nd ed. 1932.

Brown, Stephanie, ed. *Northern Rock Art: Prehistoric Carvings and Contemporary Artists*. Exh. cat. Durham: Durham Art Gallery, 1996.

Bruno, David. *Landscapes, Rock-Art, and the Dreaming: An Archaeology of Preunderstanding*. London: Leicester University Press, 2002.

Buisson, Dominique. "Les Flutes paléolithiques d'Isturitz (Pyrénées-Atlantiques)." *Bulletin de la Société Française* 87 (1990): 420–433.

Burgstaller, Ernst. *Felsbilder in Österreich*. Linz: Landesinstitut für Volksbildung und Heimatpflege, 1972.

Burkitt, Miles Crawford. *Prehistory: A Study of Early Cultures in Europe and the Mediterranean Basin*. Cambridge: The University Press, 1921.

———. *South Africa's Past in Stone and Paint*. Cambridge: The University Press, 1928.

———. *The Old Stone Age: A Study of Palaeolithic Times*. Cambridge: The University Press, 1933; 4th ed. New York: Atheneum, 1963.

Byars, A. Martin. "Symbolism and the Middle-Upper Palaeolithic Transition: A Theoretical and Methodological Critique." *Current Anthropology* 35 (1994): 369–399.

Cabré Aguiló, Juan [Aguilera y Gamboa, Enrique de, Marquis de Cerralbo]. *El arte rupestre en España (regiones septentrional y oriental)*. Madrid: Museo Nacional de Ciencias Naturales, 1915.

Calegari, Giulio, ed. *L'arte e l'ambiente del Sahara preistorico: Dati e interpretazioni. Atti del convegno organizzato dal Centro Studi Archeologia Africana e dal Museo Civico di Storia Naturale di Milano, Milano 24–27 ottobre 1990*. Milano: Società Italiana di Scienze Naturali e Museo Civico di Storia Naturale di Milano, 1993.

Campuzano Ruiz, Enrique and José Antonio Lasheras. *Santillana, Altamira*. León: Everest, 1996; Engl. ed. *Santillana, Altamira*. León: Everest, [1997].

Capell, Arthur. *Cave Painting Myths: Northern Kimberley*. Sydney, NSW: University of Sydney, 1972.

Capitan, Louis and Denis Peyrony. *L'Humanité primitive dans la région des Eyzies*. Paris: Stock, 1924.

Carballo, Jesús María. *El descubrimiento de la cueva y pinturas de Altamira por D. Marcelino S. de Sautuola*. Santander: Patronato de las Cuevas Prehistóricas de la Provincia, 1950.

———. *La cueva de Altamira y otras cuevas con pinturas en la provincia de Santander*. Santander: Patronato de las Cuevas Prehistóricas de la Provincia de Santander, [1944]; Engl. ed. *The Cave of Altamira and Other Caves Containing Paintings in the Province of Santander*. Barcelona: Patronato de las Cuevas Prehistóricas de la Provincia de Santander. 2nd ed. 1956; 3rd ed. 1963; French ed. *Les Grottes d'Altamira et les autres grottes a peintures de la province de Santander*. Santander: Patronato de las Cuevas Prehistóricas de la Provincia, 1961; German ed. *Die Höhle von Altamira und andere Höhlen mit Malereien in der Provinz Santander*. Santander: Patronato der Praehistorischen Hoehlen der Provinz, 1965.

Carmichael, David, Jane Hubert, Brian Reeves, and Audhild Schanche. *Sacred Sites, Sacred Places*. London: Routledge, 1994.

Cartailhac, Émile. *Les Ages préhistoriques de l'Espagne et du Portugal*. Paris: Reinwald, 1886.

———. "Les Cavernes ornées de dessins: La Grotte d'Altamira (Espagne). Mea culpa d'un sceptique." *L'Anthropologie* 13 (1902): 348–354.

Cartailhac, Émile and Henri Breuil. *La Caverne d'Attamira à Santillane près Santander (Espagne)*. Monaco: Imprimerie de Monaco, 1906; 2nd rev. ed. [with Hugo Obermaier] Madrid: Tipografía de Archivos, 1935; 3rd ed. Santander: Editorial Cantabria, 1954; Engl. ed. [with Hugo Obermaier] *The Cave of Altamira at Santillana del Mar, Spain*. Madrid: Tipografía de Archivos, 1935; rev. Spanish ed. *La cueva de Altamira en Santillana del Mar*. Madrid: El Viso, 1984.

Casado Lopez de Garza, María del Pilar. *Los signos en el arte paleolítico de la península ibérica*. Zaragoza: Departamento de Prehistoria y Arqueología de la Facultad de Filosofía y Letras, 1977.

Casado Lopez de Garza, Maria del Pilar, and Lorena Mirambell, eds. *El arte rupestre en México*. México, D.F.: Instituto Nacional de Antropología e Historia, 1990.

Casamiquela, Rodolfo M. *El arte rupestre de la Patagonia*. Neuquén: Siringa, 1981.

Castaño, Ana. "Aspectos ecológicos del arte parietal paleolítico en Cantabria." *Estudio de arte paleolítico*. Madrid: Ministerio de Cultura, Dirección General de Bellas Artes y Archivos, Subdirección General de Arqueología y Etnografia, 1986. 7–66.

Castleton, Kenneth Bitner. *Petroglyphs and Pictographs of Utah*. 2 vols. Salt Lake City: Utah Museum of Natural History, 1978–1979; 2nd rev. ed. 1984–1987.

Centro de Investigación y Museo de Altamira, eds. *Estudio de arte paleolítico*. Madrid: Ministerio de Cultura, Dirección General de Bellas Artes y Archivos, Subdirección General de Arqueología y Etnografía, 1986.

Cervícek, Pavel. *Catalogue of the Rock Art Collection of the Frobenius Institute*. Wiesbaden: Steiner, 1976.

Chakravarty, Kalyan Kumar, ed. *Rock-Art of India: Paintings and Engravings*. New Delhi: Arnold-Heinemann, 1984.

Chakravarty, Kalyan Kumar and Robert G. Bednarik. *Indian Rock Art and Its Global Context*. Delhi: Motilal Banarsidass, and Bhopal: Indira Gandhi Rashtriya Manav Sangrahalaya, 1997.

Chaloupka, George. *From Palaeoart to Casual Paintings: The Chronological Sequence of Arnhem Land Plateau Rock Art*. Darwin, NT: Northern Territory Museum of Arts and Sciences, 1984.

———. "Rock Paintings of the Dynamic Figures Style, Arnhem Land Plateau Region, Northern Territory, Australia." *Ars Praehistorica* 7–8 (1988–89): 329–337.

———. *Journey in Time: The World's Longest Continuing Art Tradition. The 50,000-year Story of the Australian Aboriginal Rock Art of Arnhem Land*. Chatswood, NSW: Reed, 1993.

Chapa Brunet, Teresa and Mario Menéndez Fernández, eds. *Arte paleolítico*. Madrid: Editorial Complutense, 1994.

Charrière, Georges. *La Signification des représentations érotiques dans les arts sauvages et préhistoriques*. Paris: Maisonneuve et Larose, 1970.

Chase, Philip G. "On Symbols and the Palaeolithic." *Current Anthropology* 35:5 (December 1994): 627–629.

———. "Symbolism as Reference and Symbolism as Culture." In *The Evolution of Culture: An Interdisciplinary View*, ed. Robin Dunbar, Chris Knight and Camilla Power. New Brunswick, NJ: Rutgers University Press, 1999. 34–49.

Chase, Philip G. and Harold L. Dibble. "Middle Paleolithic Symbolism: A Review of Current Evidence and Interpretations." *Journal of Anthropological Archaeology* 6 (1987): 263–296.

Chauvet, Jean-Marie, Éliette Brunel Deschamps, and Christian Hillaire. *Grotte Chauvet à Vallon-Pont-d'Arc*. Paris: Seuil, 1995: 2nd rev. ed. Paris: France Loisirs, 1997; Engl. ed. *Chauvet Cave: The Discovery of the World's Oldest Paintings*. London: Thames and Hudson, 1996; American ed. *Dawn of Art: The Chauvet Cave, the Oldest Known Paintings in the World*. New York: Abrams, 1996.

Chen, Zhao-fu: Cina. *L'arte rupestre preistorica*. Milano: Jaca Book 1988; French ed. *Découverte de l'art préhistorique en Chine*. Paris: Albin Michel, 1988.

Chernetsov, Valerii Nikolaevich. *Naskal'nye izobrazheniia Urala*. 3 vols. Moskva: "Nauka," 1964–1974.

Chiang, Chen-ming. *Timeless History: The Rock Art of China*. Beijing: New World Press, 1991.

Chippindale, Christopher. "Studying Ancient Pictures as Pictures." In *Handbook of Rock Art Research*, ed. David S. Whitley. Walnut Creek, CA: AltaMira Press, 2001. 247–272.

Chippindale, Christopher and Paul S. C. Taçon, eds. *The Archaeology of Rock-Art*. Cambridge: Cambridge University Press, 1998.

Chippindale, Christopher and George Nash, eds. *Pictures In Place: Looking at Rock Art in Its Landscape*. Cambridge: Cambridge University Press, 2002.

Chippindale, Christopher, Benjamin Smith, and Paul S.C. Taçon. "Visions of Dynamic Power: Archaic Rock-Paintings, Altered States of Consciousness and 'Clever Men' in Western Arnhem Land (NT), Australia." *Cambridge Archaeological Journal* 10 (2000): 63–101.

Chollot-Legoux, Marthe. *Les Origines du graphisme symbolique: Essai d'analyse des écritures primitives en préhistoire*. Paris: Singer Polignac, 1980.

Chollot-Legoux, Marthe, André Varagnac, and Henri Breuil, eds. *Collection Piette: Art mobilier préhistorique*. Paris: Éditions des Musées Nationaux, 1964.

Christensen, Jesper. "Heaven and Earth in Ice Age Art: Topography and Iconography at Lascaux." *Mankind Quarterly* 36 (1996): 247–259.

Chrobaczek, Christiane, ed. *Kunst der Eiszeit in Deutschland und der Schweiz*. Köln: Rheinland-Verlag, 1985.

Clark, Geoffrey A., C. Michael Barton, and Allison E. Cohen. "Explaining Art in the Franco-Cantabrian Refugium." In *Debating Complexity. Proceedings of the 26th Annual Chacmool Conference*, ed. Daniel A. Meyer, Peter C. Dawson, and Donald T. Hanna. Calgary: The Archaeological Association of the University of Calgary, 1996: 241–253.

Clewlow, Jr., C. William, ed. *Four Rock Art Studies*: Socorro, NM: Ballena Press, 1978.

Clot, André. *L'Art graphique préhistorique des Hautes-Pyrénées*. Morlaas: Éditions PGP, 1973.

Clottes, Jean. "Thematic Changes in the Upper Palaeolithic Art: A View from the Grotte Chauvet." *Antiquity* 70 (1966): 276–288.

————. "The Parietal Art of the Late Magdalenian." *Antiquity* 64 (1990): 527–548.

————. *La Grotte de Niaux*. Foix: Conseil Départemental du Tourisme de l'Ariège, 1976; Engl. ed. *The Cave of Niaux*. Boulogne: Éditions du Castelet, 1992.

————. "Eléments sur l'art rupestre paléolithique en France." *Bulletin de la Société Préhistorique de L'Ariège* 35 (1980): 79–110.

————. "Paint Analysis from Several Magdalenian Caves in the Ariège Region of France." *Journal of Archaeological Science* 20 (1993): 223–235.

————. "Dates directes pour les peintures paléolithiques." *Bulletin de la Société Préhistorique Ariège-Pyrénées* 49 (1994): 51–70.

————. *Les Cavernes de Niaux: Art préhistorique en Ariège*. Paris: Seuil, 1995.

————. "Recent Studies on Palaeolithic Art." *Cambridge Archaeological Journal* 6 (1996): 179–189.

————. *L'Art rupestre: Un message culturel universel = Rock Art: A Universal Cultural Message*. Paris: UNESCO; Comité International d'Art Rupestre, 1997.

————. *Voyage en préhistoire: L'art des cavernes et des abris, de la découverte à l'interprétation*. Paris: Maison des Roches, 1998.

————. *Le Musée des roches: L'Art rupestre dans le monde*. Paris: Seuil, 2000.

————. *La Grotte Chauvet: L'art des origines*. Paris: Seuil, 2001.

————. "Paleolithic Europe." In *Handbook of Rock Art Research*, ed. David S. Whitley. Walnut Creek, CA: AltaMira Press, 2001: 459–481.

Clottes, Jean, ed. *L'Art des objets au paléolithique: Colloque international, Foix, Le Mas-d'Azil, 16–21 novembre 1987*. 2 vols. Paris: Ministère de la Culture, 1990.

Clottes, Jean and David Lewis-Williams. *Les Chamanes de la préhistoire: Transe et magie dans les grottes ornées*. Paris: Seuil, 1996; 2nd ed. Paris: La Maison des Roches, 2001; Engl. ed. *The Shamans of Prehistory. Trance and Magic in the Painted Caves*. New York: Abrams, 1998.

————. "Upper Palaeolithic Cave Art: French and South African Collaboration." *Cambridge Archaeological Journal* 6 (1996): 137–163.

Clottes, Jean and Jean Courtin. *La Grotte Cosquer: Peintures et gravures de la caverne engloutie*. Paris: Seuil, 1994; Engl. ed. *The Cave Beneath the Sea: Paleolithic Images at Cosquer*. New York: Abrams, 1996.

Cole, Sally J. *An Analysis of the Prehistoric and Historic Rock Art of West-central Colorado*. Denver, CO: Bureau of Land Management, Colorado State Office, 1987.

————. *Legacy on Stone: Rock Art of the Colorado Plateau and the Four Corners Region*. Boulder, CO: Johnson, 1990.

Colectivo para la Ampliación de Estudios de Arqueología Prehistórica, Grupo de Espeleología e Investigaciones Subterráneas Carballo/ Raba, eds.: *Arte rupestre y mobiliar*. Santander: Impresión, 1991.

Collins, Desmond and John Onians. "The Origins of Art." *Art History* 1:1 (March 1978): 1–25.

Collins, Henry Bascom. *Prehistoric Art of the Alaskan Eskimo*. Seattle, WA: Shorey Book Store, 1969.

Colloque International: L'art paléolithique á l'air libre. Le paysage modifié par l'image. Tautavel: Faculté des Lettres et Sciencies Humaines de Perpignan, 1999.

Collot, Francis, M. Boumokra, R. Cassé. "Les Signes dans l'art pariétal: Mode d'étude des représentations non animalières." *Études préhistoriques* 3 (December 1972): 22–26.

Conkey, Margaret W. "Style and Information in Cultural Evolution: Towards a Predictive Model for the Paleolithic." In *Social Archaeology,* ed. Charles L. Redman et al. New York: Academic Press, 1978. 61–85.

———. "The Identification of Prehistoric Hunter-Gatherer Aggregation Sites: The Case of Altamira." *Current Anthropology* 21 (1980): 609–630.

———. "Context, Structure, and Efficacy in Paleolithic Art and Design." In *Symbol as Sense: New Approaches to the Analysis of Meaning,* ed. Mary LeCron Foster and Stanley H. Brandes. New York: Academic Press 1980;. 225–248.

———. "A Century of Paleolithic Cave Art: Revealing the Last Hundred Years of Scholarship." *Archaeology* 34:4 (July-August 1981): 20–28.

———. "On the Origins of Paleolithic Art: A Review and some Critical Thoughts." In *The Mousterian Legacy: Human Biocultural Change in the Upper Pleistocene,* ed. Eric Trinkaus. Oxford: British Archaeological Reports, 1983. 201–227.

———. "To Find Ourselves: Art and Social Geography of Prehistoric Hunter-gatheres." In *Past and Present in Hunter Gatherer Studies,* ed. Carmel Shrire. Orlando, FL: Academic Press, 1984: 253–276.

———. "Ritual Communication, Social Elaboration, and the Variable Trajectories of Paleolithic Material Culture." In *Prehistoric Hunter-Gatherers: The Emergence of Cultural Complexity,* ed. T. Douglas Price and James A. Brown. Orlando, FL: Academic Press, 1985: 299–323.

———. "New Approaches in the Search for Meaning? A Review of Research in 'Palaeolithic Art'." *Journal of Field Archaeology* 14 (1987): 413–430.

———. "The Structural Analysis of Paleolithic Art." In *Archaeological Thought in America,* Carl C. Lamberg-Karlovsky. Cambridge: Cambridge University Press, 1989: 135–154.

———. "Contexts for Action, Contexts for Power: Material Culture and Gender in the Magdalenian." In *Engendering Archaeology: Women and Prehistory,* ed. Joan M. Gero and Margaret W. Conkey. Oxford: Blackwell, 1991: 57–92.

———. "Humans as Materialists and Symbolists: Image Making in the Upper Paleolithic." In *The Origin and Evolution of Humans and Humanness,* ed. D. Tab Rasmussen. Boston, MA: Jones and Bartlett, 1993: 95–118.

———. "Men and Women in Prehistory: An Archaeological Challenge." In *Gender in Cross-cultural Perspectives,* ed. Caroline B. Brettell and Carolyn F. Sargent. Upper Saddle River, NJ: Prentice Hall, 1993; 2nd ed. 1997: 57–66.

———. "A History of the Interpretation of European 'Palaeolithic Art': Magic, Mythogram, and Metaphors for Modernity." In *Handbook of Human Symbolic Evolution,* ed. Andrew Lock and Charles R. Peter. Oxford: Clarendon Press, 1996: 288–344.

———. "Mobilizing Ideologies: Paleolithic 'Art,' Gender Trouble, and Thinking About Alternatives." In *Women in Human Evolution,* ed. Lori D. Hager. London: Routledge, 1997. 267–291.

———. "Beyond Art and Between the Caves: Thinking About Context in the Interpretive Process." In *Beyond Art: Pleistocene Image and Symbol,* ed. Margaret Conkey, Olga Soffer, Deborah Stratmann and Nina G. Jablonski. San Francisco, CA: California Academy of Sciences, 1997: 343–367.

———. "Hunting for Images, Gathering up Meanings: Art for Life in Hunting-gathering Societies." In *Hunter-gatherers: An Interdisciplinary Perspective*, ed. Catherine Panter-Brick, Robert H. Layton and Peter Rowley-Conwy. Cambridge: Cambridge University Press, 2001: 267–291.

———. "Structural and Semiotic Approaches." In *Handbook of Rock Art Research*, ed. David S. Whitley. Walnut Creek, CA: AltaMira Press, 2001: 273–310.

Conkey, Margaret W., Olga Soffer, Deborah Stratmann, and Nina G. Jablonski, eds. *Beyond Art: Pleistocene Image and Symbol*. San Francisco, CA: California Academy of Sciences, 1997.

Connor, Linda, Polly Schaafsma, and Keith F. Davis. *Marks in Place: Contemporary Responses to Rock Art*. Albuquerque, NM: University of New Mexico Press, 1988.

Conway, Thor. *Painted Dreams: Native American Rock Art*. Minocqua, WI: North Word Press, 1993.

Conway, William Martin. *Dawn of Art in the Ancient World: An Archaeological Sketch*. London: Percival, 1891.

Corchón, María Soledad. *El arte paleolítico cantábrico: Contexto y análisis interno*. Madrid: Ministerio de Cultura, Dirección General de Bellas Artes y Archivos, Subdirección General de Arqueología y Etnografía, 1986.

Corner, John. *Pictographs (Indian Rock Paintings) in the Interior of British Columbia*. Vernon, BC: Corner, 1968.

Cosquer, Henri, Valerie Fettu, and Bernard Franco. *La Grotte Cosquer: Plongée dans la préhistoire*. Paris: Solar, 1992.

Costas Goberna, Fernando Javier, and José Manuel Hidalgo Cuñarro. *La figura humana en los grabados rupestres prehistóricos del continente europeo*. Vigo: Asociación Arqueológica Viguesa, 1995.

———. *Los motivos de fauna y armas en los grabados prehistóricos del continente europeo*. Vigo: Asociación Arqueológica Viguesa, 1997.

Costas Goberna, Fernando Javier, and José Manuel Hidalgo Cuñarro, eds. *Reflexiones sobre el arte rupestre prehistórico de Galicia*. Vigo: Asociación Arqueológica Viguesa, 1998.

Coulson, David and Alec Campbell. *African Rock Art: Paintings and Engravings on Stone*. New York: Abrams, 2001.

Couraud, Claude. "Pour une étude méthodologique des colorants préhistoriques." *Bulletin de la Société Préhistorique Française* 80 (1983): 104–110.

———. *L'Art azilien: Origine, survivance*. Paris: Éditions du Centre National de la Recherche Scientifique, 1985.

———. "Les Pigments des grottes d'Arcy-sur-Cure (Yonne)." *Gallia Préhistoire* 33 (1991): 17–52.

Cox, J. Halley and Edward Stasack. *Hawaiian Petroglyphs*. Honolulu, HI: Bishop Museum Press, 1970.

Craig, Barbara June. *Rock Paintings and Petroglyphs of South and Central Africa: A Bibliography of Prehistoric Art*. Cape Town: School of Librarianship, University of Cape Town, 1947.

Crawford, Ian Maxwell. *The Art of the Wandjina: Aboriginal Cave Paintings in Kimberley, Western Australia*. Melbourne: Oxford University Press, 1968.

———. "Function and Change in Aboriginal Rock Art, West Australia." *World Archaeology* 3 (1972): 301–312.

Crémades, Michèle. "L'Art mobilier paléolithique: Analyse des procès technologiques." In *Arte paleolítico*, ed. Teresa Chapa Brunet and Mario Menéndez Fernández. Madrid: Editorial Complutense, 1994: 369–384.

Criado Boado, Felipe and Rafael Penedo Romero. "Art, Time and Thought: A Formal Study Comparing Palaeolithic and Postglacial Art." *World Archaeology* 25 (1993): 187–203.

Cronología del arte rupestre levantino. Valencia: Real Academia de Cultura Valencia, Sección de Prehistoria y Arqueología, 1999.

Crosby, Harry. *The Cave Paintings of Baja California: The Great Murals of an Unknown People.* La Jolla, CA: Copley Books, 1975; 2nd rev. ed. *The Cave Paintings of Baja California.* La Jolla, CA: Copley Books, 1984; 3rd rev. ed. *The Cave Paintings of Baja California: Discovering the Great Murals of an Unknown People.* San Diego, CA: Sunbelt Publications, 1997.

Cross, Ian, Ezra Zubrow, and Frank Cowan. "Musical Behaviours and the Archaeological Record: A Preliminary Study." In *Experimental Archaeology: Replicating Past Objects, Behaviors, and Processes,* ed. James R. Mathieu. Oxford: Archaeopress, 2002: 25–34.

Cueva de Altamira: Estudios fisico-químicos de la Sala de Policromos. Influencia de la presencia humana y criterios de conservación. Madrid: Ministerio de Cultura, Dirección General de Bellas Artes y Archivos, Subdirección General de Arqueología y Etnografía, 1984.

Las cuevas con arte paleolítico en Cantabria: Santander. Santander: Asociación Cántabra para la Defensa del Patrimonio Subterráneo, 1986; 2nd rev. ed. 1989; 3rd ed. edited by César González Sainz, 2002.

Curso de arte rupestre paleolítico: Con la colaboración del Excelentisimo Ayuntamiento de Santander. Zaragoza: Universidad de Zaragoza, 1977.

Curso de arte rupestre paleolítico: Universidad Internacional Menéndez Pelayo, con la colaboración del Ayuntamiento de Santander. Zaragoza: Universidad, 1978.

Dams, Lya. *Les Peintures rupestres du Levant espagnol.* Paris: Picard, 1984.

————. "Palaeolithic Lithophones: Descriptions and Comparisons." *Oxford Journal of Archaeology* 4 (1985): 31–46.

Daniel, Glyn Edmund. *Lascaux and Carnac.* London: Lutterworth Press, 1955.

Danthine, Helène. "Éléments de rituels paléolithiques." In *Santander Symposium,* ed. Martín Almagro Basch and Miguel Ángel García Guinea. Santander: Museo de Prehistoria, 1972: 83–86.

Dauvois, Michel. "Sons et musique paléolithique." *Les Dossiers de l'Archéologie* 142 (1986): 2–11.

————. "Instruments sonores et musicaux préhistoriques." *Préhistoire de la Musique.* Nemours: Musée de Préhistoire d'Île-de-France, 2002. 33–45.

Dauvois, Michel and Benoît Fabre. *Les Instruments à vent paléolithiques.* Paris: Jouve, 1999.

Dauvois, Michel and Xavier Boutillon. "Études acoustiques au Réseau Clastres: Salle des peintures et lithophones naturels." *Préhistoire Ariégoise* 45 (1990): 175–186.

David, Bruno, Ian McNiven, Josephine Flood, and Robin Frost. "Yiwarlarlay 1: Archaeological Excavations at the Lightning Brothers Site, Delamere Station, Northern Territory." *Archaeology in Oceania* 25 (1990): 79–84.

Davidson, Daniel Sutherland. *Aboriginal Australian and Tasmanian Rock Carvings and Paintings.* Philadelphia, PA: American Philosophical Society, 1936.

Davis, Whitney. "Present and Future Directions in the Study of Rock Art." *South African Archaeological Bulletin* 39 (1984): 5–10.

———. "The Origins of Image Making." *Current Anthropology* 27 (1986): 193–215.

———. "Replication and Depiction in Paleolithic Art." *Representations* 19 (Summer 1987): 117–147.

Day, Jane S., Paul D. Friedman, and Marcia J. Tate, eds.: *Rock Art of the Western Canyons.* Denver, CO: Denver Museum of Natural History, and Boulder, CO: Colorado Archaeological Society, 1989.

Deacon, Janette. *Some Views on Rock Paintings in the Cederberg.* 2nd ed. Cape Town: National Monuments Council, and Johannesburg: Thorold's Africana Books, 1998.

Delamare, Francois, Tony Hackens, and Bruno Helly: *Datation-caracterisation des peintures pariétales et murales.* Ravello: Centre Universitaire Européen pour les Biens Culturels, 1987.

Delluc, Brigitte and Giles Delluc. "Les Manifestations graphiques aurignaciennes sur support rocheux des environs des Eyzies (Dordognes)." *Gallia Préhistoire* 21 (1978): 213–438.

———. "On the Origins of Image Making." *Current Anthropology* 27 (1986): 371.

———. *L'Art pariétal archaïque en Aquitaine.* Paris: Éditions du Centre national de la recherche scientifique, 1991.

———. *Connaître Lascaux.* Bordeaux: "Sud-Ouest," 1991; Engl. ed. *Discovering Lascaux.* Bordeaux: "Sud-Ouest," 1991; German ed. *Die Höhle von Lascaux.* Bordeaux: "Sud-Ouest," 1991.

Del Pilar Casado, María and Lorena Mirambell, eds. *El arte rupestre en México.* México, D.F.: Instituto Nacional de Antropología e Historia, 1990.

Delporte, Henri. "Les Techniques de la gravure paléolithique." In *Estudios dedicados al Prof. Dr. Luis Pericot,* ed. Juan Maluquer de Motes. Barcelona: Universidad de Barcelona, Instituto de Arqueología y Prehistoria, 1973: 119–129.

———. "L'art mobilier et ses rapports avec la faune paléolithique." In *La Contribution de la zoologie et de l'éthologie à l'interprétation de l'art des peuples chasseurs préhistoriques,* ed. Hans-Georg Bandi et al. Fribourg: Éditions Universitaires, 1984: 111–142.

———. *L'Image de la femme dans l'art préhistorique.* Paris: Picard, 1979; 2nd rev. ed. 1993; Spanish ed. *La imagen de la mujer en el arte prehistórico.* Madrid: Istmo, 1982.

———. *Brassempouy: La grotte du Pape, station préhistorique. Il y a 20000 ans, l'art.* Saint-Julien-en-Born: Association Culturelle de Contis, 1980.

———. *L'Objet d'art préhistorique.* Paris: Réunion des Musées Nationaux, 1981.

———. "Note sur la structuration et la signification de l'art paléolithique mobilier." *Altamira Symposium.* Madrid: Ministerio de Cultura, 1981: 189–196.

———. *L'Image des animaux dans l'art préhistorique.* Paris: Picard, 1990; Spanish ed. *La imagen de los animales en el arte prehistórico.* Madrid: Compañía Literaria, 1995.

———. "La Notion d'image dans l'art paléolithique." *L'image et la science: Actes du 115e congrès national des sociétés savantes (Avignon, 1990). Sections d'archéologie et d'histoire de l'art, d'histoire des sciences et des techniques, et des sciences.* Paris:

Ministère de l'Éducation Nationale et de la Culture, Comité des Travaux Historiques et Scientifiques, 1992: 215–229.

———. "Gravettian Female Figurines: A Regional Survey." In *Before Lascaux: The Complex Record of the Early Upper Paleolithic*, ed. Heidi Knecht, Anne Pike-Tay and Randall White. Boca Raton, FL: CRC Press, 1993: 243–257.

Delporte, Henri, ed. *Chefs d'œuvre de l'art paléolithique*. Exh. cat. Saint-Germain-en-Laye: Musée des Antiquités Nationales, 1969. Paris: Ministère d'État Chargé des Affaires Culturelles, Réunion des Musées Nationaux, 1969.

———. *La Dame de Brassempouy: Actes du colloque de Brassempouy*. Liège: Université de Liège, 1995.

———. *L'Art préhistorique des Pyrénées*. Exh. cat. Saint-Germain-en-Laye: Musée des Antiquités Nationales 1996. Paris: Réunion des Musées Nationaux, 1996.

Delporte, Henri and Lucette Mons. "Notes de technologie de l'art préhistorique mobilier (III)." *Antiquités Nationales* 5 (1973): 20–32.

Delporte, Henri and Jean Clottes, eds. *Pyrénées préhistoriques: Arts et sociétés. Actes du 118e Congrès national des Sociétés Historiques et Scientifiques, Commission de Pré- et Protohistoire, Pau, 25–29 October 1993*. Paris: Éditions du C.T.H.S., 1996.

D'Errico, Francesco. "Palaeolithic Lunar Calendars: A Case of Wishful Thinking?" *Current Anthropology* 30 (1989): 117–118.

———. *L'Art gravé azilien: De la technique à la signification*. Paris: Centre National de la Recherche Scientifique, 1994.

D'Errico, Francesco, Christopher Henshilwood, and Peter Nilssen. "An Engraved Bone Fragment from c. 70,000-Year-Old Middle Stone Age Levels at Blombos Cave, South Africa: Implications for the Origins of Symbolism and Language." *Antiquity* 75 (2001): 309–318.

D'Errico, Francesco and Paola Villa. "Holes and Grooves: The Contribution of Microscopy and Taphonomy to the Problem of Art Origins." *Journal of Human Evolution* 33:1 (1997): 1–31.

D'Errico, Francesco, Paola, Villa, C. Ana Llona Pinto, and Rosa Idarraga Ruiz. "A Middle Paleolithic Origin of Music? Using Cave-bear Bone Accumulations to Assess the Divje Babe I Bone Flute." *Antiquity* 72 (1998): 65–79.

El deterioro en las cuevas de Cantabria. Santander: Asociación Cántabra para la Defensa del Patrimonio Subterráneo, 1988.

Dewdney, Selwyn and Kenneth E. Kidd. *Indian Rock Paintings of the Great Lakes*. Toronto: University of Toronto Press, 1962.

Dewey, William Joseph, Els de Palmenaer, and Geert Gabriel Bourgois, eds. *Legacies of Stone: Zimbabwe Past and Present*. Exh. cat. Tervuren: Royal Museum for Central Africa, 1997.

Díaz-Andreu, Margarita. "Iberian Post-palaeolithic Art and Gender: Discussing Human Representations in Levantine Art." *Journal of Iberian Archaeology* 0 (1998): 33–51.

Díaz Casado, Yolanda. *El arte rupestre esquemático en Cantabria: Una revisión crítica*. Santander: Universidad de Cantabria, 1992.

Diaz-Granados, Carol and James R. Duncan. *The Petroglyphs and Pictographs of Missouri*. Tuscaloosa, AL: University of Alabama Press, 2000.

Dickson, D. Bruce. *The Dawn of Belief: Religion in the Upper Paleolithic of Southwestern Europe.* Tucson, AZ: University of Arizona Press, 1990.

Dissanayake, Ellen. *Homo Aestheticus: Where Art Comes from and Why.* Seattle, WA: University of Washington Press, 1995; 2nd ed. New York: Free Press, 1992.

Dobres, Marcia-Anne. "Re-considering Venus Figurines: A Feminist Inspired Re-analysis." In *Ancient Images, Ancient Thought: The Archaeology of Ideology. Proceedings of the Twenty-third Annual Conference of the Archaeological Association of the University of Calgary,* ed. A. Sean Goldsmith, Sandra Garvie, David Selin and Jeanette Smith. Calgary, Alta.: University of Calgary Archaeological Association, 1992: 245–262.

———. "Re-presentations of Paleolithic Visual Imagery: Simulacra and their Alternatives." *Kroeber Anthropological Society Papers* 73–74 (1992): 1–25.

———. "Venus Figurines." In *Oxford Companion to Archaeology,* ed. Brian M. Fagan. New York: Oxford University Press, 1996: 740–741.

Domning, Jochen. *Zur Technik der Eiszeitmalereien im franco-cantabrischen Raum.* München: Verband der Deutschen Höhlen- und Karstforscher e. V. in Kommission bei der Mangold'schen Buchhandlung Blaubeuren, 1971.

Dowson, Thomas A. "Reading Art, Writing History: Rock Art and Social Change in Southern Africa." *World Archaeology* 25 (1994): 332–344.

———. "Like People in Prehistory." *World Archaeology* 29 (1998): 333–343.

Dowson, Thomas A., ed. *The State of the Art: Advances in World Rock Art Research.* Johannesburg: University of Witwatersrand, Rock Art Research Unit, 1988.

Dowson, Thomas A. and David Lewis-Williams, eds. *Contested Images: Diversity in Southern African Rock Art Research.* Johannesburg: Witwatersrand University Press, 1994.

Drew, Julie. "Depictions of Women and Gender Relations in Aboriginal Rock Art." In *Gendered Archaeology: The Second Australian Women in Archaeology,* ed. Jane Balme and Wendy Beck. Canberra, ACT: The Australian National University, Research School of Pacific Studies, 1995: 105–113.

Drössler, Rudolf. *Die Venus der Eiszeit: Entdeckung und Erforschung altsteinzeitlicher Kunst.* Leipzig: Prisma, 1967.

———. *Kunst der Eiszeit: Von Spanien bis Sibirien.* Leipzig: Koehler & Amelang, 1980.

Duff, Andrew I., Geoffrey A. Clark, and Thomas J. Chadderdon. "Symbolism in the Early Palaeolithic: A Conceptual Odyssey." *Cambridge Archaeological Journal* 2 (1992): 211–229.

Duhard, Jean-Pierre. "Le Corps féminin et son langage dans l'art paléolithique." *Oxford Journal of Archaeology* 9 (1990): 241–255.

———. "La Dichotomie sociale sexuelle dans les figurations humaines magdaléniennes." *Rock Art Research* 9 (1992): 111–118.

———. *Réalisme de l'image féminine paléolithique.* Paris: Centre National de la Recherche Scientifique, 1993.

———. *Réalisme de l'image masculine paléolithique.* Grenoble: Millon, 1996.

Dumitrescu, Vladimir. *L'Art préhistorique en Roumanie.* Bukaresti: Éditions Meridiane, 1985.

Edwards, Stephen W. "Nonutilitarian Activities in the Lower Paleolithic: A Look at the Two Kinds of Evidence." *Current Anthropology* 19 (1978): 135–137.

Ego, Renaud. *San: Art rupestre d'Afrique australe.* Paris: Biro, 2000.

Eppel, Franz. *Stationen der ältesten Kunst im Land der Steinzeithöhlen.* Wien: Schroll, 1963.

Escoriza Mateu, Trinidad. "Lecturas sobre las representaciones femininas en el arte rupestre levantino: Una revisión crítica." *Arenal* 3 (1996): 5–24.

Estévez Escalera, Jorge. "Paleoeconomia y arte prehistórico." *Altamira Symposium.* Madrid: Ministerio de Cultura, 1981: 197–205.

Estudio de arte paleolítico. Madrid: Ministerio de Cultura, Dirección General de Bellas Artes y Archivos, Subdirección General de Arqueología y Etnografia, 1986.

Evers, Dietrich. *Felsbilder: Botschaften der Vorzeit.* Leipzig: Urania, 1991.

———. *The Magic of the Image: Prehistoric Scandinavian Rock Carvings.* Warmsroth: Pulsar-Verlag, 1994; German ed. *Magie der Bilder: Prähistorische skandinavische Felsgravuren.* Warmsroth: Pulsar-Verlag, 1995.

Exposición de arte prehistórico español: Catálogo-guia. Madrid: Mateu, 1921.

Exposición de arte prehistórico español: Catálogo ilustrado. Madrid: [s.n.], 1921.

Fallue, Léon. *De l'Art récemment qualifié antédiluvien: Examen critique des graffiti provenant des grottes de la Dordogne et qui ont trouvé place à l'Exposition Universelle.* [Extrait de la "Revue artistique et littéraire"]. Paris: Vert, 1867.

Farizy, Catherine, ed. *Paléolithique moyen récent et Paléolithique supérieur ancien en Europe: Rupture et transitions. Examen critique des documents archéologiques. Actes du colloque international de Nemours, 9–10–11 mai 1988.* Nemours: Association pour la Promotion de la Recherche Archéologique en Île-de-France, 1990.

Faulstich, Paul, ed. *Rock Art as Visual Ecology: Proceedings from the Ecology of Rock Art Symposium, International Rock Art Congress, Flagstaff, Arizona, 1994.* Tucson, AZ: American Rock Art Research Association, 1997.

Faustino de Carvalho, António, João Zilhão, and Thierry Aubry. *Vale do Côa: Arte rupestre e pré-história.* Vale do Côa: Parque Arqueológico, 1996; Engl. ed. *Côa Valley: Rock Art and Prehistory.* Vale do Côa: Parque Arqueológico, 1996.

Fine, Alain, Roger Perron, and François Sacco, eds. *Psychanalyse et préhistoire.* Paris: Presses Universitaires de France, 1994.

Fischer, Eugen. *Die Rehobother Bastards.* Jena: Fischer, 1913.

Flamand, Georges Barthelémy Médéric. *Les Pierres écrites (Hadjrat-mektoubat): Gravures et inscriptions rupestres du Nord-Africain.* Paris: Masson, 1921.

Flood, Josephine. *Archaeology of the Dreamtime: The Story of Prehistoric Australia and Its People.* Sydney, NSW: Harpercollins, 1983; 3rd ed. 2000.

———. *The Riches of Ancient Australia: A Journey into Prehistory.* St. Lucia, QLD: University of Queensland Press, and Portland, OR: International Specialized Book Services, 1990.

———. "Cultures in Early Aboriginal Australia." *Cambridge Archaeological Journal* 6 (1996): 3–36.

———. *Rock Art of the Dreamtime: Images of Ancient Australia.* Sydney and New York: Angus & Robertson, 1997.

Fock, Gerhard J. and Dora Fock. *Felsbilder in Südafrika.* 2 vols. Köln: Böhlau, 1979–1984.

Forbes, Allan and Thomas R. Crowder. "The Problem of Franco-Cantabrian Abstract Signs: Agenda for a New Approach." *World Archaeology* 10 (1976): 350–366.

Formentini, Romolo. *Figure e segni nella pietra: Gli antichi cacciatori.* Torino: Antropologia Alpina, 1990.

Freeman, Leslie G., Joaquín González Echegaray, Federico Bernaldo de Quirós, and J. Ogden. *Altamira Revisited and Other Essays on Early Art.* Chicago, IL: Institute for Prehistoric Investigations, and Santander: Museo y Centro de Investigación de Altamira, 1987.

Freeman, Leslie G. and Joaquín González Echegaray. *La Grotte d'Altamira.* Paris: Maison des Roches, 2001.

Freund, Gisela. "L'Art aurignacien en Europe centrale." *Bulletin de la Société Préhistorique de l'Ariège* 12 (1957): 1–15.

Fritz, Carole. *La Gravure dans l'art mobilier magdalénien: Du geste à la représentation. Contribution de l'analyse microscopique.* Paris: Éditions de la Maison des Sciences de l'Homme, 1999.

Frobenius, Leo. *Madsimu Dsangara. Südafrikanische Felsbilderchronik.* 2 vols. Berlin: Atlantis, 1931–1932. Reprint Graz: Akademische Druck- und Verlagsanstalt, 1962.

———. *Ekade Ektab: Die Felsbilder Fezzans.* Leipzig: Harrassowitz, 1937.

Frobenius, Leo and Hugo Obermaier. *Hádschra Máktuba: Urzeitliche Felsbilder Kleinafrikas.* München: Wolff, 1925. Reprint Graz: Akademische Druck- und Verlagsanstalt, 1965.

Frolov, Boris. "L'Art paléolitique: Préhistoire de la science?" *Unión Internacional de Ciencias Prehistóricas y Protohistóricas. X congreso. Comision XI. Arte Paleolítico. Coloquio.* México D.F., Octubre 19–24, 1981. México, D.F.: UISPP, 1981: 60–81.

Gaggia, Fabio et al., eds. *Benaco '85: La cultura figurativa rupestre dalla protostoria ai nostri giorni. Archeologia e storia di un mezzo espressivo tradizionale. Atti del primo convegno internazionale di arte rupestre, Torri del Benaco 1985.* Torino: Antropologia Alpina, 1986.

Galdino, Luiz. *Itacoatiaras: Uma pre-historia da arte no Brasil = Itacoatiaras: A Prehistory of Art in Brazil.* São Paulo: Editora Rios, 1988.

Gamble, Clive. "Interaction and Alliance in Palaeolithic Society." *Man NS 17* (1982): 92–107.

———. "Culture and Society in the Upper Palaeolithic of Europe." In *Hunter-gatherer Economy in Prehistory: A European Perspective,* ed. Geoff Bailey. Cambridge: Cambridge University Press, 1983: 201–211.

———. "The Social Context for European Palaeolithic Art." *Proceedings of the Prehistoric Society* 57:1 (1991): 3–15.

Garcia, Michel-Alain and Madiha Rachad. *L'Art des origines au Yémen.* Paris: Seuil, 1997.

García Castro, Juan Antonio, ed. *Arte rupestre en España.* Madrid: Zugarto, 1987.

García Guinea, Miguel Ángel. *Cuevas prehistóricas en Santander: Altamira.* Santander: Patronato de Cuevas Prehistóricas de la Provincia, 1970.

———. *Altamira y otros cuevas de Cantabria.* Madrid: Silex, 1979; 2nd ed. 1988; German ed. *Altamira: Altamira und andere Höhlen Kantabriens. Jubiläumsausgabe zur Hundertjahrfeier der Entdeckung der Malereien von Altamira.* Madrid: Silex, 1979; French ed. *Altamira.* Madrid: Silex, 1979; Engl. ed. *Altamira.* Madrid: Silex, 1979.

———. *Altamira: Principio del arte.* Madrid: Silex, 1980; French ed. *Altamira: Origine de l'art*. Madrid: Silex, 1980; German ed. *Altamira: Anfang der Kunst*. Madrid: Silex, 1980; Engl. ed. *Altamira: The Origin of Art*. Madrid: Silex, 1980.

―――. *Descubrimiento y trascendencia de las pinturas de Altamira*. Santander: Departamento de Comunicación y Estudios del Banco de Santander, 1984.

Garfinkel, Yosef. "Dancing and the Beginnings of Art Scenes in the Early Village Communities of the Near East and Southeast Europe." *Cambridge Journal of Archaeology* 8 (1998): 207–237.

Garlake, Peter S. *The Painted Caves: An Introduction to the Prehistoric Rock Art of Zimbabwe*. Harare: Modus Publications, 1987.

―――. *The Hunter's Vision: The Prehistoric Art of Zimbabwe*. London: British Museum, 1995.

Gély, Bernard. *Grottes ornées de l'Ardèche: L'art des cavernes*. Veurey: Éditions "Le Dauphiné libéré", and Grenoble: Musée Dauphinois, 2000.

Ghilardoni, Virgilio. *Naissance de l'art*. Lausanne: La Guilde du Livre, 1948.

Giedion, Sigfried. *The Beginnings of Art*. New York: Pantheon, 1962; French ed. *La Naissance de l'art*. Bruxelles: Éditions de la Connaissance, 1965.

Gimbutas, Marija. "The Image of Woman in Prehistoric Art." *Quarterly Review of Archaeology* 2:1 (December 1981): 1, 5–6.

―――― "Vulvas, Breasts, and Buttocks of the Goddess Creatress: Commentary on the Origins of Art." In *The Shape of the Past: Studies in Honor of Franklin D. Murphy*, ed. Giorgio Buccellati and Charles Speroni. Los Angeles, CA: Institute of Archaeology and Office of the Chancellor, University of California, 1981: 16–42.

Glory, André and Henri Breuil. *Au pays du grand silence noir: Explorations souterraines*. Paris: Éditions "Alsatia", [s.d.].

Godden, Elaine. *Rock Paintings of Aboriginal Australia*. Frenchs Forest, NSW: Reed, 1982; 2nd rev. ed. Kew, VIC: Reed Books, 1997.

Goldhahn, Joakim, ed. *Rock Art as Social Representation: Papers from a Session Held at the European Association of Archaeologists Fourth Annual Meeting in Göteborg 1998*. Oxford: Archaeopress, 1999.

Gombrich, Ernst. *The Story of Art*. London: Phaidon, 1950.

Gomes, Miguel. *La cueva de Altamira (1984–1991)*. Caracas: Alfadil, 1992.

Gómez-Tabanera, José Manuel. "Significación religiosa y función semiologica en el arte rupestre astur-cantábrico." In *Symposium international sur les religions de la préhistoire: Valcamonica, 18–23 Septembre 1972*, ed. Emmanuel Anati. Capo di Ponte: Edizioni del Centro, 1975: 65–72.

―――. *Les Statuettes féminines paléolitiques dites "Venus" et leur signification dans le monde préhistorique*. Oviedo: Universidad, Seminario de Prehistoria, and RIEP Asturias-Périgord, 1978.

―――. *La presunta imagen de la diosa-madre en el paleolítico y la invención de los primeros planisferios geográficos*. Madrid: Gómez-Tabanera, 1998.

Gómez Urdáñez, José Luis, Carmen Gómez Urdáñez, Reynaldo González García, and José Luis Pano Gracia: *Os primórdios da civilização: Pré-história e primeiras culturas*. Amadora: Ediclube, 1993.

González, Reynaldo. *Las claves del arte prehistórico*. Barcelona: Ariel, 1989.

―――. *Arte prehistórico*. Barcelona: Planeta, 1995.

González Echegaray, Joaquín. *Altamira y sus pinturas rupestres*. Madrid: Ministerio de Cultura, Dirección General de Bellas Artes y Archivos, Departamento de Arqueología, 1985.

González Echegaray, Joaquín, ed. *El hombre prehistórico y el arte rupestre en España*. Bilbao: Junta de Cultura de Vizcaya, 1962.

[Festschrift Joaquín González Echegaray] José Antonio Lasheras Corruchaga, ed. *Homenaje al Dr. Joaquín González Echegaray*. Madrid: Ministerio de Cultura, Dirección General de Bellas Artes y Archivos, 1994.

González Morales, Manuel R., Rodrigo de Balbín Behrmann et al., eds. *Cien años después de Sautuola: Estudios en homenaje a Marcelino Sanz de Sautuola en el centenario de su muerte*. Santander: Consejería de Cultura, Educación y Deporte, 1989.

Goodall, Elizabeth. *Prehistoric Rock Art of the Federation of Rhodesia & Nyasaland*. Salisbury, Southern Rhodesia: National Publications Trust, 1959.

Grand, Paule Marie. *Prehistoric Art: Paleolithic Painting and Sculpture*. Greenwich, CT: New York Graphic Society, 1967.

Grande del Brío, Ramón. *La pintura rupestre esquemática en el centro-oeste de España (Salamanca y Zamora): Ensayo de interpretación del arte esquemático*. Salamanca: Diputación de Salamanca, 1987.

Grant, Campbell. *The Rock Paintings of the Chumash: A Study of a California Indian Culture*. Berkeley, CA: University of California Press, 1965.

———. *Rock Art of the American Indian*. New York: Crowell, 1967; 2nd ed. Golden, CO: Outbooks, 1981; 3rd ed. Dillon, CO: Vista Books, 1992.

———. *Rock Drawings of the Coso Range, Inyo County, California: An Ancient Sheep-Hunting Cult Pictured in Desert Rock Carvings*. China Lake, CA: Maturango Press, 1968.

———. *Rock Art of Baja California: With Notes on the Pictographs of Baja California*. Los Angeles, CA: Dawson's Book Shop, 1974.

———. *Canyon de Chelly, Its People and Rock Art*. Tucson, AZ: University of Arizona Press, 1978.

———. *The Rock Art of the North American Indians*. Cambridge: Cambridge University Press, 1983.

GRAPP (Groupe de Reflexion sur l'Art Pariétal Paléolithique). *L'Art pariétal paléolithique: Techniques et méthodes d'étude*. Paris: Ministère de l'Enseignement Supérieur et de la Recherche, Comité des Travaux Historiques et Scientifiques, 1993.

Graziosi, Paolo. *L'arte dell' antica età della pietra*. Firenze: Sansoni, 1956; Engl. ed. *Palaeolithic Art*. London: Faber and Faber, 1960.

———. *L'arte preistorica in Italia*. Firenze: Sansoni, 1973.

Grigson, Geoffrey. *Painted Caves*. London: Phoenix House, 1957.

Grimm, Robert E., ed. *Prehistoric Art: A Picture Study of Ancient America Thru Tools and Artifacts*. St. Louis, MO: Greater St. Louis Archaeological Society, 1953.

Groenen, Marc. *Ombre et lumière dans l'art des grottes*. Bruxelles: Université Libre de Bruxelles, Centre de Recherche et d'Études Technologiques des Arts Plastiques, 1997.

Groenfeldt, David. "The Interpretation of Prehistoric Art." *Rock Art Research* 2 (1985): 20–46; 166–167.

Grosse, Ernst. *Die Anfänge der Kunst.* Freiburg im Breisgau and Leipzig: Mohr, 1894.

Grottes ornées. Special Issue of *Monuments Historiques* 118 (November–December 1981).

Gudnitz, Fred. *Broncealderens monumentalkunst: De skandinaviske helleristninger.* Tanumshede: Bohusläns hällristnings-forskningsarkiv, and København: Hamburger, 1962.

Guffroy, Jean. *El arte rupestre del antiguo Perú.* Lima: Instituto Francés de Estudios Andinos IRD, 1999.

Guidon, Niède. *Peintures rupestres de Varzea Grande, Piaui, Brésil.* Paris: École des Hautes Études en Sciences Sociales, 1975.

———. *Peintures préhistoriques du Brésil: L'art rupestre du Piaui.* Paris: Éditions Recherche sur les Civilisations, 1991.

Guidon, Niède, Silvia Maranca, and Agueda Vilhena de Moraes. *Abris peints de la Serra da Capivara, région de Varzea Grande, État du Piaui, Brésil.* Paris: Institut d'Ethnologie, 1975.

Gunn, R. G. *The Prehistoric Rock Art Sites of Victoria: A Catalogue.* Victoria: Ministry for Conservation, 1981.

———. *A Second Catalogue of Victorian Rock Art Sites.* Melbourne: Victoria Archaeological Survey, 1987.

———. *Aboriginal Rock Art of Victoria.* Melbourne: Victoria Archaeological Survey, 1987.

Gutierrez, Manuel. *L'Art pariétal de l'Angola.* Paris: L'Harmattan, 1996.

Gvozdover, Marianna D. "The Typology of Female Figurines of the Kostenki Paleolithic Culture." *Soviet Anthropology and Archaeology* 27: 4 (Spring 1989): 32–94.

———. *Art of the Mammoth Hunters: The Finds from Avdeevo.* Oxford: Oxbow, 1995.

Haas, Germaine. *Symbolik und Magie in der Urgeschichte: Ihre Bedeutung für den heutigen Menschen.* Bern: Haupt, 1992.

Hachid, Malika. *Les Pierres écrites de l'Atlas Saharien.* 2 vols. Alger: ENAG, 1992.

———. *Le Tassili des Ajjer: Aux sources de l'Afrique, 50 siècles avant les pyramides.* Paris: Paris-Méditerranée, and Alger: Edif 2000, 1998.

Hadingham, Evan. *Secrets of the Stone Age: The World of the Cave Artists.* New York: Walker, 1979. London: Heinemann, 1980.

Haensch, Wolf Günter. *Die paläolithischen Menschendarstellungen aus der Sicht der somatischen Anthropologie: Menschenbildnisse auf Gravierungen, Reliefs und Malereien in Südwestfrankreich und Nordostspanien.* Bonn: Habelt, 1968.

Hahn, Joachim. "Die Stellung der männlichen Statuette aus dem Hohlenstein-Stadel in der jungpaläolithischen Kunst." *Germania* 48 (1970): 1–12.

———. "Eine jungpaläolithische Elfenbeinplastik aus dem Hohlenstein-Stadel." *Fundberichte aus Schwaben* NF 19 (1971): 11–23; French transl. "La Statuette masculin de la grotte du Hohlenstein-Stadel (Wurtemberg)." *L'Anthropologie* 75 (1971): 233–244.

———. "Aurignacian Signs, Pendants, and Art Objects in Central and Eastern Europe." *World Archaeology* 3 (1971–1972): 252–266.

———. *Aurignacien: Das ältere Jungpaläolithikum in Mittel- und Osteuropa.* Köln: Böhlau, 1977.

———. "L'Art mobilier aurignacien en Allemagne du Sud-Ouest." In *La Contri-*

bution de la zoologie et de l'éthologie à l'interprétation de l'art des peuples chasseurs préhistoriques, ed. Hans-Georg Bandi et al. Fribourg: Éditions Universitaires, 1984: 283–293.

———. "Demi-relief aurignacien en ivoire de la grotte Geissenklösterle, près d'Ulm (Allemagne Fédéral)." Bulletin de la Société Préhistorique Française 79 (1982): 73–77.

———. "Recherches sur l'art paléolithique depuis 1976." In Aurignacien et Gravettien en Europe, ed. Janusz K. Kozłowski and René Desbrosse. Vol. 3: Bilan des recherches de 1976 à 1981. Liège: Université de Liège, 1982: 79–82.

———. Kraft und Aggression: Die Botschaft der Eiszeitkunst im Aurignacien Süddeutschlands? Tübingen: Archaeologica Venatoria, 1986.

———. Die Geißenklösterle-Höhle im Achtal bei Blaubeuren. Stuttgart: Theiss, 1988.

———. "Fonction et signification des statuettes du Paléolithique Supérieur européen." In L'Art des objets au paléolithique: Colloque international, Foix, Le Mas-d'Azil, 16–21 novembre 1987, ed. Jean Clottes. Vol. 2: Paris: Ministère de la Culture, 1990: 173–184.

———. Eiszeitschmuck auf der Schwäbischen Alb. Ulm: Süddeutsche Verlagsgesellschaft, 1992.

———. "Aurignacien Art in Central Europe." In Before Lascaux: The Complex Record of the Early Upper Paleolithic, ed. Heidi Knecht, Anne Pike-Tay and Randall White. Boca Raton, FL: CRC Press, 1993: 229–241.

Hahn, Joachim, ed. Actes de la Table Ronde "Le Travail et l'Usage de l'Ivoire au Paléolithique Supérieur", Ravello, 29—31 mai 1992, Centro Universitario Europeo per i Beni Culturali, Ravello. Roma: Istituto Poligrafico e Zecca dello Stato, 1995.

Hahn, Joachim and Eberhard Wagner. "Eine jungpaläolithische Elfenbeinplastik aus dem Geißenklösterle Blaubeuren." Archäologisches Korrespondenzblatt 5 (1975): 167–170.

Hallier, Ulrich W. Die Entwicklung der Felsbildkunst Nordafrikas: Untersuchungen auf Grund neuerer Felsbildfunde in der Süd-Sahara. Stuttgart: Steiner, 1990.

———. Felsbilder früher Jägervölker der Zentral-Sahara: Rundköpfe – Schleifer – Gravierer – Punzer. Stuttgart: Steiner, 1995.

Hallier, Ulrich W. und Brigitte C. Hallier. Felsbilder der Zentral-Sahara: Untersuchungen auf Grund neuerer Felsbildfunde in der Süd-Sahara. Stuttgart: Steiner, 1992.

Hallström, Gustaf. Monumental Art of Northern Europe from the Stone Age. 2 vols. Stockholm: Thule, 1938.

———. Monumental Art of Northern Sweden from the Stone Age. Stockholm: Almqvist & Wicksell, 1960.

Halverson, John. "Art for Art's Sake in the Paleolithic." Current Anthropology 28 (1987): 63–89.

———. "The First Pictures: Perceptual Foundations of Palaeolithic Art." Perception 21 (1992): 389–404.

Hambleton, Enrique. La pintura rupestre de Baja California. Ciudad de México: Fomento Cultural Banamex, 1979.

Hameau, Philippe. Les Peintures postglaciaires en Provence: Inventaire, étude chronologique, stylistique et iconographique. Paris: Maison des Sciences de l'Homme, 1989.

Hamilton, Naomi. "Ungendering Archaeology: Concepts of Sex and Gender in

Figurine Studies in Prehistory." In *Representations of Gender from Prehistory to the Present*, ed. Moira Donald and Linda Hurcombe. Houndmills: Macmillan, 2000: 17–30.

Hamilton, Naomi, et al. "Viewpoint: Can We Interpret Figurines?" *Cambridge Archaeological Journal* 6 (1996): 281–307.

Hančar, Franz: "Zum Problem der Venusstatuetten im eurasiatischen Jungpaläolithikum." *Prähistorische Zeitschrift* 30 (1939–40): 85–156.

———. *Das Pferd in prähistorischer und früher historischer Zeit*. Wien: Herold, 1956.

Hayden, Brian. "The Cultural Capacities of Neandertals: A Review and Reevaluation." *Journal of Human Evolution* 24 (1993): 113–146.

Hedges, Ken. "Southern Californian Rock Art as Shamanic Art." *American Indian Rock Art* 2 (1976): 126–138.

———. "Phosphenes in the Context of Native American Rock Art." *American Indian Rock Art* 7 + 8 (1982): 1–10.

———. "The Shamanic Origins of Rock Art." In *Ancient Images on Stone: Rock Art of the Californias*, ed. JoAnne Van Tilburg. Los Angeles, CA: Rock Art Archive, Institute of Archaeology, University of California, Los Angeles, 1983. 46–60.

———. "Rock Art Portrayals of Shamanic Transformations and Magical Flight." *Rock Art Papers* 2 (1985): 83–94.

———. "Places to See and Places to Hear: Rock Art and Features of the Sacred Landscape." Jack Steinbring, Alan Watchman, Paul Faulstich, and Paul S. C. Taçon, eds.: *Time and Space: Dating and Considerations in Rock Art Research: Papers of Symposia F and E, Second AURA Congress, Cairns 1992*. Melbourne: Australian Rock Art Research Association, 1993: 121–127.

———. "Shamanistic Aspects of California Rock Art." In *California Indian Shamanism*, ed. Lowell John Bean. Menlo Park, CA: Ballena Press, 1992: 67–88.

Hedlund, Ann Lane, ed. *Perspectives on Anthropological Collections from the American Southwest: Proceedings of a Symposium*. Tempe, AZ: Arizona State University, 1989.

Heizer, Robert Fleming and C. William Clewlow, Jr. *Prehistoric Rock Art of California*. 2 vols. Ramona, CA: Ballena Press, 1973.

Heizer, Robert Fleming and Martin A. Baumhoff. *Prehistoric Rock Art of Nevada and Eastern California*. Berkeley, CA: University of California Press, 1962.

Helskog, Knut Arne, ed. *Theoretical Perspectives in Rock Art Research: ACRA, the Alta Conference on Rock Art*. Oslo: Novus & Instituttet for sammenlignende kulturforskning, 2001.

Helskog, Knut and Bjørnar Olsen, eds. *Perceiving Rock Art: Social and Political Perspectives. ACRA, the Alta Conference on Rock Art*. Oslo: Novus, 1995.

Hensel, Witold: *Sztuka społczeństw paleolitycznych*. Warszawa: Panstwowe Muzeum Archeologiczne, 1957.

Henshilwood, Christopher S., Francesco d'Errico, C. W. Marean, R. G. Milo, and Royden Yates. "An Early Bone Industry from the Middle Stone Age at Blombos Cave, South Africa: Implications for the Origins of Modern Human Behaviour, Symbolism and Language." *Journal of Human Evolution* 41 (2001): 631–678.

Henshilwood, Christopher S., Judith C. Sealy, Royden Yates, K. Cruz-Uribe, P. Goldberg, F. E. Grine, Richard G. Klein, C. Poggenpoel, K. van Niekerk, and Ian Watts. "Blombos Cave, Southern Cape, South Africa: Preliminary Report on the 1992–1999 Excavations of the Middle Stone Age Levels." *Journal of Archaeological Science* 28:4 (April 2001): 421–448.

Henshilwood, Christopher S., Francesco d'Errico, Royden Yates, Zenobia Jacobs, Chantal Tribolo, Geoff A. T. Duller, Norbert Mercier, Judith C. Sealy, Hélène Valladas, Ian Watts, and Ann G. Wintle. "Emergence of Modern Human Behaviour: Middle Stone Age Engravings from South Africa." *Science* 295:5558 (15 February 2002): 1278–1280.

Hernández Herrero, Gemma, ed. *Arte rupestre del arco mediterráneo de la península ibérica*. Exh. cat. Zaragoza: Departamento de Educación y Cultura, 1999. Catalan ed. *Art rupestre de l'arc mediterrani de la península ibèrica*. Barcelona: Generalitat de Catalunya, Departament de Cultura, 1999.

Hernández-Pacheco, Eduardo. *Estudios de arte prehistórico*. Madrid: Comision de Investigaciones Paleontologicas y Prehistóricas, 1918.

———. *Las pinturas prehistóricas de las Cuevas de la Araña, Valencia: Evolución del arte rupestre de España*. Madrid: Museo Nacional de Ciencias Naturales, 1924.

———. *Descubrimiento del arte prehistórico*. Madrid: Real Sociedad Española de Historia Natural, 1958. [Separata of *Boletin de la Real Sociedad Española de Historia Natural* 56 (1958): 261–285].

Hill, Beth. *Guide to Indian Rock Carvings of the Pacific Northwest Coast*. Saanichton, B.C.: Hancock House, 1975.

Hill, Beth and Ray Hill. *Indian Petroglyphs of the Pacific Northwest*. Saanichton, B.C.: Hancock House, 1974; 2nd ed. Seattle, WA: University of Washington Press, 1975.

Hill, James N. and Joel Gunn, eds. *The Individual in Prehistory: Studies of Variability in Style in Prehistoric Technologies*. New York: Academic Press, 1977.

Hirschmann, Fred. *Rock Art of the American Southwest*. Portland, OR: Graphic Arts Center, 1994.

Hodgson, Derek. "Shamanism, Phosphenes, and Early Art: An Alternative Synthesis." *Current Anthropology* 42 (2000): 866–873.

Hoernes, Moritz. *Urgeschichte der bildenden Kunst in Europa von den Anfängen bis um 500 v. Chr.* Wien: Holzhausen, 1898; 2nd rev. ed. Wien: Schroll, 1915; 3rd rev. ed. 1925.

———. *Kultur der Urzeit. 1. Steinzeit. 2. Bronzezeit. 3. Eisenzeit.* Leipzig: Göschen, 1912–17; 2nd rev. ed. Berlin: De Gruyter, 1921–23; 4th ed. Berlin: De Gruyter, 1950; Spanish ed. *Prehistoria. Segunda edición. 1. La Edad de la Piedra. 2. La Edad del Bronce 3. La Edad del Hierro.* Barcelona and Buenos Aires, 1928–1931.

Homo-Lechner, Catherine and Annie Bélis, eds. *La Pluridisciplinarité en archéologie musicale: IVe rencontres internationales d'archéologie musicale de l'ICTM.* Saint-Germain-en-Laye, 8–12 octobre 1990. 2 vols. Paris: Éditions de la Maison des Sciences de l'Homme, 1994.

Hudson, Steven C. "The Hunter's Eye: Visual Perception and Palaeolithic Art." *Archaeological Review from Cambridge* 15:1 (1998): 93–109.

Huffman, Thomas N. "The Trance Hypothesis and the Rock Art of Zimbabwe." *South African Archaeological Society Goodwin Series* 4 (1983): 49–53.

Hugot, Henri J. and Maximilien Bruggmann. *Sahara: Art rupestre*. Paris: Éditions de l'Amateur, 1999.

Huyghe, René and Emily Evershed, eds. *Larousse Encyclopedia of Prehistoric and Ancient Art: Art and Mankind*. New York: Prometheus Press, 1962; 2nd rev. ed. 1967.

Ibarra y Ruiz, Pedro. *Contribución al estudio del arte español: Instrumentos de la Edad de piedra. Cerámica y monumentos de la Edad antigua. Elche. Materiales para su historia. Ensayo demostrativo de su antigüedad e importancia histórica*. Cuenca: Ruiz de Lara, 1926.

Inskeep, Ray, ed. *Reading Art*. Special Issue of *World Archaeology* 25:3 (February 1994).

Jacobson, Esther. *The Deer Goddess of Ancient Siberia: A Study in the Ecology of Belief*. Leiden: Brill, 1993.

Jaubert, Jacques. *Chasseurs et artisans du Moustérien*. Paris: La Maison des Roches, 1999.

Jelinek, Jan. "Considérations sur l'art paléolithique mobilier." *L'Anthropologie* 92 (1988): 203–238.

———. *The Great Art of the Early Australians: The Study of the Evolution and Role of Rock Art in the Society of Australian Hunters and Gatherers*. Brno: Moravian Museum, Anthropos Institute, 1989.

Jochim, Michael A. "Palaeolithic Cave Art in Ecological Perspective." In *Hunter-gatherer Economy in Prehistory: A European Perspective*, ed. Geoff Bailey. Cambridge: Cambridge University Press, 1983: 212–219.

Johnson, R. Townley. *Major Rock Paintings of Southern Africa: Facsimile Reproductions*. Amsterdam: Meulenhoff, 1979, and Bloomington, IN: Indiana University Press, 1979.

Jones, Neville. *The Stone Age in Rhodesia*. London: Oxford University Press, 1926.

Jordá, Francisco. "Sobre técnicas, temas y etapas del arte paleolítico de la region cantábrica." *Zephyrus* 15 (1964): 5–25.

Jorge, Vítor Oliveira, ed. *Dossier Côa*. Porto: Sociedade Portuguesa de Antropologia e Etnologia, 1995.

Joubert, Sylvie, ed. *Arts primitifs dans les ateliers d'artistes*. Exh. cat. Paris: Musée de l'Homme, 1967.

Junceda Avello, Enrique. *La sexualidad primitiva y su simbología a través del arte prehistórico: "Notas a una ginecología prehistórica."* Oviedo: Grandio, 1974.

Jung, Michael. *Research on Rock Art in North Yemen*. Napoli: Istituto Universitario Orientale, 1991 [i.e., 1992]. [Supplemento n. 66 agli *Annali* 51:1 (1991).]

Kaache, Bouchra. *Archéologie de l'art rupestre: Analyse du bestiaire gravé du Présahara morocain*. Oxford: Archaeopress, 2001.

Kai, Shan-lin and Chih-hao Kai. *Chung-kuo yen hua = China's Rock Painting*. Kuang-chou: Kuang-tung lu yu chu pan she, 1996.

Keyser, James D. *Rock Art of Western South Dakota*. Sioux Falls, SD: South Dakota Archaeological Society, 1984.

———. *Indian Rock Art of the Columbia Plateau*, Seattle, WA: Douglas and McIntyre, 1992.

———. *Plains Indian Rock Art*. Seattle/WA: University of Washington Press; Vancouver: UBC Press, 2001.

Khan, Majeed. *The Prehistoric Rock Art of Northern Saudi Arabia: A Synthetic Approach to the Study of the Rock Art from Wadi Damm, Northwest of Tabuk.* [s.l.]: Department of Antiquities and Museums, Ministry of Education, 1993.

King, Mary Elizabeth. "On the Origins and Meanings of 'Art.' " *Quarterly Review of Archaeology* 4:4 (December 1983): 1, 6–7.

Kirchner, Liselore. *Jungpaläolithische Handdarstellungen der franko-kantabrischen Felsbilderzone: Ein Versuch ihrer Deutung unter Berücksichtigung ethnographischer Parallelen.* Göppingen: Werner-Müller, 1957.

Kirkland, Forrest and William Wilmon Newcomb Jr. *The Rock Art of Texas Indians.* Austin/TX: University of Texas Press, 1967.

Klíma, Bohuslav. "Les Representations animales du Paléolithique Supérieur de Dolní Veštonice (Tchecoslovaquie)." In *La Contribution de la zoologie et de l'éthologie à l'interprétation de l'art des peuples chasseurs préhistoriques,* ed. Hans-Georg Bandi et al. Fribourg: Éditions Universitaires, 1984. 323–332.

Knecht, Heidi, Anne Pike-Tay, and Randall White, eds. *Before Lascaux: The Complex Record of the Early Upper Paleolithic.* Boca Raton, FL: CRC Press, 1993.

Knight, Chris. *Blood Relations. Menstruation and the Origins of Culture.* New Haven and London: Yale University Press, 1991.

Knight, Chris, Camilla Power, and Ian Watts. "The Human Symbolic Revolution: A Darwinian Account." *Cambridge Archaeological Journal* 5:1 (1995): 75–114.

Koenigswald, Gustav Heinrich Ralph von. "Early Homo Sapiens as an Artist: The Meaning of Palaeolithic Art." In *The Origin of Homo Sapiens/Origine de l'homme moderne: Proceedings of the Paris Symposium, 2–5 September 1969, Organized by Unesco in Co-operation with the International Union for Quaternary Research (INQUA),* ed. François Bordes. Paris: Unesco, 1972. 133–139.

König, Marie E.P. "Étude des incisions rupestres comme manifestation d'un stade d'évolution de l'esprit humaine." In *Symposium international d'art préhistorique: Valcamonica, 23–28 Septembre 1968,* ed. Emmanuel Anati. Capo di Ponte: Edizioni del Centro, 1970. 515–530.

Kozłowski, Janusz Krzysztof. *L'Art de la préhistoire en Europe orientale.* Paris: Centre National de la Recherche Scientifique, 1992.

Kraft, Georg. *Der Urmensch als Schöpfer: Die geistige Welt des Eiszeitmenschen.* Tübingen: Matthiesen, 1948.

Kubler, George. "Eidetic Images and Paleolithic Art." *Journal of Psychology* 119 (1986): 557–565.

Kühn, Herbert. *Die Malerei der Eiszeit.* München: Delphin-Verlag, 1922; 2nd rev. ed. 1922; 3rd rev. ed. 1923; Spanish ed. *El arte de la epoca glacial.* México: Fondo de Cultura Económica, 1971.

———. *Kunst und Kultur der Vorzeit Europas: Das Paläolithikum.* Berlin: De Gruyter, 1929.

———. *Die Felsbilder Europas.* Berlin: Propyläen, 1935; 3rd rev. ed. Stuttgart: Kohlhammer, 1971; Engl. ed. *The Rock Pictures of Europe.* New York: October House, 1967.

———. *Auf den Spuren des Eiszeitmenschen.* Wiesbaden: Brockhaus, 1950; Engl. ed. *On the Track of Prehistoric Man.* London: Hutchinson, 1955; 2nd ed. London: Arrow Books, 1958.

———. *Eiszeitkunst: Die Geschichte ihrer Erforschung.* Berlin: Musterschmidt, 1965.

Kunej, Brago and Ivan Turk. "New Perspectives on the Beginnings of Music: Archaeological and Musical Analysis of a Middle Paleolithic Bone 'Flute.' "

The Origins of Music, ed. Nils L. Wallin, Björn Merker and Steven Brown. Cambridge, MA: MIT Press, 2000: 235–268.

Lacalle Rodríguez, Raquel. "El simbolo de la mano en el arte paleolítico." *Zephyrus* 49 (1996): 273–279.

Laing, Lloyd Robert and Jennifer Laing. *Ancient Art: The Challenge to Modern Thought.* Dublin: Irish Academic Press, 1993.

Lajoux, Jean-Dominique. *Merveilles du Tassili n'Ajjer.* Paris: Éditions du Chêne, 1962; German ed. *Wunder des Tassili n' Ajjer.* Leipzig: Edition Leipzig, 1967.

Laming-Emperaire, Annette. *Lascaux: Paintings and Engravings.* Harmondsworth: Penguin Books, 1959.

———. *La Signification de l'art rupestre paléolithique.* Paris: Picard, 1962.

———. "Système de penser et organisation sociale dans l'art rupestre paléolithique." *L'Homme de Cro-Magnon: Anthropologie et archéologie. Colloque organisé aux Eyzies du 15 au 17 juillet 1968.* Paris: Arts et Métiers Graphique, 1970: 197–211.

———. "Art rupestre et organisation sociale." In *Santander Symposium,* ed. Martín Almagro Basch and Miguel Ángel García Guinea. Santander: Museo de Prehistoria, 1972: 65–82.

[Festschrift Annette Laming-Emperaire] *Coletânea de estudos em homenagem a Annette Laming-Emperaire.* São Paulo: Universidade de São Paulo, Fundo de Pesquisas do Museu Paulista, 1978.

[Festschrift Annette Laming-Emperaire] *Hommage à Annette Laming-Emperaire.* Paris: Société des Américanistes, 1981.

Lanoue, Guy. *Images in Stone: A Theory on Interpreting Rock Art.* Roma: Art Center, 1989.

Larsson, Lar and Berta Stjernquist, eds. *The World-View of Prehistoric Man: Papers Presented at a Symposium in Lund, 5–7 May, 1997.* Stockholm: Kungl. Vitterhets, Historie och Antikvitets Akademien, 1998.

Laval, Leon. *La Caverne peinte de Lascaux.* Montignac-sur-Vezère: [Centre d'Études et de Documentation Préhistoriques], 1948.

Lawson, Andrew J. *Cave Art.* Princes Risborough: Shire, 1991.

Lawson, Andrew J., ed. *Essays in Palaeolithic Art.* Special Issue of *Proceedings of the Prehistoric Society* 57:1 (1991).

Layton, Robert. "The Cultural Context of Hunter-Gatherer Rock Art." *Man* NS 20 (1985): 434–453.

———. "The Use of Ethnographic Parallels in Interpreting Upper Palaeolithic Rock Art." Ladislav Holý, ed.: *Comparative Anthropology.* Oxford: Blackwell, 1987: 210–239.

———. "Figure, Motif and Symbol in the Hunter-Gatherer Rock Art of Europe and Australia." In *Rock Art and Prehistory: Papers Presented to Symposium G of the AURA Congress, Darwin 1988,* ed. Paul G. Bahn and Andrée Rosenfeld. Oxford: Oxbow Books, 1991: 23–38.

———. *Australian Rock Art: A New Synthesis.* Cambridge: Cambridge University Press, 1992.

Leakey, Mary Douglas. *Africa's Vanishing Art: The Rock Paintings of Tanzania.* Garden City, NY: Doubleday, 1983.

Lee, D. Neil. *Art on the Rocks of Southern Africa.* Cape Town: Purnell, 1970.

Lee, Georgia. *Rock Art of Easter Island: Symbols of Power, Prayers to the Gods.* Los

Angeles, CA: Institute of Archaeology, University of California, Los Angeles, 1992.

———. *Rock Art and Cultural Resource Management*. Calabasas, CA: Wormwood Press, 1991.

Lee, Georgia and Edward Stasack. *Spirit of Place: Petroglyphs of Hawai'i*. Los Osos, CA: Easter Island Foundation, 1999.

Lemozi, Amédée. *La Grotte-temple du Peche-Merle: Un nouveau sanctuaire préhistorique*. Paris: Picard, 1929.

———. *Pech Merle, Le Combel, Marcenac*. Graz: Akademische Druck- und Verlagsanstalt, 1969.

Lenssen-Erz, Tilman, Marie-Theres Erz, and Gerhard Bosinski, eds. *Brandberg: Der Bilderberg Namibias. Kunst und Geschichte einer Urlandschaft*. Stuttgart: Thorbecke, 2000.

Leonardi, Piero. *Sacralità, arte e grafia paleolitiche: Splendori e problemi*. Calliano: Manfrini, 1989.

Lepenski Vir: Prähistorische Plastik vom Eisernen Tor. Exh. cat. Belgrad: Nationalmuseum, and Berlin: Museum für Ur- und Frühgeschichte, 1987.

Le Quellec, Jean-Loïc. *Symbolisme et art rupestre au Sahara*. Paris: Harmattan, 1993.

———. *Art rupestre et préhistoire du Sahara: Le Messak libyen*. Paris: Payot et Rivages, 1998.

Leroi-Gourhan, André. *Documents pour l'art comparé de l'Eurasie septentrionale*. Paris: Les Éditions d'Art et d'Histoire, 1943.

———. *Archéologie du Pacifique-nord: Materiaux pour l'étude des relations entre les peuples riverains d'Asie et d'Amérique*. Paris: Institut d'Ethnologie, 1946.

———. "La Fonction des signes dans les sanctuaires paléolithiques." *Bulletin de la Société Préhistorique Française* 55 (1958): 307–321.

———. "Repartition et groupement des animaux dans l'art pariétal paléolithique." *Bulletin de la Société Préhistorique Française* 55 (1958): 515–552.

———. *Art et religion au paléolithique superieur*. 2 vols. Paris: Faculté des Lettres et Sciences Humaines, Cours Public de Préhistoire, 1959–61.

———. *Les Religions de la préhistoire (Paléolithique)*. Paris: Presses Universitaires de France, 1964.

———. *Préhistoire de l'art occidental*. Paris: Mazenot, 1965; 2nd ed. 1971; 3rd ed. 1973; 4th ed. 1995; Engl. ed. *Treasures of Prehistoric Art*. New York: Abrams, 1967; *The Art of Prehistoric Man in Western Europe*. London: Thames and Hudson, 1968.

———. "La Religion des grottes: Magie ou métaphysique?" *Sciences et Avenir* 22 (1966): 105–111, 140; Engl. transl. "The Religion of the Caves: Magic or Metaphysics?" *October* 37 (1986): 7–17.

———. "The Evolution of Paleolithic Art." *Scientific American* 218:2 (February 1968): 58–70.

———. *L'Art et les grandes civilisations*. Paris: Mazenod, 1971.

———. "Considerations sur l'organisation spatiale des figures animales dans l'art pariétal paléolithique." In *Santander Symposium*, ed. Martín Almagro Basch and Miguel Ángel García Guinea. Santander: Museo de Prehistoria, 1972: 281–308.

———. "Le Préhistorien et le chamane." *L'Ethnographie* NS 73:1 (1977): 19–25.

————. "Les Signes pariétaux comme 'marqueurs' ethniques." *Altamira Symposium*. Madrid: Ministerio de Cultura, 1981: 289–294.

————. *Più antichi artisti d'Europa*. Milano: Jaca, 1981; Engl. ed. *The Dawn of European Art: An Introduction to Palaeolithic Cave Painting*. Cambridge: Cambridge University Press, 1982; Spanish ed. *Los primeros artistas de Europa: Introducción al arte parietal paleolítico*. Madrid: Ediciones Encuentro, 1983.

————. *Arte y grafismo en la Europa prehistórica*. Madrid: ISTMO, 1984.

————. *Símbolos, artes y creencias de la prehistoria*. Madrid: ISTMO, 1984.

————. *L'Art pariétal. Langage de la préhistoire*. Grenoble: Millon, 1992.

[Festschrift André Leroi-Gourhan] *L'Homme, hier et aujourd'hui: Recueil d'études en hommage à André Leroi-Gourhan*. Edited by Marc Rodolphe Sauter. Paris: Cujas, 1973.

[Festschrift André Leroi-Gourhan] *André Leroi-Gourhan, ou, Les Voies de l'homme: Actes du colloque du CNRS, mars 1987*. Edited by Lucien Bernot. Paris: Albin Michel, 1988.

[Festschrift André Leroi-Gourhan] *Hommages au professeur André Leroi-Gourhan: Un découvreur moderne des grottes d'Arcy, 1911–1986. Journées du patrimoine 1994, grottes d'Arcy-sur-Cure*. Edited by Gabriel de La Varende. Arcy-sur-Cure: Éditions du Chastenay, 1994.

Leroi-Gourhan, André and Dominique Baffier. *Dictionnaire de la préhistoire*. Paris: Presses Universitaires de France, 1988; 2nd ed. 1997.

Leroi-Gourhan, Arlette. "The Archaeology of Lascaux Cave." *Scientific American* 246:6 (June 1982): 104–112.

Leroi-Gourhan, Arlette and Jacques Allain. *Lascaux inconnu*. Paris: Éditions du Centre National de la Recherche Scientifique, 1979.

Levine, Morton H. "Prehistoric Art and Ideology." *American Anthropologist* 59 (1957): 949–962.

Lewis, Darrell. *The Rock Paintings of Arnhem Land, Australia: Social, Ecological and Material Culture Change in the Post-glacial Period*. Oxford: British Archaeological Reports, 1988.

Lewis, Darrell J. and D. Rose. *The Shape of the Dreaming: The Cultural Significance of Victoria River Rock Art*. Canberra, ACT: Aboriginal Studies Press, 1988.

Lewis-Williams, J. David. *Believing and Seeing: Symbolic Meanings in Southern San Rock Paintings*. London: Academic Press, 1981.

————. "The Thin Red Line: Southern San Notions and Rock Paintings of Supernatural Potency." *South African Archaeological Bulletin* 36 (1981) 5–13.

————. "The Economic and Social Context of Southern San Rock Art." *Current Anthropology* 23 (1982): 429–449.

————. *The Rock Art of Southern Africa*. Cambridge: Cambridge University Press, 1983.

————. "Ideological Continuities in Prehistoric Southern Africa: The Evidence of Rock Art." In *Past and Present in Hunter Gatherer Studies*, ed. Carmel Schrire. Orlando, FL: Academic Press, 1984. 225–252.

————. "Testing the Trance Explanation of Southern African Rock Art: Depictions of Felines." *Bollettino del Centro Camuno di Studi Preistorici* 22 (1985): 47–62.

————. *The World of Man and the World of Spirit: An Interpretation of the Linton Rock Paintings*. Cape Town: South African Museum, 1988.

————. *Reality and Non-reality in San Rock Art: Twenty-fifth Raymond Dart Lecture*

Delivered 6 October 1987. Johannesburg: Witwatersrand University Press for the Institute for the Study of Man in Africa, 1988.

———. *Discovering Southern African Rock Art.* Cape Town: David Philip, 1990.

———. "Wrestling with Analogy: A Problem in Upper Palaeolithic Art Research." *Proceedings of the Prehistoric Society* 57 (1991): 149–162.

———. *Vision, Power and Dance: The Genesis of a Southern African Rock Art Panel. 14de Kroon-voordracht gehouden voor de Stichting Nederlands Museum voor Anthropologie en Praehistorie te Amsterdam op 8 Mei 1992.* Amsterdam: Enschede, 1992.

———. "Rock Art and Ritual: Southern Africa and Beyond." In *Arte paleolítico,* ed. Teresa Chapa Brunet and Mario Menéndez Fernández. Madrid: Editorial Complutense, 1994: 277–289.

———. " Modelling the Production and Consumption of Rock Art." *South African Archaeological Bulletin* 50 (1995): 143–154.

———. "Agency, Art and Altered Consciousness: A Motif in French (Quercy) Upper Palaeolithic Parietal Art." *Antiquity* 71 (1997): 810–830.

———. "Harnessing the Brain: Vision and Shamanism in Upper Palaeolithic Western Europe." In *Beyond Art: Pleistocene Image and Symbol,* ed. Margaret Conkey, Olga Soffer, Deborah Stratmann and Nina G. Jablonski. San Francisco, CA: California Academy of Sciences, 1997: 321–342.

———. *Fragile Heritage: A Rock Art Fieldguide.* Johannesburg: Witwatersrand University Press, 1998.

———. "Brainstorming Images: Neuropsychology and Rock Art Research." In *Handbook of Rock Art Research,* ed. David S. Whitley. Walnut Creek, CA: AltaMira Press, 2001: 332–357.

———. *The Mind in the Cave: Consciousness and the Origins of Art.* London: Thames and Hudson, 2002.

Lewis-Williams, J. David, ed. *New Approaches to Southern African Rock Art.* Cape Town: South African Archaeological Society, 1983.

Lewis-Williams, J. David and Geoffrey Blundell. "New Light on Finger-Dots in Southern African Rock Art: Synesthesia, Transformation and Technique." *South African Journal of Science* 93 (1997): 51–54.

Lewis-Williams, J. David and Jean Clottes. "Shamanism and Upper Palaeolithic Art: A Response to Bahn." *Rock Art Research* 15 (1998): 46–50.

Lewis-Williams, J. David and Megan Biesele. "Eland Hunting Rituals Among the Northern and Southern San Groups: Striking Similarities." *Africa* 48 (1978): 117–134.

Lewis-Williams, J. David and Johannes H.N. Loubster. "Deceptive Appearances: A Critique of Southern African Rock Art Studies." *Advances in World Archaeology* 5 (1986): 253–289.

Lewis-Williams, J. David and Thomas A. Dowson. "Signs of all Times: Entoptic Phenomena in Upper Palaeolithic Art." *Current Anthropology* 29 (1988): 201–245.

———. "Theory and Data: A Brief Critique of A. Marshack's Research Methods and Position on Upper Palaeolithic Shamanism." *Rock Art Research* 6 (1989): 38–53.

———. "Through the Veil: San Rock Painting and the Rock Face." *South African Archaeological Bulletin* 45 (1990): 5–16.

———. "On Palaeolithic Art and the Neuropsychological Model." *Current Anthropology* 31 (1990): 407–408.

———. "On Vision and Power in the Neolithic: Evidence from the Decorated Monuments." *Current Anthropology* 34 (1993): 55–65.

———. *Images of Power: Understanding Bushman Rock Art.* Johannesburg: Southern Book Publishers, 1989; 2nd ed. *Images of Power: Understanding San Rock Art.* Johannesburg: Southern, 1999.

Lhote, Henri. *A la découverte des fresques du Tassili.* Grenoble: Arthaud, 1958; Engl. ed. *The Search for the Tassili Frescoes: The Story of the Prehistoric Rock-Paintings of the Sahara.* New York, Dutton, 1959.

———. *Les Chars rupestres sahariens: Des Syrtes au Niger, par le pays des Garamantes et des Atlantes.* Toulouse: Éditions des Hespérides, 1982.

———. *Vers d'autres Tassilis: Nouvelles découvertes au Sahara.* Paris: Arthaud, 1976.

Lhote, Henri and Henri Breuil, eds. *Peintures préhistoriques du Sahara.* Exh. cat. Paris: Musée des Arts Decoratifs, 1957–1958.

Linares Málaga, Eloy. *Arte rupestre en Sudamérica prehistórica.* Lima: Universidad Nacional Mayor de San Marcos, Fondo Editorial, 1999.

Lindly, J. M. and Geoffrey A. Clark. "Symbolism and Modern Human Origins." *Current Anthropology* 31 (1990): 233–261.

Lippard, Lucy R. *Overlay: Contemporary Art and the Art of Prehistory.* New York: Pantheon Books, 1983.

Llamazares, Ana Maria. "A Semiotic Approach in Rock-Art Analysis." In *The Meanings of Things: Material Culture and Symbolic Expression,* ed. Ian Hodder. London: Unwin Hyman, 1989: 242–248.

Lommel, Andreas. *Prehistoric and Primitive Man.* New York, McGraw-Hill, 1966; German ed. *Vorgeschichte und Naturvölker: Höhlenmalerei, Totems, Schmuck, Masken, Keramik, Waffen.* Gütersloh: Bertelsmann, 1967.

———. *Die Welt der frühen Jäger, Medizinmänner, Schamanen, Künstler.* München: Callwey, 1965; 2nd ed. *Schamanen und Medizinmänner: Magie und Mystik früher Kulturen.* München: Callwey, 1980; Engl. ed. *The World of the Early Hunters, Medicine-men, Shamans and Artists.* London: Evelyn, Adams and Mackey, 1967; American ed. *Shamanism: The Beginnings of Art.* New York: McGraw-Hill, 1967.

———. "Shamanism: The Beginnings of Art. Andreas Lommel. [17 Reviews and a Reply from the Author.]" *Current Anthropology* 11 (1970): 39–48.

Lommel, Andreas and Katharina Lommel. *Die Kunst des fünften Erdteils Australien.* München: Staatliches Museum für Völkerkunde, 1959.

———. *Die Kunst des alten Australien.* München: Prestel, 1988.

Longworth, Ian, ed. *Rock Art.* Special Issue of *World Archaeology* 19:2 (October 1987).

Lorblanchet, Michel. *L'Art préhistorique en Quercy: La grotte des Escabasses, Thémines, Lot.* Saint-Jammes/Morlaas: Éditions P.G.P., 1974; 2nd ed. Portet-sur-Garonne: Éditions Loubatières, 1988.

———. "From Naturalism to Abstraction in European Prehistoric Rock Art." In *Form in Indigenous Art: Schematisation in the Art of Aboriginal Australia and Prehistoric Europe,* ed. Peter J. Ucko. Canberra, ACT: Australian Institute of Aboriginal Studies, and Atlantic Highlands, NJ: Humanities Press, 1977: 44–56.

————. "Peindre sur les parois des grottes." *Dossiers de l'Archéologie* 46 (1980): 33–39.

————. "Problèmes épistémologiques posés par l'établissement d'une chronologie d'art rupestre." *Préhistoire Ariégoise* 49 (1989): 131–152.

————. "Spitting Images: Replicating the Spotted Horse of Pech Merle." *Archaeology* 44:6 (November-December 1991): 24–31.

————. "From the Cave Art of the Reindeer Hunters to the Rock Art of the Kangaroo Hunters." *Man and Environment* 16:2 (1991): 1–38.

————. "Le Triomph du naturalisme dans l'art paléolithique." In *The Limitations of Archaeological Knowledge*, ed. Jean Clottes and Talia Shay. Liège: Otte, 1992: 115–140.

————. *Les Grottes ornées de la préhistoire: Nouveaux regards.* Paris: Errance, 1995; German ed. *Höhlenmalerei: Ein Handbuch.* 2nd rev. ed. Stuttgart: Thorbecke, 2000.

————. *Cougnac: Les grottes magiques.* Payrignac: Éditions des Grottes de Cougnac, 1997.

————. *La Naissance de l'art: Genèse de l'art préhistorique dans le monde.* Paris: Errance, 1999.

————. *La Grotte ornée de Pergouset, Saint-Gery, Lot: Un sanctuaire secret paléolithique.* Paris: Maison des Sciences de l'Homme, 2001.

Lorblanchet, Michel, ed. *Pech-Merle: Centre de préhistoire, Grotte et Musée. Musée de préhistoire Amédée Lemozi.* Cabrerets: Musée de Préhistoire Amédée Lemozi, 1981.

————. *Rock Art in the Old World: Papers Presented in Symposium A of the AURA Congress, Darwin (Australia), 1988.* New Delhi: Indira Gandhi National Centre for the Arts, 1992.

Lorblanchet, Michel and Paul G. Bahn, eds. *Rock Art Studies: The Post-stylistic Era, or, Where Do We Go from Here? Papers Presented in Symposium A of the 2nd AURA Congress, Cairns 1992.* Oxford: Oxbow, 1993.

Lorblanchet, Michel, Michel Labeau, Jean-Louis Vernet, Paul Fitte, Hélène Valladas, Hélène Cachier, and M. Arnold. "Paleolithic Pigments in the Quercy, France." *Rock Art Research* 7 (1990): 4–20.

Lumley, Henry de, ed. *Art Préhistorique.* Special issue of *L'Anthropologie* 90:4 (1986).

Lundy, Doris, ed. *CRARA '77: Papers from the Fourth Biennial Conference of the Canadian Rock Art Research Associates, October 27–30, 1977, Victoria, British Columbia.* Victoria: British Columbia Provincial Museum, 1979.

Luquet, Georges Henri. "Sur les caractères des figures humaines dans l'art paléolithique." *L'Anthropologie* 21 (1910): 409–423.

————. "Les Origines de l'art figuré." *IPEK* 2 (1926): 1–28.

————. *L'Art et la religion des hommes fossiles.* Paris: Masson, 1926; Engl. ed. *The Art and Religion of Fossil Man.* New Haven, CT: Yale University Press, 1930.

————. "La Magie dans l'art paléolithique." *Journal de Psychologie* 28 (1931): 390–427.

————. "Les Vénus paléolithiques." *Journal de Psychologie* 31 (1934): 429–460.

Lutz, Rüdiger and Gabriele Lutz. *The Secret of the Desert: The Rock Art of Messak Sattafet and Messak Mellet, Libya.* Innsbruck: Universitätsbuchhandlung Golf Verlag, 1995.

Madariaga de la Campa, Benito. *Las pinturas rupestres de animales en la región franco-*

cantábrica: Notas para su estudio e identificación. Santander: Institución Cultural de Cantabria, 1969; 2nd ed. Santander: Fundación Marcelino Botín, 2000; French ed. *Sanz de Sautuola et la découverte d'Altamira: Considérations sur les peintures.* Santander: Fundación Marcelino Botín, 2000; Engl. ed. *Sanz de Sautuola and the Discovery of the Caves of Altamira: Some Observations on the Paintings.* Santander: Fundación Marcelino Botín, 2001.

————. *Hermilio Alcalde del Río: Una escuela de prehistoria de Santander.* Santander: [s.n.], 1972.

————. "História del descubrimiento y valoración del arte rupestre español." *Altamira Symposium.* Madrid: Ministerio de Cultura, 1981: 299–310.

Malhomme, Jean. *Corpus des gravures rupestres du Grand Atlas.* 2 vols. Rabat: Service des Antiquités du Maroc, 1959–1961.

Malmer, Mats P. *A Chorological Study of North European Rock Art.* Stockholm: Almqvist & Wiksell International, 1981.

Mand, Gro. "Female Symbolism in Rock Art." In *Were They all Men?: An Examination of Sex Roles in Prehistoric Society. Acts from a Workshop Held at Utstein Kloster, Rogaland, 2.-4. November 1979 (NAM-forskningsseminar nr. 1),* ed. Reidar Bertelsen, Arnvid Lillehammer and Jenny-Rita Næss. Stavanger: Arkeologisk museum i Stavanger, 1987: 35–52.

Mania, Dietrich. *Auf den Spuren des Urmenschen: Die Funde aus der Steinrinne von Bilzingsleben.* Berlin: Deutscher Verlag der Wissenschaft, 1990.

Maringer, Johannes. *The Gods of Prehistoric Man.* New York: Knopf, 1960.

————. "Musik und Musikinstrumente in vor- und frühgeschichtlicher Zeit." *Prähistorische Zeitschrift* 57 (1982): 126–137.

Marshack, Alexander. "New Techniques in the Analysis and Interpretation of Mesolithic Notations and Symbolic Art." In *Symposium international d'art préhistorique: Valcamonica, 23–28 Septembre 1968,* ed. Emmanuel Anati. Capo di Ponte: Edizioni del Centro, 1970: 479–494.

————. *Notations dans les gravures du paléolithique supérieur: Nouvelles méthodes d'analyse.* Bordeaux: Delmas, 1970.

————. *The Roots of Civilisation: The Cognitive Beginnings of Man's First Art, Symbol, and Notation.* London: Weidenfeld and Nicolson, 1972; 2nd ed. Mt. Kisco, NY: Moyer Bell 1991.

————. "Cognitive Aspects of Upper Paleolithic Engraving." *Current Anthropology* 13 (1972): 445–477.

————. "Upper Palaeolithic Notation and Symbol." *Science* 178 (1972): 817–828.

————. "The Message in the Markings." *Horizon* 18:4 (1976): 64–72.

————. "Upper Paleolithic Symbol Systems of the Russian Plain: Cognitive and Comparative Analysis." *Current Anthropology* 20 (1979): 271–311.

————. *Hierarchical Evolution of the Human Capacity: The Paleolithic Evidence. 54th James Arthur Lecture on the Evolution of the Human Brain.* New York: American Museum of Natural History, 1985.

————. "Methodology in the Analysis and Interpretation of Upper Palaeolithic Image: Theory versus Contextual Analysis." *Rock Art Research* 6 (1989): 17–53; 149–150.

————. "Early Hominid Symbol and Evolution of the Human Capacity." In *The Emergence of Modern Humans: An Archaeological Perspective,* ed. Paul Mellars. Edinburgh: Edinburgh University Press, 1990: 457–498.

————. "An Innovative Analytical Technology: A Discussion of Its Present and Potential Use." *Rock Art Research* 9 (1991): 37–59.

————. "The Taï Plaque and Calendrical Notation in the Upper Palaeolithic." *Cambridge Archaeological Journal* 1 (1991): 25–61.

————. "The Female Image: A 'Time-factored' Symbol. A Study in Style and Aspect of Image Use in the Upper Palaeolithic." *Proceedings of the Prehistoric Society* 57:1 (1991): 17–31.

————. "Paleolithic Image Making and Symboling in Europe and the Middle East: A Comparative Review." In *Beyond Art: Pleistocene Image and Symbol,* ed. Margaret W. Conkey, Olga Soffer, Deborah Stratmann and Nina G. Jablonski. San Francisco, CA: California Academy of Sciences, 1997: 53–91.

————. "Palaeolithic Image." In *Encyclopedia of Human Evolution and Prehistory,* ed. Eric Delson, Ian Tattersall, John A. Van Couvering and Alison S. Brooks. 2nd rev. ed. New York: Garland, 2000. 519–526.

Marshack, Alexander, ed. *Ice Age Art: An Exhibition of Ice Age Art and Symbol.* Exh. cat. New York: American Museum of Natural History, 1979. San Francisco, CA: California Academy of Sciences, 1979.

Marstrander, Sverre, ed. *Acts of the International Symposium on Rock Art: Lectures at Hanko 6–12 August, 1972.* Oslo: Universitetsforlaget, 1978.

Martí Oliver, Bernardo [Bernat] and Mauro S. Hernández Pérez. *El neolitic Valencia: Art rupestre i cultura material.* València: Servei d'Investigació Prehistòrica de la Diputació Provincial, 1988.

Martín Fernández de Velasco, Miguel. *El fenómeno eldanense: Arte miles de siglos antes de Altamira.* Valladolid: [s.n.], 1996.

Martineau, LaVan. *The Rocks Begin to Speak.* Las Vegas, NV: KC Publications, 1973.

Martynov, Anatolii Ivanovich. *The Ancient Art of Northern Asia.* Urbana, IL: University of Illinois Press, 1991.

Matei, Dumitru. *Originile artei.* Bucuresti: Meridiane, 1981.

Mathpal, Yasodhar. *Rock Art in Kerala.* New Delhi: Indira Gandhi National Centre for the Arts: Aryan Book International, 1998.

Mauduit, Jacques A. *Quarante mille ans d'art moderne.* Paris: Plon, 1954; Spanish ed. *40.000 años de arte moderno.* Madrid: Taurus, 1959.

Mauny, Raymond. *Gravures, peintures et inscriptions rupestres de l'ouest africain.* Dakar: Institut Français d'Afrique Noire, 1954.

Mazel, Aron. "Rock Art and Natal Drakensberg Hunter-gatherer History: A Reply to Dowson." *Antiquity* 67 (1993): 889–892.

Mazonowicz, Douglas. *Exposición de reproducciones en serigrafía de arte rupestre de España y Francia.* Madrid: Dirección General de Bellas Artes, 1965.

————. *In Search of Cave Art.* Rohnert Park/CA: Gallery of Prehistoric Paintings, 1973.

————. *Voices from the Stone Age: A Search for Cave and Canyon Art.* New York: Crowell, 1974.

McBrearty, Sally and Alison S. Brooks. "The Revolution that Wasn't: A New Interpretation of the Origin of Modern Human Behaviour." *Journal of Human Evolution* 39 (2000): 453–463.

McDermott, LeRoy. "Self-Representation in Upper Paleolithic Female Figurines." *Current Anthroplogy* 37 (1996): 227–275.

McDonald, Josephine and Ivan Pavel Haskovec, eds. *State of the Art: Regional Rock*

Art Studies in Australia and Melanesia. Proceedings of Symposium C, "Rock Art Studies in Australia and Oceania," and Symposium D, "The Rock Art of Northern Australia," of the First AURA Congress Held in Darwin in 1988. Melbourne: Australian Rock Art Research Association, 1992.

McGowan, Charlotte. "Female Fertility and Rock Art." *American Indian Rock Art* 4 (1978): 26–40.

Medvedev, German I. "Art from Central Siberian Paleolithic Sites." In *The Paleolithic of Siberia,* ed. Anatoliy P. Derev'anko. Urbana, IL: University of Illinois Press: 132–137.

Meighan, Clement Woodward. *Indian Art and History: The Testimony of Prehispanic Rock Paintings in Baja California.* Los Angeles, CA: Dawson's Book Shop, 1969.

Meighan, Clement Woodward, ed. *Messages from the Past: Studies in California Rock Art.* Los Angeles, CA: Institute of Archaeology, University of California, Los Angeles, 1981.

Meighan, Clement Woodward and Velma Lee Pontoni. *Seven Rock Art Sites in Baja, California.* Socorro, NM: Ballena Press, 1978.

Mellars, Paul. "Symbolism, Language and the Neanderthal Mind." In *Modelling the Early Human Mind,* ed. Paul Mellars and Kathleen Gibson. Cambridge: McDonald Institute, 1996: 15–32.

Mellars, Paul, ed. *The Emergence of Modern Humans: An Archaeological Perspective.* Edinburgh: Edinburgh University Press, 1990.

Mellars, Paul and Christopher Stringer, eds. *The Human Revolution: Behavioural and Biological Perspectives on the Origin of Modern Humans.* Edinburgh: Edinburgh University Press, 1989.

Mellink, Machteld J. and Jan Filip. *Frühe Stufen der Kunst.* Berlin: Propyläen, 1974.

Menéndez Fernández, Mario. "Arte mueble y arte rupestre paleolítico: Relaciones." In *Arte paleolítico,* ed. Teresa Chapa Brunet and Mario Menéndez Fernández. Madrid: Editorial Complutense, 1994: 343–356.

Michaelsen, Per, Tasja W. Ebersole, Noel W. Smith, and Paul Biro. "Australian Ice Age Rock Art May Depict Earth's Oldest Recordings of Shamanistic Rituals." *Mankind Quarterly* 61 (2000): 131–146.

Mithen, Steven. "Looking and Learning: Upper Palaeolithic Art and Information Gathering." *World Archaeology* 19 (1987–1988): 297–327.

———. "To Hunt or to Paint? Animals and Art in the Upper Palaeolithic." *Man* 23 (1989): 671–695.

———. "Ecological Interpretations of Palaeolithic Art." *Proceedings of the Prehistoric Society* 57 (1991): 103–114.

———. *The Prehistory of the Mind: A Search for the Origins of Art, Religion and Science.* London: Thames and Hudson, 1996.

———. "On Early Palaeolithic 'Concept-mediated Marks,' Mental Modularity, and the Origins of Art." *Current Anthropology* 37 (1996): 666–670.

Mithen, Steven, ed. *Creativity in Human Evolution and Prehistory.* London: Routledge, 1998.

Mons, Lucette. "Notes de technologie de l'art paléolithique mobilier (I–II)." *Antiquités Nationales* 4 (1972): 14–21.

———. "Notes de technologie et de morphologie de l'art paléolithique mobilier (IV)." *Antiquités Nationales* 6 (1974): 29–31.

Monzon, Susana. *L'Art rupestre sud-americain: Préhistoire d'un continent.* Monaco: Rocher, 1987.

Moore, Sabra. *Petroglyphs: Ancient Language/Sacred Art.* Santa Fe, NM: Clear Light Publishers, 1998.

Morphy, Howard, ed. *Animals into Art.* London: Unwin Hyman, 1989.

Morris, Desmond. "Primate's Aesthetics: An Ape Provides Clues to the Origins of Artistic Activities." *Natural History* 70:1 (January 1961): 22–29.

———. *The Biology of Art: A Study of the Picture-making Behaviour of the Great Apes and Its Relationship to Human Art.* London: Methuen, 1962.

Morris, Ronald W. B. *The Prehistoric Rock Art of Argyll.* Poole: Dolphin Press, 1977.

———. *The Prehistoric Rock Art of Southern Scotland (except Argyll and Galloway).* Oxford: British Archaeological Reports, 1981.

Morwood, Mike J. *Visions from the Past: The Archaeology of Australian Aboriginal Art.* Crows Nest, N.S.W.: Allen & Unwin, 2002.

Morwood, Mike J. and D. R. Hobbs, eds. *Rock Art and Ethnography: Proceedings of the Ethnography Symposium (H), Australian Rock Art Research Association Congress, Darwin 1988.* Melbourne: Australian Rock Art Research Association, 1992.

Moszeik, Otto. *Die Malereien der Buschmänner in Südafrika.* Berlin: Reimer, 1910.

Moulin, Raoul-Jean. *Sources de la peinture.* Lausanne: Éditions Rencontre, 1965; Engl. ed. *Prehistoric Painting.* London: Heron, 1967.

Moure Romanillo, José Alfonso. *Las pinturas y grabados de la cueva de Tito Bustillo: Significado cronologico de las representaciones de animales.* Valladolid: Universidad de Valladolid, Departamento de Prehistoria y Arqueología, 1980.

———. "Introducción al arte rupestre paleolítico cantábrico." *Revista de arqueología* 7 (April 1987): 30–37.

———. *La cueva de Tito Bustillo: El arte y los cazadores del paleolítico.* Gijon: Trea, 1992.

———. *Arqueología del arte prehistórico en la península ibérica.* Madrid: Síntesis, 1999.

Moure Romanillo, Alfonso and César González Sainz, eds. *El final del paleolítico cantábrico: Transformaciones ambientales y culturales durante el Tardiglacial y comienzos del Holoceno en la región cantábrica.* Santander: Universidad de Cantabria, 1995.

Mourer-Chauviré, Cècile and Gilbert Fages. "La Flute en os d'oiseau de la grotte sépulcrale de Veyreau (Aveyron) et inventaire des flutes préhistoriques d'Europe." *Mémoires de la Société Préhistorique Française* 16 (1983): 95–103.

Müller-Beck, Hansjürgen and Gerd Albrecht, eds. *Die Anfänge der Kunst vor 30.000 Jahren.* Exh. cat. Tübingen: Kunsthalle, 1987; Stuttgart: Theiss, 1987; Spanish ed. *Los comienzos del arte en Europa central.* Exh. cat. Madrid: Museo Arqueológico Nacional, 1989.

Mulvaney, D. John and Johan Kamminga. *Prehistory of Australia;* 2nd rev. ed. Melbourne: Melbourne University Press, 1999.

Muñoz, Juan, ed. *La imagen del animal: Arte prehistórico, arte contemporáneo.* Exh. cat. Madrid: Caja de Ahorros y Monte de Piedad de Madrid, 1983–1984. Madrid: Ministerio de Cultura, 1983. Catalan ed. *La imatge de l'animal: Art prehistòric, art contemporani.* Exh. cat. Barcelona: Sala "Caixa de Barcelona", Obra Social, 1984.

Múzquiz Pérez-Seoane, Matilde: *Altamira.* Paris: Seuil, 1998.

Muzzolini, Alfred. *L'Art rupestre préhistorique des massifs centraux sahariens.* Oxford: British Archaeological Reports, 1986.

————. *Les Images rupestres du Sahara.* Toulouse: Muzzolini, 1995.

Myron, Robert. *Prehistoric Art.* New York: Pitman, 1965.

Naber, Friedrich B., Daniel J. Berenger, and Carlos Zalles-Flossbach. *L'Art pariétal paléolithique en Europe romane.* [Bonner Hefte zur Vorgeschichte, nos. 14–16]. Bonn: Institut für Vor- und Frühgeschichte der Rheinischen Friedrich-Wilhelms-Universität Bonn, 1976.

La naissance de l'art en Europe = El nacimiento del arte en Europa. Exh. cat. Paris: Union Latine, 1992.

Narr, Karl J. "Interpretationen altsteinzeitlicher Kunstwerke durch völkerkundliche Parallelen." *Anthropos* 5 (1955): 513–525.

————. *Urgeschichte der Kultur.* Stuttgart: Kroener, 1961.

————. "Zum Sinngehalt der altsteinzeitlichen Höhlenbilder." *Symbolon* NS 2 (1974): 105–122.

————. "Felsbild und Weltbild: Zu Magie und Schamanismus im jungpaläolithischen Jägertum." Hans Peter Duerr, ed.: *Sehnsucht nach dem Ursprung: Zu Mircea Eliade.* Frankfurt/M: Syndikat, 1983. 118–136.

Nash, George, ed. *Signifying Place and Space: World Perspectives of Rock Art and Landscape.* Oxford: Archaeopress, 2000.

Nash, George and Christopher Chippindale, eds. *European Landscapes of Rock-art.* London: Routledge, 2001.

Nayeem, Muhammed Abdul. *Rock Art of Arabia: Saudi Arabia, Oman, Qatar, the Emirates and Yemen.* Hyderabad: Hyderabad Publishers, 2000.

Nelson, D. Erle, Christopher Chippindale, Paul S.C. Taçon, George Chaloupka, and John Southon. *The Beeswax Art of Northern Australia.* CD-ROM Publication. Burnaby, BC: Simon Fraser University, Department of Archaeology, 2000.

Nelson, Sarah. "Diversity of the Upper Palaeolithic 'Venus' Figurines and Archaeological Mythology." In *Powers of Observation: Alternative Views in Archeology,* ed. Sarah M. Nelson and Alice B. Kehoe. Washington, DC: American Anthropological Association, 1990. 11–22.

Nettelton, Anitra. "San Rock Art: Image, Function and Meaning. A Reply to A. R. Willcox." *South African Archaeological Bulletin* 39 (1984): 67–68.

Neukom-Tschudi, Jolantha. *Pitture rupestri del Tasili degli Azger, Sahara Algerino.* Firenze: Sansoni, 1955.

Neumayer, Erwin. *Prehistoric Indian Rock Paintings.* Delhi: New York: Oxford University Press, 1983.

————. *Lines on Stone: The Prehistoric Rock Art of India.* New Delhi: Manohar, 1993.

————. "Bodies in Motion: India's Rock Art is a Window to Prehistoric Performing Arts." *Archaeology* 50:1 (January-February 1997): 56–59.

Nougier, Louis-René. *L'Art préhistorique.* Paris: Presses Universitaires de France, 1966; Spanish ed. *El arte prehistórico.* Barcelona: Plaza & Janés, 1968.

————. *Rouffignac.* Périgeux: Éditions du Périgord Noir, 1978.

————. *La preistoria.* [*Storia universale dell'arte. Sezione prima: Le civiltà antiche e primitive*]. Torino: UTET, 1982.

————. *Premiers Éveils de l'homme: Art, magie, sexualité dans la préhistoire.* Paris: Lieu Commun, 1984.

———. *Les Grottes préhistoriques ornées de France, d'Espagne et d'Italie.* Paris: Balland, 1990.

Nougier, Louis-René and Romain Robert. *Rouffignac, ou, La guerre des mammouths.* Paris: La Table Ronde, 1957; Engl. ed. *The Cave of Rouffignac.* London: Newnes, 1958.

Nygaard, Jon. "Rock Art and the Origin of Theatre." *Rock Art Papers* 14 (1999): 75–90.

Obermaier, Hugo. *Der Mensch der Vorzeit.* Berlin: Allgemeine Verlags-Gesellschaft, 1911; 2nd ed. 1912.

———. *Las cuevas de Altamira (Santander).* Madrid: Patronato Nacional del Turismo, 1928.

———. *Las cuevas de Altamira (Santander).* Madrid: Blass, 1928; 2nd ed. [1930?].

Obermaier, Hugo, ed. *Altamira: 4. Internationaler Archaeologischer Kongress.* Barcelona: Internationale Ausstellung, 1929.

Obermaier, Hugo and Herbert Kühn. *Buschmannkunst: Felsmalereien aus Südwestafrika.* Berlin: Brandus, 1930; Engl. ed. *Bushman Art: Rock Paintings of Southwest Africa.* London: Oxford University Press, 1930.

Obermaier, Hugo and Elias Ortiz de la Torre. *Las cuevas de Altamira y la villa de Santillana del Mar (Santander).* 3rd ed. Madrid: Espasa-Calpe, 1934.

Obermaier, Hugo and La Vega del Sella [i.e., Ricardo Duque de Estrada y Martínez de Morentín, Conde de La Vega del Sella]. *La Cueva del Buxu (Asturias).* Madrid: Museo Nacional de Ciencias Naturales, 1918.

Obermaier, Hugo, Hans-Georg Bandi, and Johannes Maringer. *Kunst der Eiszeit, Levantekunst, arktische Kunst.* Basel: Holbein, 1952; 2nd ed. 1955; French ed. *Art préhistorique: Les cavernes, le Levant espagnol, les régions arctiques.* Basel: Holbein, 1952; 2nd ed. 1956; Engl. ed. *Art in the Ice Age, Spanish Levant Art, Arctic Art.* New York: Praeger, 1953.

Okladnikov, Aleksei P. *Utro iskusstva.* Moskva: "Iskusstvo," 1967.

Orlove, Benjamin. "Editorial: The Evolution of Symbolic Capacities and Human Society." *Current Anthropology* 42 (2001): i–iii.

Osborn, Henry Fairfield. *Men of the Old Stone Age: Their Environment, Life and Art.* New York: Scribner, 1915; 3rd rev. ed. 1918.

Oster, Gerald. "The Modern Look of Ice Age Art." *Natural History* 87:8 (October 1978): 109–113.

Otte, Marcel, ed. *Sons originels: Préhistoire de la musique. Liège, 11–12–13 décembre 1992.* Liège: Université de Liège, 1994.

Otto, Josef. *Prähistorische Felsgravuren im Hohen Atlas.* Warmsroth: Pulsar, 1994.

Otto, Karl-Heinz and und Gisela Buschendorf-Otto. *Felsbilder aus dem sudanesischen Nubien.* 2 vols. Berlin: Akademie Verlag, 1993.

Pager, Harald L. *Stone Age Myth and Magic as Documented in the Rock Paintings of South Africa.* Graz: Akademische Druck- und Verlagsanstalt, 1975.

———. *The Rock Paintings of the Upper Brandberg.* Köln: Heinrich-Barth-Institut, 1989.

Pager, Harald L., Revil J. Mason, Robert G. Welbourne, and Raymond A. Dart. "San Trance Performance Documentation in the Ethnological Report and Rock Paintings of Southern Africa." *Rock Art Research* 11 (1994): 88–100.

Pager, Shirley Ann. *African Pictograms: Namibia Rock Art and Archaeology = Arte rupestre e archeologia della Namibia.* Pinerolo: Centro Studi e Museo d'Arte Preistorica, 1997.

Pager, Shirley-Ann, Ben K. Swartz, Alexander Robert Willcox, eds. *Rock Art, the Way Ahead: 25–31 August, 1991, Cathedral Peak Hotel, Natal Drakensberg. Conference Proceedings.* Parkhurst, South Africa: Southern African Rock Art Research Association, 1991.

Paillet, Patrick. *Le Bison dans les arts magdaléniens du Périgord.* Paris: Centre National de la Recherche Scientifique, 1999.

Pales, Léon. "Les ci-devant Vénus Stéapyges aurignaciennes." In *Santander Symposium,* ed. Martín Almagro Basch and Miguel Ángel García Guinea. Santander: Museo de Prehistoria, 1972: 217–261.

Pales, Léon and Marie Tassin de Saint-Péreuse. *Les Gravures de la Marches.* Bordeaux: Delmas, 1969; vol. 2: *Les Humains.* Bordeaux: Delmas 1976; vol. 3: *Équidés et bovidés.* Bordeaux: Delmas, 1981; vol. 4: *Cervidés, mammouths et divers.* Gap: Ophrys, 1989.

Parkington, John. "Symbolism in Paleolithic Cave Art." *South African Archaeological Bulletin* 24 (1969): 3–13.

Parkyn, Ernest Albert. *An Introduction to the Study of Prehistoric Art.* London: Longmans, Green and Co., 1915.

Passemard, Luce. *Les Statuettes féminines paléolithiques dites Vénus stéatopyges.* Nîmes: Teissier, 1938.

Patterson, Alex. *A Field Guide to Rock Art Symbols of the Greater Southwest.* Boulder, CO: Johnson Books, 1992.

Paulcke, Wilhelm. *Steinzeitkunst und moderne Kunst: Ein Vergleich.* Stuttgart: Schweizerbart'sche Verlagbuchhandlung E. Nägele, 1923.

Pearson, James L. *Shamanism and the Ancient Mind: A Cognitive Approach to Archaeology.* Walnut Creek, CA: AltaMira Press, 2002.

Peintres d'un monde disparu: La préhistoire vue par les artistes de la fin du XXIX siècle à nos jours. Exh. cat. Solutré: Musée Departemental de Préhistoire, 1990.

Peña Santos, Antonio de la and José Manuel Vázquez Varela. *Los petroglifos gallegos: Grabados rupestres prehistóricos al aire libre en Galicia.* Sada, La Coruña: Ediciós do Castro, 1979.

Pericot García, Luis. *Sobre el arte rupestre cantábrico: Discurso leído en el curso académico de 1953.* Santander: Librería Moderna, 1953.

Pericot García, Luis, John Galloway and Andreas Lommel. *Preistoria e i primitivi attuali.* Firenze, Sansoni, 1967; Engl. ed. *Prehistoric and Primitive Art.* New York: Abrams, 1967.

Pericot García, Luis and Eduardo Ripoll Perelló, eds. *Prehistoric Art of the Western Mediterranean and the Sahara.* New York: Wenner-Gren Foundation for Anthropological Research, 1964.

Peyrony, Denis. *Les Figures gravées à l'époque paléolithique sur les parois de la grotte de Bernifal (Dordogne).* Paris: Picard et fils, 1903. [Extrait des *Comptes rendus des séances de l'Académie des inscriptions et belles-lettres,* 1903].

———. *La Caverne de Font-de-Gaume aux Eyzies (Dordogne).* Monaco: Chêne, 1910.

———. *Les Combarelles aux Eyzies (Dordogne).* Paris: Masson, 1924.

———. *Les Eyzies, ses musées d'art préhistorique.* Paris: Laurens, 1931.

Pfeiffer, John E. *The Creative Explosion: An Inquiry into the Origins of Art and Religion.* New York: Harper & Row, 1982.

Phillipson, David W., ed. *Prehistoric Rock Paintings and Engravings of Zambia*. Exh. cat. Livingstone: Livingstone Museum, 1972.

Pietsch, Erich and Gisela Pietsch. *Altamira y la prehistoria de la tecnología química*. Madrid: Patronato de Investigación Cientifica y Tecnica "Juan de la Cierva," 1964.

Piette, Édouard. "La Station de Brassempouy et les statuettes humains de la période glyptique." *L'Anthropologie* 6 (1895): 129–151.

———. "Gravure du Mas d'Azil et statuettes de Menton." *Bulletins et Mémoires de la Société d'Anthropologie de Paris*, Series V, 3 (1902): 771–779.

———. *L'Art pendant l'Age du Renne*. Paris: Masson, 1907.

———. *Histoire de l'art primitif*. [Précédé de] *Piette, pionnier de la préhistoire, par Henri Delporte*. Paris: Picard, 1987.

———. *Gravure du Mas-d'Azil et statuettes de Menton, avec dessins de l'Abbé Breuil*. Nîmes: Lacour, 1997.

Pijoán, José. *Summa Artis: Historia general del arte*. Vol. 6: *El arte prehistórico europeo*. Madrid: Espasa-Calpe, 1996.

Plassard, Jean. *Rouffignac: Le Sanctuaire des mammouths*. Paris: Seuil, 1999.

Plassard, Jean and Marie-Odile Plassard. *La Grotte de Rouffignac*. Bordeaux: "Sud-Ouest," 1989.

Podestá, María Mercedes, María Isabel Hernández Llosas, and Susana F. Renard de Coquet, eds. *El arte rupestre en la arqueología contemporánea*. Buenos Aires: Podestá, 1991.

Poore, Anne, ed. *By Hands Unknown: Papers on Rock Art and Archaeology in Honor of James G. Bain*. Alburquerque, NM: Archaeological Society of New Mexico and Santa Fe, NM: Ancient City Press, 1986.

Poulík, Josef. *Kunst der Vorzeit*. Praha: Artia. 1956; Engl. ed. *Prehistoric Art, Including Some Recent Cave-culture Discoveries and Subsequent Developments up to Roman Times*. London: Spring Books, 1956.

Powell, Thomas George Eyre. *Prehistoric Art*. New York: Praeger, 1966; French ed. *L'Art préhistorique*. Paris: Larousse, 1967.

Power, Camilla. "Beauty Magic: The Origins of Art." In *The Evolution of Culture*, ed. Robin Dunbar, Chris Knight and Camilla Power. Edinburgh: Edinburgh University Press, 1999: 92–112.

Power, Camilla and Leslie C. Aiello. "Female Proto-symbolic Strategies." In *Women in Human Evolution*, ed. Lori D. Hager. New York and London: Routledge, 1997: 153–171.

Power, Camilla and Ian Watts. "The Woman with the Zebra's Penis: Gender, Mutability and Performance." *Journal of the Royal Anthropological Institute* (N. S.) 3:3 (September 1997): 537–560.

Poyto, Robert and Jean Claude Musso. *Corpus des peintures et gravures rupestres de Grande Kabylie*. Paris: Arts et Métiers Graphiques, 1969.

Prados García, José María. *Arte prehistórico en España*. Madrid: Servicio de Publicaciones del Ministerio de Educación y Ciencia, 1973.

Praslov, Nikolai Dmitrievich. "L'Art du paléolithique supérieure à l'est de l'Europe." *L'Anthropologie* 89 (1985): 181–192.

Préhistoire de la Musique: Sons et instruments de musique des âges du bronze et du fer en France. Exh. cat. Nemours: Musée de Préhistoire d'Île-de-France, 2002.

Prehistoric and Primitive Art and Visual Symbolism. Special edition of *Soviet Anthropology and Anthropology* 16:3–4 (Winter-Spring 1977–78).

Prehistoric Rock Pictures in Europe and Africa, from Material in the Archives of the Research Institute for the Morphology of Civilization, Frankfort-on-Main. Exh. cat. New York: The Museum of Modern Art, 1937.

Preziosi, Donald. "Constru(ct)ing the Origins of Art." *Art Journal* 42 (1982): 320–325.

Priuli, Ausilio. *Felszeichnungen in den Alpen.* Zürich: Benziger, 1984.

———. *Le più antiche manifestazioni spirituali: Arte rupestre. Paleoiconografia camuna e delle genti alpine.* Ivrea, TO: Priuli & Verlucca, 1996.

Pulligny, Félix Augustin de. *L'Art préhistorique dans l'ouest et notamment en Haute Normandie.* Evreux: Hérissey, 1879.

Ragghianti, Carlo Ludovico. *L'uomo cosciente: Arte e conoscenza nella paleostoria.* Bologna: Calderini, 1981.

Rajnovich, Grace. *Reading Rock Art: Interpreting the Indian Rock Paintings of the Canadian Shield.* Toronto: Natural Heritage/Natural History, 1994.

Ramírez, Juan Antonio. *Arte prehistórico y primitivo.* Madrid: Anaya, 1989.

Raphael, Max. *Prehistoric Cave Paintings.* New York: Pantheon Books, 1946.

Rebanda, Nélson. *Os trabalhos arqueológicos e o complexo de arte rupestre do Côa.* Lisboa: Instituto Português do Património Arquitectónico e Arqueológico, 1995.

Reinach, Salomon. "Statuette de femme nue découverte dans une des grottes de Menton." *L'Anthropologie* 9 (1898): 26–31.

———. "L'Art et la magie: A propos des peintures et des gravures de l'Age du Renne." *L'Anthropologie* 14 (1903): 257–266.

———. *Repertoire de l'art quatenaire.* Paris: Leroux, 1913.

Reinhardt, Brigitte, Kurt Wehrberger and Gerhard Bosinski, eds. *Der Löwenmensch: Tier und Mensch in der Kunst der Eiszeit.* Exh. cat. Ulm: Ulmer Museum, 1994. Sigmaringen: Thorbecke, 1994.

Resch, Walther. *Die Felsbilder Nubiens: Eine Dokumentation der ostägyptischen und nubischen Petroglyphen.* Graz: Akademische Druck- und Verlagsanstalt, 1967.

Reznikoff, Iégor and Michel Dauvois. "La Dimension sonore des grottes ornées." *Bulletin de la Société Préhistorique Française* 85 (1988): 238–246.

Riba, Daniel. *Les Gravures rupestres du Val Camonica: Haut-lieu de l'Europe préhistorique.* Paris: France-Empire, 1984.

Rice, Patricia C. "Prehistoric Venuses: Symbols of Motherhood or Womanhood?" *Journal of Anthropological Research* 37 (1981): 402–414.

Rice, Patricia C. and Ann L. Paterson. "Cave Art and Bones: Exploring Their Inter-Relationship." *American Antropologist* 87 (1985): 94–100.

———. "Validating the Cave Art—Archaeofaunal Relationship in Cantabrian Spain." *American Anthropologist* 88 (1986): 658–667.

———. "Anthropomorphs in Cave Art: A Critical Assessment." *American Anthropologist* 90 (1988): 664–674.

Riek, Gustav. *Die Eiszeitjägerstation am Vogelherd im Lonetal.* Tübingen: Heine, 1934.

Rietschel, Gerhard, et al. *Lascaux, Höhle der Eiszeit.* Exh. cat. Hildesheim: Roemer- und Pelizaeus-Museum, 1982. Mainz: Von Zabern, 1982.

Ripoll Perelló, Eduardo. *Vida y obra del abate Henri Breuil, padre de la prehistoria.*

Barcelona: Diputación Provincial, Instituto de Prehistoria y Arqueología, 1964.

———. *El arte prehistórico español.* Madrid: Instituto Español de Antropología Aplicada, 1968.

———. *Orígenes y significado del arte paleolítico.* Madrid: Silex, 1986.

———. *Sobre els origens i significat de l'art paleolitic: Discurs d'ingrés de l'academia [. . .] llegit la sala d'actes de l'Academia el día 21 de gener de 1981.* Barcelona: Reial Acadèmia Catalana de Belles Arts de Sant Jordi, 1981. Castillian ed. *Orígenes y significado del arte paleolítico.* Madrid: Silex, 1986.

———. *El arte de los cazadores paleolíticos.* Madrid: Grupo 16, 1989.

———. *El abbate Henri Breuil (1877–1961).* Madrid: Universidad Nacional de Educación a Distancia, 1994.

Ripoll Perelló, Eduardo, ed. *Miscelánea en homenaje al abate Henri Breuil (1877–1961).* 2 vols. Barcelona: Diputación Provincial. Instituto de Prehistoria y Arqueología, 1964–65.

———. *Simposio Internacional de Arte Rupestre, Barcelona, 1966.* Barcelona: Diputación Provincial de Barcelona, Instituto de Prehistoria y Arqueología, 1968.

Ripoll Perelló, Eduardo and Sergio Ripoll López. *El arte paleolítico en la península ibérica.* Madrid: Información y Revistas, 1992.

Ripoll Perelló, Eduard, Javier Arce, and Pere de Palol. *Altamira y los orígenes del arte español.* Barcelona: Círculo de Lectores, 2002.

Ritchie, Carson I. A. *Rock Art of Africa.* South Brunswick, PA: Barnes, 1977.

Robb, John E., ed. *Material Symbols: Culture and Economy in Prehistory.* Carbondale, IL: Center for Archaeological Investigations, Southern Illinois University, Carbondale, 1999.

Robinson, Judy. "Not Counting on Marshack: A Reassessment of the Work of Alexander Marshack on Notation in the Upper Paleolithic." *Journal of Mediterranean Studies* 2 (1992): 1–16.

Rodrigue, Alain. *L'Art rupestre du Haut Atlas marocain.* Paris: L'Harmattan, 1999.

Roland, Berthold, ed. *Stationen der ältesten Kunst.* Exh. cat. Mainz: Landesmuseum Mainz, 1986.

Romero, G. "El caballo en el arte rupestre paleolítico." *Estudio de arte paleolítico.* Madrid: Ministerio de Cultura, Dirección General de Bellas Artes y Archivos, Subdirección General de Arqueología y Etnografía, 1986: 67–132.

Rose, Deborah Bird. *Nourishing Terrains: Australian Aboriginal Views of Landscape and Wilderness.* Canberra, ACT: Australian Heritage Commission, 1996.

Ross, Mairi. "Emerging Trends in Rock-Art Research: Hunter-gatherer Culture, Land and Landscape." *Antiquity* 75 (2001): 543–548.

Rousseau, Michel. *Les Grands Felins dans l'art de notre préhistoire.* Paris: Picard, 1967.

Roussot, Alain, ed. *Cent ans de préhistoire en Périgord.* Exh. cat. Bordeaux: Musée d'Aquitaine, 1965.

Rowe, W. Page. "The Origin of Prehistoric Art." *Man* 30 (1930): 6–9.

Roy, Claude. *L'Art à la source: Arts premiers, arts sauvages.* Paris: Gallimard, 1992.

Rudner, Jalmar and Ione Rudner. *The Hunter and His Art: A Survey of Rock Art in Southern Africa.* Cape Town: Struik, 1970; Los Angeles: L. S. B. Leakey Foundation, 1974.

Rudwick, Martin J. S. *Scenes from Deep Time: Early Pictorial Representations of the Prehistoric World.* Chicago, IL: University of Chicago Press, 1992.

Ruiz de Samaniego, Alberto, ed. *5000 años de arte moderna: Arte rupestre prehistórica e arte contemporánea galega.* Exh. cat. Vigo: Casa das Artes, 1999. Vigo: Concello de Vigo, 1999.

Ruspoli, Mario. *The Cave of Lascaux: The Final Photographs.* New York: Abrams, 1987.

Russel, Pamela. "Men Only? The Myths About European Palaeolithic Artists." In *The Archaeology of Gender: Proceedings of the Twenty-second Annual Conference of the Archaeological Association of the University of Calgary,* ed. Dale Walde and Noreen D. Willows. Calgary, Alta.: Chacmool Archaeological Association, 1991: 346–351.

———. "The Palaeolithic Mother Goddess: Fact or Fiction?" Hilary du Cross and Laurajane Smith, eds.: *Women in Archaeology: A Feminist Critique,* Canberra, ACT: The Australian National University, Research School of Pacific Studies, Department of Prehistory, 1993: 93–97.

Saccasyn della Santa, Elisabeth. *Les Figures humaines du paléolithique supérieur eurasiatique.* Anvers: De Sikkel, 1947.

Sahly, Ali. *Les Mains mutilées dans l'art préhistorique.* Toulouse: L'Académie de Toulouse, Faculté de Lettres et Sciences Humaines, 1966.

Saint-Périer, René de. "Statuette de femme stéatopyge découverte à Lespugue (Haute-Garonne)." *L'Anthropologie* 32 (1922): 361–381.

———. *L'Art préhistorique: Époque paléolithique.* Paris: Rieder, 1932.

———. "Inventaire de l'art mobilier paléolithique du Périgord." *Centenaire de la préhistoire en Périgord (1864–1964).* Périgueux: Fanlac, 1965. [Special issue of *Bulletin. Société historique et archéologique du Périgord* 91 (1964). Supplement]: 139–159.

Sanchidrián Torti, José Luis. *Manual de arte prehistórico.* Barcelona: Ariel, 2000.

Sandars, Nancy K. *Prehistoric Art in Europe.* Harmondsworth: Penguin, 1968; 2nd ed. 1985.

Sankalia, Hasmukhlal Dhirajlal. *Pre-historic Art in India.* New Delhi: Vikas, 1978.

Sanz de Sautuola, Marcelino. *Breves appuntes sobre algunos obietos preistóricos de la Provincia de Santander.* Santander: Martínez, 1880.

Sarradet, Max. *L'Art préhistorique du Périgord: Répertoire des grottes et abris du Périgord présentant des décors pariétaux ou ayant fourni des œuvres d'art préhistoriques.* Capo di Ponte: Edizioni del Centro, 1975.

Sauvet, Georges. "La Communication graphique paléolithique: De l'analyse quantitative d'une corpus de données à son interprétation sémiologique." *L'Anthropologie* 92 (1988): 3–15.

Scarre, Christopher. *Exploring Prehistoric Europe.* New York: Oxford University Press, 1998.

Schaafsma, Polly. *Rock Art in the Navajo Reservoir District.* Santa Fe, NM: Museum of New Mexico Press, 1963.

———. *The Rock Art of Utah: A Study from the Donald Scott Collection, Peabody Museum, Harvard University.* Cambridge, MA: Peabody Museum of Archaeology and Ethnology, Harvard University, 1971.

———. *Rock Art in New Mexico.* Albuquerque, NM: University of New Mexico Press, 1972; 2nd ed. 1975; 3rd rev. ed. Santa Fe, NM: Museum of New Mexico Press, 1992.

————. *Indian Rock Art of the Southwest.* Albuquerque, NM: Museum of New Mexico Press, and Santa Fe, NM: School of American Research, 1980.

————. "Form, Content, and Function: Theory and Method in North American Rock Art Studies." *Advances in Archaeological Method and Theory* 8 (1985): 237–277.

————. *Images in Stone.* San Francisco, CA: Brown/Trout Publishers, 1995.

Schaafsma, Polly and Keith Davis. *Marks in Place: Contemporary Responses to Rock Art.* Albuquerque, NM:: University of New Mexico Press, 1988.

Schefer, Jean Louis. *Questions d'art paléolithique.* Paris: P.O.L., 1999.

Scherz, Ernst R. *Felsbilder in Südwest-Afrika.* 2 vols. Köln: Böhlau, 1970–1975.

Schlesier, Karl H. "More on the 'Venus' Figurines." *Current Anthropology* 42 (2001): 410–412.

Schmid, Eberhard. "Die altsteinzeitliche Elfenbeinstatuette aus der Höhle Stadel im Hohlenstein bei Asselfingen, Alb-Donau-Kreis." *Fundberichte aus Baden-Württemberg* 14 (1989): 33–96.

Schmid, Elisabeth. "The Human Form and the Human Face in Paleolithic Art." In *La Contribution de la zoologie et de l'éthologie à l'interprétation de l'art des peuples chasseurs préhistoriques,* ed. Hans-Georg Bandi et al. Fribourg: Éditions Universitaires, 1984: 349–352.

Schmidt, Bruno. *Messages from the Past: The Rock Art of Eastern and Southern Africa.* Warmsroth: Stone Watch, 2001.

Schmidt, Robert Rudolf. *Die Kunst der Eiszeit.* Augsburg: Filser, 1922.

————. *Der Geist der Vorzeit.* Berlin: Keil Verlag Scherl, 1934.

Schmutz-Höbarthen, Franz. *Die nordischen Felsbilder, Denkmäler des Sonnenkults: Enträtselungen und ihre Ergebnisse.* Wien: Europäischer Verlag, 1959.

Schoonraad, Murray, ed. *Rock Paintings of Southern Africa: Symposium on Rock Art [Held June 30—July 5, 1969 as Part of the 67th Annual Congress of the South African Association for the Advancement of Science in Pietermaritzburg].* Johannesburg: South African Association for the Advancement of Science, 1971. Supplement to the *South African Journal of Science.* Special Issue, no. 2.

Schulte im Walde, Thomas and Harald Braem. *Bibliographie des deutschsprachigen Schrifttums zur internationalen Felsbildforschung.* Lollschied, Rheinland-Pfalz: Kult-Ur-Institut, 1994.

Schulz, Agnes Susanne. *Northwest Australian Rock Paintings.* Melbourne: National Museum of Victoria, 1956.

————. *Felsbilder in Nord-Australien.* Wiesbaden: Steiner, 1971.

Sèbe, Alain and Tristan Roux. *Tikatoutine: 6000 ans d'art rupestre saharien.* Vidauban: Sèbe, 1991.

Seglie, Dario. *Nature and Culture in Rock Art Phenomena.* Liège: Université de Liège, 1993.

Seglie, Dario, ed. *African Pictograms: Namibia Rock Art and Archaeology = Arte rupestre e archeologia della Namibia.* Exh. cat. Pinerolo: Centro Studi e Museo d'Arte Preistorica, 1997.

[Semana de Historia de Puertollano.] *VI Semana de Historia de Puertollano.* Ciudad Real: Diputación Provincial, Área de Cultura, 1986.

————. *VII, VIII y IX Semanas de Historia de Puertollano, celebradas en 1986, 1987 y Arte rupestre del arco mediterráneo 1988.* Ciudad Real: Área de Cultura, Diputación Provincial, 1989.

Semiótica del arte prehistórico. Valencia: Conselleria de Cultura, 2001.

Shafer, Harry J. *Ancient Texans: Rock Art and Lifeways along the Lower Pecos.* Austin, TX: Witte Museum of the San Antonio Museum Association, San Antonio, Texas and Texas Monthly Press, 1986.

Sharma, Raj Kumar and K. K. Tripathi, eds. *Recent Perspectives on Prehistoric Art in India and Allied Subjects: Essays in Honour of Dr. Shyam Kumar Pandey.* New Delhi: Aryan Books International, 1996.

Sher, Iakov Abramovich. *Pervobytnoe iskusstvo.* Novosibirsk: Nauka, 1971.

Sher, Iakov Abramovich, ed. *Pervobytnoe iskusstvo: Problema proiskhozhdeniia.* Kemerovo: Kemerovskii god. in-t iskusstv i kul'tury, 1998.

Siegrist, Roland, ed. *Prehistoric Petroglyphs and Pictographs in Utah.* Salt Lake City, UT: Utah State Historical Society, 1972.

Sieveking, Ann. *The Cave Artists.* London: Thames and Hudson, 1979.

————. *A Catalogue of Palaeolithic Art in the British Museum.* London: British Museum Publications, 1987.

————. *Engraved Magdalenian Plaquettes: A Regional and Stylistic Analysis of Stone, Bone and Antler Plaquettes from Upper Palaeolithic Sites in France and Cantabric Spain.* Oxford: British Archaeological Reports, 1987.

Sieveking, Ann and Gale Sieveking. *The Caves of France and Northern Spain: A Guide.* London: Vista Books, 1962.

Skrotzky, Nicolas. *L'Abbé Breuil.* Paris: Seghers, 1964.

Slifer, Dennis. *Signs of Life: Rock Art of the Upper Rio Grande.* Santa Fe, NM: Ancient City Press, 1998.

————. *The Serpent and the Sacred Fire: Fertility Images in Southwest Rock Art.* Santa Fe, NM: Museum of New Mexico Press, 2000.

Smith, Catherine Delano. "Cartography in the Prehistoric Period in the Old Europe, the Middle East, and North Africa." In *The History of Cartography,* ed. John Brian Harley and David Woodward. Chicago, IL: Chicago University Pres, 1987: 54–101.

Smith, Claire E. "Female Artists: The Unrecognized Factor in Sacred Rock Art Production." In *Rock Art and Prehistory: Papers Presented to Symposium G of the AURA Congress, Darwin 1988,* ed. Paul G. Bahn and Andrée Rosenfeld. Oxford: Oxbow Books, 1991: 45–52.

Smith, Gerald Arthur and Wilson G. Turner. *Indian Rock Art of Southern California with Selected Petroglyph Catalog.* Redlands, CA: San Bernardino County Museum Association, 1975.

Smith, Noel W. *An Analysis of Ice Age Art: Its Psychology and Belief System.* New York: Lang, 1992.

————. *San Visions and Values: An Interpretation of the Prehistoric Rock Art of Southern Africa.* Nottingham: Smith, 2001.

Snow, Dean R. "Rock Art and the Power of Shamans." *Natural History* 86:2 (February 1977): 42–49.

Soffer, Olga, James Adovasio, and David C. Hyland. "The 'Venus' Figurines: Textiles, Basketry, Gender, and Status in the Upper Palaeolithic." *Current Anthropology* 41 (2000): 511–537.

Soffer, Olga, Pamela Vandiver, Bohuslav Klíma, and Jiří Svoboda. "The Pyrotechnology of Performance Art: Moravian Venuses and Wolverines." In *Before Lascaux: The Complex Record of the Early Upper Paleolithic,* ed. Heidi Knecht,

Anne Pike-Tay, and Randall White. Boca Raton, FL: CRC Press, 1993. 259–275.

Sognnes, Kalle. *Prehistoric Imagery and Landscapes: Rock Art in Stjørdal, Trøndelag, Norway.* Oxford, Archaeopress, 2001.

Solomon, Anne. "Gender, Representation and Power in San Ethnography and Rock Art." *Journal of Anthropological Archaeology* 11 (1992): 291–329.

———. " 'Mythic Women': A Study in Variability in San Rock Art and Narrative." In *Contested Images: Diversity in Southern African Rock Art Research,* ed. Thomas Dowson and David Lewis-Williams. Johannesburg: Witwatersrand University Press, 1994: 331–371.

———. " 'Mythic Women': A Response to Humphreys." *South African Archaeological Bulletin* 51 (1996): 33–35.

———. "Rock Art in Southern Africa." *Scientific American* 275:5 (November 1996): 106–113.

———. *The Essential Guide to San Rock Art.* Cape Town: Philip; Johannesburg: Thorold's Africana Books, 1998.

Sonin, Bill. *California Rock Art: An Annotated Site Inventory and Bibliography.* Los Angeles, CA: Rock Art Archive of the Institute of Archaeology, University of California; Bay Area Rock Art Research Association, 1995.

Soria Lerma, Miguel and Manuel Gabriel López Payer. *El arte rupestre en el sureste de la península ibérica.* Bailén (Jaén): Soria, 1989.

Spearing, Herbert Green. *The Childhood of Art; or, The Ascent of Man.* London: Paul, Trench, Trubner & Co., 1912; 2nd rev. ed. London: Benn, 1930.

Spivack, Morris Redman. *La Danse cosmique de Lascaux: Une nouvelle théorie de l'art et de la religion paléolithique.* Montignac-sur-Vézère: [s.n.], 1961.

Srejovic, Dragoslav. *Lepenski Vir: Nova praistorijska kultura u Podunavlju.* Beograd: Srpska knjizevna zadruga, 1969.

———. *Europe's First Monumental Sculpture: New Discoveries at Lepenski Vir.* New York: Stein and Day, 1972.

———. *Lepenski Vir: Eine vorgeschichtliche Geburtsstätte europäischer Kultur.* Bergisch Gladbach: Lübbe, 1973; 2nd ed. 1981.

Srejovic, Dragoslav and Ljubinka Babovic, eds. *Lepenski Vir: Menschenbilder einer frühen europäischen Kultur.* Exh. cat. Köln: Romisch-Germanisches Museum, and München: Prähistorische Staatssammlung, Museum für Vor- und Frühgeschichte, 1981.

Steinbring, Jack, ed. *Rock Art Studies in the Americas: Papers Presented to Symposium B of the AURA Congress, Darwin 1988.* Oxford: Oxbow Books, 1995.

Steinbring, Jack, Alan Watchman, Paul Faulstich, and Paul S. C. Taçon, eds. *Time and Space: Dating and Considerations in Rock Art Research: Papers of Symposia F and E, second AURA Congress, Cairns 1992.* Melbourne: Australian Rock Art Research Association, 1993.

Steinbring, Jack and Antony P. Buchner, eds. *Studies in Manitoba Rock Art.* 2 vols. Winnipeg: Department of Tourism, Recreation & Cultural Affairs, Historic Resources Branch, 1976–1978; 2nd ed. 1983–1986.

Stevens, Anthony. "Animals in Paleolithic Cave Art: Leroi-Gourhan's Hypothesis." *Antiquity* 49 (1975): 54–57.

Stevenson, Judith. "Shaman Images in San Rock Art: A Question of Gender." In

Representations of Gender from Prehistory to the Present, ed. Moira Donald and Linda Hurcombe. Houndmills: Macmillan, 2000: 45–66.

Stiebing, William H. "The Discovery of Prehistory." In *Exploring the Past: Readings in Archaeology*, ed. James M. Bayman and Miriam T. Stark. Durham, NC: Carolina Academic Press, 2000: 67–83.

Stoliar, Abram Davidovich. "On the Sociohistorical Decoding of Upper Palaeolithic Female Signs." *Soviet Anthropology and Anthropology* 16:2 (Fall 1977): 36–77.

———. *Proiskhozhdenie izobrazitel'nogo iskusstva*. Moskva: "Iskusstvo," 1985.

Straus, Lawrence G. "The Paleolithic Cave Art of Vasco-Cantabrian Spain." *Oxford Journal of Archaeology* 8 (1987): 149–163.

Strecker, Matthias. *Rock Art of East Mexico and Central America: An Annotated Bibliography*. 2nd rev. ed. Los Angeles, CA: Institute of Archaeology, University of California, Los Angeles, 1982.

Strecker Matthias and Paul Bahn, eds. *Dating and the Earliest Known Rock Art: Papers Presented at Symposia 1–3 of the SIARB Congress, Cochabamba, Bolivia, April 1997*. Oxford: Oxbow Books, 1999.

Striedter, Karl Heinz. *Felsbilder Nordafrikas und der Sahara: Ein Verfahren zu ihrer systematischen Erfassung und Auswertung*. Wiesbaden: Steiner, 1983.

———. *Rock Paintings from Zimbabwe: Collections of the Frobenius-Institut*. Wiesbaden: Steiner, 1983.

———. *Felsbilder der Sahara*. München: Prestel, 1984.

Strube, León. *Arte rupestre en Sudamérica, con especial descripción de los petroglifos de la provincia de Coquimbo, Chile*. Concepción: Imprenta Alemana, 1926.

Svoboda, Jiří: *Mistri kamenného dláta: Umení pravekých lovcu*. Praha: Panorama, 1986.

Swartz, Ben K. and Thomas S. Hurlbutt. "Space, Place and Territory in Rock Art Interpretation." *Rock Art Research* 11 (1994): 13–22.

Taborin, Yvette. "Les Prémices de l'expression symbolique." In *De Néandertal à Cro-Magnon*, ed. Catherine Farizy. Exh. cat. Nemours: Musée de Préhistoire d'Îsle de France, 1988: 73–75.

Taçon, Paul S. C. "Australia." In *Handbook of Rock Art Research*, ed. David S. Whitley. Walnut Creek, CA: AltaMira Press, 2001: 530–575.

Taçon, Paul S. C. and Christopher Chippindale. "Najombolmi's People: From Rock Painting to National Icon." In *Histories of Old Ages: Essays In Honour of Rhys Jones*, ed. Atholl Anderson, Ian Lilley and Sue O'Connor. Canberra, ACT: Pandanus Research School of Pacific and Asian Studies, Australian National University, 2001: 301–310.

Taçon, Paul S. C., Meredith Wilson and Christopher Chippindale. "Birth of the Rainbow Serpent in Arnhem Land Rock Art and Oral History." *Archaeology in Oceania* 31 (1996): 103–124.

Tassé, Gilles and Selwyn Dewdney. *Relevés et travaux récents sur l'art rupestre amérindien*. Montréal: Laboratoire d'Archéologie de l'Université du Québec à Montréal, 1977.

Thiault, Marie-Hélène and Jean-Bernard Roy, eds. *L'Art préhistorique des Pyrénées*. Exh. cat. Paris: Château de Saint-Germain-en-Laye, 1996. Paris: Éditions de la Réunion des Musées Nationaux, 1996.

Thompson, Paul. *Maori Rock Art: An Ink that Will Stand Forever*. Wellington: GP Books, 1989.

Tiwari, Shiv Kumar. *Riddles of Indian Rockshelter Paintings*. New Delhi: Sarup & Sons, 2000.

Topper, Uwe and Uta, Topper. *Arte rupestre en la provincia de Cádiz*. Cádiz: Diputación de Cádiz, 1988.

Trezise, Percy J. *Quinkan Country: Adventures in Search of Aboriginal Cave Paintings in Cape York*. Sydney, NSW: Reed, 1969.

———. *Rock Art of South-east Cape York*. Canberra, ACT: Australian Institute of Aboriginal Studies, 1971.

———. *Dream Road: A Journey of Discovery*. St. Leonards, NSW: Allen & Unwin, 1993.

Tringham, Ruth and Margaret Conkey. "Rethinking Figurines: A Critical View from Archaeology of Gimbutas, the 'Goddess' and Popular Culture." In *Ancient Goddesses: The Myths and the Evidence*, ed. Lucy Goodison and Christine Morris Madison. London: British Museum Press, 1998: 22–45.

Trotter, Michael Malthus and Beverley McCulloch. *Prehistoric Rock Art of New Zealand*. Wellington: Reed, 1971; 2nd ed. Auckland: Longman Paul, 1981.

Turpin, Solveig A. "Speculations on the Age and Origin of the Pecos River Style." *American Indian Rock Art* 16 (1990): 99–122.

———. "Rock Art and Its Contribution to Hunter Gatherer Archaeology: A Case Study from the Lower Pecos River Region of Southwest Texas and Northern Mexico." *Journal of Field Archaeology* 17:3 (1990): 263–281.

———. "The Were-Cougar Theme in Pecos River-Style Art and Its Implications for Traditional Archaeology." In *New Light on Old Art*, ed. David S. Whitley and Lawrence L. Loendorf. Los Angeles, CA: University of California at Los Angeles: Institute of Archaeology, 1994: 75–80.

———. "On a Wing and a Prayer: Flight Metaphors in Pecos River Art." In *Shamanism and Rock Art in North America*, ed. S. A. Turpin. San Antonio, TX: Rock Art Foundation, 1995: 73–102.

———. "Archaic North America." In *Handbook of Rock Art Research*, ed. David S. Whitley. Walnut Creek, CA: AltaMira Press, 2001: 361–413.

Turpin, Solveig A. and Herbert H. Eling, Jr. *Cueva Pilote: Ritual Bloodletting Among the Prehistoric Hunters and Gatherers of Northern Coahuila, Mexico*. Austin, TX: The University of Texas at Austin, Institute of Latin American Studies, and Saltillo, Coahuila: Instituto Nacional de Antropología e Historia, 1999.

Turpin, Solveig A., Herbert H. Eling, Jr., and Moisés Valadez Moreno. "From Marshland to Desert: The Late Prehistoric Environment of Boca de Potrerillos, Nuevo León, Mexico." *North American Archaeologist* 14: 4 (1993): 305–323.

———. "The Archaic Environment of Boca de Potrerillos, Northeastern Mexico." *North American Archaeologist* 15:4 (1994): 331–357.

———. "Boca de Potrerillos, Nuevo León: Adaptación prehispánica a las áridas del noreste de México." In *Arqueologia del Occidente y Norte de México*, ed. Eduardo Williams and Phil C. Weigand. Zamora, México: El Colegio de Michoacán, 1995. 177–224.

———. "The Mobiliary Art of Boca de Potrerillos, Nuevo León, Mexico." *Plains Anthropologist* 41:156 (1996): 105–116.

Turpin, Solveig A., ed. *Papers on Lower Pecos Prehistory*. Austin, TX: The University of Texas at Austin, 1991.

———. *Shamanism and Rock Art in North America*. San Antonio, TX: Rock Art Foundation, 1994.

Ucko, Peter J., ed. *Form in Indigenous Art: Schematisation in the Art of Aboriginal Australia and Prehistoric Europe*. Canberra, ACT: Australian Institute of Aboriginal Studies; Atlantic Highlands/NJ: Humanities Press, 1977.

Ucko, Peter J. and Andrée Rosenfeld. *L'Art paléolithique*. Paris: Hachette, 1966; Engl. ed. *Palaeolithic Cave Art*. London: Thames and Hudson, 1967.

———. "Critical Analysis of Interpretations and Conclusions and Problems from Palaeolithic Cave Art." In *Anthropology and Art: Readings in Cross-cultural Aesthetics*, ed. Charlotte M. Otten. Austin, TX: University of Texas Press, 1971. 247–281.

———. "Anthropomorphic Representations in Palaeolithic Art." In *Santander Symposium*, ed. Martín Almagro Basch and Miguel Ángel García Guinea. Santander: Museo de Prehistoria, 1972: 149–211.

Ucko, Peter J. and Layton, Robert, eds. *The Archaeology and Anthropology of Landscape: Shaping Your Landscape*. London: Routledge, 1999.

Unión Internacional de Ciencias Prehistóricas y Protohistóricas. X congreso. Comision XI. Arte Paleolítico. Coloquio. México D.F., Octubre 19–24, 1981. 2 vols. Mexico, D.F.: UISPP, 1981.

Van Riet Lowe, Clarence: *Prehistoric Art in South Africa: An Explanation of a Map and Index of Sites Showing the Distribution of Prehistoric Rock Engravings and Paintings in the Union of South Africa*. Pretoria: Government Printer, 1941.

Van Tilburg, JoAnne, ed. *Ancient Images on Stone: Rock Art of the Californias*. Los Angeles/CA: Rock Art Archive, Institute of Archaeology, University of California, Los Angeles, 1983.

Van Tilburg, JoAnne and Clement W. Meighan, eds. *Prehistoric Indian Rock Art: Issues and Concerns. Report of the 1980 Conference Proceedings, Institute of Archaeology, the Rock Art Archive, University of California, Los Angeles*. Los Angeles, CA: Institute of Archaeology, University of California, Los Angeles, 1981.

Vaquero-Turcios, Joaquín. *Maestros subterráneos: Una visión cercana del arte rupestre, sus creadores y las técnicas que utilizaron*. Madrid: Celeste, 1995.

Vasil'evskii, Ruslan Sergeevich, ed. *Pervobytnoe iskusstvo*. 2 vols. Novosibirsk: Izdatel'stvo "Nauka," Sibirskoe otdelenie, 1971–1976.

———. *Zveri v kamne: [Sbornik statei]*. Novosibirsk: "Nauka," Sibirskoe otdelenie, 1980.

———. *Plastika i risunki drevnikh kul'tur*. Novosibirsk: Izdatel'stvo "Nauka," Sibirskoe otdelenie, 1983.

———. *Proiskhozhdeniia izobrazitel'nogo iskusstva*. Moskva: Iskusstvo, 1985.

———. *Naskal'nye risunki Evrazii: Sbornik nauchnych trudov*. Novosibirsk: Nauka, 1992.

Vázquez Varela, José Manuel. *Os petroglifos de Galicia*. Santiago de Compostela: Servicio de Publicacións da Universidade, 1990.

———. *Antepasados, guerreros y visiones: Análisis antropológico del arte prehistórico de Galicia*. Pontevedra: Deputación Provincial de Pontevedra, Servicio de Publicacións, 1995.

Verbrugge, Amand Raymond. *Le Symbole de la main dans la préhistoire.* Courances: L'Auteur, 1958; 2nd rev. ed. 1969; Engl. ed. *Corpus of the Hand Figurations in Primitive Australia.* Gap: Éditions Ophrys, 1970.

Verworn, Max. *Die Anfänge der Kunst: Ein Vortrag.* Jena: Fischer, 1909.

———. *Zur Psychologie der primitiven Kunst: Ein Vortrag;* 2nd ed. Jena: Fischer, 1917.

Vialou, Denis. *Guide des grottes ornées paléolithiques ouvertes au public.* Paris: Masson, 1976.

———. "L'Art préhistorique: Questions d'interprétation." *Monuments Historiques* 118 (November–December 1981): 75–82.

———. *L'Art pariétal en Ariège magdalénienne.* 3 vols. Paris: Musée National d'Histoire Naturelle, Musée de l'Homme, Laboratoire de Paléontologie Humaine et de Préhistoire, 1981.

———. "Art paléolithique et art rupestre brasilien: Methodologie des approches." *Unión Internacional de Ciencias Prehistóricas y Protohistóricas. X congreso. Comision XI. Arte Paleolítico. Coloquio. México D.F., Octubre 19–24, 1981.* México, D.F.: UISPP, 1981: 111–122.

———. *L'Art des grottes en Ariège magdalénienne.* Paris: Éditions du Centre National de la Recherche Scientifique, 1986.

———. *L'Art des cavernes.* Monaco: Le Rocher, 1987.

———. *La Préhistoire.* Paris: Gallimard, 1991.

———. *Au Cœur de la préhistoire: Chasseurs et artistes.* Paris: Gallimard, 1996; Engl. ed. *Prehistoric Art and Civilization.* New York: Abrams, 1998.

———. *L'Art des grottes.* Paris: Scala, 1998.

———. "L'Art paléolithique." In *La préhistoire,* Marcel Otte, Denis Vialou and Patrick Plumet. Bruxelles: De Boeck & Larcier, 1999: 213–289.

Vialou, Denis, ed. *Séminaire 'Représentations préhistoriques' 1983–1984.* Special issue of *L'Anthropologie* 88:4 (1984).

Vieira, Antonio Bracinha. "Mythe e magie dans l'art pariétal: La logique de la caverne." *Trabalhos de Antropologia e Etnologia* 36 (1996): 169–191.

Vigliardi, Alda, ed. "Art in the Palaeolithic and Mesolithic." *Proceedings of the XIII Congress of Prehistoric and Protohistoric Sciences, Forlì—Italia, 1996, 8–14 September.* Vol. 3 ed. by Renata Grifoni Cremonesi, Carlo Tozzi, Alda Vigliardi and Carlo Peretto. Forlì: A.B.A.C.O., 1998: 73–130.

Vilanova y Piera, Juan. *Conferencias dadas en Santander.* Torrelavega: Rueda, 1881; 2nd ed. Edited by Orestes Cendrero Uceda. Santander: Universidad de Cantabria. Servicio de Publicaciones/Santillana del Mar: Ayuntamiento de Santillana del Mar, 1997.

Vinnicombe, Patricia. *People of the Eland: Rock Paintings of the Drakensberg Bushmen as a Reflection of Their Life and Thought.* Pietermaritzburg: University of Natal Press, 1976.

Vouvé, Jean, Jacques Brunet, Pierre Vidal, and Jacques Marsal. *Lascaux en Périgord Noir: Environnement, art pariétal et conservation.* Périgeux: Fanlac, 1982.

Wagner, Eberhard. "Eine Löwenkopfplastik aus Elfenbein von der Vogelherdhöhle." *Fundberichte aus Baden-Württemberg* 6 (1981): 29–58.

Walker, Michael. "Spanish Levantine Rock Art." *Man* NS 6 (1971): 553–589.

Waller, Steven J. "Sound Reflection as an Explanation for the Content and Context of Rock Art." *Rock Art Research* 10 (1993): 91–101.

————. "Taphonomic Considerations of Rock Art Acoustics." *Rock Art Research* 11 (1994): 120–121.

Wallin, Nils L. "The Origins of Music." In *The Origins of Music*, ed. Nils L. Wallin, Björn Merker and Steven Brown. Cambridge: MIT Press, 2000: 235–268.

Walsh, Grahame Leslie. *Australia's Greatest Rock Art*. Bathurst, NSW: E. J. Brill, Robert Brown and Associates, 1989.

————. *Bradshaws: Ancient Rock Paintings of North-west Australia*. Genève: Bradshaw Foundation, and Édition Limitaee, 1994.

Wanke, Lothar. *Zentralindische Felsbilder*. Graz: Akademische Druck- und Verlagsanstalt, 1977.

Watts, Ian. "The Origin of Symbolic Culture." In *The Evolution of Culture*, ed. Robin Dunbar, Chris Knight and Camilla Power. Edinburgh: Edinburgh University Press, 1999: 113–146.

Weaver, Donald Edgar. *Hieroglyphic Canyon: A Petroglyph Record of a Changing Subsistence Pattern*. El Toro, CA: American Rock Art Research Association, 1985.

Weigert, Hans, ed. *Kleine Kunstgeschichte der Vorzeit und der Naturvölker*. Berlin: Propyläen, 1942; 2nd rev. ed. Stuttgart: Kohlhammer, 1956.

Weisse Dame – roter Riese: Felsbilder aus Namibia. Texte der Ausstellung. Exh. cat. Köln: Universität zu Köln, Institut für Ur- und Frühgeschichte, Forschungsstelle Afrika. Köln: Heinrich-Barth-Institut, 1996.

Wellmann, Klaus F. "A Bibliography of North American Rock Art." *The Artifact* 16 (1978): 1–109.

————. "Rock Art, Shamans, Phosphenes and Hallucinogens in North America." *Bollettino del Centro Camuno di Studi Preistorici* 18 (1981): 89–103.

————. *A Survey of North American Indian Rock Art*. Graz: Akademische Druck- und Verlagsanstalt, 1979.

Welsh, Liz. *Rock-Art of the Southwest: A Visitor's Companion*. Berkeley, CA: Wilderness Press, 2000.

Weltfish, Gene. *The Origins of Art*. Indianapolis, IN: Bobbs-Merrill, 1953.

Wendt, Wolfgang E. "Art mobilier aus der Apollo 11 Grotte in Südwest-Africa." *Acta Praehistoria et Archaeologica* 5 (1974): 1–42; Engl. summary " 'Art mobilier' from the Apollo 11 Cave, South West Africa: Africa's Oldest Dated Works of Art." *South African Archaeological Bulletin* 31 (1976): 5–11.

Wernert, Paul. *Representaciones de antepasados en el arte paleolítico*. Madrid: Museo Nacional de Ciencias Naturales, 1916.

————. *Nuevos datos etnográficos para la cronología del arte rupestre de estilo naturalista en el Oriente de España*. Madrid: Museo Nacional de Ciencias Naturales, 1917.

White, Randall. "Visual Thinking in the Ice Age." *Scientific American* 261:1 (July 1969): 92–99.

————. "Beyond Art: Toward an Understanding of the Origins of Material Representation in Europe." *Annual Review of Anthropology* 21 (1992): 537–564.

————. *Dark Caves, Bright Visions: Life in Ice Age Europe*. Exh. cat. New York: American Museum of Natural History, Saint-Germain-en-Laye: Musée des Antiquités Nationales. New York: Norton, 1986.

————. " Technological and Social Dimensions of 'Augignacian-Age' Body Ornaments across Europe." In *Before Lascaux: The Complex Record of the Early*

Upper Paleolithic, ed. Heidi Knecht, Anne Pike-Tay and Randall White. Boca Raton, FL: CRC Press, 1993: 277–299.

———. " Substantial Acts: From Materials to Meaning in Upper Paleolithic Representation." In *Beyond Art: Pleistocene Image and Symbol,* ed. Margaret W. Conkey, Olga Soffer, Deborah Stratmann and Nina G. Jablonski. San Francisco, CA: California Academy of Sciences, 1997: 93–121.

———. "The Dawn of Adornment." In *Exploring the Past: Readings in Archaeology,* ed. James M. Bayman and Miriam T. Stark. Durham, NC: Carolina Academic Press, 2000: 391–395.

Whitley, David S. "Shamanism and Rock Art in Far Western North America." *Cambridge Archaeological Journal* 2 (1992): 89–113.

———. *A Guide to Rock Art Sites: Southern California and Southern Nevada.* Missoula, MT: Mountain Press, 1996.

———. *L'Art des chamanes de Californie: Le monde des Amérindiens.* Paris: Seuil, 2000; Engl. ed. *The Art of the Shaman: Rock Art of California.* Salt Lake City, UT: University of Utah Press, 2000.

———. "Reading the Minds of Rock Artists." In *Exploring the Past: Readings in Archaeology,* ed. James M. Bayman and Miriam T. Stark. Durham, NC: Carolina Academic Press, 2000: 373–379.

Whitley, David S., ed. *Handbook of Rock Art Research.* Walnut Creek, CA: AltaMira Press, 2001.

Whitley, David S. and Lawrence L. Loendorf. *New Light on Old Art: Recent Advances in Hunter-gatherer Rock Art Research.* Los Angeles, CA: Institute of Archaeology, University of California, Los Angeles, 1994.

Whitley, David S., Joseph M. Simon, and Ronald I. Dorn. "The Vision Quest in the Coso Range." *American Indian Rock Art* 25 (1999): 1–31.

Wiber, Melanie. *Erect Men, Undulating Women: The Visual Imagery of Gender, Race and Progress in Reconstructive Illustrations of Human Evolution.* Waterloo, Ont.: Wilfrid Laurier University Press, 1997.

Willcox, Alexander Robert. *Rock Paintings of the Drakensberg, Natal and Griqualand East.* London: Parrish, 1956.

———. *The Rock Art of South Africa.* Johannesburg: Nelson, 1963.

———. "An Analysis of the Function of Rock Art." *South African Journal of Science* 74 (1978): 59–64.

———. *The Rock Art of Africa.* New York: Holmes & Meier, 1984.

———. *The Drakensberg Bushmen and Their Art: With a Guide to the Rock Painting Sites.* Winterton, Natal: Drakensberg Publications, 1984.

Wilson, Thomas. *Prehistoric Art; or, The Origin of Art as Manifested in the Works of Prehistoric Man.* Washington, DC: Government Printing Office, 1898.

Windels, Fernand. *La Capilla Sixtina del arte cuaternario: La cueva de Altamira.* [S.l.]: Edi España, [1945?]; 2nd ed. Madrid: Delblan, 1968; French ed. *Lascaux: "Chapelle Sixtine" de la préhistoire.* Montignac: Centre d'Études et de Documentation Préhistoriques, 1948; Engl. ed. *The Lascaux Cave Paintings.* London: Faber and Faber, 1949.

Wingert, Paul S., ed. *Prehistoric Stone Sculpture of the Pacific Northwest.* Exh. cat. Portland, OR: Portland Art Museum, 1952.

Winkler, Hans Alexander. *Rock-drawings of Southern Upper Egypt.* 2 vols. London: The Egypt Exploration Society, and Oxford University Press, 1938–39.

Winkler, Traute, ed. *Früheste Kunst der Menschheit: Bilder und Kleinkunst aus französischen Höhlen der Eiszeit.* Exh. cat. Dortmund: Geschichtliches Museum der Stadt, 1959.

Wreschner, Ernst E. "Red Ochre and Human Evolution: A Case for Discussion." *Current Anthropology* 21 (1980): 631–644.

———. "Red Ochre, the Transition between Lower and Middle Palaeolithic and the Origins of Modern Man." In *The Transition from Lower to Middle Palaeolithic and the Origins of Modern Man,* ed. Avraham Ronen. Oxford: British Archaeological Reports, 1982: 35–39.

Yates, Royden. *Pictures from the Past: A History of the Interpretation of Rock Paintings and Engravings of Southern Africa.* Pietermaritzburg: Centaur, 1990.

Yates, Royden and Anthony Manhire. "Shamanism and Rock Paintings: Aspects of the Use of Rock Art in the South-west Cape, South Africa." *South African Archaeological Bulletin* 46 (1991): 3–11.

Yates, Royden, Jo Golson, and Martin Hall. "Trance Performance: The Rock Art of Boontjeskloof and Sevilla." *South African Archaeological Bulletin* 40 (1985): 70–80.

Young, M. Jane. *Signs from the Ancestors: Zuni Cultural Symbolism and Perceptions of Rock Art.* Albuquerque, NM: University of New Mexico Press, 1988.

Younkin, Elva, ed. *Coso Rock Art: A New Perspective.* Ridgecrest, CA: Maturango Museum Press, 1998.

Zerbst, Fritz. *Steinzeit heute: Gelbe Buschmänner im Süden Afrikas und die europäische Vorzeit.* Wien: Böhlau, 1983.

Zervos, Christian and Henri Breuil. *L'Art de l'epoque du Renne en France, avec une étude sur la formation de la science préhistorique.* Paris: Éditions "Cahiers d'art", 1959.

Zhurov, R. I A. "On One Hypothesis Relating to the Origin of Art." *Soviet Anthropology and Archaeology* 16:3–4 (Winter-Spring 1977–78): 43–63.

Zilhão, João and António Faustino de Carvalho, eds. *Arte rupestre e pré-história do Vale do Côa: Trabalhos de 1995–1996.* Lisboa: Ministério da Cultura, Instituto Português do Património Arquitectónico e Arqueológico, 1997.

Zintgraff, Jim. *Pecos River Rock Art: A Photographic Essay.* San Antonio, TX: McPherson, 1991.

Index

About the Contributors

LAWRENCE S. BARHAM is a Senior Lecturer in the Department of Archaeology, University of Bristol. He has worked in Africa for more than twenty years, most recently in Zambia, where he is investigating the environmental and social factors that contributed to the emergence of modern human behaviours, including art. He is the author of *In Search of Cheddar Man* (Tempus 1999), *The Middle Stone Age of Zambia, Southcentral Africa* (Western Academic & Specialist Press, 2000) and co-editor of *Human Roots: Africa and Asia in the Middle Pleistocene* (Western Academic & Specialist Press, 2001).

GÜNTER BERGHAUS is a Reader in Theatre History and Performance Studies at the Drama Department, University of Bristol, and has been visiting professor at the State University of Rio de Janeiro and at Brown University. He has published extensively on theatre anthropology, ritual studies, avant-garde performance, Renaissance and Baroque theatre. He has directed numerous plays from the classical and modern repertoire and devised many productions of an experimental nature. He has been principal organizer of several international conferences and has held research awards from the Polish Academy of Sciences, the German Research Foundation, the Italian Ministry of Culture, the British Academy, and the Brazilian Ministry of Education

ROGER CARDINAL is Professor of Literary and Visual Studies at the University of Kent at Canterbury. He is an international authority on Surrealism and the European avant-garde, and has written widely on artists and writers in the modern period. His books include *Surrealism* (1970, with Robert Short), *Figures of Reality* (1981) and *Expressionism* (1984). He has edited collective volumes on modern French poetry (*Sensibility and Creation*, 1977) and on collecting (*The Cultures of Collecting*, 1994, with John Elsner). He has also written monographs on Paul Nash (1989) and Henry Moore (2000), as well as articles on Kurt Schwitters, Giorgio de Chirico, Alberto Giacometti, André Masson, Hans Bellmer and Wols. He has curated several international exhibitions in England, France and the United States concerning the linked fields of Art Brut, Naive Art and Folk Art. Associated publications include: *Outsider Art* (1972), *Primitive Painters* (1978), *Outsiders* (1979), *Private Worlds* (1998, with John Beardsley), *Messages d'outre-monde* (1999, with Martine Lusardy) and *Marginalia* (2001, with Ans van Berkum, Jos ten Berge and Colin Rhodes). He is currently writing a book which approaches the arts of prehistory from an art-historical perspective.

CHRISTOPHER CHIPPINDALE is Reader in Archaeology at Cambridge University, and an archaeology curator in its Museum of Archaeology & Anthropology. Rock art is one of his major research fields, especially in northern Australia, where singular circumstances offer unusual possibilities. He also works on varied other aspects to archaeology, such as the consequences of antiquities collecting and Stonehenge.

J. DAVID LEWIS-WILLIAMS is professor emeritus and senior mentor in the Rock Art Research Institute, University of the Witwatersrand, Johannesburg, South Africa. He spent forty years studying the hunter-gatherer rock art of southern Africa. His publications include: *Believing and Seeing: Symbolic Meanings in Southern African Rock Art* (London: Academic Press, 1981), *Rock Art of Southern Africa* (Cambridge: Cambridge University Press, 1983) and *Images of Mystery* (Cape Town: Double Storey, 2003). Recently, he was asked to translate the new South African national motto into the now-extinct /Xam San language. He has also worked in and published extensively on the Upper Palaeolithic cave art of western Europe. His books on this topic include (with Jean Clottes) *Shamans of Prehistory: Trance and Magic in the Painted Caves* (New York: Harry Abrams, 1998), and *The Mind in the Cave: Consciousness and the Origins of Art* (London: Thames & Hudson, 2002).

YANN-PIERRE MONTELLE is a Ph.D. candidate in Anthropology and Performance Studies at Brown University in the USA. He is currently finishing his dissertation, which looks at the emergence of theatricality in human behavior in the Upper Paleolithic. In the context of his research, he has investigated many caves in the Franco-cantabrian region, and has been doing extensive fieldwork in Galicia, Australia, and New Zealand. He has sampled aspects of his research in rock art and performance in international conferences. He has two articles in press about rock art and liminality, and rock art and cognitive mapping.

JON NYGAARD is Professor of Theatre Studies at University of Oslo, Norway. His research interests have centred on the theory of theatre, theatre policy, theatre history and performance studies, especially on the origins of theatre and performance. Over the last ten years, his main research field has been rock art and performative processes in the Arctic Region. He has published extensively on Norwegian theatre policy and contemporary theatre and is the author of textbooks on *Theory and Methods in Theatre Studies, The History of Theatre in Europe* and *Theatre as an Expression of Culture and Identity among the Indigenous People in the Arctic Region.*

CAMILLA POWER has a B.A in Mathematics from Oxford University, and took a M.Sc. and Ph.D. in anthropology at the University of London (UCL). She is currently Senior Lecturer in Anthropology at University of East London. Her research interests have centred on models for the evolution of symbolic culture with special attention to language, art and ritual. She has published extensively on gender relations, ritual and cosmology of African hunter-gatherers with specific focus on women's initiation practice and its representation in rock art.

SOLVEIG A. TURPIN is a Research Fellow at the Institute of Latin American Studies, The University of Texas at Austin. Until her retirement in 1998, she served as director or associate director of two of the University archaeological research programs. She has published extensively on the archaeology and rock art of northern Mexico and southwestern Texas as well as the contact period in the more remote regions of northern Mexico. She was a founder of the Rock Art Foundation, Inc. and continues to supervise research and conservation at specific rock art sites as well as conducting field work in her areas of interest.